THE ORIGIN OF THE ARAB–ISRAELI ARMS RACE

The Origin of the Arab–Israeli Arms Race

Arms, Embargo, Military Power and Decision in the 1948 Palestine War

AMITZUR ILAN
Department of American Studies
The Hebrew University, Jerusalem

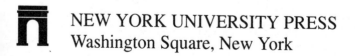
NEW YORK UNIVERSITY PRESS
Washington Square, New York

First published in the U.S.A. in 1996 by
NEW YORK UNIVERSITY PRESS
Washington Square
New York, N.Y. 10003

Library of Congress Cataloging-in-Publication Data
Ilan, Amitzur, 1932–
The origin of the Arab–Israeli arms race: arms, embargo, military
power and decision in the 1948 Palestine war / Amitzur Ilan.
p.   cm.
Includes bibliographical references and index.
ISBN 0–8147–3758–7
1. Israel–Arab War, 1948–1949—Diplomatic history.   2. Arms race–
–Middle East—History—20th century.   I. Title.
DS126.92.I425   1996
956.04'2—dc20   95–2923
                                                                          CIP

Printed in Great Britain

To Shlomit

Contents

List of Tables

Preface

This book is a study in the interdiscipline of military logistical studies and international relations. It deals with the provision of military aid to the rival parties of the 1948–9 Palestine war.

The 1948 war brought about a revolutionary and durable change in the status and future of Palestine, which was to have a lasting effect on the future of the Middle East and the world at large. No wonder that so much has been written on it since. However, its historiography has suffered from a deep schism emanating, in the first place, from disagreement over the evaluation of the moral and political consequences of the war.

Supporters of Zionism regard the outcome of the war as a divine redemption of the Jewish people from the curse of dispersion and persecution; supporters of the Arabs, on the other hand, view it as a colossal blow both to the Palestinian Arabs and to the Arab cause in general. This historiographical schism is partly due to the fact that, unlike most other conflicts of this century, the cleavage between Arabism and Zionism today is almost the same as it was then, and partly due to the lack of sufficient documentary sources. Historians can hardly avoid taking sides, although many pretend that they do not. This schism is also manifest in a mutual suspicion between historians about the value of the sources used by those with whom they disagree. In consequence, various interpretations are given to the same events, to the point where there is not even agreement as to what had actually happened. As E. H. Carr pointed out with regard to another historical dispute, 'It is the argument over the priority of causes about which the historical argument revolves.'* My issue is not the consequences of war but its course. More particularly, it is about the moulding of the warring parties' military power, seen in relation to the crucial turning-points in the war where the outcome was decided. By arguing my case I hope at least to set up a more correct order of the priority of the causes which affected the course of the war.

This book originated from research carried out at my suggestion in the History Department of the Israeli Defence Forces between 1990

---

* E. H. Carr, *What is History?* (London, 1961) p. 90.

and 1993, which aimed, at the outset, to explore the impact of the arms embargo on the course of the war. It gradually gained a somewhat wider outlook. I am grateful for the hospitality and the assistance given to me by that Department, both financially and in access to documentary sources. I am grateful to General Doron Rubin and Colonel Benny Michelson who approved my project, and to Lt Cols Noah Hershkovitz, Elhanan Oren, Ze'ev Lachish and Zvi Offer, and to Major Avi Cohen, who were ready to listen to my ideas, read sections of the work while still in crude form and often helped me find a lost track. I am also grateful to the above Department for giving me the opportunity to test my ideas before a wider audience. While I did not always meet with full approval as to my conclusions, I never sustained any doctrinaire pressure in drawing them. It goes without saying that these conclusions, for good or bad, are mine and I alone bear the responsibility for them.

I am also grateful to colleagues in academia, particularly to Professors Yehoshua Ariely and Uri Bialer of the Hebrew University, to Dr Derek Hopwood of St Antony's College, Oxford, and to Professor Aharon Shai of Tel Aviv University, who were aware of and supportive of my research and who inspired me with confidence. I acknowledge with thanks the help received from the staff of various Israeli Archives, particularly from Mr Mickey Kaufman, Mr Morris Kantor and Dr Yehoshua Freundlich and to the helpful staff of the British Public Record Office at Kew, London, the USA National Archives in Washington, DC, and Suitland, Maryland, and the UN Archives in New York City. I am grateful to Dr Ian Gaskin of St Antony's College for helping me establish contact with former British and Arab military personnel, and to the late Mrs Joy Ungerleider Mayerson, Director of the Dorot Foundation, New York.

Finally, I am grateful for the interest shown in my book by the Editorial Committee of the St Antony's College Series, by Mr T. M. Farmiloe of Macmillan and by Mr Simon Winder of St Martin's Press. I want to thank Ms Grainne Twomey, Commissioning Editor of Macmillan, for her cordial and efficient work with me. This book was originally written in Hebrew. I translated into English myself and I am much obliged to my wife, Shlomit, and to Mrs Valery Rose of Longworth, Oxford, for their help in this endeavour.

A. I.

Jerusalem

Main Sources and Abbreviations

BRITISH ARCHIVES: PRO

ADM	Admiralty Office
CAB	Cabinet Office
CO	Colonial Office
COS	Chiefs of Staff Committee
DEFE	Office of Defence
FO	Foreign Office
WO	War Office

USA ARCHIVES

FRUS	*Foreign Relations of the United States* (a published series)
HSTL	Harry S. Truman Library, Independence, MO
SA	Papers of Abba H. Silver, Cleveland, OH
USNA	US National Archives, Washington DC
WNRC	US National Archives, Suitland MD

ISRAELI ARCHIVES AND MAJOR SOURCES

BGD	David Ben Gurion's Diaries, IDFA
CZA	Central Zionist Archives, Jerusalem
DFPI	*Documents of Israel's Foreign Policy* (a published series)
HA	Haganah Archives, Tel Aviv
IDFA	Israeli Defence Army Archives
ISA	Israel State Archives, Jerusalem
KMA	Kibbutz Meuchad Archives, Ef'al
SHA	*The Roots of Israeli Air Force* (a published series; in Hebrew)
TRBA	Telegrams Record Book, Avigur's Office, Geneva
TRBS	Telegrams Record Book, Sapir's Office, Geneva

ARAB SOURCES

ANBL	Arab News Bulletin, London
IPI	'Taqrir Lajnat al-Tahqiq al-niyabiyah fi qadiyat philastin' (Iraqi Parliamentary Inquiry), 1949

UNITED NATIONS ARCHIVES AND MAJOR UN SOURCES

UNA	United Nations Archives, New York, NY
UNGAOR	Records of the UN General Assembly
UNSCOR	Records of the UN Security Council
UNWB	*UN Weekly Bulletin*
NYT	*New York Times*

A LIST OF OTHER ABBREVIATIONS COMMONLY USED

AA	Anti-aircraft
AFV	Armoured Fighting Vehicle
AT	Anti-tank (and Armour)
AZEC	American Zionist Emergency Council, New York
BMEO	British Middle East Office, Cairo
CIA	USA Central Intelligence Agency
FBI	USA Federal Bureau of Investigation
FLC	USA Foreign Liquidation Commissioner (arms, etc.)
IDF	Israeli Defence Forces
LL	Lend Lease (equipment)
LST	Landing Ship (Tanks)
MD	Munition Division, USA Department of State
MELF	Middle East Land Forces Command, Britain
NSC	National Security Council, USA Government
OB	Order of the Battle
OFLC	Office of Liquidation Commissioner (USA)
PAC	Committee of Arms and Armament Policy (USA)
SC	Security Council
SinC	Second in Command

SY	Security Division, USA Department of State
UJA	United Jewish Appeal, USA
UNTSO	United States Truce Supervision Operations (force)
WAA	War Assets Administration (USA)

Introduction

On 29 May 1948, 2 weeks after five regular Arab armies invaded Palestine in an attempt to erase the lately established Jewish state, the UN Security Council imposed an embargo, which banned the supply of arms, war materials and other forms of military aid to the parties directly involved in the Palestine conflict. This embargo, initiated by Britain and the USA, remained in force approximately 15 months. In fact, withholding of military aid to these Middle Eastern countries began earlier. On 14 December 1947, the United States imposed a unilateral such embargo, based on her 'Neutrality Acts' of the previous decade and from about February 1948 Britain drastically cut down her own military aid to the Arab countries, except Transjordan. Earlier still, the British military aid to Egypt and Iraq had thinned down as a result of the deterioration of Britain's relations with these countries.

During the embargo period, the first Arab–Israeli war was fought and decided and the concluding armistice of 1949 between the rival parties marked a new era in the history of the Middle East. Is there a link between these events? If there is – exactly what is it? From reading documents pertaining to the Arab–Israeli conflict in its 1948 international context, one gets the feeling that there is still important – yet hardly treated – material concerning arms supply and embargo, which may contribute immensely to our understanding of what happened in that war, and without which the history of these events may remain subject to emotive, contradictory presentation and myth. Such an examination is the aim of this study.

THE INCERTITUDE OF EXPLAINING WAR RESULTS ACCORDING TO FORMAL ORDERS OF THE BATTLE IN THE 1948 PALESTINE CASE

The Israeli victory in 1948 was supposedly a surprise. During most of the preliminary civil war in Palestine, which began the morning after the UN Assembly recommended partition and lasted until 15 May, the armed forces of the Jewish Yishuv had at their disposal only a limited amount of small arms with very few stocks of ammunition, and they

1

found it very difficult to cope even with the local Palestinian Arab militia, reinforced by merely a few thousand foreign volunteers. Soon thereafter, that Yishuv which turned Israel had to cope with an offensive by a coalition of five regular Arab armies, some of them British trained and assisted, who had artillery, armour, air forces and navies at their disposal. Indeed, in mid-May, the infant Israeli Defence Forces (IDF) were still genuinely inferior in armaments. Their weapons still consisted almost exclusively of small arms, which at that point were insufficient to arm even one third of the troops Israel could mobilize.[1] As the end of the British mandate coincided with the Arab general offensive, Israel was already engaged in fighting.at once on all fronts when she only began importing heavy weapons on a large scale. Soon after came the Security Council's embargo which threatened to put Israel's arms import plans in jeopardy. Conventional wisdom would then be that the Arab armies, representing a population of over 30 million and established years earlier, should have been able to increase their initial edge over the IDF, due to their bigger man-power reserves and established supply relations, and with this supposed advantage, win. But as it turned out, the war ended up in Israel's military and political favour due to an undenied Israeli military advantage. How so?

Notwithstanding the David versus Goliath myth, the answer to this question has already been partly given: the Arab armies failed to take advantage of their opening edge over the Israelis. They launched their offensive with relatively small Orders of the Battle, ignored some basic principles of war, and by the time they began reinforcing their forces, a truce was imposed by the UN, after which their advantage shrunk due to Israel's superior sources of armaments and conduct in the war. When Israel was eventually sufficiently invigorated, she broke the truce in defiance of the UN orders and, unpunished for this violation, due to a divided Security Council, took her adversaries one by one, defeated some of them, changed the balance of power in her favour and forced all her neighbours to sign an armistice with her. The terms of this armistice, largely influenced by the war results, left Israel in control of a wider territory than recommended either by the UN Assembly in November 1947 or by the UN Mediator supported by the Western Powers in 1948. Thereafter, Israel stood fast against taking in large numbers of Arab refugees who in the course of the war lost their homes inside the territory she now held and against giving up territory conquered in the war. This explanation, however, even if not incorrect, lacks at least one major component: it does not explain how exactly the change in the balance of power in Israel's favour occurred under the embargo.

Historians dealing with the emergence of the state of Israel have one problem in common: they find it hard to avoid taking sides. While this shortcoming is understandable against the background of the continuity of the Arab–Israeli dispute along similar political divides as 1948, the lack of clarity with regard to historical military facts adds a confusing schism to the assessment of the military balance between Israel and the Arabs in the 1948 war. Depending on which side a particular historian is on emotionally, the tendency is, as a rule, to depict the opposite side as stronger, so as to introduce one's favourite side in a more heroic or helpless light. We find a serious Arab historian such as Walid Khalidy claiming that as early as May 1948 the IDF had already enjoyed an overall superiority in men and weapons[2] and respected Israeli military historians who, in presenting the Arab strength, literally put together all the implements of war the Arab armies had, or supposedly had at their disposal, on paper.[3] Both interpretations fail to take into consideration that only a minor part of the arms on their lists (if those lists were correct in the first place) could have, in the circumstances, been put to effective military use. The presentation of such lists and diagrams, with no regard for the effectiveness of the weapons in question or to the availability of ammunition and the know-how pertaining to them, contributes little to the understanding of what happened in the battlefield and much to befog it. For while one may count tanks, guns, aircraft and so on, how can one illustrate an artillery suffering from a debilitating shortage of ammunition or a heavy wear of bore? How does one go about air-forces of five dozen aircraft which are totally grounded for lack of parts, trained pilots and proper ground maintenance?

The 1948 Palestine war under the embargo must be viewed as a *sui generis* case. The bad standard of weapons in use, of supplies and the low level of military expertise on both sides, make it imperative, first and foremost, to check *not numbers of weapons but their residual utility after the depreciation caused by factors which diminished their military effectiveness*. In our case these factors were predominant and the embargo was dominant among them. Considering the trivial, yet often ignored historical rule, that it is always the stronger party which wins wars, the real process to look for, in our case, is the crippling versus invigoration processes on both sides or, in other words, the parties' ability, at various stages of the summer of 1948, to wage war under the embargo limitations. When all is said, the results of the 1948 war were the outcome of the aggregate balance of addition and depreciation of the effectiveness of troops and implements of war.

To reconstruct such a 'balance' is not an easy task; not one that can be accomplished by simply presenting a yet revised set of tables and diagrams, nor by means of statistics of nominal arsenals alone; it must depend on *description* of the diminishing effectiveness of arms, on the level of ammunition stores and on the chances, viewed through the prism of the then war-lords, of their hopes of replenishing and maintaining their armies.

A supposedly equal embargo imposed on two warring parties may affect the balance of power in three ways: it may diminish an existing military power, it may hamper efforts to invigorate and it may work to the advantage of a specific party even when that party was hit, by hitting its adversary harder. Even an embargo which hits both parties hard, may still bring about a marked *relative* advantage to one of them, by hitting it less. If one party suffers relatively less, provided it still retains its basic military machinery intact, this may give it a crucial strategic advantage despite its own losses. Thus, in considering the balance of power in the 1948 Palestine war, it is not the formal OB that must be so much considered, as the aggregate power output of war machines after the embargo and other factors had taken their toll.

Having made our point in various ways, let us now add that the embargo was not the only factor which made a difference. While there is no concrete proof that the Israelis were on average better soldiers, they definitely enjoyed higher morale and determination and they better adhered to the principles of war. They also enjoyed the situation of fighting in 'internal lines'[4] and a few other advantages. We intend to show, however, that Israel's ability to cope better with the embargo situation was, by far, her greatest strategic asset.

AN EXAMPLE FOR THE INCERTITUDE OF ANALYSING A BALANCE OF POWER UNDER EMBARGO BY FORMAL ORDERS OF THE BATTLE

As an example of the difficulty, indeed the futility of reconstructing the balance of military power in this war using formal OBs, let us introduce the balance of air power between the Arabs and Israel in mid-October, which we shall explain in detail later on.

By the criterion of OBs, the Arab Air Forces still had an edge over the IDF. The combined air forces of Iraq, Egypt and Syria consisted of over 160 aircraft and Egypt had by then bought an additional 40 fighters and nine bombers, the delivery or assembly of which was delayed, bringing the total number to over 200. Against these figures, the total number of aircraft bought by Israel amounted to some 120, but due to the embargo conditions Israel only managed to import and make servicable approximately 75 of them, excluding most of the better aircraft.

Now, how many airplanes could each party at this point master and send into combat? The answer in *both* cases is very few indeed. The Iraqi Air Force with 60 aircraft, among them 30 Ansons and Gladiators used as bombers and ten modern Sea Fury fighter-bombers, was, for all practical purposes, grounded for lack of equipment, spare parts, ammunition and trained men.[5] The Egyptian Air Force had nine squadrons, consisting, all in all, of 82 aircraft of which 32 were modern fighters (Spitfires and Macchi) and 16 bombers, some of them converted transport planes. In practice, however, the airworthy Egyptian air combat power amounted to approximately 10–12 fighters (three were destroyed on the ground in an opening Israeli strike) and four to five serviceable bombers.[6] The Syrian Air Force had some 20 aircraft of which 12 were trainer Harvards converted to fighter-bombers and the rest either non-combatants or unserviceable. The marked inferiority of the Syrian Air Force and ammunition shortage, brought the Syrian command to use airplanes only when the Syrian skies were penetrated,[7] but the October campaigns barely touched the Syrian front section.

At this point Israel had already bought some 120 aircraft, approximately 90 of them modern fighters. But most of these planes either had not arrived yet or were no longer or ever serviceable. The Israeli Air Force now numbered eight squadrons, but most of the planes were available for limited service only. For instance, of the 25 Czech-produced Messerschmit fighters, bought in March and delivered between May and July, disappointingly only eight remained in use and by order these were 'confined to escorting missions only'. Of the 50 British Second World War Czech Spitfires, bought in August, only three arrived in time for the October offensive and an additional Spitfire was locally assembled. Excluding these aircraft, Israel had two not yet servicable Mustang, ten bombers (some of them converted from transport planes), nine transport planes fully engaged in importing war materials, and a diverse collection of small civil aircraft used for multi-purposes, including ground support. But quite a few of these last, as well as transport aircraft, by definition 'belonged to a high-risk group'.[8]

While there is no way in which one would be able to deduce from these figures alone which of the two air forces had the upper hand in battle, history has it that between 15 and 23 October, during which the Egyptian Army suffered its main defeat, Israel fully controlled the skies, with a ratio of combat sorties of approximately one to six in its favour. In the subsequent campaigns the Arabs hardly used air power at all.[9] However, Israel's capability did not stem from any advantage in the number of aircraft or their particular quality, but from a few other factors, including the service in the IDF of a large number of foreign airmen and ground technicians, which enabled her to use aircraft around the clock, the total condemnation of Arab Air Forces except that of Egypt and the latter's inaptitude in using her still serviceable aircraft due to lack of similar staff and spare parts. In addition, the conversion of over 20 Israeli civil aircraft to combatants, enabled the IDF, due to its general control of the air, to provide some air support to its ground forces. The ample supply of air ammunition and bombs, partly home-made, added to the Israeli advantage. Still, when all is said, the campaign of October was *not* decided in the air.

A THEORETICAL LOOK: EMBARGO AS A MEANS OF ACHIEVING POLITICAL AIMS

'Embargo' denotes an international policy aimed at attaining political aims, through pressure put to bear on certain subjects. It usually involves blocking the supply of essential goods, mostly weapons and strategic materials, to a state or a group of states, until they yield to a demand. This is a relatively young term (not a policy). At the beginning of this century 'embargo' still meant confiscation of cargo in ports of a plaintiff state to bring pressure to bear on the cargo's owner. Between the two World Wars, what we now call 'embargo' was usually termed 'boycott' and was used mainly in the context of collective security sanctions against a defined 'aggressor'. When the UN Charter was written, early in 1945 and the Security Council was given teeth to apply a variety of punitive measures against a potential aggressor, ranging from economic sanctions to a collective use of military power, the word embargo was not mentioned, as it was not in the early 1950s, when the UN Assembly too was given power to legislate for the use of punitive measures. But in the United States, particularly in the State

Department, that term was already in use when discussing measures derived from Articles 39, 41 and 42 of Chapter 7 of the UN Charter. In December 1947, when the United States announced her Palestine embargo, it used the term but based it legally not on any UN instrument but on her own 'Neutrality Acts', which back in the 1930s forbade sales of arms to countries which were at war *with each other*. When the UN decided on an *international* drive to ban war materials from Palestine in May 1948, it adopted the American intention, but judicially introduced it as a collective security measure. In fact it was not exactly that either.

TWO TYPES OF EMBARGO: 'COERCIVE' AND 'NEUTRALIZING'

We can distinguish between two types of embargo: one aimed at imposing submission to some terms on a subject and another, imposed equally on two or more parties who fight each other, in order to put down a conflict or prevent one side from subduing the other. The 1948 Palestine embargo was, by intention, of the second type. An early example of applying the first type of embargo was the abortive attempt by the League of Nations in 1935 to force Italy to give up her conquest of Ethiopia. The League's measures then included banning the export of arms, war materials and the suspension of credit. Further examples are the UN Assembly decision of May 1951 to ban 'strategic materials' from China and North Korea, the economic embargo set against Cuba by most countries of the Western hemisphere in 1962, the boycotting in October 1973 by the Arab states of export of oil to the USA, Portugal, South Africa and Zimbabwe, the suspension of American export of cereals to the USSR in 1980 and the Security Council embargo on Iraq 1990.[10]

We may well call the first type of embargo 'coercive' and the second one 'neutralising'. An early example of the second is the Anglo-French non-intervention policy in the Spanish Civil War of 1936–9 and, by intention, the USA early 'Neutrality Acts' already mentioned. Better examples still are the USA ban on the sales of arms to both India and Pakistan in February 1975 and the current embargo attempted by the UN Security Council in the complicated conflict in former Yugoslavia.

THE PROBLEM OF APPLYING AN EMBARGO

While a decision to impose embargo of both types is relatively easy, compared to a decision to take other punitive measures, it is never a step in which success is guaranteed. Embargo may not usually require the use of force and one may relatively easily withdraw from it when it does not work or relax it and even put up with its futility. However, the violation of the embargo by signatories and non-signatories is its *tendon Achillis*. For even a minor violation or laxity may irrevocably damage its effectiveness. Experience shows that even in countries where the government and the public at large fully adhere to the embargo's aims, there are always elements interested and active in its infringement, all the more so when such a public consensus does not exist. The enlargement of the circle of participants, which is essential for its success, tends to compromise the embargo terms. An embargo may not be a great deterrent measure, because it comes after a crisis has already developed. Thus, even when it severely hit the subject, it still does not easily cause it to yield. Rather, that subject would try to bypass the embargo through chinks in the fences built around the existing sources of supply and experience has it that they may succeed.

But it is particularly difficult to run a successful neutralizing embargo. In this case, the signatories may predominantly have different interests or sentiments in favour of one party or the other, with a resultant divergence as to the practical conduct of the embargo. A minor failure to treat the sides to the conflict equally or more often *because* they were treated so, may result in a failure to keep the signatories together. Since two parties subject to the same neutralizing embargo are not equal in character, the mere attempt to treat them equally may help to widen the gap between them, rather than to close it. Clearly, if one party is hit harder, the other may yet get relatively stronger and use it's advantage on the battlefield. To apply a perfect neutralizing embargo, that is, to have an equalizing effect on both parties, the embargo must in fact treat the parties *unequally*, according to each one's strong or weak points. But it is doubtful whether such an 'equalizing' policy would ever succeed in prescribing an agreed dosage of military help to the supposedly weaker party when the embargo is imposed by several or many partners.

THE ORIGIN OF THE IDEA OF A PALESTINE EMBARGO

The idea of preventing one side in Palestine subduing the other after the end of the British mandate, by freezing up a military balance until a political solution would ripen, stemmed from the British Foreign Office. It cropped up towards the end of the British mandate in Palestine, not because of a neutrality in sympathy (the Foreign office sympathy was clearly with the Arabs), but because it recognized that the development of a wide armed conflict in Palestine might put Britain's and Western strategic interests in jeopardy. Outstanding in propagating that idea was Harold Beeley, an Oxford historian turned Foreign Office expert, who held the Foreign Office's Palestine Desk. As from December 1947, Beeley's idea was that before any political settlement could be reached between the Arabs and Jews in Palestine, there should be some violent encounter between them, during which a partition would 'sort itself out'. To help such a process, the big Western Powers must see that the hostilities were short, were not getting out of control and would end up bringing both parties to political terms. Later on, a new factor forced itself into Beeley's prescription; it was the British wish to allow King Abdullah of Transjordan to annex the Arab part of Palestine to his kingdom instead of following the UN recommendation of establishing a Palestinian Arab state there. Britain's Foreign Secretary, Ernest Bevin, was well disposed towards Beeley's idea and at the end of May he managed to persuade the US State Department to subscribe to this policy as well.

In an unofficial stock-taking of the Palestine situation which took place in London early in January 1948, Beeley talked to the Cairo-positioned Intelligence Chief Brigadier Iltyd N. Clayton and to an American friend, a Middle East expert and a diplomat stationed in London, Lewis G. Jones. A civil war was already mounting in Palestine and the conferees expected worse still to come. Yet, when Beeley was asked to make an appreciation of the likely course of events he sounded inadvertantly optimistic and produced the following scenario:

> Although the Arab states are in an ugly mood, there is a chance that they can be caused to refrain from (military) interference (in Palestine) because it may breed disorders inside their own borders. Arab–Jewish fighting inside Palestine is inevitable (but) there is a sporting chance that if left undisturbed by foreign intervention or aid, the parties will tire sooner or later of the conflict... outline of a defensible Jewish State would emerge, i.e. the area which the Jews

proved they can defend ... a great part of the Arab population in
the Jewish state would probably make its way through the lines to
the safety of the Arab area; by the same token, the more exposed
Jewish settlements would be abandoned.... When a stalemate oc-
curs, there is a good prospect that the moderates on both sides will
be ready to negotiate a settlement....[11]

Clearly, Beeley's prophecy was not a very successful one, since the
Arab states did intervene in Palestine when the British mandate ended.
But his general concept remained intact and his advice was now sought
by Bevin. The idea of sealing Palestine off to external military aid
turned a corner-stone of the British policy in Palestine, with one important amendment, namely, that besides accepting the establishment
of a 'compact' Jewish state 'in areas defensible by the Jews', it was
agreed that Transjordan would annex the Arab parts of Palestine, for
the time being excluding Jerusalem. This policy was secretly approved
at a meeting of the British Cabinet on 22 March.[12] As for the United
States, it succumbed to that British policy, but only after its own plan
of revoking the 29 November resolution and putting Palestine under a
'temporary' UN trusteeship, came to a dead end at the special UN
Assembly and after the flabbergasted President Truman recognized Israel
without warning the State Department or his UN Delegation.

A further elaboration of Beeley's concept of a settlement which 'sorts
itself out' while the big powers dry out the parties' ability to fight,
was the passing on 29 May of a resolution imposing a combination of
truce and embargo supervised by UN observers, at the Security Council.

BASIC SUPPOSITIONS, AND OBJECTIVES FOR STUDY

As the basis of our study there is a series of suppositions. They are,
briefly, as follows:

1. The Palestine war of 1948 was not a continuous warfare, but a
prolonged, imperfect truce, interrupted by short, intensive outbursts of
fighting in which the war was decided. It was exactly what the Western Powers and Security Council tried to avoid. The understanding of
what happened, under these circumstances to the contrasting efforts of
the truce promoters, on the one hand and of the rival parties, on the
other is an important key in understanding the results of the war. But

they must be checked chronologically correctly and with the correct details as to the state of the war machineries on both sides at every point.

2. The relative military strength of each of the warring parties and the *real* balance of power between them at every deciding juncture, depended mainly on the degree of their success in importing or locally producing implements of war and essential military supplies.

3. The Israeli military strength, more than that of the Arabs, stemmed from aid obtained from abroad in weapons and personnel. But a careful check must be done on Israel's success to obtain these deliveries in time for the decisive military campaigns. It is clear that, generally speaking, military historians have so far failed to do so. A careful check must particularly be made on the impact of Britain's slowing down of military assistance to the Arab states *prior* to the imposition of the UN embargo and even more so on Britain's conduct with regard to military aid to the Arabs during the course of the embargo.

4. The history of the Palestine war indicates *prima facie* that the embargo was fairly efficient. Why and how then did it fail to prevent Israel from turning the balance in her favour when her advantage was largely based on external aid? Was it because of loopholes in the embargo execution? Or because Israel managed to import much equipment in the twilight period before the embargo was elaborated? Or was it generally because the embargo was imposed equally on unequal parties?

5. A series of additional questions arise, in view of our basic supposition that the war was, by and large, decided in the realm of foreign assistance and in the prevention of such assistance. What exactly motivated the initiators of the embargo to launch it and what, in particular, made the British so interested in it? Why did the American Zionists, who in 1948 scored great political victories affecting America's Palestine policy, fail to bring about an American decision to lift the embargo in favour of Israel? As for the Soviet Union, if it was true, as is commonplace, that East–West antagonism was the main factor which brought about Soviet acts of undermining the embargo, why did the USSR fail (or did it?) to give any direct or even efficient indirect military aid to Israel? Why did it continue to offer and give aid to the Arabs? What, when all is said, was the effect of the military aid sent to the rival parties from the Communist Bloc? Who else, if any, in the international arena violated the embargo or turned a blind eye to it?

6. A series of questions also arise regarding the timing of the military decisions. Did the embargo at any time help to prevent the breaking of the truce? How did the governments of Israel and the Arab

states, and their respective High Commands, see their chances and make their plans under the embargo restrictions?

7. It is clear that the embargo did not work symmetrically. But how exactly? Did Israel really win *because* of the embargo, perhaps *despite* the embargo or, maybe, without any strong causal relation to its existence? In other words, was the difference between the damage caused by the embargo on each side a major factor in the war results? And, if so, is the effect clear and simple or is it a complex combination of damage and utility, which only in aggregate and only at specific junctures turned so crucial?

PERIODIZATION OF THE 1948 PALESTINE WAR

The special character of the Palestine war of 1948 and the fact that some of the outbreaks of fighting which interrupted the UN-sponsored truce had irrevocable historical consequences, add weight to the need for a definition just when exactly this war was decided, by act or by default. From our point of view, it adds qualification to the consideration of the *real* balance of power between the warring parties. Since the real balance continuously changed, due to the impact of the embargo and of the parties' efforts to overcome it, the task of the military historian is to draw the correct power ratios at these specific junctures. This brings us to a suggestion of a somewhat different periodization of the war than has so far been acceptable.[13] We distinguish four junctures in which the war was decided.

1. Juncture 1: the determination of the Palestine Civil War between the irregular Jewish forces and the local Arab militia aided by a volunteer corps, which took place between mid-April and mid-May 1948. In its course the Jewish forces, which until then suffered an incapacitating shortage of weapons, ammunition and lack of general strategic direction, managed to obtain additional small arms from Czechoslovakia. Gaining this advantage just when the last phase of the British evacuation of Palestine took place, the Jewish forces, in an offensive improvisingly extended during its execution, managed to conquer much of the area in the centre of the country, along its valleys and the coastal plain and provided their state-in-the-making control over a continuous territory consisting of its main urban areas, the most vital communication lines, sea- and airports, etc. When this was followed by a massive

flight of the local Arab population, it reinforced Jewish self-confidence and their leaders' determination to proclaim their sovereignty in defiance of a warning from the US Department of State to refrain from doing so.

2. Juncture 2: the consequences of the offensive of the regular Arab forces against Israel between the middle and the end of May 1948. During that stage, forces of five Arab states failed in their attempt to subdue the Israeli army before it had a chance to absorb masses of weapons purchased in advance but not yet imported because of the presence of the British in Palestine. At the end of these 2 weeks, the IDF had already brought in and assimilated part of these implements of war and launched a series of ambitious though ill-managed, counter-offensives on all fronts. Although none of the Israeli onslaughts attained their original goals, the Arab offensive was checked and their commands switched to defensive positions, still before the imposition of the truce by the UN. With this, the Arabs apparently lost their only frail chance to decide the war in their favour.

3. Juncture 3: the major IDF offensive in the second part of October, which first shuttered the Egyptian defences, encircled part of their army and pushed the remainder far to an unsustainable position further south. It was followed by an attack on the Qawukji forces in Central Galilee, resulting in a complete uprooting of these forces and, in consequence, in a drastic change of the frontlines and the balance of power between the parties, with a devastating effect on the so-called 'Bernadotte plan' under consideration at the UN Assembly and the Security Council. This was followed by an almost unchecked, creeping extension of the areas under the IDF control, in the Negev, the Jerusalem corridor and even inside Lebanon. It also helped to thwart a belated Palestinian Arab attempt to proclaim sovereignty in the Gaza area. Due to complex political considerations Israel refrained from attacking the Arab Legion and the Iraqis on the Central Front, by which (though Israel might not have known it) it prevented a possible British military intervention to save the Arab Legion. The consequences of this development, combined with the prevalence of the embargo, eliminated whatever wish there remained in the Arab command to carry on their military expedition in Palestine. Taking advantage of that situation, the IDF command initiated a further operation which utterly broke the backbone of the Egyptian Army, furthered the opening of the armistice talks and brought about a bloodless attainment of Israeli control over the mandatory territorial salient reaching out to the Red Sea.

4. Juncture 4: this one, partly overlaps its former juncture, extends

over the period of armistice talks, starting 7 January and ending 20 July 1949. In its course, no serious fighting occurred, but the results of the earlier warfare, combined with Israel's improved strategic position, Israel's success in overcoming bottle-necks which earlier blocked her imports of arms and the continuous failure of the Arabs to stop the process of paralysation in their own armies as a result of the embargo, enabled the Israeli negotiators to take a firm stand in the four sets of armistice talks, using, among other means, military threats against their counter-Arab negotiators, particulalry Transjordan and Syria.

We shall treat our subject in the following order: starting with the background to the introduction of the Security Council's embargo of 29 May 1948, we shall then set up the military balance at the end of May 1948 and then the conduct of the main actors in the international arena on the issues of embargo and arms supply to the warring parties throughout the entire period. Finally, we shall discuss the outcome of the contradictory trends to impose the embargo and to bypass it and its aggregate consequences on the war.

The purport of our conclusion is that although the Arab armies started the war better equipped than the Israeli army, their organization was from the start badly lacking and their stores of ammunition and spare parts were nearly empty. Thereafter, due to the embargo restrictions, their former sources of supply and military know-how were cut off and they failed to find any meaningful replacement of them. Throughout the war, the Arab exertions to obtain additional effective weapons, ammunition, spare parts and know-how were in vain. In contrast, the Israeli forces, which were also badly hit by the embargo, nevertheless managed to import a considerable number of weapons and supplies and to produce some at home as well, and to attain considerable foreign military expertise. The difference provided the necessary and sufficient conditions for an Israeli advantage.

1 The Security Council's Arms Embargo of May 1948 and its Precursors

Withholding military assistance from the parties involved in the Palestine conflict in 1948, was an Anglo-American policy, which the two powers successfully extended to the UN.

PALESTINE, THE COLD WAR AND ANGLO-AMERICAN JOINT STRATEGY

Shortly after the end of World War II, Britain and the United States renewed their traditional strategic bond, this time out of fear of Soviet expansionism. In the Middle East, the main landmark for this trend was the Truman Doctrine of March 1947. In this region, Anglo-American policies dovetailed on most issues, but not always on Palestine. American foreign policy makers were basically sympathetic to Britain's Middle East policy, including Palestine. They viewed Britain's simultaneous seeking of the friendship and the domination of the Arab countries favourably, so long as US economic and other interests were not impaired. The USA never challenged Britain's sponsorship of the Arab armies of Iraq, Egypt and Transjordan or even occasional British assistance to other Arab armies. But on Palestine, the USA government was increasingly under effective internal domestic pro-Zionist pressure, which tended quickly to spill over to USA foreign policy. Thus, while the two English speaking powers saw eye to eye on the needs of their containment policy *vis à vis* the USSR, almost every British move on Palestine since the fall of 1945, to which the US State Department first gave its blessing, was subsequently undone at a top political level. This was often also the case in 1948.

The eruption of the war between the Arabs and Jews in Palestine in 1948 was viewed both in London and in Washington as a threat to the interests of both powers and to Western strategy. The war fanned anti-British and anti-American sentiments in the Arab public; it threatened the stability of regimes of the Arab world, which were considered the foundation of Western regional strategy. The Arab–Israeli war seemed to be ideal circumstances for a Soviet or a Soviet-inspired penetration of Communist agents and subversive elements, which might try to pave the way for a Soviet take-over. In the spring of 1948, the British and the American Chiefs of Staff seriously considered how to hold a Soviet military thrust towards the Suez Canal.[1] The disruption of oil production in the Arab world, which was needed to reconstruct the West European economies, was also considered a potential calamity.

At the same time, the inflammation of the Arab–Zionist conflict and the prospect of the establishment of a Jewish state in Palestine, fanned pro-Zionist sentiments in the USA and a strong drive, not only among Jews there, to see the UN recommendation of establishing a Jewish state carried out. For these reasons, a strong need was felt, both in London and Washington, for an agreed Anglo-American Palestine policy. 'I am convinced', warned the US Ambassador at the Court of St James, Lewis W. Douglas, on 22 May 1948,

> that the crevasses widening between US and Britain over Palestine cannot be confined to Palestine or even to the Middle East: it is already seriously jeopardizing the foundation-stone of US policy in Europe. . . . Far beyond the substance of the act of US de facto recognition (of Israel) . . . Worst prospect I can see on the horizon [is] the possibility that we may raise [our] embargo on Middle East arm shipments to favour Jews . . . only a short step until British Government may lift [its] embargo on arms to the Arabs. When this happens, the two great Democratic partners will indirectly be ranged on opposite sides of the battle line scarcely three years after May 8 1945.[2]

Bevin himself likewise liked to portray the situation in strong colours. 'It was', he later wrote, a situation which required both Britain and the USA 'to make sacrifices' so as 'to prevent a sorry spectacle of Britain arming one side in Palestine and the US the other, with the Russians the sole permanent beneficiaries'.[3]

In mid-May 1948, when the British rule of Palestine came to an end, an urgent reassessment of the Palestine situation was made in Anglo-American channels in search for the real order of priorities. This is the background for the Anglo-American truce and embargo initiative, worked out jointly at the highest level of policy makers and then dictated to the two powers' respective delegations at the Security Council, leading to the Security Council resolution of 29 May 1948.

THE UN AND PALESTINE: FROM CONFLICT RESOLUTION TO TROUBLE-SHOOTING

Solving the Palestine problem was the boldest and the most ambitious project undertaken by the United Nations up to 1948. To carry it out the UN resuscitated segments of its Charter and built instruments which had never been tested: a special Assembly, an Assembly inquiry commission, an *ad hoc* committee in the Assembly and Assembly debate on issues usually reserved for the Security Council. Following the planning stage, so to speak, on 29 November 1947 the Assembly decided on a partition scheme and created administrative tools to implement it. In the early months of 1948, the partition implementing body, UNPAC and the UN Trusteeship Council, which sponsored the establishment of the future government of Jerusalem, recruited many experts and officials to the UN payroll and frantically engaged them in designing government instruments for the proposed partition.[4] But the partition was extremely inept. It envisaged two new sovereign states to succeed the British mandate, one Arab and one Jewish, coupled by a third entity, a UN-sponsored enclave of Jerusalem, subsisting in seven fragmented regions, clasped in the bosom of each other and saved, so to speak, from total physical loss, by an impossible scheme of 'economic union', which required the best of goodwill and not a nurtured, uncompromising mutual hatred. Indeed, this design had to be abandoned following spasmatic Arab–Jewish intercommunal violence which errupted the next day after the Assembly decision and soon amounted to a civil war.

The situation was further aggravated by the British attitude. For Britain, sick and tired of Palestine, set her mind on ending the mandate as soon as possible, saving as much as possible on British blood, resources and prestige among the Arabs. This ruled out any British help to the implementation of the UN partition or any other scheme. Early in February, UNPAC was at a loss and requested the Security Council's intervention. The SC was then convened on 22 February, but contrary to the previous November, the USA and the USSR were no longer at one on the desired way to resolve the problem. While the Americans would not even think of sending troops to Palestine to enforce partition, this was exactly what the Soviets demanded and seemed keen to participate in such a force. Now the USA looked for deferment of decision on any final scheme. Their new policy was to turn the clock half-way back, seek abrogation of the partition resolution and place Palestine under UN Trusteeship, hoping that Britain might be persuaded to extend her presence in Palestine. To attain this, it called for yet another session of the special UN Assembly.

The American government had its own peculiar difficulties. 1948 was to be a Presidential election year and this had already been manifest in the thoughts and actions of White House advisers and other political office holders. Typically, the gap between politicians on the one hand and of the State Department and top military on the other hand, was widening with regard to Palestine. In mid-March, Truman reluctantly agreed to the Trusteeship formula, but insisted that the word 'temporary' must be attached to it. Angry Zionist reaction made him unwilling to endorse that scheme in public, particularly when he learned what the prospects of that scheme at the UN Assembly were. In May, early when the trusteeship proposal at the Assembly was dead, the State Department toyed with a new idea of appointing a temporary UN commissioner, who would take over the sovereignty from the British. Trying to help Truman in his domestic agony, the State Department refrained from involving him any further in this and a few other Palestine improvisations, conjured up at the last moment. But rather than comforting the President, it brought to a head his old distrust of the 'striped pants boys'. While the State Department was engaged in exerting pressure on leaders of the Yishuv to refrain from proclaiming the Jewish state upon the termination of the mandate, Truman, helped by some of his political advisers, quietly planned a *de facto* recognition of the Jewish State, if and when it was proclaimed, without telling the State Department or his country's delegation at the UN. When on 14 May he did as much, the exasperated Secretary of State George Marshall retorted, that the USA prestige at the UN 'had hit its all time low',[5] and State Department officials were panic-strickened lest the worse was still to come, namely, a likewise Presidential decision to lift the December 1947 American Arms embargo and help Israel. British diplomats in Washington (at this point there was no Ambassador in office) were affected by that same fear.

In mid-May 1948, the first anniversary of the UN taking up Palestine, rather than navigating the problem towards a resolution, the UN found itself escalating it to new records of violence, culminating in the announcement of the Secretary General of the Arab League, that the Arab armies 'entered Palestine to restore order'. This brought the Assembly hastily to convert the task of 'commissioner' to 'mediator', with the candidate himself, Count Bernadotte of Sweden, appointed a few days later by a committee of the Big Five,[6] only arriving in the arena on 27 May. Shocked by the genii it had helped to let out of the bottle, the UN tried to salvage its diminishing authority by legitimizing various palliatives which cropped up in the ruins of its original scheme. One such palliative was the truce regime and the international embargo, imposed by the Security Council.

Meanwhile in London, the British Palestine policy went further away from the American one. As early as 22 March, in response to the trusteeship proposal of 19 March, the British Cabinet secretly accepted a future *de facto* partition of Palestine between Jews and Arabs, the establishment of a 'compact' Jewish State and the annexation of the residual Arab parts of Palestine to Transjordan.[7]

The middle of May was a juncture rich with dramatic initiatives by various parties, taken in an opaque scenery. Unyielding to American requests for a delay, the British terminated the mandate on schedule. The state of Israel was immediately proclaimed with no Arab counterpart state announced. President Truman promptly recognized Israel and the USSR followed suit within 36 hours. Following a decision by the government of Egypt made on 12 May, to send the army to Palestine, the armies of Iraq, Syria and Lebanon acted likewise, as their governments had already decided, and to the British dismay, on 18 May the Arab Legion, which London had hoped would avoid fighting the Israeli forces, joined the Arab offensive. The UN Secretary General, Trygve Lie, reacted with an angry statement, pointing out a 'danger to the very foundation of the UN', and immediately reconvened the Security Council, where he and the Soviet delegation demanded the use of sanctions against the Arab states. At the same time, following Truman's act, the UN Assembly ended up in pandemonium, and it looked touch and go whether the Security Council would be able to take any effective measures to bring about an effective step towards a truce, because of a looming Soviet veto. Indeed, three deadlines fixed by the Security Council for such a truce had elapsed and the fighting went on unabated. Only a fourth deadline, fixed by Bernadotte for 11 June, at last brought about the cease-fire.

Bernadotte's success was attained partly because of the exhaustion of the fighting armies. It was further enhanced by a firmer resolution passed by the Security Council on 29 May, at the initiative of Britain and the US, with a Soviet abstention.

THE ANGLO-AMERICAN AGREEMENT AND 29 MAY RESOLUTION

Anglo-American disagreement was not the only hurdle in the way of an effective action by the Security Council: the Soviet delegation stubbornly demanded the identification of the Arabs as 'the aggressor', and called for the invocation of sanctions against them according to Chapter 7 of the UN Charter. This caused the British delegation to warn that if such a resolution was brought up, they would cast their veto against it. Soon the Soviets realized that they could gain little from paralysing the debate, but perhaps could gain something if they allowed it to proceed. On 22 May, when the USA delegation raised a mild resolution calling for a truce 'within 36 hours' without identifying the 'aggressor', the Soviet delegate abstained. But there was much doubt as to the value of that resolution, since the US and the British were not yet in agreement about what to do next. But on the same day, the two powers entered a hectic negotiation at the highest level, which continued until 27 May and ended up with an agreement.[8]

The leading figures in this hasty Anglo-American negotiation were Foreign Minister Bevin on the British side and Acting Secretary of State Robert Lovett for the Americans. The US Ambassador in London, William Douglas, was acting as a go-between. The two governments, fully conscious of many incidents of discord in their past Palestine relations, were doubly cautious not to fail this time. Attentive to a warning from the British Embassy in Washington that the only way to keep the US government from lifting its own embargo was to stop the British arms supply to the Arab countries,[9] Bevin became convinced that a British *quid pro quo* was essential in an honest, complete stoppage of British military aid to the Arab armies, including the Arab Legion.[10] Ambassador Douglas met daily with top British Ministers, including Prime Minister Clement Attlee, Bevin and Defence Minister Victor Alexander and often with top British military as well, absorbing a good deal of British views as to how the war in Palestine risked Western strategic interests. Douglas passed the British message on to Washington and in return put to Bevin American queries on the role of the Arab Legion in Palestine, the status of British arms-supply contracts to Arab governments, etc. The exchange also included intelligence appreciations of the military situation and the balance of power in Palestine, after which it was accepted, with some relief, that the rival parties were 'at a near equal strength'.[11] During the negotiation, high-ranking State Department officials visited the White House several times, to keep the President *au fait* and to obtain his endorsement of the agreement which was in the making. The end result was that a multistage plan, suggested by Britain, became acceptable to the Americans. The main points of this plan were as follows.

1. A truce must immediately be established in Palestine under a firm Security Council order, with the help of the UN Mediator. A party failing to comply with this order or who later violated the truce would be subject to UN sanctions.

2. The USA would continue her embargo and all British aid to the Arab armies, including delivery of implements of war which had already been promised but not yet sent, should be suspended. British personnel would be withdrawn from service with Arab armies, including the Arab Legion (but this included only British officers and non-commissioned officers 'seconded' to Arab armies and not such soldiers who were sworn to other governments).

3. All former schemes for political settlement recommended by or to the UN, including the partition scheme recommended by the UN Assembly on 29 November 1947 and the trusteeship scheme recommended by the USA on 19 March 1948 were impracticable and must be scrapped.

4. Britain and the USA would now seek a new partition of Palestine, based, *mutatis mutandis*, on the present front lines and the partners to this partition should be Israel and Transjordan. The question of the future of Jerusalem and the final demarcation of boundaries would remain open. Britain should recognize the state of Israel as soon as the foundation was laid for such a settlement.

5. As an interim measure, the Security Council should see to it that once a truce was established, no change should be allowed in the front lines, unless through negotiation and agreement between the Arabs and the Jews, under the aegis of the UN Mediator and the Security Council.

6. Meanwhile, the Security Council should impose an international embargo, so that none of the parties in Palestine would be able to obtain military assistance from any external source. Britain and the USA on their part should act as leaders of this policy and see that it was fully kept, world-wide.[12]

When the SC renewed the Palestine debate on 27 May, Douglas had already passed on to London his government's acceptance of these British views, including President Truman's concurrence. The next day Douglas breakfasted with Bevin at the Foreign Office, where 'it was understood' that the British and the US delegations at the UN would act in concert to pass a resolution that would help launch that policy. A cable sent on the evening of that day to Douglas confirmed oral assurance which, in the Ambassador's own words, 'was the best news he had received in many weary weeks'. And when Bevin heard it he 'was glad that US and UK relations are back on the track again'.[13]

The new Anglo-American initiative not only paved the way for extending the Anglo-American policy to the UN, but contained a durable, built-in mechanism of checks and balances, which was expected to secure both governments' adherence to the embargo. Britain could at any time renew her military aid to the Arab armies as an effective potential sanction against an American lifting of the embargo on such aid to Israel.

Reporters and political commentators at the UN quickly sensed the change of spirit and the confidence injected in the British and the American delegations.[14] The atmosphere of frustration which followed the failure to implement the 22 May resolution changed into a cautious optimism. The Soviet delegation too bowed to the new trend by accepting a call for the establishment of a truce without pointing out aggressors.[15] More reasons for optimism was intelligence to the effect that the parties in Palestine were close to exhaustion, the Arabs because they began the war badly equipped and with relatively small armies, and the Israelis because they had now spent all their reserves on abortive counter-attacks. Israel, which had already accepted the 22 May resolution, seemed certain to accept the new one, while it was learned that Arab procrastination in accepting the truce stemmed not from a bland rejection but rather from internal confusion and bad inter-Arab relations. British diplomats reported that the only real obstacle for the Arab acceptance of the truce was their demand for a complete stoppage of Jewish immigration to Israel, which Israel still rejected.[16] On 28 May, a British resolution was tabled at the SC to compete with a surprisingly moderate Soviet resolution put up earlier. In the vote that took place early on 29 May, the Soviet resolution failed to obtain sufficient affirmative votes and immediately afterwards the British resolution was accepted with minor alterations.[17]

The new resolution ordered a cease-fire for a period of 4 weeks without prejudice to the parties' claims and pointed to the UN Mediator and the Truce Commission as the UN representatives negotiating the truce. It fixed a deadline of 36 hours for the parties to state their acceptance of the order. Articles 2 and 4 of the resolution called upon all governments and authorities in the world to undertake not to introduce armed forces and war materials to Palestine, as well as to Egypt, Iraq, Lebanon, Saudi Arabia, Syria, Transjordan or Yemen. Article 11 warned that any party failing to do so or who violated the truce later might be subject to sanction under Chapter 7 of the Charter.[18]

Even this deadline (2 June) was not kept. However, on 9 June, when Bernadotte was given full control of the negotiation and the widest authority to dictate terms and a new deadline, the Arab and the Israeli governments replied positively to his call and 2 days later the fire ceased. The truce and the embargo went into effect.[19]

THE DURATION AND TERMINATION OF THE PALESTINE EMBARGO

Contrary to the Anglo-American plan, the truce, which began on 11 June did not end the war and the front lines of that date did not remain intact in order to form the frontiers of the settlement. The fighting was renewed on 9 July at the initiative of the Arab League and on 15 July the Security Council ordered a new truce, this time without any time limit. That truce went into effect on 18 July. The embargo was never regarded as having abated. But again, rather than bringing about stabilization and eventually a settlement, the second truce began in a worse atmosphere than the first and a state of no peace–no war remained throughout the 3 months of its duration. Military activities on both sides, aimed at improving positions and gaining ground, took place all the time. The truce came to an end in mid-October when a well-planned Israeli offensive was opened. By the end of the month the Israeli victories and territorial gains in three sections of the front pulled out the rug from under the Anglo-American original design of partition, embodied in the so-called 'second Bernadotte plan'. The Security Council, convened every now and then, continued to warn the parties to keep the truce and then Israel to withdraw to the pre-October lines or face the invocation of sanctions. But this was a most inconvenient moment to apply such sanctions, because the US Presidential election campaign was at its peak and both major candidates had already committed themselves to not forcing Israel to give up territory (the Negev) allotted to it by the 29 November resolution. Under these circumstances the Anglo-American agreement collapsed and the Security Council watched Israel not only retaining the areas conquered in October, but expanding further into southern Palestine. The USA gave up on the most important facets of her joint policy with Britain, yet the embargo stayed put and continued to be run quite efficiently.

The Security Council abrogated the embargo only after the Acting Mediator, Dr Ralph Bunche, reported to it the successful signing of four armistice agreements between Israel and her Arab neighbours. His report was discussed by the Security Council on 11 August 1949 and in consequence it decided, with the USSR and the Ukraine abstaining and Israel protesting (*sic*), that the armistice 'supersedes the truce provided for in the Security Council's resolution No. 50 of 29 May 1948'. The governments of Britain and the USA, in separate statements, regarded this decision as making the embargo null and void.[20]

2 The Warring Parties in Palestine at the End of May 1948

At the outset of our study of the evolvement of the change in the military balance between the Arabs and Israelis in 1948, we face a methodical question: where to start? A civil war began in Palestine as early as 30 November 1947, following the UN Assembly vote for partition. That civil war then escalated apace. But at its turning point, which only occurred between mid-April and mid-May 1948, the warring parties were still different from those which fought the same war a short while later. On the Arab side, irregular forces, consisting of local Arabs and foreign volunteers were fighting, using mostly arms smuggled from the neighbouring Arab countries. On the Jewish side, irregular militias, which served as a skeleton for the future Israeli Defence Forces, did not yet amalgamate into one united army and were unable to ship in many weapons from abroad because of the British presence. Then the British mandate came to its end, the irregular Arab forces disintegrated (except for the Qawukji troops, which temporarily retreated to Syria), and the regular armies of the neighbouring Arab countries joined the war in their stead, though first with relatively small forces. Now, on the Jewish side a regular, united army was quickly forming and a large-scale importation of arms abroad had began, though, for the most part it had not yet arrived. Significantly, for 2–3 weeks there was not yet a UN embargo and when that embargo was declared its practical imposition procrastinated for some time. Britain did not completely cease sending 'in the pipeline' military equipment to some Arab armies until the first week of June; in some cases it even intensified these deliveries, in view of the forthcoming embargo.[1] It was 2 June when the British Foreign, Defence, War and Supply Offices instructed their subordinates to withhold military equipment destined to the countries involved in the war,[2] but an order to this effect was issued by the British Middle East Land Forces Command (MELF) only on 7 June.[3] Other governments engaged in supplying arms to the Arabs or the Jews, saw the 11 June as a deadline to start respecting the embargo; France put it off even further and Czechoslovakia ignored it.[4]

The end of May is perhaps the most appropriate date from which to begin checking the change in the parties military strength. At this point, regular armies were fighting on both sides of the front, in a situation of a near military draw, under an official UN arms embargo. From this juncture, whenever necessary, we shall refer back to earlier phases of the war and to the earlier balance of power.

THE ORIGIN OF THE ARAB–ISRAELI ARMS RACE

Until the end of World War II, the Middle East was void of modern armies and weapons, except for the British army. The armed forces of the quasi-sovereign Arab states were all based upon the traditional colonial army, which was never a multiarms machinery, but forces aimed at securing the internal security. Only in the case of the Transjordanian Arab Legion was part of a colonial force upgraded to an auxiliary contingent of the British army garrison. These armies were equipped with near obsolete weapons, supplied by their respective colonial or ex-colonial military nursing powers. British and French commitment to build, equip and train modern armies in their respective domains appeared during the twilight of their official rule. Political disagreement between the ultra-nationalist independent Arab governments which were installed as a colonial concession and their former colonial patrons who remained involved in their affairs by the letter of their mutual agreements, caused further delays.

There was also weapons in the hands of non-governmental, usually illegal groups, like Arab and Jewish militias in Palestine or the Kurds in Iraq. But much as some of it played a role in the attrition of the British willpower to rule these countries, its value in modern warfare would be negligible.[5]

The growth of modern national armies and the beginning of the arms race in the Middle East originated from two post-World War II developments: the impending termination of the British empire in the Middle East, which intensified the British military assistance to certain Arab states, and the emergence of a Jewish state in Palestine.

Tired of empire in the traditional sense, the post-war British Labour government hoped to come to new terms with their former colonial vassals in the region. They intended to offer them, what to the British looked a benevolent package deal, aimed at securing Britain's strategic rights, formerly taken for granted, in return for giving symbolic satisfaction to local national aspirations and allocation of technical and military assistance. In April 1946, Bevin told the Cabinet Defence Committee that if the Arab governments would be willing to help cement the British strategic position in the Middle East, 'we on our part would do our best to bring their armies to a capability of running modern warfare'.[6] Still having approximately a quarter of a million troops under their wider Mediterranean Command, supported by a strong navy and air force, the British took the negotiation with the Arab governments as between equals. The specific partners to these negotiations were the governments of Iraq, Egypt and Transjordan, with which Britain had already had previous agreements. From both sides' point of view, these agreements were now in need of modification, though the new terms were viewed differently. For instance, the British were willing to evacuate their army from Nile Valley and Delta, but intended increasing their garrison at the Suez Canal Zone; the Egyptian Government wanted them out, period.

As a trust-building measure, the British Government offered the local governments a multistage programme to build the local military forces as modern armies and began to carry that programme out before any political agreement was signed. But it turned out that the British bargaining power was smaller than thought, and Arab nuisance value underestimated. A zeal among the public in the Arab world for full sovereignty, suspicion of the British (even more – the French) ulterior motives and Britain's evident financial exhaustion, rendered it difficult for Bevin to offer anything that the Arabs did not expect to receive anyway.

While this process was taking place, the Jewish Yishuv in Palestine was growing impatient with Britain's Palestine policy and launched its own struggle for statehood. Aware of the deep Arab hostility to Zionism, leaders of the Yishuv regarded the British plans to arm the Arabs a direct – if not a deliberate – act against their aspirations. As early as the summer of 1945, the Chairman of the Jewish Agency, David Ben Gurion, turned his mind to the possibility of a general Arab armed opposition to the establishment of a Jewish state, when circumstances brought it about and took the first practical steps to plant abroad the seeds of a machinery to procure war materials for the future Jewish state.

The British negotiation with the governments of Iraq and Egypt failed to develop as the British hoped. In Egypt it went on the rocks in October 1946. With deadlock over the issues of the presence of the British army in Egypt and the future of Sudan and during 1947 this disagreement turned ugly. A similar development followed in Iraq in

January 1948. But just when the army-building plans in Egypt and Iraq came to a halt, in Transjordan the negotiations came out very well and stimulated a plan to extend the Arab Legion. But this drive occurred very late in the British timetable for pulling out of Palestine. On 15 May, therefore, none of the British-sponsored Arab armies was in any way near the mark set by the original army-building plan. At the same time, these armies were geared to British standards, calibres, supplies and doctrine and the British helped that situation by omitting to create autonomous stocks of ammunition and spare parts in these armies or by helping to build local military industry. These armies became desperately dependent on the continuation of British supply and assistance. The political advantage of such dependence with regard to Palestine is evident, for instance, from remarks contained in British military reports from Iraq in the autumn of 1947, suggesting curbing Iraq's zeal to intervene in Palestine by withholding military supplies.[7]

THE IRAQI ARMY IN THE SPRING OF 1948

The fact that until 1948 the building of the Iraqi Army never came close to completion, should be ascribed mainly to the course of the Anglo-Iraqi relations. The Iraqi Army was established by Britain in the 1930s, to comply with the Anglo-Iraqi agreement of 1930. But there was no British intention of modernizing it, yet. Iraq's leaning towards the Axis in the early part of World War II was a lesson which did not encourage doing so even after the deposition, in May 1941, of Rashid Ali al Gaylani. Some British military were of the opinion that the delay in building the army was the reason for the pro-Axis attitude among the Iraqi military corps in the first place, but their opinion was out of line with London. Under the Labour Government, a 5-year plan was redrawn for the construction, equipping and training of a multi-arms, modern army, consisting of three infantry divisions, one armoured brigade and a five-squadron air force. Equipment was to be provided under easy terms, with Iraq's growing output of oil securing the payment of the debt. In the summer of 1946, Britain's Prime Minister, Clement Attlee, acting as a caretaker Minister of Defence, approved the plan. A British Military Advisory Mission was established in Baghdad, headed by Major General J. M. L. Renton, whose curriculum vitae included long service in Iraq with some years of teaching at the military Staff College in Britain; now his title was 'Inspector General of the Iraqi

Army'. His second in command was Colonel J. A. Hopwood, an expert on quartermaster matters. The rest of the mission included some 30 officers, acting as school of war, staff college, airmen training school and arms-acquisition council.[8] In seasonal reports sent by Renton to the War and Foreign Office, the General sounds highly critical of the standard of the Iraqi soldiers, yet full of hopes of improving them. After completing a series of comprehensive formations training and some staff exercises, he talks of a possible British cooperation with the Iraqi army in the defence of the Middle East against a Soviet attack.[9]

During 1947, relations between the Iraqi government headed by the Shi'ite Saleh Jabr and the British Ambassador Sir Henry Mack and between General Renton and the General Iraqi Command were fairly good. But underneath the thin, pragmatic political surface, strong anti-British sentiments fomented, always in danger of eruption and of being played off by the opposition to pull down the government. When in mid-January 1948, the opposition got wind of the terms of the agreement with Britain, signed by Jabr in Portsmouth, street riots in Baghdad were so intense that they not only caused the revocation of the Anglo-Iraqi agreement but the resignation of the government. New elections were called, but they could not be held immediately. The weak caretaker government under Mohammad al Sadr either failed to see the connection between coming back to terms with Britain and preparing the army for possible intervention in Palestine, which was already high on the national agenda, or was too weak to carry this conclusion consistently into effect. The fact remains that after the Portsmouth fiasco, helplessness in preparing the army for intervention in Palestine increased.[10]

There was no clear line of reaction to the Portsmouth event on the British side either. Renton suggested that Anglo-Iraqi relations 'were still extremely good' and that the military aid should continue as a gesture of goodwill. But apparently he and Ambassador Mack failed to impress Bevin. The execution of the 5-year plan was now suspended and Renton's contract, which was due to expire in April, was not to be renewed.[11] Renton's departure was postponed only so that he could complete an immediate programme of training. Meanwhile, he also managed to supply the Iraqi combat formations with ammunition 'to the level of first- and second-line stores standards', under the pretext that it was deemed for general exercises, planned for February and March. It meant that fighting echelons and their immediate rear were replenished to their full capacity according to the Standing Orders for Operations. The army manoeuvres were then held almost as if Portsmouth had never happened. But what the army procured during these exercises turned out to be the last meaningful supply of British ammunition and expendable materials to Iraq in 1948 and most of 1949.

At the end of March, Renton reported the successful completion of three major military exercises of the Iraqi army.[12] His detailed report, *ipso facto* sheds light not only on that army's capability, but on Britain's search for a new *modus vivendi* with Baghdad after Portsmouth. The military exercises included testing the function of Iraqi brigade groups in operation and logistics (operations 'Endurance' and 'Administration') and a tactical exercise without troops (TEWT, code named 'Fabius') held in the presence of the Iraqi high command and British military superior to Renton. The army exercised the defence of Iraq's territory against attack from the north, including counter-attacks with British air support. Britain's Air Vice Marshall, Robert Foster, who was also present, was impressed and joined Renton in assessing that the Iraqi army might well take part in the Western defence of the Middle East, now under planning as operation 'Sandown'. Indeed, later Foster was among the stronger protagonists in Britain's easing of the embargo on supplies to Iraq.[13] This TWET, however, did not include offensive tactics.

Following the March manoeuvres, Ambassador Mack reported that 'the army is built well for its missions'.[14] He did not specify what these 'missions' were, but it is clear that by British standards they did not include a war expedition to Palestine. Not only did Iraqi intervention in Palestine stand in contradiction to their plans that Transjordan and a 'compact' Jewish state should share Palestine, embodied in the Cabinet decision of 22 March, but they continued to have a low opinion of the offensive capability of the Iraqi army, as well as of its intelligence and logistics.[15] All the same, the Iraqi army was at this stage the Arab army which had reached the highest standard of formation training.

Iraq's army Commander-in-Chief was Lieutenant General (Farik) Saleh Saib al Juburi, who from September 1948 also assumed direct command of the Iraqi expeditionary force in Palestine. In May 1948 the army included two infantry divisions, the first commanded by Major General (Amir Liwa) Noor al Din Mahmoud and the second by Major-General Noustafa Raghib. There was also a third, training 'division', which, among other tasks, was in charge of home security and the permanent danger of Kurdish insurgence.[16] But the divisional formation was merely formal. In April, General Mahmoud was appointed by the Military Committee of the Arab League Commander-in-Chief of all the Arab armies in Palestine, a task left meaningless with the appointment, shortly afterwards, of King Abdullah as 'supreme' commander of these forces. But Mahmoud did not return to his division, nor was anyone appointed in his stead. As for General Raghib, in May he was appointed Commander of the Iraqi forces in Palestine and, again, no substitute was made for his position in the command of his division. The basic tactical formation remained the brigade groups (Jahpal), consisting of infantry brigades with the addition of artillery, armour, engineering and other supporting units, in a varying dosage.[17]

In addition to the infantry divisions, the Iraqis had an armour brigade, commanded by Brigadier Taher Mohamad, which, again, served merely as a logistic and training framework of the armoured forces. It consisted of some 120 armoured fighting vehicles (AFV), including new Daimlers and Humber 4 cars, supplied as late as early 1948 and older ones, including Morris and GMC. Approximately 60–70 of the Iraqi AFVs were armed with two- or six-pounder guns. One AFV battalion (No.1) served as the general staff reserve; the rest belonged to three regular battalions (Faisel, Hashem and Mansur) bound to be incorporated in Jahpals. The Iraqi artillery consisted of some 70–80 field guns of a variety of types. Some were 3.7 and 4.5 inch howitzers, with excessive wear of bore (WOB) and old ammunition, which made their accuracy dubious. The better part of the artillery were the fairly new British 25 pounders. These were the core of the Iraqi artillery, along with some of the better howitzers. Together they formed the Fifth Artillery Battalion, which had reached a fairly high standard in shooting. A second artillery battalion included substandard howitzers and a third battalion included two batteries of 6 inch howitzers, which never left Iraq. Artillery ammunition included only two kinds of shells: explosive and smoke. While all the 25 pounder shells were in good condition, their stock in 1948 was only 18 000 in all. An additional delivery of this sort, due to arrive from Britain in March, was withheld and was never released. The Iraqi anti-tank artillery included several 17 and 6 pounders and the anti-aircraft units, eight 40 mm Bofors and a few light 20 mm Iseta Fraskini. The Artillery Corps suffered from a shortage of organic transportation. Its standard of signalling was described as 'poor' yet its actual firing and fire observance obtained the British mark 'good'.[18]

The Iraqi Air Force, commanded by Brigadier Sami Fattah, was in 1948 based on old aircraft, but was on the threshold of modernization. In March 1948, Wing Commander H. W. Fisher, the Chief British Instructor, reported that it included four squadrons with a total number of 62 aircraft, among them 21 Anson, which could be converted into bombers, and 11 old Gladiator fighter bombers. Among the light aircraft it included 15 Tiger Moths, 3 Doves, and 9 Audaxes. In February 1948, the Iraqis received three new Fury fighter bombers, the first of the 32 promised which were due to arrive during 1948 and early 1949.

With the exception of the Fury and the Dove, all the aircraft were in poor condition, for which Fisher partly blamed his superiors in London. His complaint was that various kinds of equipment ordered 'simply did not arrive'. But the main reason why the aircrafts were in a poor state was the low standard of maintenance. In Fisher's opinion, 'the IRAF as it is today would be useless against any modern air force of the same size, nor would it be possible [for Britain] to rely on them for any major task'. In 1948, Iraq's hope was pinned on the promised supply from Britain of new types of aircraft, namely Furies, Bolton Pauls and Chipmunks, which had been promised prior to the Portsmouth crisis. Their supply was considered, in Fisher's word's, 'a big jump from anything the Iraqis have ever flown or maintained before'. Since most of the Iraqi pilots in 1948 were elderly and of poor competence, Fisher 'reckoned' that 'fresh blood' was essential, including the Chief Commander. Indeed, a group of 24 young Iraqi (and three Syrian) cadets were about to complete elementary training at Habbania, while a group of eight advanced flight cadets had just returned from Britain. Courses for ground maintenance, which started in Iraq in 1947, produced a few Iraqi ground teams, but these last could not yet function without British supervision.[19]

At that point, Iraq needed more than a year of intensive British coaching and continuation of British supply to be able to run her air force as planned. However, at the time when Fisher's report was written, British assistance to Iraq was axed. The delivery of the Furies via Cyprus continued up to a strength of 11 (one crashed, ten remained) and then stopped. Three British engineers who were helping to prepare these aircraft were ordered to leave. The Furies, which arrived without their respective guns, machine-guns, 20-mm ammunition and spare parts, did not get this equipment throughout the Palestine war. At best, therefore, they could fly, but not fight.[20]

Iraq's desperate dependence on British supply was not confined to air. A British War Office report of March 1948 opines that the Iraqi army was dependent on Britain for all its supplies, 'including ammunition, spare parts, even uniform, webbing, tents etc'. 'The stoppage of British supply', concludes an IDF intelligence appreciation after the war, 'could paralyse Iraq's ability to fight'. Probably Iraq did not even exploit to the full the twilight period before the full imposition of the embargo. After the war General Raghib told the British Consul in Mosul that shortly before the first truce in Palestine came into effect, the

MELF Quartermaster in Fayid sent an urgent cable to the Iraqi General Staff that if they could act quickly and send transportation to a British base in the Canal Zone, they could still obtain consignments of war-like stores before the embargo commenced in practice. But the officer on duty in Baghdad was so absorbed in card playing when he received the message, that he failed to act before it was too late.[21]

THE IRAQI ARMY IN PALESTINE.

Iraq began her involvement in the Palestinian war as early as February 1948, by sending volunteers, some of them members of her armed forces, to fight with the irregular Arab forces in Palestine. Following an Arab League Cairo decision of December 1947, Ismail Safwat, Assistant Chief of Staff of the Iraqi army, was appointed supreme commander of the Arab volunteer corps. But for all practical purposes the management of this 'Army of Deliverance' was in the hands of Syria, which provided most of the volunteers and the command of this force and trained its men. After the collapse of the Jabr Government, in January, fear of a pro-British stigma stuck to the Iraqi Royal Family and spurred the Iraqi Regent, Abd al Ilah, to join the popular cry to send the regular army 'immediately' to Palestine as well. Late in February, two 'battalions' of volunteers actually went to Palestine.

But sending the regular army was a different matter. Actually, the Sader Government considered sending a regular army battalion, but in early April King Abdullah, bound by his undertaking to the British Government, made it clear that he would not allow the Iraqi unit to cross his country, at least not before the termination of the British mandate in Palestine. On the general Arab scene, on 25 April, Abd al Illah arrived in Cairo at the head of a military mission determined to persuade the Arab League to sanction a general Arab intervention in Palestine as soon as the British mandate ended. On 30 April, a gathering of Arab Chiefs of Staff in Amman heard General Safwat's report on the situation in Palestine and approved a plan for a joint military intervention, which required 'no less than five fully equipped army divisions and six air squadrons of bombers and fighters'.[22] On paper, but only so, the Arab countries put together had more than such forces at their disposal, but the Egyptian Government did not yet commit itself to such an endeavour. Nevertheless, the decision to intervene on 15 May was made.

The government in Baghdad for its part, decided to send the army to Palestine as early as 21 April. Accepting Abdullah's proviso, that no crossing into Palestine was to begin prior to 15 May, the Iraqi High Command had time for preparations. From 25 April, three Iraqi Jahpals were formed at Washsash, north of Baghdad, on the basis of the regular infantry brigades Nos 1, 2 and 3, to include elements of armour, artillery and engineers. Jahpal 2, destined to be the main striking force, received under its command the quality Hashem AFV battalion, most of the 25 pounder artillery battalion and an engineer contingent. It arrived at the bank of the River Jordan, near Naharayim on 13 May and set up a bridgehead. Jahpal 3 arrived 5 days later, and Jahpal 1, serving as a reserve, arrived early in June.[23] And yet the Iraqi attack in the Upper Jordan Valley was launched before the rest of the force had arrived and thus not with all the forces available. The explanation for this obvious inefficiency is in the first place the need to show action and at the same time the terribly slow movement of the Iraqi army across the desert to Transjordan, resulting from the availability of only one highway and from what the British described as a 'dilapidated system of transportation'. It must also be ascribed to lack of confidence on the part of the Iraqi command, resulting from its almost total intelligence blackout about the location and the OB of the Jewish forces.

In its attack, between 16 and 22 May, Jahpal 2 failed to attain any of its objectives. It failed to capture Gesher, then the Kaukab al Hawa ridge and, finally, Beit Yosef. When the other Jahpals finally arrived, the offensive at that bridgehead was called off and the Iraqi expeditionary force turned southwards, crossing the Jordan again further south at Damia, where there was no IDF presence at all. It then deployed its forces over the northern and middle part of the Samaria area. A retrospective British appreciation was amazed at what followed:

> Adequate planning based on the use of the principles of war and those of logistic, were completely foreign to the (Iraqi) General Staff or the commanders in the field. Clearly ... [a better] planning in May 1948 and close co-operation with armies of the other Arab states could well have enabled the Iraqi Army to advance to the Mediterranean before the beginning of the first truce ...[24]

There is evidence of Iraqi surprise at being unexpectedly fired at by the Israeli 65-mm guns, and the straffing of a couple of Israeli Messerschmits, which the Iraqis had no idea the Israelis had at that point. Thereafter, the Iraqi command chose to take a defensive position, showing a better performance in defence than in attack. They managed to repulse and frustrate the IDF offensive on 2 June in Jennin and later in the Gilboa area. But the Israeli intelligence, too, was amazed that 'the Iraqis failed to make the slightest attempt to take advantage of capturing the Triangle [Samaria region] in order to develop an offensive against the thin (coastal) area held by the IDF.'[25]

Apparently, the Iraqi command immediately began to feel vulnerable when it undertook the defence of a relatively long, undulating front line in Samaria, disturbed by brazen Israeli attacks on it from the north at Jennin and from the west at Kakoun and were unfamiliar with the real strength of the IDF. Fearing an encirclement, General Raghib demanded reinforcement and the General Command in Baghdad then constructed and sent to Palestine Jahpals 4 and 5 – literally all the troops it could muster. These forces arrived later, during the first truce. Meanwhile, the Iraqi Air Force was sent to Transjordan with a total strength of four Gladiators, six Ansons and a few light aircraft.

When that build-up took place, General Renton was no longer in Iraq. But Colonel Hopwood and some of his men did remain until the end of May and their advice was valuable in the building of the Jhapal's. Sharp orders from London made them leave Iraq as well.[26]

THE EGYPTIAN ARMY IN THE SPRING OF 1948

There is some similarity between the poor state of the Iraqi and the Egyptian Armies, resulting from the deterioration of their relations with Britain. But since Anglo-Egyptian relations deteriorated first, Egypt's preparation for the war suffered more than Iraq's. According to the 1936 Anglo-Egyptian treaty, Egypt's army was to be built and assisted by Britain only. As early as December 1938 the British worked out a 5-year plan for the modernization of the army, which included equipment worth £80 million. The plan never got off the ground. During World War II the army was neither expanded nor modernized, with the exception of anti-aircraft contingents, which served the British Army. But the British maintained a military academy in Egypt, which, as it happened, turned out officers dedicated to liberating the army from British control.[27]

The supply of British military equipment, but not new equipment, was renewed after the war. For the Labour Government it was an advance payment for Egypt's signing of a new Anglo-Egyptian treaty, a 'protocol' about which Bevin and Egypt's Prime Minister, Ismail Sidky (a signatory of the 1936 agreement), signed in October 1946. But dis-agreement over the interpretation of sections in the protocol dealing with the future of Sudan and the evacuation of British troops from Egypt, coupled with violent street demonstrations, protesting against the protocol and populism of Egypt's King, Farouk, enhanced its revo-cation and the resignation of his government. The new government, headed by Mohammed Nokrashi, sworn in December 1947, was politi-cally weaker than its predecessor, but seemingly more militant. It took the dispute with Britain to the Security Council, where in August 1947 it won the dubious support of the USSR but failed to have its com-plaint passed through. Meanwhile, Anglo-Egyptian relations were fur-ther tainted and the British military assistance to Egypt was obviously affected.

Prior to the deterioration of Anglo-Egyptian relations in 1946, the British nurtured a long-range plan to build an Egyptian army of 3 divisions, one of them armoured, and an interim target of one infantry division, with small armour, artillery and engineer contingents, as well as an air-force and a navy, to be completed in 1949. Early in 1948 the skeleton for the interim plan already existed, but equipment was slow in coming. The political crisis slackened the progress of the rearma-ment long before the possibility of an Egyptian intervention in Pales-tine was discernible in London or in Cairo.[28]

The British assistance to the Egyptian army was conducted by a team of approximately 50 British officers, headed by Major-General Robert Arbuthnot, with two deputies: Colonel G. F. Stephens, who was in charge of the army's reorganization and equipment and Colo-nel C. D. Consett, who ran a nine-section military academy, for infan-try, gunners, armour, engineers, scouts, signallers, ordnance, logistic and the air force. Training included among other subjects: tactical courses for minor officers, occasional company, battalion command courses, logistic and standing operation procedure (SOP). But according to Arbuthnot's report of December 1947, 'the army cannot be said to have made much progress in 1947' and in another section he even says that 'The Army has remained static and has not progressed at all'. Thus, for instance, the British trainers never reached the stage of exercising cooperation between infantry, armour, artillery etc.[29] Un-like Renton in Iraq, Arbuthnot gave little hope to his students. He continuously lamented the poor quality of the Egyptian soldier and, even more, the incompetence of the High Command in Cairo. His re-port is splattered with negative characterizations of members of the Egyptian military elite, which in his words, were 'corrupt', 'lazy', 'egotists', even 'stupid'. Despite evident temperamental differences between Arbuthnot and Renton, it is clear that from the three British-supported Arab armies, the Egyptian army was the least prepared for war.

Despite the bad state of the army, Prime Minister Nokrashi and his newly appointed Minister of War, Mohammed Haidar, decided to 'suspend' the work of the British military mission in Egypt and caused 'bewilderment' in army circles.[30] General Haidar was politically a strong man, but no military expert. He attained his position and rank through nepotism; after serving first in the state prison service, he moved to become the King's adjutant, a position from which he developed influence both on the King and on Azzam Pasha, Secretary-General of the Arab League.[31] When Arbuthnot left Egypt in January 1948, the British Ambassador in Cairo, Sir Ronald Campbell, noted Haidar's satisfaction. But when he asked the Foreign Minister, Ahmed Khashaba, 'who will fill the gap' created by the departure of the British officers, Khashaba replied honestly that he 'had no idea'.[32] Haidar probably still did not think that this would affect British supply to Egypt, but it did.[33]

Indeed, the Egyptians continued to ask the British for military supplies as if nothing had happened, as well as sending feelers to Belgium and Czechoslovakia, to buy British standard ammunition there (*sic*). The British Embassy, as well as the Supreme Command of the British Forces in the Middle East, supported these requests, for the sake of maintaining good working relations.[34] As a result, in February 1948 – weeks after Arbuthnot's mission had left – a British gesture of ammunition replenishment to Egyptian formations 'up to the level of first- and second-line ammunition', was sanctioned by the War Office in London, provided the items in question were not in short supply for the British forces themselves.[35] Unfortunately, the British did suffer from a temporary shortage of artillery and mortar shells, so the Egyptians received less than was intended.[36] One of the King's courtiers, who was later involved in negotiating with foreign freelance arms dealers, wrote that he was told that the army went to war in Palestine with 'merely 3 days of logistic stores' ammunition.[37] The Egyptian army, reported an IDF intelligence source during the war, 'remained absolutely dependent on supply from the British Army'.[38] But the deficit was temporarily offset by the seizure, on 22 May, of some 350 tons of gun and mortar ammunition earmarked for the Arab Legion, loaded on the ship *Ramses* at Suez. The injections of supply, however, were the last received by Egypt from British sources for many months. Another, British gesture made at the end of 1947 was the completion of a long overdue supply of a few Spitfire aircraft to the Egyptian Air Force.

The poor state of the army, resulting from the deterioration in the Anglo-Egyptian relations, was one reason for the lack of enthusiasm in the Egyptian Government to send the regular army to Palestine. Another, at least by argument, was the Prime Minister's reluctance 'to wage war with the British Army at his back'.[39] Ambassador Campbell on his part, did not perhaps want to encourage Egypt to send the army to Palestine – he would lose favour with Bevin if he did – but did not like such arguments made either. He refused to accept that Britain would forsake Egypt in her difficult hour, rather than seize the opportunity and demonstrate her friendship and helpfulness. Campbell, therefore, made it a habit to 'warmly' support Egyptian requests, sent to London right before 15 May or even after that date, for the supply of weapons promised long ago, which should have now been in Egypt. He endorsed requests for 50 medium tanks, 28 armoured cars, 30 25-pounder guns with 1000 shells per barrel, 2000 army trucks, five new Vampire jet fighters, 25 Harvard trainers and a dozen light Auster VIIs. Campbell also asked for consideration of the acceptance of 33 Egyptian flight cadets for an advance combat air course. But in London these requests were turned down.[40].

Nokrashi was evidently hoping that a direct military intervention in Palestine would not be necessary. His hesitation was shared by a handful of other sober politicians and military, but not by the ultra-nationalistic, vociferous political opposition, the foolhardy King or by the Minister of War Haidar. Nokrashi himself represented a small political party (Saadist) and was threatened by larger oppositions and by a King who could and probably would fire him if he failed to do his wish. At the same time, it was not as clear what was the risk of sending the army to Palestine. Nokrashi wanted to believe that there were still various escape routes open if things went wrong. Talking to the worried General, Ahmed Ali al Muwawi, who assumed command on 26 April over a force sent to El Arish, he described the impending mission in Palestine as 'policing' and said he was sure that 'the UN would soon intervene'. On 11 May speaking at Egypt's Upper House, he raised a similar argument, saying that 'it is not a real war, but rather an act of restoring law and order in the Arab regions of a country were sovereignty ceased to exist'. He also reported sending feelers through the Jewish community in Egypt to some 'wealthy Egyptian Jews abroad', suggesting a *modus vivendi* in Palestine, by which the Egyptian army would abstain from attacking Jewish settlements in return for the Jews going back on their claim of sovereignty.[41]

For the Egyptian Army command, however, the tormenting question was, what if after all there would be a real war? What effective OB could they amass from the disorganized army? What objectives can such a force at best attempt to attain in Palestine? There was neither a shelf plan, nor a clear intelligence basis to plan upon. The plan adopted was simply to move into Palestine along a trafficable axis and try and crush any Jewish resistance encountered.

The Egyptian Government did not make any financial preparations for a state of war either, until the last moment. Accustomed to the British assistance terms, the government saw no need to depart from its traditional balanced-budget policy until mid-May. Suddenly it realized that it might need an extraordinary budget for the war spending, particularly for buying war materials which the British had failed to supply. This enhanced provisions for a deficit budget made on 13 May and allowed the Minister of War to draw unlimited funds to finance the war, without having to report details on spending to the Exchequer's Comptroller. Had this measure been taken long before the UN embargo, or at least been efficiently managed now, it might still have compensated Egypt for the British omission. But, as we shall see, this measure was almost totally wasted.[42]

THE EGYPTIAN ARMY: END OF MAY 1948

What was the real strength of the Egyptian Army in May 1948? Formally, it consisted of three infantry and one armour brigades an air force and a navy. Its effective strength, however, was far smaller, because sections of the army were in disarray and could not be sent to battle. The infantry barely amounted to two Brigades and the armour according to far exaggerated Israeli sources, included two light tank Battalions of Mark 6 and Locust types and over a battalion of other AFVs.[43] In fact, in May 1948 the Egyptian tank force included one under-standard battalion of Mark 6s, approximately 30 tanks not armed with guns and a variety of AFVs – Humber 4 and Humber 3 cars, a few half-tracks and many armed Bren carriers – not organized in any standard, combat formation. The Egyptian artillery consisted of a Battalion of 30 25 pounder guns, of which 24 were new.[44] It also included three batteries of old 18 pounders and howitzers 3.7 and 4.5 inch, suffering from a heavy WOB and a small number of anti-aircraft and anti-tank guns. As regards modern artillery, only the 25 pounders were dependable.[45]

The Egyptian Air Force was the best among the Arab armies. On paper it consisted of seven squadrons, of which two consisted of some 40 Spitfire IXs, 32 of which were considered serviceable, in addition to two bombing squadrons, based on C47 Dakota aircraft and many medium and small aircraft, used for transportation and communication. As a result of the withdrawal of the British military mission, the effectivity of the force rapidly deteriorated. In a memorandum addressed to the Ministry of Defence in London, Colonel Patrick Ryan, a former RAF man, who represented the British Ministry of Air in Egypt, opined that the Egyptian Air Force 'would come to a stand still within two months due to shortage of pilots, spare parts and proper maintenance'.[46] This proved a somewhat too pessimistic prediction, but not by far. As early as the first truce, the number of serviceable aircraft drastically dropped, particularly after ten of the best Spitfires were lost in action.[47] Ryan was not alone in giving such a low appreciation of the Egyptian maintenance ability. As early as December 1947, notwithstanding the embargo yet, General Arbuthnot opined that the future of the independent Egyptian army was 'totally obscure' and that after the departure of the British mission, 'inertia . . . together with ignorance and lack of interest displayed by politicians . . . (would lead) to the falling off from the efficiency which has been achieved'.[48]

In mid-May, the only available combat force ready to move to Palestine was a combined group assembled at El Arish 2 weeks earlier, which was indeed the force that entered Palestine on 15 May. It included one brigade group of three infantry battalions (Nos 1, 6 and 9), an auxiliary support battalion of machine guns and 3 inch mortars, one field artillery battalion of 24 25 pounders, two companies of armoured cars (24 AFVs), an engineer detachment and a few anti-aircraft and anti-tank pieces.[49] When this force was already fighting in Palestine, under the command of General al Muwawi, hasty steps were taken to amass more units, which included a tank battalion of 30 light tanks and a few medium Sherman tanks (according to Arbuthnot 'non-runners'). After more delay, two additional infantry battalions (Nos 4 and 7) and some of the old howitzers were sent as reinforcement, and reservist units began to arrive, piecemeal, as well.

Upon entering Palestine, General al Muwawi assumed command over the irregular Egyptian forces which entered Palestine earlier, now called 'Light Forces'. These included mainly members of the fundamentalist 'Moslem Brotherhood', whose despatch to Palestine in March, under the command of regular army command,[50] served the government's wish to get rid of a subversive element in the public and register points in the fulfilment of Egypt's duty to the Arab cause. The Egyptian command also took charge of the Gazan Palestinian irregulars, with whom Ehwan had influence. At the end of April, the irregular Arab force in Southern Palestine numbered some 2000 men. But notwithstanding their zeal to fight the Zionists, most of them belonged to the 'loaners', ('zoua'ran') whose standard of training, organization and discipline was poor. Enjoying a numerical and fire superiority, they still failed three times to capture their main target: the isolated Jewish Kibbutz Kfar Darom.

The air force put at the disposal of the expeditionary force at El Arish in May, included 16–18 Spitfires, three to five Dakotas converted to bombers and a number of non-combatant airplanes. These amounted to all the serviceable aircraft the Egyptian command had at that point.[51]

THE SUPPLY AND MAINTENANCE OF THE EGYPTIAN EXPEDITIONARY FORCE

In January, after the withdrawal of his mission, General Arbuthnot's opinion was that 'now ... none of the Administrative Service Corps (of the Egyptian Army) could be described as fit for war'. The withdrawal of the British supply depot from Egypt's mainland a few months earlier along with the entire British pull out of the Nile Valley, created a situation in which 'the Egyptian army had no warlike stores of its own at all'; no ammunition or spare parts reserve.[52] There were still occasional supplies of war materials from British bases in the Canal Zone – general supplies came from Fayid, ammunition and other expendable war-like stores from Tel al Kebir and Geneifa, navy supplies from Timsah and air force needs from Abu Sultan –[53] but every item required formal allocation from the the MELF Q Branch in Fayid and an endorsement by the Ministries of War or Supply in London. As from February, it required permission from the Foreign Office. The Egyptians paid for the supplies from their Sterling balances, which had been frozen during the war and of which up to one-quarter of the total sum had lately been released. Officials at the Ministry of Defence in London viewed the new situation with a sneer. 'Our treaty relations with Egypt', wrote one of them 'and the easy approach to our depots made them accustomed to (our) supplying all their needs'.[54] But it must be born in mind that even the Suez area, where the main

British stores were located, was recognized even by the British government as sovereign Egyptian soil. This state of affairs, accounts for Ambassador Campbell's and General Crocker's wish to continue to keep the supply going.

However, in London other factors weighed heavier. In the Cabinet, the Minister of Defence, Victor Alexander, representing the interest of continuing to supply the Arabs, was in the minority and he too bowed to Bevin's view, which put Britain's relations with the USA as their first priority. Bevin and Alexander were old political friends from their joint association with the Labour Party in Bristol. But when they disagreed in Cabinet, as a rule Bevin's opinion prevailed, because he enjoyed Prime Minister Attlee's highest confidence. When the first restrictions on the supply of war materials to the Arab armies were imposed in February 1948 Alexander did not realize that this was the start of a period of more than a year in which he would not allow General Crocker to supply a single item to any Arab force.[55] This British blindness explains much of that of the Egyptians too.

In Palestine, the Egyptian logistic layout was based on temporary depots deployed in the El Arish area, themselves supplied by boats and railways. Down to the combat units, the method changed to a supply-point disposition (SPD). Formations were expected to arrange for their own transportation, because the army had no vehicular means to do it.[56] Army commanders thus hired or confiscated civil vehicles in Raffah, Khan Yunis and Ghaza for their needs.[57] Between 15 May and the beginning of the first truce, the Egyptian Command shipped most of its ammunition stores to El Arish, including the one consignment destined for Transjordan which Egypt confiscated. Literally, no worthy ammunition reserve was left at this point in the Egyptian bases. Egypt had no ammunition factory of her own, nor the technical capability to build one or to ease the basic shortage of ammunition by 'refreshing' the old one.[58]

During the first truce, Egypt continued to reinforce her troops in Palestine by sending more formations. The number of troops rose gradually from approximately 6000 at the end of May to approximately 14 000 in September.[59] However, the efficiency of that build up was to a great extent ineffective, since no real improvement occurred in the supply situation.

TRANSJORDAN AND HER ARMY IN 1948

In 1948 the new independent Arab state of Transjordan and her army, the Arab Legion, enjoyed a special status among British policy-makers. Three things made Transjordan such a favourite: the country's special demographic and geographic situation, Britain's strategic needs, and Britain's political failure to come to terms with the governments of Iraq and Egypt. While there was never an identity of interests between the aims of the governments of Britain and Transjordan, Soviet and Zionist propaganda successfully portrayed King Abdullah as a British puppet, because the juxtaposition was close enough.

However, Abdullah was nothing of the sort. His goal was to cement his political and military power, depending on British aid, to materialize what he believed the British had once promised his father (in 1916!) namely, the establishment of 'Greater Syria' under his throne, which should include Syria, Transjordan and Palestine. In 1948, of course, this was not what the British Government had in mind, if it ever had. An interim step towards attaining that goal was Abdullah's hope of annexing Palestine or at least the Arab parts allotted by the UN resolution to a Palestinian Arab state, which the UN now clearly failed to implement and in which the Mufti-controlled Arab community was practically disintegrating. Depending on the British to build and keep his army, Abdullah tried to gain more independence from the British by building himself a position of importance in inter-Arab affairs as well, and by independently cultivating special relations with the Jewish Yishuv in Palestine. He still aspired to the Palestine Jews becoming future subjects of his kingdom. But respecting Jewish technical capability and international influence pushed him to seek agreement with them at this time, to help secure his share in Palestine instead of the Mufti's.

In British eyes, Abdullah's value increased in 1948 because the Legion was considered an actual, even more a potential, strategic asset: Abdullah proved to be the only Arab ruler who was unlikely to lose his position upon signing an agreement with them and because a chance was discerned to use his aspirations as a lever to turn the tormenting Palestine issue into a political solution that would fit Britain's ends.

The collapse of the British treaty negotiation with Egypt and Iraq occurred at the same time as the British decision to withdraw from Palestine. The UN failure to implement its partition design took place when it seemed apparent that Britain would have no authority to hand Palestine sovereignty over to. At the same time, British experts had already grasped the possibility that a *de facto* partition, different from what the UN design envisaged, but a better one from their point of view, was forming up, by which a 'compact' area, defensible by the Jews, would, after the British withdrawal, form a Jewish state and another, a much larger one, where the local Arab community was in a process of disintegration, would be annexed to Transjordan, excluding, for the time being, Jerusalem. This seemed almost too good to be true, since the Legion had already stayed in Palestine on garrison duties. But to ward off accusations, increasingly made by the Zionists in the USA and by the USSR, that the Legion was re-occupying Palestine for Britain, the British Middle East Command was ordered to see to it that the Legion left Palestine when the British mandate was over. If it returned to it the next day, it was supposedly Abdullah's business. Bevin, who supervised the drawing of this scenario, regarded it essential that Abdullah knew what the Legion would rather not do. In a telegram in February, sent to Britain's Minister in Amman, Sir Alec Kirkbride, Bevin summed up what he made clear to Abdullah's Prime and Foreign Ministers, who had recently held talks in London:

> It was understood that the Legion would have to leave Palestine before 15th May . . . (but) it would be to the public benefit if it returned to the Arab areas of Palestine to maintain law and order . . . but not the Jewish areas, unless the Jews invaded Arab areas.

With Jerusalem very much in mind, Bevin also insisted that the occupation of parts of Palestine by the Legion should be pending a political settlement and that the Legion's actions must not be in contrast to any decision that the UN had made or might still make.[60] A Transjordanian delegation was in London as early as the end of January 1948 to discuss Abdullah's plans; typically it included Arabs (Prime Minister Tawfiq Abu'l Huda and Foreign Minister Pawzi al Mulki), as well as Britons (Brigadier General John Glubb, Commander of the Arab Legion and Pirie-Gordon, Kirkbride's deputy). However, it was too early for solid commitments on the British part. New vistas actually began to appear immediately after that mission returned to Amman, following the reopening of the issue of the future of Palestine at the Security Council in early February. The US proposal of 19 March to place Palestine under UN temporary trusteeship made it urgent to come before the British Cabinet and on 22 March the Cabinet approved Bevin's resolution that there should be no change in the date fixed for the end of the mandate and that Britain 'should make no effort to oppose the setting up of a Jewish state or a move into Palestine from Transjordan'.[61] The result was a speeding up of the enlargement of the Legion, which got into a full gear in February 1948.

The 'Legion' originated from a post-World War I British gendarmerie whose task was to flaunt the British rule over the area between Hijaz, the Red Sea and Syria, before political boundaries of the modern Middle East were demarcated. Soon Transjordan was established as a British Emirate under Abdullah, controlled by the British High Commissioner in Jerusalem. Captain Frederick Peake, the founder and first commander of that Legion, continued to hold his position but thereafter served two masters: the British army and Abdullah. The relatively high standard of soldiering in the Legion, compared with other colonial armies of the time stemmed from the persistent allocation of British officers and resources to the Legion, which turned it into the only Arab army where British soldiers regularly served. In fact, the high and medium command was almost totally British. The Legion quality also stemmed from the dedication and originality of some British military, such as the Royal Engineer Corps officer John B. Glubb, who entered service with the Legion in 1930 and assumed command of it in 1939. Glubb preferred to take Bedouins for service, rather than townsmen. His romanticism and pragmatism created a pattern of mock assimilation of British officers with the Bedouin costume, language and manners and moulded a working synthesis between the British and the Bedouin war traditions. The Legion proved to be a disciplined unit with high *esprit de corps*. In 1948, the number of the British officers serving in the Legion grew to 46, not counting a few additional NCOs. But these Britons were of two kinds: soldiers who, as from 1946 were sworn-in Transjordanian soldiers, whose allegiance was to King Abdullah only, and the others who were British army regulars, 'seconded' to the Legion by the War Office in London.

Up until early 1948, the Legion included three different services: a well-trained mechanized unit built to act at long range, garrison companies whose standard of training was lower and a police force. A fourth unit under British command, the Transjordan Frontier Force (TJFF), was not directly under the command of the Legion (even Palestinian Jews sometimes served in it) but it was of similar character. When the TJFF was dismantled in 1947, some of its men and most of its equipment were absorbed into the Legion.

The Legion's value to Britain was dramatically proved in May–June 1941, when a relatively small mechanized force helped to topple the pro-Axis government of al Gylani in Baghdad and to capture Syria and Lebanon from the pro-Nazi Vichy forces. After the war the Legion's best units were engaged in routine security tasks in Palestine but none the less had been reduced to half their size. While during the Second World War it counted some 12 000 men, at the end of 1947 it had no more than 6000 men. In 1948 both Britain and Abdullah again needed a bigger force.[62]

THE ENLARGEMENT OF THE LEGION IN 1948[63]

In January 1948 the Legion was a deficient brigade group, lacking various standard auxiliary units, but with excessive fire-power and high mobility. It had good quality British vehicles, both modern AFVs armed with 2 pounder guns and non-armoured four-wheel-driven cars armed with machine-guns. This weapon was in use while guarding installations and the Iraq oil pipeline in Palestine. The fighting echelon of the Legion numbered less than 5000 men, including seven, under-trained garrison companies. In Glubb's drawer there was for some time an ambitious programme to extend the Legion into a standard army division; he also planned an air force. Suddenly, in early 1948, the Ministries of Defence and Foreign Affairs in London began to show interest in this plan, because, as the chief the British Middle East Office (BMEO) in Cairo wrote, following the Portsmouth débâcle, 'The tendency is to hold fast to Transjordan . . . our only reliable ally, and let the rest (of the Arab states) go hang'.[64]

Transjordan with poor resources could not support such an army, so the British exchequer paid the entire cost of this extension and the maintenance with the Transjordanian budget of 1948, now two and a half time larger than that of 1947 (over £6 million) of which 65% came as a British grant-in-aid. It did not mean, however, that Glubb received a lump sum with which he was free to operate. According to Glubb's biographer, 'allocation had been painfully slow because of bureaucrats in London'.[65] Probably it was simply too short a time for a fully-fledged division to form up. Still, the Legion gained in vigour. The main changes included additional weapons, extension of existing formations, reorganization of headquarters and a nucleus of artillery and engineering units. Three battalions were turned into brigades, which themselves absorbed new manpower from the garrison companies, veteran Legionaires, released TJFFs[66] and new recruits. But this reorganization was not completed by 15 May; it continued throughout 1948 and was completed in the spring of 1949, when the Legion's strength reached approximately 14 000 men. At the end of May 1948 the Legion's total strength including new recruits was in the vicinity of 9000.[67] Further-more, the Legion's service in Palestine up until May prevented its best units from undergoing formation training or even command TEWT exercises. But then, quite a few in its senior command had good divi-sion procedure experience from their service with the British army during World War II. Thus, while the Legion lacked unit training, its command was professionally of the highest standard among all the other armies in Palestine in 1948.

THE LEGION ORDER OF THE BATTLE AT THE WAR'S OUTSET

At the end of May 1948, the Legion's OB was as follows: the Legion High Command in Transjordan under General Glubb. A Division, com-manded by Brigadier Norman Lash in Palestine, consisting of two bri-gades, the First and the Third, with only two battalions in each (Nos 1–4) and a skeleton of a third brigade (No. 4) which at that point consisted of the seven garrison companies. Battalions 1–4 were well trained and fully equipped, including support weapons, with an addi-tional 12–14 Humber 4 and Marmon Harrington armoured vehicles per battalion, armed with 2 pounder guns.[68] The total number of the ar-moured fighting vehicles was 72, not counting other combat vehicles without armour but with strong fire-power. So long as the Legion had ammunition, its relatively small size was offset by a fire strike unparalleled in any other army in Palestine. The Legion's guns and AFVs were brand new and its gunners were among the few who man-aged to be well-trained before mid-May. However, the entire field artillery at its disposal was one squadron of 25 pounders (i.e. two batteries with four guns in each) with another squadron being established. All artillery officers were British and their deputies were Arabs. In June, Lieutenant Hassuna was the first Arab officer to assume command of a battery. In addition, the Legion had 24 6-pounder anti-tank guns allocated to subunits.[69] There was also a small Engineers Corps de-tachment and an improvised but highly efficient ordnance unit (REME) run by British technicians. The Legion had no aircraft, but a unit of air-support liaison, aimed at using British air support, was included. Finally, the Legion had two permanent liaison offices, one with the MELF Command in Fayid, and another in London.[70]

The source of the Legion quality was its British command, albeit not all of it, notably Glubb and Lash.[71] Most of the Legion officers had World War II experience. All the new brigade commanders were former battalion commanders and most of the newly appointed battalion CinCs and their deputies, as well as Heads of Staff Branches, came from the best of the regular British army.[72]

PROBLEMS OF BRITISH COMMAND AND SUPPLY IN THE LEGION IN 1948

The enlargement of the Legion probably doubled its fire-power, but made it more dependent on the British. If, for some reason, the British officers were withdrawn or the supply of ammunition withheld, the Legion's power would be curtailed drastically. But total withdrawal of the British officers was unlikely to happen, because most of them no longer subordinated to London or Fayid. The problem was different with regard to supply. Since the British did not put any meaningful independent stores at the disposal of the Legion, its superior fire-power was bound to evaporate quickly if the British supply was cut off.

One more reason for the lack of independent stores of ammunition in the Legion was that this unit was counted as part of the Order of the Battle of the British army in the Middle East.[73] According to British logistic doctrine, a brigade or a division does not independently hold supplies on top of its immediate standard battle orders, but what its next mission requires. Expendable supplies in particular were re-calculated by the standard of 'contact days', defined as 'ammunition of all natures, petrol, oil and lubrications (POL) and stores expended by a formation or a unit per day when in contact with the enemy'.[74] The exact contents of this measurement vary according to the OB of the formation in question and its type of mission. Officers who served with the Legion in 1948 remembered the use of this standard, but admitted that very few outside the Q Branch staff were ever able to quantify it in detail.[75] But in 1948 the continuation of the British supply to the Legion became a top international issue. Thus, Prime and Foreign Ministers too were often discussing 'contact days'.

So what did the Legion obtain when it entered Palestine? In February it received supplies for 10 contact days and towards 15 May an additional portion of 30 contact days were allotted to it. On 16 May it had been sent by means of railway from the Tel al Kebir base in the Canal Zone to Suez, where it was said to be loaded onto two boats.

But only the first shipload, which included small-arms ammunition and 2 pounder shells had reached its destination by 20 May. The second one, consisting of some 350 tons of 25 pounder gun and 3 inch mortar ammunition, loaded on the *Ramses* on 22 May, was seized by the Egyptian authorities, unloaded and sent to the Egyptian ammunition depot at El Arish. The British never compensated the Legion for this loss, because, by then, the Legion, in spite of Bevin's and Kirkbride's warning, entered the battle in Jerusalem, at a time when the British were desperately trying to keep the USA from lifting her embargo and sending arms to Israel. Soon the two governments had reached a gentleman's agreement to withhold all supplies to the Arabs and the Jews and to extend the embargo to all UN members. Obviously, at this point no one in the British government dared violating that agreement, but at the same time no one expected the embargo to last more than a few weeks.

So, later, 'the Legion', as General Glubb wrote in his emotional pleading for ammunition in August, 'had fought forty days on a ten Contact Days allotment'. In fact, Glubb was truthful only with regard to artillery and mortar ammunition. As a matter of fact, the Legion's small-arms ammunition was not exhausted, both because such ammunition was on board the first boat which had arrived safely in Aqaba on 20 May and because in February, while on duty in Palestine, its quartermasters made a deal with the command of the British army in Palestine (which had a very short deadline to clear big stores) that the Legion would take all the spare small-arms ammunition it could. But this arrangement did not included artillery and mortars, because these were in short supply in the British army too.[76] What is clear is that after 22 May the Legion could no longer depend on future replenishment of ammunition from British sources and had nowhere else to look to. When the Legion became engaged in bitter fighting in northern Jerusalem and Latrun, its units used heavy gun and mortar fire. Belatedly its command realized that it could no longer afford to squander heavy ammunition. On 30 May, when the Legion's Fourth Battalion managed for the second time to ward off an IDF attack on Latrun, its artillery support was at the very end of its ammunition.[77].

THE LEGION'S ENTRY INTO THE WAR

When the British mandate came to an end and the Legion crossed the River Jordan back to Palestine, it was not yet clear to its command what their task was. Troops had just returned from Palestine by an order from London, except for one infantry company, reinforced by a few AFVs, which on 12 May captured the Jewish Etzion settlements between Bethlehem and Hebron, and stayed put in the Bethlehem area, with the High Command turning a blind eye to it. Upon re-entering Palestine, the Legion did not take the main Jericho–Jerusalem highway but a side road to Rammallah. Their immediate assembly location was between Ramallah and Nablus. A distance was kept from the Jewish forces for a full 3 days, until King Abdullah, now a titular 'Commander-in-Chief' of all the Arab forces, made up his mind not to comply with the British warning to him to refrain from engagement in fighting the Jews. Abdullah was aware of the relatively small size of his army and the limits of his ability to involve it in heavy fighting. He knew that he was acting against Bevin's warning and that if his army was to suffer heavy losses or be defeated, the British might not be able to come to his rescue. If his army was enfeebled or lost, he would lose the main support of his political power and the hope of fulfilling his ambitions. Yet he also knew he must do something to impress the world that he was now in Palestine. He was deeply disturbed by the fast Jewish advances in the Jerusalem area (Operations 'Yivoussi', 'Maccabi' and 'Kilshon'), particularly those outside the Jewish-inhabited suburbs, considering that Jerusalem was never included in the Jewish area under the UN partition scheme either. It was utterly disagreeable to him, what seemed imminent, that the Jews would now get control of the Old City of Jerusalem. Swept by a sentiment of mission on behalf of the Arab cause, bestowed upon him by the Arab League, after 3 days of waiting, which an Arab historian of the Legion termed 'the foresaken days', Abdullah made up his mind. On 17 May he ordered the hesitating Glubb to leave the positions held by the Legion earlier and take Jerusalem by force.[78]

Glubb then launched three simultaneous moves: he sent Brigade 1 to attack the northern section of Jerusalem, to secure a corridor between the Ramallah heights and the Old City, he sent the garrison companies from Brigade 4 into the Old City to aid the irregular Arab forces inside and he captured, with Battalion 4 of Brigade 3 (later reinforced by more contingents of the same brigade) the momentarily vacant Latrun stronghold, blocking the Jewish supply route to Jerusalem. At this point the Legion enjoyed a clear fire-superiority over the Jewish forces and made full use of it.[79] The Jewish troops in the greater Jerusalem sector were equal in number to the Arab forces, including the Legion, but they had no artillery, and were engaged with a contingent of the Qawukji forces at the Bab al Wad passage and expected an Egyptian column to appear any moment at the southern entrance to Jerusalem. Thus Glubb managed to form a connection to the Old City from the North, to encircle the Jewish forces on Mount Scoupus and to block the only highway from the Coastal plain to Jewish Jerusalem at Latrun. However, he failed to make an advance into the Northern section of the modern Jewish city, where he suffered heavy casualties, which served as a warning as to what might happen if the Legion continued to attack in a built-up area. With increasing IDF pressure on Latrun and every reinforcement sent to augment defences around that stronghold, the Legion pressure in the city itself focused on capturing the Old City. Little cooperation was attained between the Legion and the other Arab forces, nor a proper overlapping. As a result, the Arab siege of Jewish Jerusalem was incomplete. Soon Jews managed to develop an alternative route of supply south of Latrun, a situation which apparently was not known to the Legion command when the first truce began.[80]

THE ARMIES OF SYRIA AND LEBANON IN 1948

The Syrian and Lebanese armies were established as colonial forces by France during her mandatory rule in the Levant countries. In the annexes to two treaties of independence 'initialled' respectively in September and November 1936, France undertook to modernize these armies. But since these treaties were not ratified in Paris until World War II broke out, random supply of second-rate equipment substituted the promised modernization.[81] In April 1946, The French mandate was over. When command over these armies was transferred to the governments of the two new republics, a local, French-educated officers corps was left behind with still more plans for modernization. But the practical French military assistance to these governments continued at random, amidst mutual political distrust between the two sides. The stability of the government and unity of purpose of establishing good relations with the Arab world, which characterized Britain at that point was lacking in France. The governments of Syria and Lebanon, lacked the resources and often the interest to have a too strong army, for fear of a too strong military elite which might interfere in politics. But in 1948 there came a stronger Syrian drive to strengthen the army. By then the original French modernization plan, however, developed one step forwards and then one step backwards. The weapons supplied by France were defined in CIA reports as 'obsolete'. Low-level maintenance caused some of it to deteriorate still further. The result was that out of a supposedly large Syrian OB, only a small fighting force could in reality be extracted.[82]

Between Syria and Lebanon, the former had by far the biggest army. In 1948 it consisted of two parts: the old one (including gendarmerie, horse and camel cavalry) and the supposedly modern one (a skeleton for a division of three brigade-groups). But this modernization was largely only on paper. In May 1948, the only formation in shape was Brigade 1 with two infantry battalions, and a pool of one mixed armoured battalion, consisting of one light Renault R35 and R39 tank company with 37-mm guns and two AFV companies, supported by a deficient artillery of 3–4 75-mm and 1–2 105-mm guns batteries. The armour was a mixture of GMC, Panard, White, Staghound, Marmon Harring-ton and Dodge, some with and some without turrets or guns, others with a variety of 37-mm, 47-mm and 25-mm guns stripped off the gendarmerie or picked up in former World War II battlefields. Brigade 2 also consisted of two batallions, but it was generally in a worse shape. Brigade 3 was in the process of conversion from the gendarmerie.

The weakest point of the Syrian army, however, was small arms. The army's 7.5 and 8-mm French rifles and sub-machine guns, according to CIA sources, were unreliable, because of neglect. Rifles of other sorts, British and German, including some new ones, recently bought in Czechoslovakia, complicated the management of the supply of ammunition. Syria was keen to replace the old rifles with new ones and meanwhile donated many of the old to the volunteer 'Army of Deliverance' which was forming in the Kataneh base in Syria, destined for Palestine. Ammunition stores were very limited, since unlike Iraq or Egypt, even before the embargo, Syria never had an assured source for replenishment.

The Syrian Air Force (Lebanon had none) was at its very beginning. Its core was 20 light American training Harvards, converted to combat and a handful of light Tiger Moths, Piper-cubs and Fairchilds. One-third of all these were unserviceable in 1948 and the number of trained Syrian pilots capable of performing combat flights hardly sufficed to fly even the few serviceable Harvards. A group of Syrian cadets finished their training in February. A few more were about to finish training in Iraq. At that point, the only experienced combat pilots were mercenaries. The shooting down of two Syrian Harvards in May, by

IDF ground fire in Eastern Galilee, deterred the Syrian command from further air incursions into Israel.[83]

Following the Palestine debate at the UN Assembly in 1947, and in anticipation of both the UN attempt to establish a Jewish state and of Syria's arch-rival, King Abdullah, to get control over the other parts of Palestine, the Syrian government intensified its effort to improve the state of its army and to augment and control the Arab irregular forces which were fighting against the Jews there. Syria, therefore became the moving power behind the Arab League's initiated Army of Deliverance. Unable to depend on any external military nursing power to supply her army and mistrusting France, she sent feelers in various other directions to look for military equipment, particularly small arms.

In November 1947, Syria asked Britain for several thousand rifles and machine-guns, but the British government had no interest in selling weapons to Syria and the Syrian application was hanging about in London, rejected time and again with various excuses. In December Syria was told that it had missed the 'normal' deadline for such applications, which was September. In February 1948, Syria was reprimanded for her part in the incursion of irregulars into the still British-controlled Palestine and in April the British simply told Syria that the current British policy was the suspension of all military deliveries to Arab countries, 'except for contract signed before the present situation'. Finally, in May, Syria was advised that 'it will be in the benefit of the Arabs if Britain will not give the USA an excuse to lift their embargo'.[84]

In the fall of 1947 Syrian feelers also reached Czechoslovakia. In November, Prague agreed to sell Syria all her needs in small-arms and small-arms ammunition. Now it turned out that the Syrian government was unable or unwilling to pay immediate hard currency in cash. The delivery of the Syrian consignment was delayed and, meanwhile (as we shall show), emmisaries from the Yishuv, with a better means of payment at their disposal, snatched much of the small arms immediately available. When the delivery to Syria finally began, late in March 1948, security negligence enabled a Hagana commando to sink the main shipload of this consignment and only some 1000 rifles and a few submachine guns reached Syria in different ways.[85] This left the Syrian Army supplies in an even worse situation than that of the Arab armies which depended on British sources. The situation of the smaller Lebanese Army was none better.

In Syria and Lebanon there were the beginnings of ammunition factories. IDF intelligence reported such a plant in the al Kadem suburb of Damascus and CIA sources told of a such a factory in Beirut.[86]

However, the production of these plants was such that it could not relieve the ammunition distress of main ammunition sorts in any Arab army.

THE ARMIES OF SYRIA AND LEBANON AT THE WAR'S OUTSET

Despite the poor state of her army, Syria was among the Arab states which vigorously demanded military intervention in Palestine. The Syrian and Lebanese share in the first phase of the invasion after 15 May, however improvised, contributed a good deal to the difficulties of the IDF command to hold the defence of its controlled area. However, later on their impact on the war and their zeal to fight greatly declined.

The first Syrian attack, between 17 and 22 May, took place south of the Sea of Galilee, depending on their left flank being secured by the Iraqis. In their onslaught they used their best available forces, namely Brigade 1, including the 75-mm guns and the armour and air force, spending a good deal of their sparse artillery ammunition. After capturing certain IDF positions, including two abandoned Kibbutzim, they were repulsed with heavy losses in their attempt to take two other Kibbutzim, the Daganias. The unexpected appearance of four IDF 65-mm guns, the main cause of their casualties, having not expected to face guns and like the Iraqis, not realizing that these were the only field artillery pieces Israel had at that point, having lost four AFVs, including three tanks and two aircraft, and, lastly, seeing the Iraqi clearing off their left flank and being threatened by an Israeli commando raid on their rear, the Syrian command decided to move its effort to the northern section, under a destructive attack on Kibbutz Ein Gev. Now their assault focused on the Israeli salient along the Upper Jordan Valley. Helped by reinforcements from Brigade 2 and by a rare instance of two-army coordination with the Lebanese, who attacked the same salient from the East, on 7 June the Syrians attacked south of Lake Hulle, scoring their greatest success in the war by capturing, on 9 June, Mishmar Hayarden and forming a threat to the Israeli defences in the entire northernmost part of the country.

The Lebanese army entered the war at the northernmost section of Upper Galilee. On paper it had four infantry battalions, an AFV company and two Batteries of 75-mm guns. Their actual attacks at the Naftali Heights was carried out by two infantry battalions and an AFV company. On 16 May they captured the stronghold of Mallakiya, lost it again as a result of a counter-attack held by an IDF mechanized force at their back and gained control of it again on 6 June.[87]

ARAB IRREGULAR FORCES IN PALESTINE UP UNTIL THE END OF MAY 1948

In the civil war which erupted in Palestine in December 1948, the Palestine Arab community did not have at their disposal a military force to match the Jewish one. 'A population of 1 300 000 Arab Palestinians', wonders an Israeli scholar in a later study of military preparedness of the Palestinian Arab, 'could amass only a scant number of men to shoulder the task of saving their national survival'.[88] Yet, their violent activities, under the conceding-nothing leadership of the Mufti, Amin al Hussiany, was the oil poured on the Palestine flame. A prompt aid seemed forthcoming from other Arab countries, at least according to statements made by heads of the Arab League. However, that help was hampered by the presence of the British Army in Palestine, by political disagreement between Arab governments and mostly by the poor arsenal at the disposal of the Arab countries. But since the arsenal of the Jewish Yishuv was also terribly poor, it delayed the military decision in favour of the Jewish forces until late April.

According to the decision of the Arab League of 8 December 1947, the Palestinian Arabs were to get Arab volunteers, arms and funds, for which quotas were fixed for each Arab country. This resistance, was aimed less at an immediate military decision and more at a political sabotaging of the UN action. Syria's Prime Minister, Jamil Mardam, defined that aim as putting in great doubt the implementation of the UN partition plan by peaceful means, which would cause its suspension. According to what transpired at the UN between the months of February and April, it seemed that this goal was well within reach. But the Arab military effort was far too weak, the Jewish envigoration and military successes in April were too decisive and the inability of the new UN Special Assembly convention to reach a decision too baffling to substantiate that hope. In a series of Jewish military operations, beginning in April (actually concurrently with some Arab offensives) the Arab forces, local as well as the volunteer corps, suffered a series of defeats. The Yishuv forces managed to consolidate their military position and, still before the end of the British mandate, establish their control over a necessary and sufficient strategic area to be able to proclaim their state and hold their own against the subsequent attack by the regular Arab armies. These events affected the international arena in a direction very different from what it seemed to the Arabs earlier.

Earlier, the Arab League had delegated the overall command of the irregular military activities in Palestine to Assistant Chief-of-Staff of the Iraqi army, Ismail Saffwat and the planning of the military activities to a veteran Iraqi soldier, General Taha al Hashemi.[89] In fact, the control of the Army of Deliverance was in Syrian hands. Syria provided most of the men, commands and weapons, giving the direct command in the field to pro-Syrian officers like Fawzi al Qawukji and Adib Shishakly, who could be trusted to supplant the anti-Syrian influence of Abdullah as well as the Mufti. That intensive Syrian involvement helped to split the irregular Arab force into four separate 'armies' which 'divided the country between themselves', but acted with little coordination, sometimes double-crossing each other.[90]

Qawukji forces were active in Northern Samaria, Lower Galilee and in May at the Jerusalem approaches. Later they withdrew to reorganize in Syria and returned to Lower Galilee in early June. During the rest of the summer, this Army of Deliverance, along with some Lebanese contingents, controlled the longest section of front any Arab army held alone, officially considered a part of the Lebanese forces, being under Syrian influence, but all in all keeping their independence.[91] At the peak of their strength they numbered six battalions with approximately 5000 men – an international mosaic of Syrians, Iraqis, even Germans, Bosnians, etc. Their equipment was the poorest among all the Arab armies in Palestine: non-standard small arms (the men were the owners of their arms), a few medium mortars and four to five 75-mm and 105-mm guns received from Syria. The amount of ammunition at the disposal of this artillery was very limited.

Up until the spring, there were two smaller irregular forces in the centre of the country, under the control of the Mufti. One was active in the Rmleh-Lyda area under the command of Hassan Salameh and the other in the Jerusalem section under Abd al Qader al Hussayni. These forces were manned almost entirely by local Arabs, who were called to duty by the traditional alarm (Faz'a) method. Together they counted some 1000 men, perhaps less. In southern Palestine there was a fourth irregular force, consisting of local Palestinians and volunteers mainly from Egypt, by and large controlled by Egypt's General Staff. Finally, there were, semi-autonomous irregular forces in Jaffa, Haifa, the Druz community, etc., led by officers from Syria, Iraq and Transjordan.

The Jewish offensive which began early in April ended with the disintegration of the local Palestinian Arab community, the escape of its leadership and the breaking of the backbone of three out of four of the local Arab armies. All the mixed cities in the country, with the exception of the old quarter of Jerusalem and hundreds of Arab villages, many of them now empty, were also captured by the Jewish forces, together with two wholly Arab cities. In the process, the top Palestinian Arab leadership left the Jewish-controlled area, making the defenceless Arab population prone to escape or be easily driven away by Jews. Abd al Qader and Salameh were killed. With the exception of Qawukji forces, the irregular Arab troops deserted their units or joined the Arab armies which entered their respective sections.

After mid-May there was a new pattern of the participation of Arab 'irregulars' in the war. While Qawukji remained independently active, in matters of supply he was treated as an aberrant son. Having been a Syrian satellite, with Syria herself almost running out of ammunition, Qawukji tried to use the Arab League's channels to improve his supplies, reminding them that supplying his army was a League's solemn undertaking, even threatening to resign, but to little effect.[92] Nonetheless, after returning from the reorganization in Syria, in early June his contingents were again a hard nut for the IDF to crack. Their help was material in the Lebanese recapture Mallakiya and in Lower Galilee he seriously threatened to capture the Sejera junction. So long as there was a truce or that the IDF did not open a direct offensive against his forces, Qawukji's existence counted a great deal among the Arab expeditionary forces, if only for holding the longest Arab front section facing Israel.

THE ISRAELI ARMED FORCES AT THE END OF MAY 1948

In May 1948 Israel's Defence Forces had just emerged from underground militias. They had no respite to reorganize when they were attacked by five regular Arab armies, simultaneously though not concertedly, along several axes. They had to form up while defending the very physical survival of the new Jewish state and the Jewish community in Palestine. This effort was followed by a desperate dash to import or to produce weapons and to equip a just mobilized army.

Indeed, the most acute problem of the forming up of the IDF was not a shortage of manpower or finance, but of weapons. When the UN

Assembly voted for the partition of Palestine, the total number of members of the Yishuv who received some military training surpassed 60 000, but the number of rifles at their disposal was approximately 12 000. All the other small and medium arms pieces, including pistols, amounted to some additional 6000 pieces. At the end of April 1948, the Jewish forces still had just over 16 000 rifles, some 1000 light and 150 medium machine-guns and a few hundred light and medium mortars and their ammunition stores for small arms amounted to less than a million rounds. It was still very far from possible to provide every new recruit with personal arms. In access to these, the IDF had lately obtained and used six 20-mm guns, 25 odd AFVs of all sorts and approximately a dozen serviceable light aircraft.[93]

Other basic needs of the army beside weapons, were mobilization and the attainment of a unity of command. The IDF General Staff sprang from the *Mifkada Artzit*, the Overall Command of the Haganah during the mandate period. This body did not always or necessarily consist of men of military distinction and expertese. Rather, it was composed of underground individuals proportionally representing political parties in the so-called 'Organized Yishuv', the overwhelming majority in the Jewish community who accepted the leadership of the official Zionist Executive. In May 1948 circumstances necessitated a wider consensus and the abolishment of the anachronistic political composition of the supreme command. While the establishment of provisional legislature and the cabinet were attained by an interparty agreement, reached in late April, depolitization of the High Command and the direct subordination of a united army to a professional General Staff, remained the subject of disagreement, often nearing insurgency. The main issues under dispute were the future position of former Chief of the *Mifkadah Artzit*, the subordination of the dissident IZL and LHI to the army command and the abolishment of the independent Palmach command. The relegation of Yisrael Galili, a leading political figure in the left-wing Mapam Party and the appointment of the politically unaffiliated General Yacov Dori Chief of General Staff subordinated to the Minister of Defence, was still considered by many as a political step by the new Prime and Defence Minister, David Ben Gurion, leader of the majority Labour Party Mapai, to cement his party's position in the army. Opposition to this and other appointments made by Ben Gurion, perforated to many walks of the army, creating an atmosphere close to disobedience on the one hand or the resignation Ben Gurion on the other hand.[94] As for the dissident IZL and LHI, although these were relatively small, they commanded public sympathy in wider circles and were a potential nuisance value with regard to discipline in the army and a threat to Israel's foreign relations.

The vast majority of early members of the IDF came from ranks of the Haganah. From the 1920s, every healthy young man and woman in the Yishuv were supposedly Haganah members. In practice, a far smaller group manned the active ranks of the Haganah's four major formations: Palmach, Hish, Him and Gadna. Mobilization among these began as early as December 1947, but general mobilization started only in early May, more so after mid-May. A preliminary major problem was also finance. The Yishuv defence budget for 1947–8 (the Jewish calender year) was originally merely $3.5 million.[95] What was needed now including the cost of weapons, amounted to 30 times that amount.

The general mobilization, under charge of the Centre for National Service, an arm of the Haganah, was transferred *per se* to the Israeli Ministry of Defence. But even when this body was established, early in 1948, many units were already long mobilized and engaged in some of the most bitter battles. Palmach, the elite formation of the General Staff including its reserves, continued to take new recruits from the youth of the Kibbutz movements and eventually also from among foreign volunteers. In mid-May Palmach numbered approximately 6000 men and women.[96] But it was the Hish, the 'Field Troops', which formed the core of the Haganah trained manpower, from which the main corps of the IDF first-line brigades, the 'Hativot' came. The better-trained regulars of the Haganah belonged to this force, among them former servicemen of the British army, who brought with them experience of command, staff work and army routine, rarely known in the Palmach. Hish also included some 1800 members of the British-sponsored 'Settlements Added Police'. The number of Hish mobilized recruits rose by the day, although until May many members continued to share civil occupation with part-time military activity.

By 1 April, over 90 000 men and unmarried women were registered for service, but only approximately 36 000 received a call to report. For on top of administrative and bureaucratic difficulties, there was simply not yet enough arms to give to new recruits. In the third week of May this situation began to change. Every able man and unmarried woman of the ages 18–35 years, with the exception of 'vital workers', were now called and soon there was a call also for men of the ages 35–45 years.[97] Beyond that direct mobilization into the regular IDF, the Him arm engaged men and women in and beyond conscription in local defence of cities, towns and settlements. Often, Him soldiers were in the first line of fire. Finally, Gadna, the youth troops, considered the General Staff's reserve, were still largely under the age of 17 years. After a bitter public debate, men born in 1931 were called and by mid-summer were mobilized too. By then hundreds of that age group had already volunteered earlier to Palmach, Hish or the dissident organizations. Women in the regular army amounted to some 10% of the total recruits.[98]

The absorption into the IDF of the dissident organizations raised a series of tormenting problems and involved mutual distrust, sleuthing, clashes, arrests, even shooting and casualties. The main stumbling block for full amalgamation were the conditions put up by these organizations to the High Command; they demanded autonomous units of their own men within the IDF and the retainment of their 'freedom of action' in Jerusalem. As a *modus vivendi* IZL and LHI announced their disbandment 'in the low country only'. On May 29 several hundred members of LEHI joined the newly organized Armour Brigade 8 and a few days later two IZL 'battalions' joined IDF Brigades 3 and 5. According to the IZL historian, 'five more battalions' were about to join when the Altalena incident took place, as a result of which members of the IZL had, henceforth, to join the army individually.[99] The two organizations, however, continued to act separately in Jerusalem, up until the assassination of the UN Mediator, Count Bernadotte, on 17 September when they were forced to dismember. Three weeks later the special headquarters of the Palmach was also disbanded.

Finally, the IDF conscripted over 20 000 foreigners: immigrants, volunteers and soldiers of fortune from abroad. The majority of these last came from European Displaced Persons Centres, from Eastern Europe and North Africa, and from British detention camps in Cyprus. The latter became *bona fide* IDF soldiers in the category of *Gahal*, recruits from abroad. A smaller, yet highly valuable group of recruits, called *Mahal*, consisted of experienced soldiers who either volunteered to serve for solidarity motives or served under special terms, some for considerable salaries. This service, of course, was contrary to the terms of the UN embargo and against their own countries' laws.

The Israeli mass recruitment went well and could have gone even better. The sense of national emergency coupled with excitement in the Jewish diaspora were partly responsible for this success. But the main reason for the success was the unique demographic advantage enjoyed by the Yishuv, having been a community with an abnormal young age stratification; a young society with high conscription potential. This was the result of a persistent Zionist selective immigration policy. For although the British controlled and continuously curtailed

Table 1 Age groups of Jewish immigrants to Palestine, 1928–47 by
per cent[101]

Age/years	0–14	15–29	30–44	45 and above
1928–32	13.2	65.1	11.4	13.3
1933–4	20.2	43.4	22.7	13.7
1935–8	18.1	42.7	19.6	19.6
1939–47	10.5	40.6	21.1	17.6
Illegal immigration	6.1	53.3	27.2	12.5
Average	17.7	46.6	20.1	15.6

the immigration quotas, they left the allocation of immigration certifi-
cates within the quotas to the Zionist Executive, which always preferred to take in young immigrants and children. This criterion was
even further severed in selecting candidates for the illegal immigration, after 1945. In consequence the mean age of Jewish immigrants,
up until 1945 was 16 years and afterwords 19 years. The Israeli advantage drawn for that policy is all the more ostentatious considering
that in 1928 the Jewish community in Palestine numbered only 152 000
and in May 1948, 649 000 and that of the 300 000 young men and
women who immigrated to Palestine since 1929, the majority came
after 1934.[101] From Table 1 it is clear that in 1948 the majority of the
64.3% (46.6+17.7) of men and women immigrants and some of their
offspring were conscripts. Even those who immigrated as youths earlier
were still capable of contributing to production and defence while almost all their offspring were in the service ages. Indeed, in 1948 males
aged 20–44 years in the Yishuv formed 22% of the entire Jewish population, while in the Arab sector of Palestine, the figures were 14%.[102]
In fact, members of the IDF fighting formations were on average younger;
most of them were aged between 17 and 24 years. The share of that
native group in the total number killed in action (indicating their share
in battles) was 64.8%.[103]

This is the demographic foundation of Israel's extraordinary ability to raise an army that in December 1948 numbered over 104 000
conscripts, notwithstanding casualties and it continued to grow.[104] And
although over 24 000 members of the IDF, approximately one-quarter
of the entire army at this point were not members of the Yishuv prior
to 1948, without them Israel's rate of direct military mobilization had
surpassed any precedence in military history: 13% of the population
served in the army, in addition to considerable sections which were

not formally mobilized, yet contributed tremendously to the military effort. Such a rate would put the strength of the British-born army in World War II at 6.5–7 million, the USA at 21–2 million and the Red Army at 24 million.

Indeed, there was never a moment in the 1948 Palestine war that the Jewish forces suffered a numerical inferiority against the Arab forces which they fought. There was, however, an interim period, that is, until the main general mobilization was completed, during which the number of IDF combat troops only equalled the attacking armies. Early in June, the number of soldiers in the IDF combat formations (Hativot and Heilot) was 30 000, only slightly in excess compared to approximately 28 000 on the Arab side, but that number included over 1000 or more women and those in headquarters which in the Arab case usually stayed in their own countries. Again, the IDF problem was not the number of troops, but arming them and teaching them modern warfare. How was it that the Arabs failed to set up a bigger army at such a crucial moment in their history – is history. Here we shall endeavour to answer a somewhat close but different question: why did the Arabs fail to be better armed and equipped and how, relatively speaking, Israel managed to do better?

If Israel's major problem was not the number of troops, it was ultimately not financial, either. While the governments of Iraq and Transjordan incurred a financial crisis right upon entering the war and while Egypt and Syria, which were in a relatively better financial form were unable by their own means to find alternative sources of war materials to those which became closed to them, the Jewish communities in the Western world, stimulated by Yishuv emissaries, provided Israel literally with more funds than needed to finance the war, including arms purchase. In 1948, fund raising to aid Israel in the diaspora amounted, cash and commitments, to approximately $129 million, including $4.5 million raised by the IZL and LHI. What Israel spent on arms acquisition and other external expenditure pertaining to the war amounted to only approximately $78.3 million, of which $55.5 million were spent in Europe and $18.3 million elsewhere.[105]

Thus, Israel's difficulties in financing the war were at worst a problem of temporary delays of payments, but never a real lack of dollar cash flow. Despite occasional exhaustion of dollars, Israeli arms purchasers in 1948 became renown for their capability to put millions of Dollars as a down-payment and pay the rest of their bills. This power was increased by the fact that often allocations bypassed the Israeli exchequer and went directly to the chief purchasers. While this practice evaded proper financial supervision and apparently encouraged a degree of embezzlement (*Iee Nikion Kapayim*) to which the IDF records occasionally allude, it definitely speeded up the process.

ISRAEL'S ARMS PURCHASING ORGANIZATION AND PROJECTS IN 1948

Immediately after World War II, some Yishuv leaders had already anticipated the possibility that if circumstances enabled them to establish a Jewish state in Palestine, they might have to fight not only the Palestinian Arabs but regular armies of the Arab states. The foundation was laid quite early for a clandestine organization in the USA and in other countries to finance and buy 'heavy arms'. The Haganah and later also the dissidents, were meanwhile accumulating small arms abroad, hoping to be able to ship it to Palestine. But it was simply impossible to import arms in big bulk up until the very end of the British rule. A 'most dangerous bottle-neck' was therefore expected to occur before the Yishuv had time to ship in and absorb the military equipment purchased abroad, even if this equipment was ready in time. This, indeed is what transpired, only earlier than expected. Long before 15 May, the Yishuv shortage of arms and ammunition put their future at great risk. According to General Ygael Yadin, the IDF Chief of Operations in 1948, 'of all the war period . . . the month of March was the most terrible and most critical, because there was nothing to fight with.[106] The picture drawn by Yadin, plausibly implies that all the financial, demographic, strategic, morale and administrative advantages enjoyed by Israel later on and all the arms it had purchased by then abroad, might not have helped the Jews had they lost the battle over the control of roads and the supply of isolated settlements and of Jerusalem in March, while still fighting against irregular Arab forces only, because they lacked arms and ammunition. They nearly did.

It was only the first deliveries of arms and ammunition from Czechoslovakia in early April and a similar bulk of arms which arrived at the end of that month, which dramatically changed the situation in the Yishuv's favour.[107] In fact, the arms received in April were not much, but it acted as a critical mass. It amounted to some 5000 rifles, 240 machine-guns and 5 million rounds of ammunition at the beginning of April and a similar load arrived on 28 April. Furthermore, since unloading was still clandestine and could only be done sparsely and since the next consignment of Czech small arms did not arrive until 28 May, a second 'terrible' period of shortage occurred between the termination of the British mandate and the arrival, within a further 3 weeks of several additional boats and aircraft, carrying more arms, including artillery. Just before the embargo came into effect, Israel managed to bring in such a large amount of arms and ammunition, that a telegram in June from the Chief of Israel's arms acquisition to Israel's Ministry of Defence, victoriously tells the good tidings: 'we have reached a saturation (revaiah) in small-arms' and that the 'heavy' arms are very useful.[108]

But the IDF inferiority in 'heavy' weapons, that is, artillery, armour and air and sea powers, could not be wiped off at once and numerically it never did. It was not any devastating impact of the new Israeli weapon which stopped the Arab invasion, but a combination of several factors pertaining to the very appearance of such weapons in Israeli hands: surprise, Arab bad intelligence, brazen Israeli counter-attacks, exhaustion of much of the Arab ammunition reserves and a sudden realization that with the embargo now on, British supply of ammunition was not forthcoming. For the time being, anyway, the effect of the Israeli artillery and aircraft was psychological. The few Israeli 65-mm guns, which the IDF command kept rotating between the fronts, the few 20-mm anti-aircraft guns put to use as anti-tank weapons (without armour-piercing shells), the handful of light aircraft which threw unzeroed home-made bombs on Arab positions and towns and the two sorties of four Israeli Messerschmidts over the Eyptian and the Iraqi fronts, after which only one Messerschmidt survived, were largely responsible, as the documents show, for the switch of the Arab armies, early in June, (save, for a while Syria and Lebanon) to defensive positions.[109] At the end of May 1948, Israel's *tendon Achillis* was neither troops nor financial resources, but the fact that it only started to import arms after 15 May and suddenly the staggering news about the imposition of the embargo came, just when the flow of arms increased.

At the helm of Israel's arms acquisition organization, as of many of her other security arms, stood Ben Gurion. But the practical execution was at the hand of the Chief of Rechesh, an old organization, in which structure, method and personnel changed little, but to which a new mission was assigned.[110] It was none but the old Mossad, which formerly organized illegal immigration and which since late 1947 gradually switched to arms. In March 1948, the veteran chief of the Mossad, Shaul Avigour, was appointed Chief of Rechesh, with all former Aliya Beit agents, Yishuv seamen and emissaries in other clandestine tasks abroad, including the Haganah missions in Europe and the USA, sub-ordinated to him.

Avigour's appointment was made by Ben Gurion on 20 March, when it became apparent that the acquisition efforts were out of focus. Avigour then moved the Mossad headquarters from Paris to Geneva and went to Rome to meet with the 'Big Three' of the acquisition operations: Yehuda Arazi, Ehud Avriel and Mounya Mardur. He informed this triumvirate of his authority and introduced a detailed plan of objectives and priorities in the allocation of funds.[111] None of these three agents was new to Avigour (all had worked under him as illegal immigration agents) nor was the plan introduced utterly new; it was already partly in execution. Yet Ben Gurion and Avigour realized that these agents must be disciplined if the delicate arms supply was to work, and that the new acquisition plan might still be subject to alterations following growing difficulties in arms purchase in the USA, and the spectacle of new opportunity in Czechoslovakia and, possibly, in France.

According to the new arrangements, there were three major centres under Geneva: Prague, Rome and New York, and a number of secondary centres, namely Paris, London, Brussels and Geneva itself. It was a network created by the changing picture of armament sources. Prague became paramount early in 1948, when the special relations which began to form between Yishuv and the government of Czechoslovakia now seemed expandable to other Communist countries. The Prague branch was headed by Avriel, who was installed there in December 1947. The New York *Rechesh* headquarters, covering the entire Western hemisphere, was first viewed as the main future source of armament and then turned out a great disappointment, was put under Ben Gurion's favourite, the young Teddy Kollek. Soon, however, most of the funds collected in the USA were diverted elsewhere. As for Rome, it grew in importance because Italy was found to be a huge dumping ground for US military surpluses, and law enforcement there was loose and the Italian ports were approachable and familiar to the *Mossad* agents. The leading spirit in Italy, as in France, was Arazi, the most experienced secret agent of Haganah abroad, who had been buying arms for it since 1938. Arazi knew the world of arms-trade better than anyone else in Palestine and was at his best in inventing cunning techniques of illegal shipment and licensing. However, he was hopelessly individualistic, disobedient, careless with money and could never plan more than one or two steps at a time. After incurring disgraceful failures in the USA earlier that year, Arazi was excluded from working across the Atlantic, and Avigour's relations with him grew strained. In fact, Avigour was looking for a way to sack Arazi altogether, but in the months of May and June Arazi was again brilliantly successful in France and Italy, so his deposition was deferred.[112]

Because of the nature of the clandestine work, of diehard habits and the fast-changing circumstances, Avigour hardly controlled the Rechesh organization. Agents disdained him and his superiors (except, perhaps, Ben Gurion) and seemed to have been convinced that the new centralism was bound to defeat their efforts. Ben Gurion on his part often felt likewise, and allowed additional 'loners' to penetrate the system and bypass the hierarchy – adding chaos to the prevailing situation. A plan set in Tel Aviv or Geneva could the next morning be subject for on-the-spot alterations. New agents, who grew within the system and became chiefs of independent networks, made their own decisions and spending. Hundreds of thousands of dollars in cash were delivered across the USA and Europe, changing hands without registration of any kind. It was told that airmen, only recently recruited, were carrying Rechesh dollars by the thousands in their inner pockets. 'How can we ever find out where the millions of dollars were spent?' lamented the Director General of the Ministry of Defence in a letter to Avigour 'what happened to eight million dollars taken by Alon?; 'there is not a single proper financial report!' Rechesh history is littered with failed projects for which no one claimed responsibility. Avigour, in any event, grew increasingly bitter. At the end of his service in Geneva he wrote that he 'wished . . . never again to be thrown into this kind of responsibility'.[113] In July Avigour lost his son in the war, and two weeks later he was replaced by Pinhas Sapir, a less charismatic figure, but a better administrator. Sapir undertook to overhaul the system by way of reprimands and dismissals, and managed to improve Geneva's control over the organization,[114] but whether this worked is not clear. It, anyway, came too late to affect the decisive phase of the 1948 war.

Anyway, in the race against the clock and the embargo, it is doubtful whether centralization could have produced better results. Almost none of the original *Rechesh* initiative went according to plan. However, there were some individual, locally improvised enterprises which bore brilliant success, such as the Israeli purchase of cargo aircraft in the USA, and artillery in France.[115]

Table 2 Formal Order of Battle in the Palestine front at the end of May 1948

Army Formations	Strength		Inf. btns.		AFVs		Artillery		Serviceable combat aircraft	
	Men	Bgds.	Stand.	Others	Tanks	Other	Field	Other	Fighters	Others
Iraq	4 500	3*	7	2**		40	48	12	13	15
Egypt	5 500	2*	3	3**	30***	24	24	16	32	12
Transjordan	6 500	3*	4	2**	–	120	12***	16	–	–
Syria	6 000	3	7	–	12	35	36	30	–	15
Lebanon	2 000	–	4	–	–	12	16	–	–	–
Irregulars	3 000	–	–	4	–	5	6	–	–	–
Total	27 500	11	25	10	42	237	142	74	45	42
Israel	32* 000	9** (12)	27 (32)		13	15	45***	30****	7	32

Iraq: *brigade groups (Gahpals), **local Arab units.
Egypt: *including the Light Forces, **plus some foreign units, ***Mark 6 tanks not armed with guns.
Transjordan: *2 battalions in brigades 1 and 2 + skeleton brigades, **seven garrison companies, ***Another 12 guns in units under establishment.
Irregulars *Forces under Qawukji.
Israel: *The entire IDF, including services and some 10 000 in recruitment process. Not including about 900 IZL and LHI troops in Jerusalem, **Three more brigades under advanced construction, ***including 120-mm mortars, ****mainly 20-mm.

Table 3 Formal Order of Battle in the Palestine front in mid October 1948

Army Formations	Strength		Inf. btns.		AFVs		Artillery		Serviceable combat aircraft	
	Men	Bgd.	Stand.	Others	Tanks	Other	Field	Other	Fighters	Others
Iraq	18 000	5*	13	3**	–	2	58	18	13	15
Egypt	15 000	3*	7	8+**	16***	40	40	20	36	46
Transjordan	13 000	3	6	2*	–	110	24	30	–	–
Syria	15 000	3	7	–	–	50	30	12	–	14
Lebanon	3 000	–	4	–	–	12	16	?	–	–
Irregulars	4 000	–	–	5	–	8	6	–	–	–
Total	68 000	14	37	18	16	222	174	80	49	75
Israel	88** 000	12	33	–	13	60	150*	75	16	56

Iraq: *brigade groups (Gahpals), **local Arab units, ***practically all aircraft grounded.
Egypt: *including the Light Forces, **eight reserve battalions + 8–9 foreign companies, ***Mark 6 tanks, additional 32 Locusts under reconditioning.
Transjordan: *local Arabs.
Irregulars: *Forces under Qawukji.
Israel: *The entire IDF, including services, **including 120-mm mortars.

ISRAEL'S MILITARY INDUSTRY IN 1948

Another major Israeli advantage over the Arabs under the embargo conditions was her capability to produce essential war materials at home. Stemming from a small clandestine factory and following a massive illegal import in 1947 of equipment for military production from the US, in 1948 the Israeli military industry quickly developed into an organization capable of helping to equip a large army. At the end of May 1948 this industry was supplying the IDF with sub-machine-guns (Stans). Early in June, some 7000 locally produced Stans were already in use and in October the number in use was 16 000. It produced all Israel's needs in 2 and 3 inch mortars, in short-range infantry anti-tank launchers (PIAT) and in most types of hand grenades and air bombs. It supplied most of the IDF needs in low, high and propellant explosives, in mines and in demolition materials. It also gave essential services to the artilley and armoured corps by mending old artillery pieces and aged ammunition imported from abroad, though it was beyond its capability to recondition gun barrels. The armour factory, which began with armour-plating tractors and tracks, moved to build AFVs on civil carriages, upon which rotating turrets were built and, when available, guns were installed. It also fitted half tracks and jeeps for combat tasks. These locally produced AFVs, though cumbersome to operate and not particularly trafficable in bad terrain, none the less compensated the IDF for the lack of tanks and made the subsequent IDF fire-power ovewelming.

The military industry was, however, unsuccessful in many of its other ambitious projects. In 1948 it failed to produce an infantry machine-gun and it was late in producing 7.92 mm ammunition, perhaps because supply was assured from Czechoslovakia. It painfully failed to recon-dition unserviceable 75-mm guns and ammunition imported from Mexico. It could not producee the most needed 120-mm mortar ammunition, and its home-made 160-mm mortars (Fritz) proved inaccurate and a risk to its users. Inability to renovate gun barrels was particularly calamitious in the Israeli failure to use medium tanks, purchased in Italy.[116]

THE IDF ORDER OF BATTLE, MAY 1948

A report from the end of the third week of May depicts the IDF strength, including some 10 000 recruits still in the recruiting centres, as 36 500.

These figures did not include IZL and LHI. A week later, the figures surpassed 42 000.[117] Nine brigades, some still far from standard strength, were already deployed in the front, and three more were in the process of establishment.[118] This OB did not include many hundreds of members of settlements in the line of fire, which, with or without the help of small *Palmach* or *Hish* contingents, played a role in containing the initial onslaught of the regular Arab forces. The Kibbutzim Nirim, Kfar Darom, Negba, Yad Mordechai, Gesher and Degania each at some time engaged a full Battalion attack, supported by armour and artillery. Most of these settlements not only held their own, but along with other settlements often remained thorny spots on the Arab lines of communication, and important Israeli intelligence 'eyes'.

Towards early June the IDF stocks of weapon and ammunition greatly improved. Now the number of service rifles reached approximately 36 000,[119] and the number of sub-machine guns was about 7000. The number of light machine-guns was 6500, and the number of medium machine-guns reached 300. A large amount of ammunition for these weapons also arrived in Israel. Whereas in mid-April the total amount of 7.92-mm ammunition was half a million rounds, now it was now 33 million. The number of medium infantry weapons, particularly 81-mm mortars and ZB37 Czech machine-guns was still below standard, but this gap was closed in July. The Israeli artillery made as yet only moderate progress. At the end of May it had at its disposal five 65-mm guns, 12 120-mm heavy mortars, 25 20-mm Hispano-Swizza guns and two 25 pounder guns to which no ammunition was found. Israel's armour was still AFVs stolen from the British, including one Sherman and two Cromwell tanks (ammunition for their guns was non-existent), 13 armoured cars of various sorts, 16 half tracks and two dozen home-made AFVs.[120]

In May 1948, the Israeli Air Force, was almost non-existent, since some of its few light aicraft were destroyed on 15 May in an Egyptian air raid on Tel Aviv airport. Out of 24 light Austers, bought from the mandatory authorities in January (some for use, some for parts) a few entered service in March, but after 15 May only four could fly. Two Norsemen which arrived early in May were lost and a C47 Dakota, confiscated from Air France, was also in ruins. Still, half a dozen light passengers aircraft (Bonanza, Fairchild and Rapid) were still used for primitive bombing of the enemy.[121] The most valuable surviving part of the air force was its transport wing, consisting of nine American C46 Commandos and one Constellation, bought and reconditioned in the USA. Most of these planes had just arrived from across the

Atlantic, and were destined to carry arms from Czechoslovakia.

Israel's high hopes were pinned at 25 Czech ME109 Messerschmidt fighters, which began to arrive dismantled; it took two C46 flights to carry one Messerschmidt. Their assembly in Israel involved a further complicated process which augured disappointment. The Czech technicians who worked on these aircraft in Israel found it difficult to solve problems such as the timing between the guns and the propeller. Meanwhile, five Israeli pilots, who went to Czechoslovakia to learn to fly Messerschmidts were already back waiting. On 29 May the first four Messerschmidts could take off and did, but three of them were lost within 24 hours, while the assembly of seven more has vacillated. Israeli technicians were also busy rebuilding a British Spitfire, out of a crushed Egyptian plane and from parts found in an evacuated British base. All these planes, however, could not take off before the commencement of the truce on 11 June.[122]

The Israeli Navy had a great project of acquisition, since earlier it was feared that an Arab blockade would be attempted against Israeli navigation. But there was no such blockade and at the same time, despite heavy spending in the USA and Italy, by the end of May Israel was unsuccessful in acquiring any war-like ships. Its Navy included two old civilian vessels converted into gunboats (SS *Eilat* and *Drom Africa*) and a third ship (*Wedgewood*) still under repairs.[123]

What was the standard of the IDF troops at this point? Evidently they enjoyed high morale, but they were far from mastering the military profession. 'Our men in the army are very good Zionists', was Ben Gurion's conclusion as late as October, 'but they are not yet soldiers'.[124] Indeed, even elementary military doctrine and expertise, which the British taught the Arab armies, was lacking in the IDF combat corps. The heavy losses suffered by some of the best IDF units up until May, brought about even a drop in the standard of junior commanders. Knowledge of modern warfare, tactics and strategy, was badly lacking among the medium and high echelons of command, where promotion was quick for the bold and the natural leaders, but where very few had a chance to study war. The highest standard course for officers was a Platoon commanders and even in these courses not much expertise was learned about the use of weapons. There was no time even for a proper individual training of new recruits, let alone formations. No battalion or brigade had undergone any joint exercises or even TWET until well after the war. Following consultation with Colonel Mickey Stone, an American Mahal volunteer who from March acted as a super-expert for the High Command, Ben Gurion confided to his diary that there was no officer in the Hagana-turning-regular army who knew how to command a company or battalion in battle. A fundamental blackout in the education of IDF officers was fighting an enemy's fortified position. When Stone suggested a course for Battalion commanders, the Chief of Staff, General Yacov Dori said he could not spare his best officer and suggested that they should 'take a correspondence course . . .'[125] The situation was somewhat better in the Israeli Air Force, due to the large number of experienced Mahal air and ground crews (note: out of 232 air-crew members in the IDF in October 1948, only 38 did not come from abroad in 1948).[126] The trouble was that there were too few aircraft for these men to fly.

To sum up: at the end of May, the professional standard of the armies on both sides was low, except the Arab Legion; the Israelis had advantages in morale and the unity of command, which the Arabs were lacking. The Arabs started with great superiority in the number of heavy weapons, but their immediate attack was made with relatively small OBs. The reinforcement of their forces later on went hand in hand with the Israeli mass mobilization and absorption of new arms and ammunition during early June and during the first truce. After the collapse of the main corps of irregular Arab forces in Palestine, just when the mandate drew to its end, the numbers of troops on both sides of the front were approximately equal. When the first truce came into effect, the Arabs were still far superior in the number of weapons, particularly artillery, armour and aircraft, but they had already missed their real chance to make use of their superiority and so the value of their advantage shrunk, due to both the embargo situation and the appearance of similar weapons on the IDF side. However, at the end of May it was still too early to predict how Israel's future arms acquisition plans would be affected by the embargo.

We may safely, therefore, accept the British definition of late May[127] that 2 weeks after the regular Arab armies attacked Israel, the two parties were in a state of a near military draw. The Anglo-American initiative at the UN was to keep them in this state.

3 The United States, the War in Palestine and the Embargo, 1947–9

The Second World War elevated the USA to a position of superpower and dwarfed her traditional peacetime isolationist approach to foreign policy. In the bipolar international setting which followed, the USA led the Western democracies against the Communist realignment led by the USSR. This was one of the main reasons, though not the only one, which brought about America's increasing involvement in the Middle East, a region which until recently had been a British domain. Three factors brought about this change: first, the US determination to contain the Soviet threat to countries in the northern part of the Middle East, which Britain could no longer sustain alone; secondly, a search for new sources of oil, either for the US economy or to strengthen her European allies (or prevent Soviet access to them); and, thirdly, the upsurge of the pro-Zionist sentiment, and influence in US domestic politics. To most American foreign and defence policymakers of the time, the first two factors stood in a sharp contradiction to the third, but historically speaking, all three helped to augment America's new involvement in the region. For although Zionist aspirations were viewed by US State and Defence Department officials as detrimental to US economic and strategic interests, most American politicians, including President Harry S. Truman, increasingly bowed to the Zionist influence in America's politics and often acted contrary to the experts' opinion. It was this schism which since 1946 caused the US Palestine policy to look wanton and which in 1948 helped the emergence of the state of Israel.

THE UNITED STATES AS A POTENTIAL SOURCE OF ARMAMENT

The US involvement in the Palestine conflict of 1948 had another result. Following the massive war production of weapons, the drastic

72

post-war reduction of the US armed forces from 12.5 million to a mere 1.5 million,[1] and the formal end to the Lend Lease programme (henceforth – LL), resulted in the dumping of an immense amount of military equipment both inside the USA and in many overseas countries. Washington saw little use in keeping this equipment serviceable or in transporting home equipment stockpiled aboard. In a massive operation, it gathered ships, aircraft, armoured and other vehicles, guns, ammunition, explosives, electronic equipment and much building material, in yards, hangars, bunkers, harbours and airports within the USA and on foreign soil. Its policy was to 'liquidate the equipment in bulks' and get 'the best scrap-yard price' for it. But to avoid the chance that this equipment might find its way into military use against US interests, war-like equipment had first to be 'neutralized'. According to a set of detailed instructions, sent to US agents world-wide, unless the War or Navy Departments in Washington instructed otherwise, every weapon, ammunition, etc., was to be 'mutilated, disarmed, or otherwise rendered ineffectual for military use'.[2] To this end, holes were drilled in gun barrels, radio, radar and weapons were removed from aircraft and vessels, shells and bombs were emptied and so on. Millions of pieces of equipment were catalogued and, as from the autumn of 1946, it began to be sold to the public. In some cases it was sold in bulk to local governments, as means of securing neutralization and payment. Local governments were often permitted by the USA government to keep certain weapons intact, for use in their armed forces.[3]

To carry out this vast operation, the US government established two federal agencies. Within the USA the War Assets Administration (WAA), subordinated to the Departments of Defence and Commerce, was put in charge. Overseas, the Office of the Foreign Liquidation Commissioner (OFLC), subordinated to the State Department was in control, working through a world-wide system of local liquidation bosses, attached to US diplomatic missions in over 20 countries. Rome, Paris, Cairo and the Office of the Military Governor in Germany were the main OFLC headquarters abroad. Quite a few dumps, particularly of equipment formerly lent to the British army, were located in Arab states, still guarded by the British army. Dumps in Egypt were located at Hexstaf, Tel al Kebir, Kassasim and even on the Palestine border at Raffah. Their worth was assessed at $110 million. In Iraq there was a dump near the British base at Shuiba.[4]

From the point of view of the US government, by the autumn of 1947 the liquidation process abroad was close to its end. But reduced FLC teams continued to have vigil over the equipment's use. Now the civil markets in these countries had a glut of American equipment, traded by private entrepreneurs. Scrap-dealers were quick to grasp that a neglect neutralization would increase the price of their assets, and they often managed to prevent or to mitigate the act of mutilation. Weapons were not always efficiently neutralized or when they were, much of the demand for them was still for military purposes. There was also a lot of 'non-combatant' equipment, such as uniforms, tents, communication equipment and vehicles, which were sold intact. All in all, much of the equipment did go, with or without permission, to stocks or to the use of local armies and militias. Radio and other communication equipment was one case in point. In 1947, even the Haganah bought such radio sets in Egypt.

Up until the war in Palestine, the Arab governments had shown little interest in buying such American equipment from the OFLC. They expected their British trainers either to get them British equipment in a better condition or to negotiate on their behalf with the OFLC, with better expertise and purpose. Furthermore, by their very military treaties with Britain, the armies of Transjordan, Iraq and Egypt were not permitted to buy equipment independently from sources other than the British. The Americans for their part were far from ready to put their relations with Britain in jeopardy by selling the Arabs OFLC equipment without British permission. The only way the Arab armies could acquire military equipment from these stockpiles bypassing the British was through foreign middlemen or organized thefts.

Actually, in 1947 Washington was more strict than the British, though not always consistent, in refusing to supply military equipment to the Arabs. At the end of January 1947 it rejected a British recommendation to transfer 40 used M4 Sherman tanks, stationed near Ismailiya, to the Egyptian Army, despite the recommendation of the US Military Attaché in Cairo, Colonel Stevens. When the Anglo-Egyptian relations sunk into crisis in the autumn of 1947, the Egyptian Government sent feelers to the USA scrap market and obtained a promise from Lawrence Ives, a USA ex-army colonel turned scrap-dealer, who promised them 'unneutralized tanks'. The State Department was on guard and held 50 light M5 tanks which the Egyptian Military Attaché bought from Ives. Yet, the State Department itself sanctioned the sale of a dozen Dakota planes and nine old American mine sweepers, anchored in Malta and the UK, to the Egyptian Navy.[5]

THE UNITED STATES' ARMS POLICY IN THE MIDDLE EAST, 1947

On 12 March 1947, following Britain's admission that she could no longer carry the burden of defending the Middle East against Soviet threats alone, the USA launched the Truman Doctrine. Ten days later, Congress approved the allocation of $400 million for immediate aid to Turkey, Greece and 'other free people who are resisting subjugation . . . by outside pressure'. An immediate American step in this vein was the reconditioning of certain US obsolete weapons dumped in Egypt and their transfer to the Turkish Army.[6]

The US Constitution requires that an alliance with a foreign government must obtain Congress's consent. But there are lesser degrees of rapprochement under which military aid can be given. In 1947, such jurisdiction was at the hands of the interdepartmental Policy Committee on Arms and Armament (PCA) chaired by the Secretary of State or his representative, which also included representatives of the Department of Defence and the sub-Departments of the Army and Navy. This body was formulating the US policy of arming foreign governments.[7] But practically, much influence was in the hands of the medium-rank echelon of the Munition Division (MD) of the State Department, established in May 1946 with the aim of 'administering legislation and agreements pertaining the control of international trafficking of arms, ammunition and implements of war'. The MD's task was to licence the export of arms from the US and to collect intelligence, in concert with the Federal Bureau of Investigation (FBI) about firms and individuals in the US and outside, who were engaged in arms trafficking and to assist the Departments of State and Justice in cases where subversive or other illegal activity connected with the sale of arms was suspected.[8]

At the head of the MD stood, in 1948, Elmer Cummins, with John Elliot as Deputy and Charles Saltzman as the officer in charge of intelligence coordination about arms trafficking. These officials were the most knowledgeable on the subject and thus developed a wider, if unofficial authority on US arms sales as well. Their view was that the task was to object to any extension of US arms sales to foreigners. Their memoranda reveal a persistent attempt to persuade their superiors not to interpret military foreign obligations widely, particularly not in the Middle East.

Cummins and Elliot were largely responsible for thwarting the supply of tanks to Egypt in 1947, mentioned above. It did not matter to them that Colonel Haieba, the Egyptian Military Attaché in Washington had already paid Colonel Ives US $60 000 downpayment for '60 servicable tanks armed with 37-mm guns at the price of 6000 each' and that it was soon found that many of these said tanks were without guns and suited for spare parts only. When the MD was approached to licence the deal, it opposed it for 'reason of high policy', finding no different thinking at the PCA level. (This did not prevent Colonel Ives selling some of the same tanks again to Israel through Arazi, who too paid their price but was unable to take them out of the country.)[9] It was also Cummins, in cooperation with the highly vigilant Director of the Office of Near East and Africa (NED), Loy Henderson, who proposed a quick and well-timed *fait accompli* snatch act of imposing a US arms embargo on countries involved in the Palestine conflict. The PCA and the Secretaries of State and Defence, gave their full support to all these initiatives without hesitation, in view of American commitments already made and others which seemed forthcoming.

ARAB AND JEWISH ATTEMPTS TO OBTAIN AMERICAN MILITARY ASSISTANCE IN 1947

Early in 1947, there were those in the US who believed that the Truman Doctrine created a channel for military aid to Middle Eastern countries other than Greece, Turkey or Iran. The MD and the PCA thought otherwise. In March, they faced requests for military aid from Egypt and Syria; and in December from the Jewish Agency.[10] In the case of Syria, the request was backed by Robert Meminger, US chargé d'affaires in Damascus, and by US former envoy in Damascus, George Wadsworth, now the Chief of the Greece–Turkey Division of the State Department. The Syrians asked for assistance in building a '25 000 mean strong land force . . . and an Air Force of 100 trained pilots', for which the chances first looked good. Syria had no military nursing-power as did Iraq, Egypt and Transjordan, and it was located in the proximity of the Soviet frontiers. There were also fears in Washington that, unless given such aid, Syria might ask for Soviet military assistance.[11] As for Egypt, although US Minister in Cairo, Pinckney Tuck 'warmly' backed the Egyptian request, the MD pointed out that the Anglo-Egyptian Treaty of 1936 precluded Egypt from obtaining American assistance. But even that request was not rejected out of hand, but was put on ice.[12]

The Syrian request came under discussion at the same time as the

Truman Doctrine.[13] Cummins argued against it on the grounds that it would 'be against the traditional French interest in the Levant' and that there was 'no legislation enabling us to act along this line'. Still, for a while supporters of the military assistance to Syria had the upper hand. On 17 May 1947, the US Minister Designate for Damascus, James Keely, was told in the NEA that 'part of the request was met with approval'.[14] As a gesture of goodwill Syria immediately received 'almost as a gift' 20 reconditioned AT6 Harvard and two Piper Cub aircraft, as well as 150 medium machine-guns and thousands of uniform sets, tents, etc. More encouraging for Syria was the decision in principle, to train 100 Syrian pilots in the USA, 'subject to Congress approval'. But in October 1947 the process of approval was withheld when, during the Palestine debate at the UN Assembly, Syrian army units made threatening moves near the Palestine frontiers.[15]

Meanwhile, Anglo-Egyptian confrontation at the Security Council worked to the curtailment of British military supplies to Egypt. In view of that, Prime Minister Nokrashi sent his Ambassador in Washington to see Secretary of Defence James Forestall and Acting Secretary of State Robert Lovett, to see if 'an American military mission could be located in Cairo', and to replace the British mission. But Egypt underestimated Anglo-American solidarity. The State Department replied to the Ambassador that his request was being 'discussed with the British government', while indoors Lovett pointed out three reasons why the Egyptian request must be turned down: first, its irrelevance to the objectives of the Truman Doctrine; secondly, America's reluctance to get involved in the Anglo-Egyptian dispute; and thirdly, that the defence of Egypt was in any event a major objective of Britain. Early in September 1947 the Egyptian government was told that its request was refused for 'absence of legislation'. As some compensation, American assistance in building the Egyptian military industry was offered, but the idea evaporated into thin air.[16]

Following the passing of the UN partition resolution on 29 November 1947, the Zionists joined the applicants for US military assistance. Yishuv leaders, who had long pinned their hopes of building the army of their yearned-for Jewish state with American help, soon approached the State Department with requests which, in the eyes of US officials, promptly gave the problem a new, alarming dimension.

The Yishuv arms acquisition in America was planned to be done in two courses; not necessarily contradictory, but by design totally separate from one another. One course was to persuade the US government to undertake to train and arm the Yishuv militia to a regular army. While the UN Assembly was still in session, representatives of the Jewish Agency began to send feelers to the State Department on this matter. The other course was to work clandestinely with a small group of American Jews to raise money and buy arms illegally, with the quiet consent of the Administration or, if necessary, without such a consent.[17]

The Zionist move promptly caused the mild interest which existed in the State Department to provide military assistance to Syria to evaporate. For Henderson and Cummins it now seemed imperative to withdraw quickly from any former commitment to supply arms to the Arabs, in order to avoid an imminent bigger pro-Zionist commitment. For this last seemed to work diametrically against the best American and Western interests in the Middle East. It was prophesized that it might fuel the Arab–Jewish war, which would play into the hands of the Soviets at a time when the Pentagon had no reserves even to deal with likely European troubles.[18] Such a consideration triggered a fast-moving departmental initiative which led to the imposition of a unilateral American arms embargo on Palestine in mid-December.

THE AMERICAN ARMS EMBARGO OF 14 DECEMBER 1947

Early in November, Henderson was very frustrated for not being able to undo American–Soviet cooperation on Palestine at the UN. Leaving Long Island, New York, which he visited for that purpose, he wasted no more time in Washington. In anticipation of a pro-partition resolution at the UN Assembly,[19] and familiar with the existence of the Haganah branch in New York, preparing to buy arms illegally,[20] Henderson launched an act of legislation, aimed at blocking US military aid to any party involved in the Arab–Zionist conflict. He was encouraged to do so by important quarters of the State Department, among them the venerated Chief of the Policy Planning Staff (PPS), George Kennan, Acting Secretary of State, Robert Lovett, the Chief of the Legal Division, Ernest Gross, who provided him with legal advice and the Chief of the Political Division, Norman Armour.[21] All these officials expressed the conviction that it should be far easier to snatch such a decision now, while attention was still focused on the Assembly, than after the partition resolution became a political fact. On 10 November Henderson distributed to a carefully selected list of State Department pigeon-holes, a top secret memorandum suggesting a prompt publication of Executive Order based on the USA pre-War Neutrality Acts, which would impose a total ban on the export of war materials to the countries and organizations involved in the Palestine dispute.

It took only a few hours until the officials addressed – Gordon Merriam, Chief of the Near East desk (NE), Norman Armour, Ernest Gross and Cummins – all endorsed the memorandum, to which Lovett added his own signature. Four days later, the memo was tabled at a PCA meeting, but action was deferred until 26 November, pending Secretary of State Marshall's return from Europe. Eventually the Secretary signed the document on 5 December, after President Truman's endorsement was obtained. Truman for his part waited to see what the UN Assembly would decide (which explains the delay). According to David Niles, the Jewish White House adviser on minorities, Truman was persuaded to endorse the embargo after being told that the embargo would 'improve the US position among the Arabs after what has been going on at the Assembly' and that it was 'not necessarily against the Zionists'. The embargo became official policy on 14 December, by being published in the State Department *Bulletin*.[22]

According to the new policy, all military assistance to Palestine and her neighbouring states was to be banned, including deliveries and services already committed to. For enforcement, a 'Task Force' was created inside the State Department, chaired by the Cummins and including representatives of Henderson's NEA Office, the UN Office (SPA) and the Security Divisions (SY), as well as of federal agencies outside the State Department such as the FBI, the CIA and the custom and port authorities. A special line of information-exchange on arms trafficking was established between Washington and London. The list of materials under restriction had been worked out, and extended to non-military goods as well, such as iron sheets, and vehicles.[23] On 26 March Presidential Executive Order 2776 was published. It originally aimed at preventing export of strategic materials to Communist countries, but was made to fit the Middle East embargo as well.

Order 2776, due to come into effect on 15 April, was a major blow to the *Haganah* acquisition plans. It forbade the export of non-combatant aircraft, vessels, radio and other electronic devices which its agents were purchasing. Explaining that step to a Congressional sub-committee, Dean Rusk, Director of the Special Affairs Office at the State Department explained: 'we do not wish our citizens to act as gun-runners and tangle with the UK and the UN while the Palestine mandate still exist'.[24]

THE YISHUV EFFORTS TO OBTAIN AN OFFICIAL AMERICAN MILITARY AID

Back in November 1947, while the State Department was processing the embargo decrees, the UN Assembly session at Lake Success came to an end with the partition resolution. Almost immediately, a civil war erupted in Palestine, with manifest the Arab aim of thwarting the UN recommendation. Leaders of the Yishuv now hoped that the US government, which struggled hard to push the partition resolution through at the Assembly, would feel obliged to support the UN project, financially and, if necessary, militarily. Early in December the treasurer of the Jewish Agency Executive, Eliezer Kaplan, was at the State Department, suggesting a $500 million American participation in the project of partition, of which $75 million might come from the US Export–Import Bank and the rest as a grant-in-aid or as a US subscription to the UN. Moshe Sharett, chief of the Jewish Agency Political Department, came on Kaplan's his heels, holding 'two working sessions', on 8 and 12 December, at the State Department, one with Henderson and another with Armour. Sharet asked for American help in arming and training a Jewish militia 'to take over, gradually, from the British . . . as they withdrew their armed forces'. Sharett had already heard rumours about the imminent embargo, but hoped that it would not apply to the implementation of the UN resolution. Like Kaplan, he was thinking big, requesting 'reasonable quantities of all types of small arms plus heavier equipment including planes, machine guns, mortars, anti-aircraft and tanks'. Sharett added that the Yishuv turned to the US in the first place, but if their request is not answered, they 'would perforce be obliged to turn elsewhere'.[25]

The possibility of obtaining arms elsewhere was not an empty warning, though Henderson, possibly even Sharett had not yet learned that exactly at that time Haganah agents had reached a concrete agreement in Prague on a small-arms deal. But certainly Sharett was trying to manipulate a paranoid American vexation, nourished by British intelligence, according to which 'hundreds of Soviet trained agents' were about to sail from Romania to Palestine on board the two illegal immigrants ships *Pan York* and *Pan Crescent*. Being himself convinced that the allegation was basically nonsense, Sharett tried to use it to prod Washington to consider military aid to the Yishuv more seriously.[26] Hendersons' far from intending to broach to Sharret the true thoughts of the State Department, answered vaguely that he would pass the contents of their talk, evidently a dialogue of the deaf, to his superiors. It took Sharett a few more weeks to realize that he was wasting his time. Meanwhile on 14 December the American embargo became public.

THE IMPOSITION OF THE US EMBARGO AND ARAB AND ZIONIST REACTION

There were different reactions to the American embargo from the Arabs and the Zionists. The Arab total abstention from protesting should be ascribed to the success of the British Foreign office thesis, diffused to British diplomats in Arab capitals and onto Arab governments, that the US embargo would mainly hit the Zionists. In practice, the only injured Arab party was Syria, which had been waiting for the extension of the aid to her from the USA which had already begun and was now suspended.[27] But it is important to note that from this moment, up until late 1950, the USA arena was totally abandoned by the Arab rearmament efforts.

The Zionist reaction, on the other hand, was bitter, prompting a vociferous protest. Zionist propaganda introduced the US embargo as a cynical, hardly disguised anti-Semitic conspiracy, concocted at the State Department to undermine UN decisions, prevent the establishment of a Jewish state, and caring nothing about the possibility of the physical extermination of the Yishuv.[28] Almost as a conditioned reflex the American Zionists woke up. Congress, the White House and the State Department were flooded with telegrams from American citizens, demanding an active American role in the implementation of the UN recommendations, including sending arms to the Palestine Jews. Lovett said that he 'believed' that 'the pressure was just beginning to build up'. Early in February the Zionist Emergency Council (AZEC) called for a conference in which representatives of 400 branches of the Zionist political lobby gathered to get advice on how to 'Save the UN Resolution'. A campaign was planned under the slogan 'lift the embargo now!', and Congressmen, Senators and Governors were mobilized to support arming the Palestine Jews. That pressure was assessed as 'among the strongest ever remembered'.[29]

ZIONIST POLITICAL POWER IN THE USA IN 1948

In 1948 the American Zionists had at their disposal an efficient organization of propaganda and political pressure. They commanded thousands of devoted activists, organized in a country-wide network of cells, geared to exert grassroot pressure on politicians' respective constituencies, a strategy which proved no less effective than lobbying these same politicians in Washington, which the Zionists did well too. Their machinery was controlled from New York by a body which, although autonomous, was attentive to an 'Advisory Committee' (consisting of representatives of major political parties of the Palestine Yishuv) as well as to the American branch of the Jewish Agency. At short notice, they could launch a nation-wide political campaign focused on a specific objective, which would soon be felt in Washington. Their extraordinary political power stemmed neither from the size of the Jewish community in the USA, nor very much from accessive Jewish representation in political positions, but from a special combination of Jewish demographic dispersion across the USA, from the Jewish and non-Jewish political mood in the post-Holocaust era, and from the very nature of the political process in the USA. In 1948, the problem faced by the American Zionists was not their ability to manage a strong campaign, but to time it well. As it turned out, the 'lift the embargo' campaign was ill-timed and unfocused.

Between 1943 and 1948 there was a tremendous upsurge in Zionist influence in American politics, emanating from such psycho-political factors as the shock suffered by Americans, Jews and gentile alike, over the horrors of the Holocaust, and the fascination of many American Protestants over the return of the Jews to Zion, as well as the imagined parallels between the Zionist settlement of Palestine and America's frontier myth. The number of Zionist sympathisers increased inside and outside the Jewish community, and this support was moulded into a political power by painstaking Zionist organizational work, and a ruthless struggle against opposition within and without the Jewish community. Jewish organizations were renowned for their propensity to help finance political campaigns of individuals who committed themselves to the Zionist cause. The great number of Jews in the media, the arts and in academia, was also a factor in producing more votes. In 1948 the Jews formed approximately only 3.5 per cent of the US population, but the Jewish proportion in highly populated states, which weighed heavily in the Electoral College, was between 5 and 14 per cent, and Jewish voting habits indicated a high turnout in ballots and a high homogeneity in voting.

Thus, in a political process where a winner takes all, the Jewish vote looked decisive in almost every close race, including the composition of the Presidential Electoral College. However, although from the early 1930s, most American Jews voted for the Democrats – in 1944 elections this vote was 92 per cent – Democratic candidates never felt that the Jewish vote was secured for them.[30] Republican candidates had their own Jewish campaigners and their hopes to gnaw at the Jewish vote never abated. 'In the USA', noted Thomas P. O'Neil, a venerate Congressman, 'elections are always local, even when the issue is foreign affairs.' In 1948 there was not the slightest doubt that to win the Jewish vote one must demonstrate a *bona fide* pro-Israeli policy.

The first half of 1948 was characterized by a strong worry about the chances of Truman being re-elected. Back in the biennial election of 1946, the Democrats lost their majority in both Houses of Congress over Truman's domestic policy. Now, as time progressed, public polls indicated a still growing dissatisfaction with Truman. Disenchanted leading Democrats wished to have a more attractive Presidential candidate – perhaps General D. D. Eisenhower. To make things worse, there was a strong undercurrent of Jewish agitation condemning the late Democratic President, F. D. Roosevelt, for beguiling Jews to vote for him and then doing nothing to save their brethren from the Nazis, or to oppose the anti-Zionist British White Paper policy of 1939. When Truman had secured his Party nomination (and in consequence two dissident Democrats, Henry Wallace and Storm Thurmond stood independently for election), leading Democrats prepared themselves for the inevitable defeat. At the same time, devoted members of the Truman administration felt that only an extraordinary election strategy might snatch the victory from the Republicans, and this must include a marked pro-Zionist policy.

Throughout 1946 and 1947, Truman had already gained on points with the American Zionists on the Palestine issue, but early in 1948 he seemed to have lost favour with them again due to America's withdrawal from supporting partition. Truman's so-called 'election cabinet', consisting of special political advisers including notably the young Clark M. Clifford, put it to him that if he wanted to defeat the Republican candidate 'solely on political appraisal' he could not afford to lose the vote of 'ethnic and deprived' groups which once formed the so-called 'Roosevelt coalition'. These 'groups' included blacks, Labour, farmers etc.,[31] and last but not least the Jews – 'important in winning New York . . . and who are today primarily interested in Palestine'. Indeed, in the election of 1948 Truman and the Democrats tried to win back the support of these groups by adopting a liberal policy, and in the Jewish case, a pro-Israeli line, whenever the President thought he could afford to adopt it.[32]

There is little doubt that Truman believed that this line would help him win the Presidency in 1948, even though he eventually did not carry New York. It also helped Israel to gain international legitimacy in the crucial hour of her establishment and to substantiate her existence by retaining her military victories in the autumn. But this trend was not immediately discerned. The Zionist drive early in 1948 to lift the US embargo failed, and throughout most of the election of 1948 a bi-partisan agreement excluded Palestine from the campaign issues.

THE FAILURE OF THE ZIONISTS TO LIFT THE AMERICAN EMBARGO

The campaign to lift the embargo was the first shot in a series of Zionist domestic campaigns held in the USA in 1948. However, the Zionists saw literally all their objectives attained, but not that one. They saw the State Department plan to substitute partition with trusteeship die out at the UN Assembly; they attained Truman's recognition of Israel immediately upon her proclamation, without telling the State Department and the US UN delegation; the establishment of a USA diplomatic relationship with Israel; a dramatic withdrawal of the US delegation at the Security Council, following Truman's re-election, from the policy of forcing Israel to withdraw from areas which the IDF conquered in defiance of the Security Council's orders; the shelving of the Bernadotte plan, and so on. After the war, they won American financial support for Israel. Why then, did they fail to get America to lift her embargo on military aid to Israel?

There are two clear reasons for this omission: first, it gradually became apparent to Truman that it would be more beneficial to his policy if, in return for a British undertaking not to supply arms to the Arabs, the US embargo should be sustained. Soon he realized, as indeed did well-informed Zionist leaders, that the embargo was working in favour of Israel and not the other way round. Secondly, the US Government, jointly with the British Government, were convinced that the combination of an embargo and a truce in Palestine was an essential requisite for the settlement of the whole issue, in a way which did not appear contradictory to the basic Zionist aspirations.

However, in early 1948, this perspective was still befogged and lifting the embargo was the main Zionist objective. Early in December the President of the World Zionist Organization, Dr Chaim Weizmann, who a month earlier was seen by Truman to ask for the retention of the Negev in the boundaries of the projected Jewish state, then debated at the UN Assembly, sent a cable to the White House. Weizmann tried to make Truman feel as being a partner to a promising project, which however, now needed further support. 'The only matter which causes us anxiety now', wrote Weizmann, 'is our people's deficiency in the equipment necessary for their defence. The Arabs obviously suffer no such lack.' Similar cables arrived in the White House from pro-Zionist Congressmen. But Truman consulted his pro-Zionist advisers, Niles and Clifford and became convinced that the embargo was a stitch in time, provided Britain followed suit. Following that conclusion, he snubbed Weizmann, writing that 'it was essential that restraint and tolerance be exercised in Palestine from now on . . .'[33]

Meanwhile, the Zionist campaign was gathering momentum. Letters and cables poured into the offices of Congressmen, Governors and the Truman Administration. The State Department alone reported 86 000 such messages.[34] Private archives of American politicians of the time are, indeed, packed with identical letters and cables calling for the US to arm the Yishuv.[35] On 26 January the British Ambassador, Lord Inverchapel, was invited to see Under-Secretary of State Lovett and was told that if Britain did not impose a restriction on her own supply of arms to Arabs, 'Congress may impose on us to remove ours'. The Ambassador on his part pointed out a resolution calling on the lifting of the American embargo, about to be introduced in the House of Representatives by Representative C. Buckley, and to a similar grouping in the Senate as well.[36] Early in February the campaign seemed stronger still. Thirty Republican Representatives endorsed a petition calling for a lifting of the embargo, and many newspapers' leaders took up the issue favourably. On 12 March, the *New York Times* published a letter to the Secretary of State signed by 45 Congressmen in this vein. Democratic Party leaders, particularly in the state of New York, made fiery speeches, calling for the 'immediate' arming of the Palestine Jews. The mayor of New York, William O'Dweyer, participated in several such rallies.[37] All this time, the State Department position remained a mystery for the Zionists, and they were rightly vexed.

They tried to find out what was going, on through Mrs Eleanor Roosevelt, wife of the late President, now a member of the US UN delegation and a great friend of them. But, unwittingly, the former

First Lady contributed to their leaping in the dark, by letting them know and they leaked it to the *New York Times*, that she herself had written to the Secretary of State, advising him that 'the quicker we remove the embargo and see the Jews and any UN police force . . . equipped with modern armaments . . . the better it will be for the whole situation'. Since it seemed unreasonable that Mrs Roosevelt's expressed an opinion utterly in contrast to policy makers', the Zionists loosened their vigil. But Secretary of State Marshall, who did not bring Mrs Roosevelt into the secrets of the plan to reverse the UN resolution, only wrote to her that in his opinion, 'sending arms to Palestine would facilitate acts of violence and further shedding of blood'. With the convening of the Security Council early in February to discuss the situation in Palestine, Marshall had already made up his mind that an intervention by the Security Council to implement partition was out of the question, 'because the USSR is the only nation that would gain from it'.[38]

The Zionists were taken completely by surprise when the State Department's *volte face* on the partition issue was announced on 19 March by Senator Warren Austin, the Chief of the US Delegation at the Security Council. The USA, he said, wished to abolish the partition resolution and put Palestine under a temporary UN trusteeship regime. The Zionists were shocked. Within a few days their 'lift the embargo' campaign came to a halt.[39] But the State Department's own hope to be able to convene yet another special UN Assembly and to master enough vote to pass the new resolution had proved without foundation. This failure enraged Truman, after he reluctantly endorsed the Department's policy in mid-March. When, early in May members of his 'election cabinet' recommended that he would announce his intention to recognize the Jewish state if it was established upon the termination of the British mandate, it was utterly against the State Department policy of putting pressure to bear on the Jews *not* to proclaim the Jewish state. When Marshall was told, on 12 May of the President's intention, he threatened to resign, so Truman decided to recognize Israel without giving the Secretary of State notice. When this was done, on 14 May, many expected Marshall indeed to resign, but he controlled his anger and, realizing that his own policy at the Assembly had itself reached a dead end, he allegedly said that 'you do not accept a post (like mine) and then resign when the man who has the Constitutional authority to make a decision makes one'. It appears that he realized that the President was not altogether nonsensical in this constraint, after the Yishuv leaders did not heed Marshall's warnings and did proclaim their state.[40]

It took approximately 2 weeks until the military situation in Palestine cleared up for Washington policy makers. During that time, the attacks of the Arab regular armies were in full swing. The Egyptian bombing of Tel Aviv, which still lacked any air defences, served as a strong argument for Dr Weizmann who came again to the USA to plead with Truman to arm Israel. The State Department was to be asked clearly 'yes or no' about the supply to Israel of 'fighter-bombers, anti-aircraft and anti-tank artillery'.[41] At that point, however, the Americans were fully immersed in talks with the British Government about the Palestine embargo. Truce and embargo became a redeeming formula, that should have helped both Israel's security and Western Middle East more than ever. Soon, Lovett was able to tell Israel's envoy Eilat that his hands were tied by the Security Council decision.[42] When the 4 weeks truce elapsed on 9 July and the fighting was resumed, Israel's military strength was already evident. On 18 July, when the Security Council imposed a new truce, it was far more difficult to convince even sympathetic Americans, that their country should infringe the Security Council decision, while the IDF was doing so well. Indeed, after the IDF victories of October 1948, very few among Israel's well-wishers in the USA thought Israel was still in danger of elimination.

But now the American elections neared and Zionist pressure was mobilized to substantiate Israel's military gains. Late in the summer of 1948, when the elections entered their final phase, Zionist representatives, respectively, associated with both major political parties and Presidential candidates, laboured successfully to include pro-Israeli planks in their Parties' platforms. Now the issues of lifting the embargo and the boundaries of Israel were included. The Republican plank of July, treated these issues somewhat prudently, by only pledging 'full recognition of Israel with her boundaries as sanctioned by the UN'. But after Bernadotte's plan of September was put before the third UN Assembly, which envisaged far smaller boundaries for Israel, a pledge to oppose that plan was difficult to obtain from the Republican nominee, Dewey. However, he made it 'known' that he 'had committed himself to modification of the embargo act'. The Democratic Palestine plank was more outspoken, stating 'We approve the the claims of the state of Israel to the boundaries set forth by the UN Resolution of November 29 . . . modifications should be made only if fully acceptable to Israel' and 'We favour the revision of the arms embargo to accord . . . Israel the right of self-defence . . . (and the) modification of any UN resolution which prevented such revision'.[43]

However, lifting the embargo at this stage was out of question because it would jeopardize not only the Anglo-American agreement of 26 May and the SC resolution of 29 May, but stood contrary to a new Anglo-American basic plan for the settlement of the Palestine issue, approved in August by Truman and Marshall.[44] Furthermore, it did not need much sense of prophecy to predict that if the USA lifted her embargo, so would Britain and this, among other things, might work in favour of the Arab armies rather than in favour of the IDF. Finally, as from August, Truman and Dewey maintained a secret gentleman's agreement of imposing a complete silence in their own campaigns on the Palestine issue.[45] The Zionists therefore focused their efforts on extracting a statement from one of the candidates, in order to invoke a reaction from the other. Eilat, for instance, tried to persuade Truman's advisers that the president should 'warn the Arabs' that they must respond to Israel's peace proposals or he would see himself 'unable to stand against the pressure' and lift the embargo; it was clear that the Arabs could not accept such a proposal.[46] But until the last week of October, when Dewey broke the bipartisan agreement, these efforts were unsuccessful. A week before polling day, opinion polls indicated that Dewey was losing ground to Truman, after leading comfortably all throughout the summer. Dewey then allowed a statement on his behalf that he 'supported the Palestine plank in the Republican Platform', and Truman was quick react. On 25 October, Truman pledged himself not to press Israel to give up areas given to her by the 29 November resolution. It meant the Negev, where the IDF had just defeated the Egyptian army.

Truman won the Presidency race and inspired a change in the Security Council position about Israel's need to withdraw in the Negev. But no change took place on the issue of arms supply. The IDF was now victorious. Truman may have privately been pleased with these results, but he could not give a prize of military aid to the side which had just violated the SC resolutions and got away with it. Since now the British began to argue with the USA about allowing some military supplies to the Arabs, Israel became a proponent of keeping the embargo intact.

All this time, the Zionist campaign in the USA to lift the embargo constantly fed the British fears that Truman would yield to pressure and unilaterally do so. This reinforced Anglo-American keen cooperation and Britain's earnest adherence to the embargo. While the deterioration of Britain's relations with the Arabs worried Bevin a great deal, Anglo-American strategic cooperation remained paramount for him.

ISRAEL'S EFFORTS TO BYPASS THE AMERICAN EMBARGO ILLEGALLY

Quite apart from the Zionist struggle against the American embargo, almost without the knowledge of the official Zionist leadership, a Jewish underground organization was meanwhile engaged in smuggling implements of war from the USA to the Yishuv and to Israel.[47]

The foundation for this clandestine organization was laid more than 2 years earlier by David Ben Gurion, who, while the Second World War was still being fought, began to regard the USA as a potential lever with which to push through the Jewish state project, and as a major potential arms supply for the future Jewish army.

During Ben Gurion's visit to the USA in the summer of 1945, he met not only with the lately reinvigorated militant Zionist leadership there, but with a special group which had no part in politics, but which gave a promise to work in underground. Aided by his intelligence expert, Reuven Shiloah, Ben Gurion was able to build a body that would collect intelligence and make contacts pertaining to the acquisition of military equipment and recruit military experts, in anticipation of an imminent encounter between the Yishuv and the Arab world, if and when the Jewish state became a reality. Familiar with what he termed the 'double loyalty' complex of many American Jews, Ben Gurion was anxious to avoid embarrassing the official Zionist establishment by tainting their American patriotism. His search focused on 'daring and true Zionists who would be ready to follow me and do what I tell them to do without asking questions'. He was particularly interested in businessmen who would volunteer to contribute both their finance and time to this end, with a high likelihood of having to transgress the US law. The need for secrecy, at that point, was dictated more by the imperative of hiding it from the British CID, than from the US FBI. On 1 July 1945 a meeting was organized for Ben Gurion with 18 selected American and Canadian Jews with little or no record at all of political activity. The meeting was held at the Manhattan home of Rudolf G. Sonneborn, a chemical engineer and industrialist from Baltimore, who thereafter became the leader of that group. None of those convened shunned from joining the activity described, while AZEC and even the Jewish Agency Executive in the USA were not informed about it. The organization was camouflaged under the title 'Sonneborn Institute'. Its task was in the field of intelligence, judicial and financial services, extramurally to the regular Zionist activity in America. It was to be controlled by the 'Haganah Mission' in the USA.[48]

During the years 1946–7, the 'Institute' activities were divided between purchasing vessels for illegal Jewish immigration to Palestine and machinery and raw materials for the Yishuv infant arms industry. As from December 1947, it focused on the acquisition of war materials destined to reach the Yishuv towards the end of the British mandate and on recruitment of volunteers and mercenaries.[49] Operations were directed from the Haganah headquarters at 'Hotel 14', on 60st Street, Manhattan, which up until the spring of 1947 was headed by Yacov Dory, later the IDF Chief of General Staff, who was substituted by Shlomo Shamir, another top Haganah officer, with a young Jewish Agency intelligence agent, Teddy Kollek, as his second in command. From mid-May 1948, Kollek headed the mission. On the American part, Sonneborn was the chief. He selected agents, saw to training them by experts and was in charge of raising funds which amounted to millions of dollars, to finance the Institute operations. Hush-money was a big part of it.

Under the guise of business dinners, held at the McAlpin Hotel, Sonneborn and his right hand, Harold Jaffer, a public relations expert with an office at Columbus Centre, managed the Institute activities. They established radio contact with the Haganah headquarters in Tel Aviv which, soon enough, the FBI began to monitor. But apparently, the FBI was not very successful in decoding messages sent in this way, because they used an 'intuitive' code, based on the 'Sabra' subculture and the native Yishuv Hebrew slang, that even a fluent American Hebrew speaker would fail to understand. But crowning it all, this network was amateurish. The Institute's offices, for instance, were all concentrated in a small area in mid-Manhattan, which made the FBI job of tailing them easy. The FBI uncovered their agents names, particularly after some of them were caught red-handed. Indeed, from the time when the FBI decided to close in on the Institute, it was barely able function and some of its chief agents had to flee from the USA.

Kollek, who ran the arms acquisition operations during the peak of the embargo, was a team person, different from some of the former freelance agents who meteored in the American scene earlier. But these qualities did not necessarily improve the results of the acquisition work, while making him and some of his lieutenants an easier target for the FBI checking. In his memoirs Kollek described himself as a lost 'traffic policeman' who tried to control a mess of men and capital equipment moving by their own rules, usually contrary to his orders.[50]

While the Haganah mission was giving general guidances to the Institute, the actual activities were carried out by American citizens or by Palestinian Jewish students, who stayed long-term in the USA. Some of the Institute's agents developed independent networks, as did Adolph (Al) Schwimmer, a TWA flight engineer who grew to be a boss of the aircraft purchasing section; Sam Sloan, a scrap-dealer who became a chief purchaser of AFVs; Dan Fliderblum, an RCA engineer who became chief buyer of electronic equipment; Leonard Weisman, who became a liaison to underworld dealers and to corrupt Latin American rulers; Joe Boxenbaum, a former Marine officer who controlled the purchasing of vessels and the recruitment of marine crews; and, last but not least, the Corporate Lawyer, Nahum Bernstein, who carried out two jobs, helping the Institute to establish dummy corporations, through which the purchasing was done and, as a former OSS man, he trained Institute recruits in hand-to-hand combat, use of radios, household burglary, etc.[51] Occasionally, additional freelancer purchasers would come from Tel Aviv and add diversion to the already highly diversified activity, not to mention Yehuda Arazi, who was arriving and departing by rules known to himself only.

The main acquisition method used was buying equipment from either a civil scrap-dealer or, in WAA tenders, for dummy corporations, and then trying to smuggle them out.[52] A description of some of these last and their tasks, give some idea of the nature of the Institute work. The 'Machinery Processing and Converting Company' was founded in the spring of 1947 to camouflage the export of equipment to produce arms and ammunition in Palestine. Early in 1948 this company established two subcorporations, the 'Oved Trading Company' and the 'New England Plastic Novelty Company'. One was to cover up Arazi's massive export of explosives and the other ran port warehouses, where goods arriving to ports of disembarkation were kept. 'Materials for Palestine' was established in December 1947, with the aim of sending legal aid to the Haganah; its establishment was even publicized in the press, along with AZEC's campaign 'save the UN'. Through the services of that company, permitted materials were sent, for example, permissible goods including medical supplies, tents, blankets, hats, etc. More and more such goods were later restricted, including helmets, barbed wire, fortification materials, steel plates, oil and aviation spirits, military handbooks, etc. After such severance of the embargo rules 'Material for Israel' had two facets: one legal and the other illegal, according to the goods in question. The 'Eastern Development Co.' and 'Inland Machinery and Metal Co.' were established early in 1948 to cover up Arazi's project of buying various weapons including rockets. The 'Sherman Metropolitan Corp.' served as a substitute instrument to ownership of warehouses in the vicinity of ports. The 'Radio and Communication Engineering Co.' dealt with the purchase and export of radio, telephones and radar equipment. 'Land and Labor for Palestine' tried to appear as a Zionist youth movement for agricultural settlement, while serving as a recruitment office for Mahal.[53]

Among the many companies and corporations which were formed and then abandoned, those of the aircraft acquisition were a special brand. Schwimmer and Bernstein first established the 'Schwimmer Aviation Services' as a civil cargo and passenger airline. When an opportunity arose to buy a bankrupt company called 'Aviation Service' from a Jewish owner, who agreed to go on heading his company, they used it to buy neutralized aircraft and to recondition them. As time became short and the delivery of these aircraft to Palestine by boats was too long and risky, Schwimmer decided to overhaul the aircraft in the Lockheed workshops, at Burbank, California, and when they were under threat of being confiscated, a third company was established, no less than the 'national' airline of Panama, 'Lineas Aereas de Panama' (LAPSA), registered in Panama City for a bribe of $100 000.

THE FRUITS OF ISRAEL'S ARMS ACQUISITION IN THE USA

The signal to begin buying arms in the USA was given immediately after the UN Assembly recommended partition. In December, Arazi arrived in New York, equipped with a list of orders, which included armour, guns, aircraft and ships, and with such inside information about the armament market in the USA, bought from an old acquaintance, the international arms dealer Count Stefan Czarnecki. Soon, Golda Meir, formerly Chief of the Jewish Agency Political Department, arrived in the USA, to open a fund-raising campaign for the infant Jewish state, and soon she reported that she was definitely raising 'over 50 million Dollars till the end of the month'. This brought Arazi to believe that his budget would be literally unlimited. But Arazi was not particularly familiar with the American arena, less still with the nature of the American embargo. Thus, although he had taught the 'Institute' some useful tricks, the damage which he caused by his activities offset his achievements. He shrugged off the FBI and let his fantasies run wild. When the magnitude of his spending and failures became known in Tel Aviv and in Geneva, he was ordered to stop all his activities in the USA.

A sarcastic account of Arazi's activities was given a few months later by the leader of the American Zionists, Abba Hilel Silver, at a special meeting of the Jewish Agency (the US Branch Executive):

> ... the anarchy which has crept into the Zionist picture ... may be traced to ... a man who comes from Palestine and sets up an organization of a hand-picked people, *sub rosa*, without consulting the Zionist movement. [He and his] people have since come to think of themselves as superior to any Zionist authority on the American scene, and accordingly acted as such. These were the people behind 'Material for Palestine' and 'Friends of Israel', who now actually attempt to break the UPA (fund raising). ...

As to a question 'who in the American Zionist organization gave Arazi that authority', Silver assured his listeners: 'No one did'. The opinion in Geneva was perhaps less injured, but no less critical.[54]

The balance sheet of the Yishuv–Israel arms purchase in the USA, however, although far from fulfilling the hopes pinned to this source by Ben Gurion and the Haganah command, is, nevertheless, not at all just failure. There were clearly two stages in its development. During the first stage, which ended when Executive Order No. 2776 entered into effect on April 15, a significant number of equipment, aircraft and half tracks and many miscellaneous items were sent, and most of them were absorbed in the IDF in time and played part in the military decision. The second phase occurred after that date or as soon as the enforcement of the new order became effective. Now the US authorities brought the Israeli arms acquisition operation in the USA almost to a complete standstill. Weapons and equipment bought or attempted to be sent after mid-April, arrived only in small amounts and their contribution to the military decision has either very limited or they came too late to take part in the military decision.

The first operation of the Institute towards arming the Yishuv was the purchase of equipment and raw materials for the Yishuv arms industry. It was carried out during 1946 under the supervision of a Haganah arms expert, Haim Slavin, a capable engineer, but one who did not know America and could not even speak English. The Institute rendered him invaluable help by establishing a dummy company for his activities, taking him to scrap-yards, monitoring WAA tenders for him and by cataloguing information for him on second-hand arms-producing machines for sale. They paid some 2.5 million dollars for the equipment he bought and much of the hush-money when needed. They helped him pack and ship the equipment to Palestine bit by bit,

Table 4   Israeli illegal arms acquisition in the USA and Latin America in 1948, plan and execution

Sort	Original deal amount, date		Absorbed in IDF amount, date		Notes
Carrier aircraft					
C46 Commando	12	December 47	9	May–June 48	
C69 Constellation	3	November 47	1	June–1948	2 confiscated
Skymaster	2	April 1948	2	May–June 48	Chartered
Original bombers					
B17 'Fortress'	4	March 1948	3	July 1948	
B25 Mitchell	10	May 1948	–	–	Abandoned
A2OG Havoc	4	June 1948	–	–	Confiscated
Improvised bombers					
C47 Dakota	5	June 1948	2	October	(Chartered?)
T6 Harvard	17	March 1948	9	November	The rest in 1949
Fighter aircraft					
P51 Mustang	8	May 1948	1	November 48	Some in 1949
Light aircraft					
L4 Piper Cub	8	May 1948	8	From November till March 49	
T13 Trainer	2	February 48	–		Not used
PT13 Steerman	15	May 1948		Entered service in 1949	
AFVs					
M5Tanks	38	March 1948	–		
M3 Half tracks	100	January 48	13	March 1948	40 were
			18	Sept. 1948	confiscated
			24	During 1949	by Egypt in November 48
Jeeps	?		40	June–Decem.	
Artillery					
75 mm (Mexican)	35	June 1948	32	September	Not used
Navy vessels					
Aircraft carrier	1	February 48		Sold for scrap, May 1948	
LCT and guard bts	3	April–June	3		In 1949
Ammunition					
75 mm shells	20 tons	June 1948		September	Not used
0.3, 0.5 Inch	2 million	April 48	–	?	
Air bombs	3 thousands			?	
Miscellaneous					
Machine guns	500	April–May	?	September	
Aviation fuel	15000 tons				
Radio & Telephone	2000	January 48	most	April 1948	Provided for all IDF needs
Various equipment & Military stores					
Sub-machine guns	500	April–May	most	August–Sept	
R2800 aircraft	50–60	April–May	30–5	Early 1949	
engines	50	April–May	most	October	

in some 950 wooden crates marked 'textile machines', over a period
of a year – 'not one cog was lost'. On the basis of this equipment, the
then primitive arms factory of the Yishuv quickly sprang into 12 arms
producing plants, which by mid-1948 supplied a good deal of the IDF
needs in small and medium arms, ammunition and armoured vehicles.[55]

Slavin's success created an atmosphere of great expectation in the
Haganah command about the possibilities of arms import from the USA.
But 1948 started with a bad luck and continued with worse. On 3
January a cargo of 50 tons of explosives, part of it pertained to Slavin's
period and some 250 tons to Arazi's, was discovered by the port authorities at pier 'F' of Jersey City, upon being loaded on the ship *Executor*.
The consignment had already gone a long way from Mexico to warehouses around New York City, and now there was a danger that the
whole lot would be confiscated. As a matter of fact, only part of it
was lost. The worse part of the blunder was the publicity which the
case received, due to the densely populated urban area where it was
discovered, and that six young Jewish employees of the Institute were
caught red-handed. Indeed, the interrogation of these men by the FBI
provided the latter with ample information about the Institute and strings
to enable it to follow the Institute's future activities. Slavin, who was
no longer in the USA and Arazi, who quickly fled from the country,
were declared 'wanted'. To prevent a collapse, the Haganah headquarters sent a new man, Eliahu Sakharov, to reorganize the underground. But, meanwhile, the lenient attitude of the judicial arm soon
soothed the Haganah. The mayors of New York City and Jersey City,
and Senator Robert Wagner of New York, worked successfully to persuade the judicial authorities to substitute the charges to the lightest
possible and the judge in the Federal Court which took the case even
expressed a moderate 'sympathy with the young people's ideals . . .
not methods'. They were fined $1000 each and put on 1 year's proba-
tion. In February, Arazi was back under a new identity and business
seemed as usual. In fact, Arazi now extended his activities, stimulated
by a new list of 'most urgent' items, made by Ben Gurion himself.[56]

Arazi's project pivotted around the purchase of the 102 000 ton aircraft carrier *Attu*, which stood for sale at Norfolk, Virginia, for which
he paid $125 000, intending to spend an additional $200 000 on fitting
the ship to carry on board a huge sailing arsenal. A bigger still sum of
money was thus to be spent on weapons which *Attu* was to carry to
the shores of the Jewish state when the mandate came to its end. His
idea about licensing was no less fantastic: he thought of offering a
deal to the United States Department of Defence, according to which
part of *Attu*'s capacity would be allotted to equipment destined to Turkey

under the Truman Doctrine, and the rest to the Haganah. With the help of 'Institute', Arazi contacted various scrap-dealers and also entered WAA tenders. His emissaries negotiated the purchase of a large number of aircraft, 50–60 light tanks, over 100 half tracks, several dozen field-guns and hundreds of other items, including rockets. He handed out generous advance payments everywhere, and to secure the continuation of his cash-flow he used Teddy Kollek's line to Ben Gurion in order to bypass Avigour and the Jewish Agency treasury. In a cable to Ben Gurion in January, Kollek timidly asked permission to 'take 15 million Dollars from Golda . . . after which we shall have no more financial problems'. Meanwhile Arazi lived on the Institute funds.[57]

Early in March Arazi left for Europe where he had more projects. He was not present in the USA when it turned out that *Attu* was unlikely to be able to sail away, with or without the equipment, and that under the new restrictions and vigil by the US authorities most of the equipment itself was also unlikely to leave the country. Moreover, by Avigour's order, Arazi was to confine his activities to Europe. It became apparent that all Arazi's projects in the USA had one problem in common, namely, that it was easy and cheap to buy the equipment, but almost impossible to get it out. In his last visit to the USA in April, Arazi tried to save face by selling *Attu*. The work to rebuild the ship had long stopped and creditors started a court order to seize it.[58] An additional blow was the decision taken in Tel Aviv in March to divert most of the funds to Czechoslovakia.

For the remainder of the equipment Arazi faced the choice between keeping it 'dormant' in scrap-yards or trying to sneak it piecemeal to Latin American countries, with the help of corrupt rulers. When he had finally quit the American scene, he left his successors the ruins of a large plan on which a lot of money was spent and an emergency scheme to rescue some of the operation. Much equipment was just left where it was, and it was eventually either confiscated by the authorities or lost, although a thin trickle of it did finally reach Israel towards the end of the war.

The Latin American project, code-named 'Dromi', was to become an alternative focus of Israeli arms-purchase activities in America in the post-Arazi period. But here, too, the fruits bore no resemblance to the magnitude of the planning or indeed to the needs of the IDF. The most successful among these Latin American rescue operations was LAPSA, through which 12 C46 cargo plans were to be smuggled to Israel (nine arrived). But the success in this case must be ascribed mainly to the fact that the aircraft were flown out of the USA before

Executive Order 2776 came into effect. In Mexico, which was intended to become a main collecting station for equipment smuggled out from the USA, the rulers procrastinated too long, partly because they did not get as big a bribe as they had demanded and partly because of a lack of determination or understanding of the situation at the Geneva headquarters. In March–April, two Institute agents, Greenspan and Silberman, opened a relief station for equipment in Haiti and in the Dominican Republic, by establishing a dummy plant of a zipper factory at San Cristobal, a suburb of San Domingo; and a warehouse for imported agricultural equipment near Port au Prince. Through these posts, they managed to get out of the USA two consignments of vehicles, including some half tracks, supposedly ordered by the local rulers. But this route, too, functioned only prior to 15 April, before a firm warning from American diplomats shut that door too.[59] Belatedly, a more elaborate network was established in Mexico, but as will be seen later, this, too, failed to bear much fruit.

Still, while Arazi's big project in the USA went to pieces, other projects did go well, because they were smaller, better sheltered and executed faster and with precision. Among these last was the purchase of telephone and radio equipment. But, again, this was done before Order 2776 entered into effect.

In January 1948, the chief of communication in the Haganah, Yacov Yanai, asked for permission to go to the USA to buy the requirement of the future Jewish army in radio and telephone equipment. The communication inventory of the Haganah until then was poor: some 200 radio sets in all. The Jewish Agency purse was at that point empty, unable to grant the quarter of a million dollars needed and the Chief of Operation of the Haganah was reluctant to relieve Yanai from duty. Ben Gurion supported Yanai's request so he was given leave of absence, but no funds. In New York, the Institute took care of Yanai and with the help of the knowledgeable Fliderblum, some 250 tons of equipment was bought within days. It included 12 high powered AM/FRCL transmitters, which later served the General Staff and major front commands, hundreds of medium-distance Mobil radio Sets SCR 19, 610 and 300, hundreds of short-distance radio sets MAB and Motorola, some 1000 field telephone sets, 200 telephone exchange units, hundreds of miles of cord and many parts from which the home-made MK18 was later assembled. By mid-May this equipment was safe in Palestine (except for one air consignment captured in Cairo). Almost immediately, the infant Israeli army had all it literally needed in communication equipment.[60]

All Israel's efforts to obtain tanks from the USA failed.[61] However, some success was the importation of armoured half tracks. Over 100 such vehicles were purchased in January at Harrisburg, Pennsylvania, and most of the vehicles indeed left the USA. Much fewer, however, arrived in Israel, for when the *Attu* project collapsed, the half tracks were painted red and agricultural factory 'international' stickers were put over them. Some were sent in small numbers in February. The Isbrandtsen Shipping Co., which ran a line to the Far East via the Mediterranean, took a small number of half-braves and successfully unloaded them at the port of Haifa, with the permission of William G. Peasley, the British Acting Director of Haifa harbour. Clearly, Peasley had either been misled into believing that these were tractors or he had been bribed. But when 53 more half tracks were sent to Haifa on board the *Flying Arrow*, the FBI tipped off the State Department and the latter warned its Consulate in Haifa, which woke up the British authorities. The *Arrow* managed to unload only 13 vehicles before the British Inspector of Custom came on board and removed the red paint, exposing a US military number. The ship was ordered to sail out, and it unloaded the 40 remaining odd vehicles in Bombay, where they stayed for a few months. Towards October the IDF badly needed them, but they only left Bombay on board the *Flying Trader* in November. On 15 November, when the ship passed through the Suez Canal, it was searched and the half tracks were confiscated by the Egyptian authorities. A handful of the remainder in the USA were smuggled out to Mexico and were sent to Israel in December or January.[62]

The severing of the embargo measures in the USA also hit hard Israel's aviation project. Like the *Attu* project, the dimension of the disaster could be illustrated by comparing the initial plan to the number of aircraft which eventually served in the Israeli Air Force during the war.

At the outset, the low prices of aircraft up for sale in WAA tenders in the USA raised hopes both in the Institute and in Tel Aviv of being able to build a massive air force. It was hoped that the airforce would be flown by mixed cadres of native Israelis pilots and Jewish volunteers from abroad. Early in February 1948, Ben Gurion endorsed a purchasing plan under the code 'Yakum Purkan' and the list of the desired planes was given to Arazi. It consisted of 36 fighters, six to eight bombers, three twin-engine training aircraft and quite a few other planes, including helicopters. When that list was shown to Al Schwimmer in the USA, he had already been working on a purchase of aircraft according to a plan of his own and he refused to abandon this effort.

Instead, he amalgamated both lists and even added more items, based on what was available on the market.[63] In view of the good tidings about Golda Meir's successful fund-raising, Tel Aviv then approved the extended list. Now the purchasing list consisted of over 120 aircraft, including three giant Constellations, 12 C46 Commandos, five C47 Dakota, 12 marine PVI Ventures, five training BT13s, ten naval fighter F6F Hellcats, six to seven P51 Mustang fighters, four B17 Fortress bombers, ten B25 Mitchel bombers, seven A20 bombers, two TBF torpedo carriers and some 35 light Harvards, Piper-Cubs and Steerman.[64] But in the middle of Schwimmer's hectic shuttle between one scrapyard and another, on 26 March came Order 2776. Schwimmer realized better than his superior in Tel Aviv, Geneva or even in New York, that it offset the ambitious aircraft purchase. He then dropped the ambitious list and set himself about saving what he already had in hand.

It just so happened, that at exactly the same time, the Czech Government agreed to sell to the Haganah large amounts of small arms as well as Messerschmidt fighters, whereas the few aircraft which Schwimmer had already been reconditioning at the Lockheed workshop in Burbank, California and Melville, New Jersey, were Commando and Constellation carriers. Since the problem of transportation of the Czech purchases to Israel was not satisfactorily solved, an idea cropped up to try to combine both deals. Of course, it necessitated that the American carriers would be out of the USA before 15 April. Thus, it was decided in Tel Aviv to shift financial resources from New York to Prague, and at the same time try and get Schwimmer's transport planes to come to Czechoslovakia – exactly what Order 2776 has meant to prevent. To be on the safe side, the Institute was also asked to charter Skymaster cargo planes from civil American airlines and send them to Czechoslovakia as soon as conditions in Palestine would allow it. This endeavour was, in the circumstances, none too easy either, but this is how the airlift 'Balak' operation came into being. The FBI had long known what Schwimmer's dummy companies were up to, but until 15 April they had no legal way to stop the aircraft from getting out of the country. They tried various legal tactics to sabotage the licensing of the cargo planes departure but Schwimmer and Bernstein outwitted them by establishing LAPSA, which made the aircraft supposedly the property of the government of Panama.[65]

Helped by the Institute's contacts, Schwimmer managed to get 12 C46s out of the USA before 15 April, as well as one of the three Constellations and two of the five BT13s purchased in the USA. Two C46s were flown via Italy as early as mid-March (but only one reached

Israel). The rest then flew via Panama City, Brazil and West Africa. They joined the Balak operation after mid-May. The BT13s were flown on board two C46s but were not actually in use during the war. An improvised 'bonus' to the operation of Schwimmer's network was the smuggling to Mexico of scores of R2800 10W Pratt and Witney planes engines, a gift from a Jewish scrap dealer in Honolulu and some 500 machine-guns, with ammunition, stolen from a nearby WAA yard.[66]

SUBSEQUENT EFFORTS TO SALVAGE THE ISRAELI ARMS PROJECTS IN THE USA

Following Arazi's removal from the USA, the reduction of fund allocation to the US purchasing mission, and the severe measures taken against the 'Institute' activities by the FBI, the new chief of the IDF mission in the USA, Teddy Kollek, searched for chinks in the walls of the embargo measures to salvage equipment already bought. He and Sakharov continued to receive desperate requests from Tel Aviv for armoured fighting vehicles and vessels, which they actually had, but could not send. The solution sought was to develop the so-far dormant Mexican ties and turn all this equipment to a supposed Mexican order. In addition, Schwimmer planned a sudden illegal escape of 11 aircraft, including nine bombers (five A20s and four B17s) and the two remaining Constellations. To prepare for this operation, he cut the reconditioning work to the bare minimum required for one transatlantic leap, relying on further work to be carried out on these aircraft once they were in Czechoslovakia.[67] The operation was to begin by arranging distracting inland 'test-flights' to put the FBI off guard and then to hop to an offshore destination such as New Foundland or Puerto Rico, refuel, and then cross the Atlantic via the Santa Maria air field at the Azores, where refueling was secured through a local contact. Three B17s managed to do just that and arrived safely in Czechoslovakia in mid-June. They were then reconditioned in Czech workshops, equipped with bombing facilities and other necessary equipment. In mid-July, they flew to Israel, bombing Cairo and Gaza on their way.[68] Schwimmer did not manage to do the same with the other aircraft, because it was impossible to time all the flights on the same date. By now the FBI was increasingly tailing his men. The fourth B17 later managed to reach as far as the Azores, but due to a strong US intervention with Lisbon, it was unable to refuel and its American crew was persuaded to return to the USA and to cooperate with FBI investigation. Two Constellations were also confiscated just when they were about to take off from Melville, New Jersey, on 10 July.[69]

Schwimmer now clearly transgressed the law by sending his company's aircraft to a country beyond the Iron Curtain under false documents. He had to flee from the USA and entered service with the Israeli Air Force.

On 22 September the Iraqi *Chargé d'Affaires* in Washington tipped the Munition Division that the ship *Bunty*, carrying a Panamanian flag, was about to load 36 light M5 tanks at the port of Galvaston, documented to Mexico, but in fact destined to Yugoslavia, that is, to Israel. The tanks were seized by an ambush of the customs authorities, and the $140 000 paid earlier to Colonel Ives were lost.[70]

In the absence of Arazi and Schwimmer from the American scene, the style of the Israeli acquisition work became less individualistic, more cautious, and more sophisticated, but on the whole it was no more successful. The major improvement was the substitution of internal American dummy corporations with Latin American government ones, and the development of better packing technique of military goods for shipment. In fact, the use of corrupt Latin governments for a cover-up was the same ploy long used by Arazi. As early as 1938 he bought small arms for the Haganah, using letters of introduction bought from Latin American rulers, particularly from Nicaragua and this is how, in 1948, he bought most of the equipment in Europe. Equipped with a Nicaraguan diplomatic passport and letters from Nicaragua's Ministry of Foreign Affairs and the Ministry of Defence, Nicaraguan missions in European were obliged to render 'Dr Joze Y. Arazi' 'any help he needed' as 'our representative who buy arms for our government'.[71] He used the Institute services to also establish 'working relations' with the governments of the Dominican Republic, Haiti, Panama, and, finally, Mexico. A year after Arazi left the USA, Kollek's still owed the heads of state of Mexico and Nicaragua between 2–3.5% of every purchase made in the USA, whether the goods were eventually delivered or not.[72] The establishment of LAPSA and the rights for the one-off landing of the C46 planes involved a payment of $100 000 to the president of Panama and according to British sources, the President of Mexico earned 1 million dollars from the Zionists in 1948.[73] Evident to the rigidity of the payment conditions is a warning which Arazi sent Kollek in 1949, to the effect that 'if the debt to the President is not forfeited, all Stefan's (USA acquisition business) would go down the drain'.[74]

Now, Mexico–Dromi became the pivot of Hadod (Kollek), and equipment loaded on ships in American ports was said to sail for Mexico with 'only the Captain knowing the true destination'. Whether these ships later called at Mexican ports or sailed from America across the Atlantic remained immaterial.[75]

But the ploy was not clever enough to hide the operations from British and American intelligence. Both now viewed the Zionist network with hidden admiration as almost an omnipotent conspiracy. A British report from Ciudad Trojillo of July wrote about a supposed 'inter-continental Zionist conspiracy for arms trafficking' focusing on Mexico, where the 'Minister of Defence General Limon (*sic*) sells big quantities of arms to Israel via the port of Tampico, including tanks ... owing to corruption all along the line up to the very top'.[76] In contrast to this portrait, the view from Kollek's angle indicates loss, frustration and often great despair on the Israeli side:

> In March ... When we first offered the deal [he and Sakharov wrote] Dromi was very keen. He needed the cash in his pocket. But then you decided to put it off although we have already invested over 100 000 Dollars as down payment. Then he began to hesitate ... but his greed for cash made him easy to persuade. The tractors (tanks, halftracks) which we bought from the surpluses of that country (USA) were already ours, along with the licence to get the merchandise out. We have bought 38 (tanks) with 37 (mm. guns) but it will be necessary to equip each with two (machine guns) when they arrive. The amount of ammunition ... we'll try [to get] 1000 [each]. No spare parts obtainable but by dismantling other tanks. By the first contract 25 were due to us and the rest to him. We proposed that the whole lot should remain ours and he agreed to accept [more] money instead. He also promised to give us those heavy [guns] which he had in 75 (mm). As for tracks (aircraft), he set up a difficult condition that a big firm would also appear as a party ... and we are still trying our best in the Far East.[77]

The first successful consignment of equipment via Mexico sailed on board the ship *Enterprise*, which left the USA on 18 July. Its cargo included four dismantled P51 Mustang fighters, two light Piper Cub aircraft and 32 75 mm guns, bought from the Mexican army, with 16 000 shells. The ship arrived in Israel in mid-August, but the Mustangs were difficult to reassemble and were not even ready for the mid-October deadline. As for the guns, they were the biggest disappointment of the artillery purchaser for their ammunition was unserviceable and no technique was found to remodel it.[78] 'In Arnon (Tel Aviv), Sapir wrote Kollek, 'they ceased to believe that a single useful item will come from the USA so long as the embargo is in effect.'[79] 'We do not want scratch your wounds', he telephoned Kollek again in January 1949, after the promised tanks did not arrive neither to the 'Yoav' nor towards the Horev operations, 'but I am sure you know that that to date we did not receive a single tank', to which Kollek replied:

> You can imagine our frustration . . . one hundred and fifty FBI men are sleuthing us non-stop. We have at hand machines but without leveling a road for them there is no chance that they would manage to get through. We keep them still until a passage is secured both for them and for those which follow.[80]

With no major road 'levelled', the equipment was dismantled, atomized, and hidden underneath legal material, but this made the assembly very slow and difficult. Transports became more numerous late in the autumn. On 20 October, nine out of 17 'Harvard' aircraft arrived in Israel. Five of them later took part in an improvised bombing of the Egyptian position in Faluja.[81] Only one of four Mustangs brought in August, became serviceable while the war was still on, that is, on 20 November. Flown by an American Mahal pilot, it immediately shot down a British reconnaissance Mosquito, which regularly photographed Israeli military installations. The alarmed British Chiefs of Staff pondered over the continuation of such British flights and eventually in mid-December decided to renew them.[82]

Israel's plans to build a navy from scrapped American vessels was. also a failure which was a disappointment in view of the earlier successful purchase of vessels for illegal immigration in the USA. Following the *Attu* affair and the tightening of inspection at ports and coasts, the Israeli harvest amounted to three vessels bought before mid-April, none of which proved very useful. PC *Noga*, bought in March, and reconditioned at Marseilles, France, joined the navy in mid-October, but was soon sent back to the docks. Two LCIs, *Ramat Rahel* and *Nitzanim*, entered service in January 1949. 'Naval acquisition in the USA', wrote the historian of the Israeli Navy, 'played no meaningful role in the naval campaigns of 1948'.[83] A successful endeavour, however, was the delivery of aviation spirit in barrels, also restricted by the embargo. Towards the October operations, two ships carrying such fuel arrived in Haifa with over 2 million litres, sufficient for the full operation of the Israeli Air Force for approximately 6 months.[84] Other useful supplies which arrived abundantly from the USA were clothing, medicines, tents and military engineering materials.

The American embargo, however, had little effect on Israel's recruitment of American and Canadian servicemen to the IDF, which was a success. North American servicemen played an important role in the command and professional instruction of IDF units. Most outstanding in this group was Colonel David Stone (Marcus), who served as chief military adviser to Ben Gurion in the position of Deputy Chief of Staff and late in May he was appointed commander in chief of the Jerusalem front. Unfortunately, he was mistakenly shot by a Haganah sentry. The Canadian Infantry Major, Benjamin Dunkelman, commanded IDF Brigade 7 and a former US Navy frigate commander, Paul Shulman, became Commander-in-Chief of the infant Israeli Navy. But nowhere was the contribution of Mahal as vital as in the Israeli Air Force. In fact, it is unthinkable that this force would have been able to operate or, indeed, get aircraft in the first place, without the help of foreign air and ground crews. The number of aircrew personnel from the USA and Canada, who served with the IDF in 1948 was 198, of which 118 were pilots. The total number of citizens of those two countries who served in the Israeli Air Force in 1948 was over 300 and the total number of North Americans who served in the IDF surpassed 1500.[85] Some of the Mahal were highly paid; in some cases more than their compatriots earned in their own countries' air force.[86]

THE UNITED STATES AS AN INTERNATIONAL POLICEMAN OF THE EMBARGO

The United States and Britain, which from May until late October viewed the Palestine settlement eye to eye, fully adhered to the embargo. There idea continued to be to retain the military and the territorial *status quo* in Palestine until they could jointly bring the Security Council to impose their new partition scheme – if possible labelled 'Made in Sweden', as Count Bernadotte, advised by his American chief aid, Dr Bunche, was forwarding a very similar scheme to the UN. The assassination of Bernadotte by Israeli extremists on 17 September, and the fact that before his death Bernadotte had asked the UN Secretary General to put his scheme before the forthcoming UN Assembly, was then regarded as a sacred will, and this forced Bevin and Marshall to announce their support of putting the scheme on the Assembly's agenda, although earlier they preferred to leave it to further secret contacts.

Meanwhile, in mid-August it became apparent to British and American intelligence that, owing to on its recently gained superiority over the Arab armies, Israel was determined to renew the fighting. But they continued to appreciate that strict imposition of the embargo was the safest way to cripple that Israeli intention, and eventually bring about the desired settlement along their own territorial ideas.[87]

Thus, the Divisions of Armament and Security (MD and SY) in the State Department kept good contact with their counterpart Special Department of the British Foreign office, headed by Lancelot Thirkel, and exchanged intelligence, advice and suggestions for measures which the two governments must take to enforce the embargo. The two governments jointly kept the pressure on other governments to stick to the embargo, and the CIA and the international section of the FBI worked around the clock to keep governments *au fait* with breaches of the embargo within their realms.[88] There was also a mutual Anglo-American watch over one another, and a mutual consultation on such fringe cases as the supply of spare parts to Egypt's civil national airline 'Misr', which had reached the point of paralysation.[89] Of course, these contacts were kept top secret, as their exposure might have greatly embarrassed the two governments. On the one hand it would have shown Britain's responsibility for starving the Arab armies of ammunition, or on the other hand the USA's 'abandonment of Israel'.

There were also some red-lines which these governments hesitated to cross. In August the State Department flatly dismissed a proposal by the Director of the CIA, Rosco Hillenkoetter, to intercept or to shoot down Israeli cargo planes carrying supplies from Czechoslovakia when they crossed the US military zone in southern Germany.[90] Britain anticipated the need to stop holding supplies to the Arab Legion, which after July suffered a great shortage of ammunition when it appeared exposed to the danger of elimination by the imminent Israeli offensive.

But the Anglo-American vigil and diplomatic pressure was an effective tool in reducing embargo infringements by other UN members. Among its noticeable successes on this score were:

(1) stopping the airlift of small arms from Prague to the Haganah in April for over a month, after only one such flight took place on 31 March;[91]

(2) bringing to a quick halt the transit to Israel of equipment bought in the USA through the Dominican Republic and Haiti;

(3) interrupting or slowing down of various deliveries made with

the help of the governments of Panama, Mexico and Nicaragua;

(4) the closure, on 11 August, of the Czech Zatec air-base, which earlier served as a major Israeli despatch post;

(5) causing much hesitation and delay in the actions of the governments of Finland, Yugoslavia, Bulgaria and Greece, regarding the transit of arms to Israel through their territories;[92]

(6) stopping the refuelling of Israeli cargo planes in Corsica and in Portuguese territory;

(7) The cessation of Egyptian purchases of arms and ammunition in Spain and Switzerland, in the autumn of 1948;[93]

(8) Finally, the reluctance of the USSR herself to get directly involved in any act of violating the embargo, was also the result of the American pressure.[94]

Indeed, the contention held *prima facie* by Western intelligence, that the USSR was by design directly involved in sending arms and trained men to Israel, had finally been shaken following a statement of the Soviet news agency TASS of 8 August, which firmly insisted that the USSR was observing the embargo. That statement was read in Washington with much instruction and served as a starting point for a reassessment of the fear that there was a Soviet drive to get control of the government of Israel.[95]

But this was not the only wrong appreciation made by the Western intelligence, which had been overoptimistic about the effect of the embargo. Early in August a CIA report was still satisfied that although Israel was receiving military assistance from Czechoslovakia and other sources, as did some Arab states,

> The application of the UN arms embargo would probably result in a military stalemate. . . . The Arabs would find themselves incapable of prosecuting a large scale offensive (and) the Jews would also be unable to wage offensive war.[96]

Bernadotte and Bunche contributed to that wrong conclusion by sweeping under the carpet information they had about the failure of their observers to prevent arms smuggling.[97] It was only towards the end of August that this optimism changed into a fast-growing anxiety that IDF was gathering strength, and that Israel intended to open a major offensive in defiance of the Security Council's warnings.

THE USA AND THE MILITARY BALANCE IN THE PALESTINE
WAR: A CONCLUSION

In 1948, the embargo was the only consistent element in Palestine
policy. American foreign and defence policy-makers (though not the
President himself) viewed their country's commitment to establish a
Jewish state as a domestic issue which had quite mistakenly spilled
over into foreign policy. They were sceptical about the feasibility of
the UN partition resolution, and about its utility to their country's foreign and defence policy. But the attitude of the less informed and more
sentimental public was different. When the state of Israel was proclaimed, in spite of the State Department's attempt to prevent it, the
President felt that he must recognize it promptly. The USA government then sought, jointly with Britain, new partition boundaries, and
only reluctantly parted from that Anglo-American scheme as a result
of a combination of Israel's military success and Truman's bowing to
his powerful pro-Zionist voters on the eve of the 1948 elections.

Throughout 1948 and well into 1949, the USA adhered to an active
policy of embargo. On this issue, both the White House and the Departments of State and Defence acted in concert – a harmony explained
the fact that the same set of considerations which brought Truman to
act against these Departments in making various concessions to his
pro-Zionist public, led him to retain the embargo. The progress of the
war further convinced the President and his political advisers that considering the constrained British situation, lifting the embargo would,
in the end, undermine Israel's strength (possibly even its survival) and
do more harm than good to Truman's chances of being re-elected. There
were still plenty of other scores on which the President could act and
win the pro-Zionist vote: granting Israel recognition, arranging for normal
diplomatic relations between the two countries, promising Israel financial
aid, and refraining from forcing her to cede the territories which she
captured during the war.[98] One may only speculate what would have
been his action had the effect of the embargo been against Israel.

By and large, the Israeli arms purchase in America had been a mir-
age. American military scrap-yards were indeed unlimited, and on the
face of it very cheap: an aircraft-carrier for $125 000 was less than the
price Israel paid for one Czech 'Messerschmidt'; a 4-engined B17
American bomber costs only $15 000; an A20 Bomber costs $6000; a
twin-engine C46 costs $5000; a 'Constellation' $15 000; an M5 tank,
$8200, and so on. The cargo ship *Kefalos*, which made several trips
from the USA to Israel via Mexico, cost about the same as one Czech

Messerschmidt.[99] But the real cost of the American equipment – covering reconditioning, transportation, hush money, and in particular considering the equipment which was lost or had been confiscated by US authorities – explains why the relatively small volume of equipment imported from America in 1948 cost the Israelis over $18 million. Had Israel not found alternative sources to substitute her deceptive American dream, the outcome of the war would have certainly been different. Most of the Israeli failures in America resulted from her inability to overcome the embargo restrictions. However, methods which failed in the US, and which sent most of the efforts there down the drain and were bitterly criticized in Tel Aviv and Geneva, worked surprisingly well in France, at just the same time, and saved the day for Israel.[100]

Israel failed in her plan to obtain official military aid from the USA, or illegally to import arms purchased there. Particularly painful and costly was her failure to import tanks and fighter aircraft.

By far Israel's greatest help from the USA was the vast dollar cash-flow which came during the war from pro-Israeli fund-raising. As well as this, Israel did score important successes in four other areas: (a) the procurement of machines to establish her local arms production; (b) the obtainment of a fleet of cargo planes made prior to the severance of the embargo on 15 April; (c) the purchase of a great number of radio and other signalling equipment, completed before 15 April; and (d) the recruitment of many experienced North American servicemen to the IDF, without whom the IDF Air Force in particular might not have been able to function. Other sorts of aid and procurement cannot be regarded as in the same category of importance to the outcome of the war.

4 Britain's Middle Eastern Policies and Military Aid, 1948–9

However keenly Britain wished in 1948 to shake off the burden of the Palestine mandate, her past role in the mandate, her share in the Western defence of the Middle East, her interest in the Arab world and her growing dependence on the USA, made her continue to play a key role in shaping the Palestine situation, either by action or by default. The mere fact that for years she supplied weapons and military know-how to the main Arab armies, left these armies dependent on the continuation of such British aid. Britain's hope to mould a new, pro-British Middle East without antagonizing the USA, and her momentary relations with some of the Arab governments, made her keen to impose the arms embargo. However, while her motive was to create a stalemate in the hostilities in Palestine as prerequisite for a settlement, her withholding of military aid from the Arabs, albeit followed by an American withholding of such aid from the Jews, worked faster than expected at diminishing Arab military capability, giving the military advantage to Israel.

Although Britain came out of the Second World War as a winner, by the same token she was relegated to a second-rate power on the international scale. Her Labour Party, which came to power in 1945 partly aware of this fact, was stocked with plans to reform the British Empire, which now became, a liability. Labour ministers, particularly Ernest Bevin, took to the road with the intention of dismantling the old empire, but at the same time tried to hedge it by preserving British economic, strategic and cultural interests in the countries now candidates for sovereignty. Bevin knew that in all these countries, there were internal as well as external issues pending decision, which he tried, open-mindedly and creatively, to solve with patience and goodwill. During his early years in office, he was renowned for his confidence 'to stake his political future' on solving such problems as Palestine, Egypt and

Iraq. Only gradually did he realize that his country had little to give to the peoples of the former empire, and less still power to enforce his plans. 'Bevin's . . . "Arab policy" ', wrote Elizabeth Monroe, 'had been "pro-Arab" only to non-Arabs; by Arab standards it had accomplished nothing'.[1]

The new British policy was defeated by four major factors. The first was the development of the Cold War. In wartime summit meetings, both the Soviets and the Americans recognized the Middle East as a British domain. But the post-War crises of Iran and Greece, the tension created by the Soviet desire to obtain control of the Black Sea straits and the extremization of ideological East–West confrontation, gnawed at that recognition. Between 1946 and 1947, the Soviet policy towards the Middle East was imbued with threats and pressure against local governments, combined with verbal attacks on the British policy. Early in 1948, experts in London feared that this propaganda was a precursor for:

> a Soviet plan . . . to undermine our position in the Middle East, to dominate the Mediterranean . . . confident that their success in Greece would bring about the collapse of Turkey . . . and in Palestine, Jewish immigration from Eastern Europe be used as an instrument of Soviet penetration.[2]

In 1948 the British military feared a Soviet land offensive towards the Suez Canal, and made plans to face such an attack in co-operation with their American Allies. These considerations required revision of earlier British plans for the withdrawal of the British army from the Middle East. Now the British Chiefs of Staff maintained that the Suez Canal Zone must be held for the foreseeable future, and the Order of the Battle of the British forces there be increased far beyond what the 1936 Anglo-Egyptian Treaty provided for. Similar thoughts followed with regard to Iraq.[3] If, none the less, Bevin considered the evacuation of Egypt, the Chiefs of Staff told him that they must reinforce the British forces in Palestine.[4] Palestine was, however, already thrown into the UN lap.

The second factor was psycho-political. Years of British rule fermented hatred towards them among the public in the region, which, along with anti-Zionism, became a tool in the hands of local oppositions to totter local governments. It became customary in the Arab world, that whenever an Arab government was about to reach a rapprochement with Britain, it was in immediate danger of collapse under pressure of mob, led by political oppositions.

The third factor which hindered the post-imperial design was Britain's economic exhaustion. Early in 1947 it became apparent in London that the British resources would not be sufficient to maintain the defence of the region *vis à vis* the Soviet pressure, and Britain urgently requested the USA to support her on this score. An American commitment to such effect came promptly, in the form of the Truman Doctrine, which although it still left the British army in charge, financed the local armies in the so-called 'Northern Tier' and enhanced a joint Anglo-American military planning in case of war with the USSR. But this did not improve Britain's own ability to give military and economic aid to countries in the region, except for old American LL equipment which the British army no longer wanted and occasionally gave to Arab armies. Furthermore, Britain's growing dependence on the USA required due bowing to America's special domestic–foreign policy problem pertaining to the Arab–Zionist dispute. Typically, Bevin tried to see advantages in bringing the Americans to cooperate with Britain on Palestine, but the report of the Anglo-American Committee of Inquiry on Palestine, and what followed its conclusions, began to mar Anglo-American relations with disagreement. Now the USA got involved deeper in Palestine.

The fourth hindering factor was the severance of the Arab–Zionist dispute. The decision to turn Palestine to the UN 'without recommendations' must be viewed as symptomatic of the general British mood of frustration over its inability to come to terms with the Arab governments. It was Britain which initiated new treaties with these governments. Legally speaking, there was no need to do it. The Anglo-Iraqi Treaty of 1930 was due to expire only in 1950; the Anglo-Egyptian Treaty in 1956, and the Anglo-Transjordan Treaty would expire in the 1960s. Bevin wanted to offer these governments generous terms out of his own initiative, including committing Britain to give the Arab governments 'a worthy' military assistance by truly modernizing them. It was probably only because the signing of these new treaties did not develop as Bevin hoped that British military aid to the Arabs did not come about.

There were four phases in the British military assistance to the Arabs. The first was from mid-1946 up until the deadlock in the negotiation for the treaties which coincided with the appearance of a fear of Arab military intervention in Palestine; the second was from that deadlock up until the imposition of the UN embargo in May 1948, and the third was from June 1948 up until the abrogation of that embargo in August 1949. The fourth phase began with the renewal of the military aid programme, starting from the end of 1949. Britain's policy during the second phase was already tantamount to a partial embargo, and in the third phase aid to the Arabs stopped completely.

THE RECONSIDERATION OF THE MILITARY AID TO THE ARAB COUNTRIES

On 18 December 1947, in reply to an arranged question at the House of Commons, Christopher Mayhew, Labour's Parliamentary Under-secretary-of-State for Foreign Affairs, announced that 'in view of the possibilities of trouble in the Middle East it was decided recently that all orders for war materials from Middle Eastern countries would be very carefully scrutinised.'[5]

The statement came shortly after the passing of the partition resolution at the UN Assembly, which was followed by the unilateral American embargo. Mr Mayhew's statement was not yet a full undertaking to stop all military assistance to the Arabs and it was aimed mainly at reassuring the USA, where the British Ambassador Sir Oliver Franks, continuously reported the American concern about Britain's arming the Arab states, which recently threatened to intervene in Palestine. State Department officials told Franks that if the British aid went on, it might eventually force the US Government to lift its own embargo and come to the aid of the Jews in Palestine. Bevin, who grasped the danger of Anglo-American cooperation in the defence of the Middle East, accepted that this tie was paramount to any other consideration, including Anglo-Arab relations. Despite objection from within his own Ministry, as well as from the Ministry of Defence and the Chiefs of Staff, Bevin manipulated his immense influence in the Cabinet to enact a slow-down policy on military aid to the Arabs and on this he received full support from Prime Minister Attlee. His position, however, might not have been so strong had the treaties with the Arab governments not been torn to pieces by rebellious mobs in these countries. The British adherence to the embargo in 1948 was cemented not only by consideration of the Anglo-American cooperation, but also by the depressing feeling that there was no one to talk sense to in Cairo and Baghdad.

The delivery of the British military aid to the Arabs, suffered delays anyway, as a result of bureaucratic and technical problems. When the slow down was enacted, a tug-of-war developed inside the British government as to whether at least that gap should be closed or not.[6]

BRITISH MILITARY ASSISTANCE TO EGYPT UNTIL 1948

In negotiating Egypt's demand for full independence, both in 1936 and in 1946, the British readily offered the Egyptians attributes of sovereignty, to the extent that they did not tresspass on British strategic interests.[7] Britain committed herself to defending the integrity of Egypt, but retained the right to hold military bases and ports in Egyptian territory. In both cases Britain undertook to build the Egyptian Army and to train, arm and supply it and Egypt undertook not to ask for military assistance from any other source. But, although from time to time plans were made for a 3 or a 5 year army-building programme, the pace of building the army remained linked to British interests. For this reason, the military assistance to Egypt slowed down during World War II and again in 1946. During the Second World War, Britain lacked a real motive to go on with building the Egyptian Army except the establishment of Egyptian anti-aircraft contingents. In the spring of 1946, as British negotiation with the government of Ismail Sidki about a new treaty began to take shape, anti-British demonstrations and street riots occurred in Cairo. In the Autumn, the talks moved to London.

The Egyptian demands included the evacuation of the British Army from Egypt earlier than it was prescribed by the 1936 Treaty and the 'Unity of the Nile Valley', which meant the annexation of Sudan to Egypt. The British, who ruled Sudan 'in condominium with Egypt' were opposed to the annexation of Sudan to Egypt. But Bevin, in disagreement with his Chiefs of Staff, accepted a British pull out from Egypt by the end of 1949, provided the British right for a military redeployment in case of emergency was recognized by Egypt. In May 1946, Britain unilaterally announced her withdrawal from the Nile Valley and Delta and soon did it. In October 1946, the Anglo-Egyptian negotiations in London came to a successful conclusion. Bevin and Sidky both made concessions and signed a 'protocol' in which Sidky recognized Sudan's right for a national self-determination and Bevin committed Britain to an early withdrawal.[8]

But this protocol was met with angry reaction both in Egypt and London. Conservative Party critics, including those who firmly preached abandonment of Palestine, were unwilling to forgive the government giving up on matters 'concerning the foundation of the Empire and Democracy'. Many in the British defence establishment stood aghast. And although Bevin withstood these public attacks well, he felt strongly that he had reached the limit of his concessions to Egypt. Worse awaited Sidky when he returned to Egypt. He faced angry demonstrations organized by the Wafdist opposition and by radical elements, who protested against his alleged submission to the British. In distress, Sidky made a statement to the effect that the protocol actually provided for an Egyptian rule in Sudan, which the British promptly denied. King Farouk now joined the critics of Sidky, who in December was forced to resign, while the protocol was never ratified. Mahmoud Noqrashi, a less acceptable politician to the British was appointed as the new Prime Minister and Anglo-Egyptian efforts to mend differences laxed. In the summer of 1947 Egypt took her dispute with Britain to the Security Council, where she failed to obtain a favourable verdict. Bevin's reaction was 'I stick to the 1936 Treaty'.[9]

The victim of these developments was the British military assistance to Egypt. In the autumn of 1947, Noqrashi denounced the British military mission, led by General Arbuthnot and the Foreign Office informed the Cairo Government that the mission's work would terminate when Arbuthnot's contract expired, which was the end of December 1947. Noqrashi hinted that he would seek military assistance from other governments, including the USA, but the withdrawal of the military mission was carried out as announced.[10] In fact, Noqrashi was far from demanding the cessation of British aid to Egypt and the British also muffled their decision not to renew the work of the mission. But neither of the two governments went out of its way to ask for the continuation of its work either. This state of affairs was enough for the British supply bureaucracy to slow the process to a halt. Other factors helped the slow down. From Arbuthnot's reports it is clear that he grew to hate his job and saw the modernization of the Egyptian Army hopeless. His complaints about 'corruption', 'laziness' and 'stupidity' at the top echelons of the Egyptian military establishment, had their effect on the Defence and War establishment in London. The military mission was back in London on the first day of 1948.

British policy-makers were not at all certain what to do now. On the one hand, they had political *and* economic motives to go on supplying arms to Egypt, particularly since one-quarter of Egypt's (World War II) blocked Sterling balance in London, amounting to approximately £400 million, had in June 1947 been unfrozen and their spending on products of Britain's arms industry seemed good for Britain's economy.[11] Another argument in favour of going on with the supply of arms was raised by the British Ambassador in Cairo, Sir Ronald Campbell and by General Crocker, who argued that whatever the political disagreements, such supplies were requisite for 'day to day working relations'. But American pressure and the approach of the deadline of the British evacuation of Palestine weighed heavier. Disagreement within the British Government now switched to the question of the equipment already 'in the pipeline', that is, equipment already in the process of dispatch. In February 1948 the British War Office believed that, technically speaking, there was 'little chance to clear that equipment', anyway. But while the War and Defence Offices were willing to continue sending arms which had already been committed, as an act of good faith, the Foreign Office demanded it be stopped completely, even when the equipment in question was stored in Egyptian territory. In the end, each item of equipment was dealt with on its merit. For instance, a long pending deal for supplying Egypt with two squadrons of Spitfire aircraft had then been completed. But three British frigates, long promised, were withheld.[12]

As early as January 1948, in a meeting held at the Prime Minister's Office, with Bevin and the Minister of Defence, Alexander, present, Bevin pushed through his point that both Britain and the USA must agree to refrain completely from any further supply of war materials to the Jews or the Arabs. 'It could be shown to the Arabs', Bevin argued, 'that probably they would be the net losers if the State Department raises the US embargo upon arms for the Jews'.[13] In March this tendency became a policy. Internal correspondence of April, in the Ministry of Defence, explained that

> The overriding political consideration now is that His Majesty's Government should take no action which might give the United States an excuse for lifting their embargo on arms to the Middle East'[14]

It thus went without saying that new requests for sales of arms and ammunition by Syria, with which the British had no treaty, but in normal times would have been considered positively, were turned down. 'We cannot allow such order to be fulfilled during a period of civil strife in Palestine', wrote the Foreign Office desk officer in charge of military assistance.[15]

In the spring of 1948, notwithstanding the absence from Egypt of the British military mission, Egypt's interest in buying arms in Britain had grown. Prime Minister Noqrashi, far from enthusiastic about sending the ill-prepared army to Palestine, in April began to suspect that this intervention might be inevitable. Egypt's Minister of War, Haidar, 'representing the King', then asked Ambassador Campbell for much more than what remained 'in the pipe line'. His list of requests included vehicles, including AFVs, ammunition and aircraft. While these requests were turned down in London, the Egyptians managed to get one more injection of 'first and second line ammunition' from British stores in the Canal Zone (which in normal times would be given almost automatically). Unfortunately, this last portion did not include ammunition for 3-inch mortars and 25-pounder guns, because such items were in short supply in the British army as well. In any event it was the last ration of ammunition – indeed of any British military supply to Egypt for over a year. Even when King Farouk himself swallowed his pride and asked Campbell to support the new requests, this was to no avail.[16]

BRITISH MILITARY ASSISTANCE TO IRAQ UNTIL MAY 1948

In Iraq, as in Egypt, Bevin tried to be the initiating party in the negotiation for the new treaty. In view of the Egyptian débâcle, he was ready to offer concessions which some in Britain thought outrageous. 'It would be wiser', he argued, 'to avoid fighting a diplomatic rearguard action to defend a position which we are bound to give up in the end.'[17] The Iraqi negotiators, headed by the Shi'ite Prime Minister Saleh Jabr, demanded the evacuation of the British military bases of Habbaniya and Shuiba, to which General Crocker and the Chiefs of Staff strongly objected, but Bevin, encouraged by the advice of his Ambassador in Baghdad; Sir Henry Mack, thought otherwise. The British idea was, again, to find a *modus vivendi* with the Iraqis, which in view of the proximity of the Soviet border to Iraq and the threat of Kurdish insurrection, seemed more likely to be attained.[18] Towards the opening of the talks, Bevin closed ranks with Alexander on the terms Britain would be ready to accept.

The negotiations opened in London on 6 January 1948, against a background of Arab anxiety and bitterness following the Palestine decision at the UN Assembly. This did not help the Iraqi public to look favourably on the forthcoming Anglo-Iraqi agreement. Still, there were those in London and Baghdad who argued that the anti-Arab development at the UN and the British concessions to Iraq in the forthcoming negotiation might reinforce Iraq's confidence in the British friendship. Bevin talked of 'stabilizing the situation in Palestine by making separate agreements with countries such as Iraq'. This should be viewed as a hope of controlling Iraqi military policy through Iraq's dependence on British aid.[19]

On 6 January 1948, Prime Minister Jabr, followed by a battery of

Ministers and two former Prime Ministers, arrived in Portsmouth, England, for the final phase of the negotiations. The atmosphere in the talks was described as 'excellent'. Nine days later, the two sides signed an agreement in which Britain recognized Iraq's absolute sovereignty over her entire territory, but none the less, allowed the British RAF to continue using the Habbaniya and Shueiba bases. It was also agreed to give a push to the so-far procrastinated 5 year plan of building the Iraqi army. The British military mission in Iraq was up-graded to a 'Defence Council' and instead of the old equipment which had been supplied so far, new equipment was promised, including fighter aircraft and new AFVs.[20] The British press then jumped to the conclusion that 'everything that was objectionable in the Treaty of 1930 had been removed' and that the new treaty 'established Anglo-Iraqi relations . . . for some time, on equal terms'.[21] An Iraqi purchasing mission, which had been based in London since October, received from the Iraqi Ministry of Defence additions to its already large list of orders.[22]

But the fate of the Portsmouth agreement of January 1948 was not better than that of the Bevin–Sidri protocol of October 1946. In reaction to news about the new treaty on 16 January, the Iraqi opposition amassed thousands on the streets of Baghdad to protest and the demonstration, which developed into riots, lasted for a few days, with some 50 dead. Jabr returned home and found a situation which not only forced him to resign, but to flee from the country. The usually pro-British regent, Abdul Illah, felt obliged to join the protest and declared the Portsmouth Treaty null and void. He also announced a new election for parliament and, in order that the deposition of Jabr would not be considered as an anti-Shi'ite step, he appointed another Shi'ite, the politically weak Mohammad As Sader, as a caretaker Prime Minister. It was under that government and under fear of the Baghdad mob, that the fate of the Portsmouth Treaty was sealed. It was also this government which drifted Iraq into the war in Palestine.

The new débâcle perplexed London. Bevin, however, kept his nerve and reacted in the same way as he did when his protocol with Sidki was torn to pieces. He said that for him the 1930 treaty remained in effect and that he 'would not propose . . . any move to the Iraqis until the they themselves asked' him to,[23] which they didn't. General Renton tried to persuade his superiors in London that what had happened was 'having little effect on the (army's) Excellent relation with our mission'[24] and that the rearmament programme must go on. Indeed, the delivery of in the pipeline equipment continued for a while, with the approval of the Ministry of Defence. But in February these deliveries slowed down and in March they came to a halt.

Bevin and Alexander were in disagreement, but still friends. Their struggle over the continuation of the military assistance to the three treaty countries, with Alexander always pushing towards continuation and Bevin for stoppage, always took an intimate form of 'Dear Ernie' and 'My Dear Victor'. But Bevin kept the upper hand. Harold Wilson, – then President of the Board of Trade, remembered Bevin as 'the only Cabinet member whom Attlee never criticized'.[25] Thus, as early as January, Attlee instructed the Cabinet that no war material of any kind could go to Middle Eastern countries without explicit permission from Bevin.[26] But this did not put an end to pressure on the Foreign Office from the Chiefs of Staff and the War and Defence offices to allow small deliveries, particularly ammunition, to reach the Arab armies. Thus, on 13 March Bevin wrote to Alexander suggesting, 'in the light of the Palestine situation at this moment', a lull 'of say, three months' in the supply of war materials, 'after which we shall reconsider the matter'.[27]

The last consignments of military equipment to Iraq, left Britain on board the *City of Florence* and the *Cheltenham* on 3 and 18 of March, respectively. They included, among other items, 30 Daimler armoured cars and several 25 pounder guns. Eight additional Sea Fury aircraft, of which one crashed in Cyprus, also arrived during that period. But although by a contract signed in September 1947, during 1948 Iraq was to receive 34 such aircraft (30 one-seated, four double-seated) fully equipped and their crews be trained, the eight brought now were also the last aircraft delivered.[28] At about the same time a transport of spare parts for Egypt's Spitfires was also shipped, perhaps because George Strauss, the Minister of Supply, 'admitted' that this consignment had been due a year earlier and it was his office's fault that it was held up. Two ships with military equipment, 'not weapon or ammunition' left for Britain late in April, for a long sailing and were due to arrive in Basra in June.[29] Beyond that, all movement of war materials to the Arab countries now stopped.[30] An urgent Egyptian application in April, to complete the supply of 16 million rounds of 0.303 ammunition and 135 000 mortar bombs, said to have been in the pipeline, was turned down, as were Iraqi requests to supply the missing weapons for the Fury planes. Bevin repeatedly explained to British representatives in Arab capitals that the continuation of supply to the Arabs might provoke Truman to lift the American embargo because of Jewish pressure in the USA.[31] However, Bevin did not realize that he was stopping these supplies for 18 months.

The Portsmouth agreement was intended to give the Iraqi army a big leap forwards. The equipment 'temporarily withheld', included not only many implements of war, but much ammunition, part of which was long overdue. It also included the equipment without which the Fury aircraft could not become serviceable. The equipment withheld included at least 40 25 pounder guns, 64 Mermon Harrington and Dingo AFVs, 18 40 mm anti-aircraft guns and millions of small arms and ammunition items. A British report of May 1949, notes that

> By an unfortunate oversight none of the ammunition requirements of Iraq for 1947 were delivered before the embargo . . . (and that) Iraq was two years behind in matters of ammunition.[32]

Additional damage was caused to Iraq indirectly. As early as May 1947, General Renton offered, with American permission, to build an Iraqi tank regiment from old American Land Lease M4 Shermans. These tanks were returned by the British Army to an OFLC yard in Egypt. Over 500 such tanks were then rusting on Egyptian soil, and with British help the 40 requisite tanks could have definitely been reparable. However, the Iraqis, expecting modern AFVs, turned the offer down.[33]

THE BRITISH MILITARY AID TO TRANSJORDAN BEFORE THE EMBARGO

Britain's failure to reach agreement with Egypt and Iraq dramatically augmented the importance of Transjordan in her Middle East strategy. Sir John Troutbeck, Chief of the BMEO wrote on 3 March that British experts felt that Britain must now: 'hold fast to Transjordan which is our only reliable ally, and let the rest (Arab governments) go hang'.[34]

The depreciation of Iraq's potential OB, resulting from the British withholding of deliveries in March 1948 is summed up in Tables 5 and 6 below.

But it was not only the lack of other Arab partners who would allow Britain a strategic hold in their domains which increased Transjordan's importance in the British eyes, but a new hope of supplementing their withdrawal from Palestine with a partition of a new kind, between Transjordan and a 'compact' Jewish state – a settlement which seemed to be 'sorting itself out', as Harold Beeley propagated it around the Foreign Office. With Britain unable, the USA unwilling, and only the USSR keen to participate in the enforcement of the original UN

Table 5 Supply of British equipment to Iraq in 1948, plan and
implementation (selected items)[35]

Item	Plan	Implementation
Fury fighters	34	10
25-pounder guns	72	12 (24?)
40-mm AA guns	54	10
17-pounder guns	48	8
4.2-inch mortars	16	0
20-mm guns	54	4
Daimler, Humber AFVs	126	59
Light tanks	39	0
Cruiser (medium) tanks	82	0
Special tanks (sic)	30	0

Table 6 Ammunition committed and not sent to the Iraqi army in 1948
(selected items)

Item	Amount withheld
25-pounder gun shells	42 000
17-pounder gun shells	2 000
40-mm gun shells	13 800
2-Pounder gun shells	24 300
20-mm gun shells	Un-quantified
0.303-rounds ammunition	4 000 000
PIAT ammunition	19 200

partition scheme, there seemed to be a new hope that most of the UN
members should now realize that they could not afford to turn down
this new kind of partition, although it ruled out the establishment of
an independent Palestinian Arab state. The Arab Legion seemed the
perfect agent to help implement the new scheme, provided it did not
enter into areas originally allotted to the Jews or those which were
heavily populated by them. How exactly would the new boundaries
eventually be drawn, and what would be the fate of Jerusalem and the
flow of oil from Iraq to Haifa, was still far from clear. But Bevin was
experienced and disillusioned enough to believe that such questions
would have to be resolved later on.

In the light of these considerations, the new Anglo-Transjordanian
treaty was negotiated, signed and ratified without a hitch. The flow of
British military aid to Transjordan – all brand new equipment – in-

creased just as supplies to other Arab armies slowed down. At the time when British advisers left or intended to quit their work with other Arab armies, over 20 new British officers were seconded to the Legion, in addition to those who had already served in it. While the King of Egypt and the Regent of Iraq appealled to King Abdullah not to sign the treaty with Britain, and while Syrian hand bills tried to persuade the public in Amman to get out and protest,[36] there were few in Transjordan who would follow that advice. Abdullah himself, viewing the Arab areas of Palestine as being for the taking, was convinced that it was his chance to start realizing his political grand design of Greater Syria. It is unlikely that at this point either he or the British considered the Legion's involvement in the war against the Jews.[37]

Precursors of this new British policy cropped up in London in January. Following an exchange of appreciations between the Foreign Office and its representatives in Amman, Sir Alec Kirkbride and Christopher Pirie-Gordon, it was agreed to invite a Transjordanian delegation to London, which would typically include two Arabs (Prime Minister Taufiq Abu L'Huda and Foreign Minister Fawzi al Mulki) and two Britains (General Glubb and Pirie-Gordon). The official aim of the visit was a new treaty, but no less important was the need for agreement on the future action of the Legion. Bevin's summary of his meetings with Abu L'Huda goes as follows:

> It was well understood that the Arab Legion would have to leave (its present engagement in) Palestine before 15th May (but) it would be to the public benefit if it returned to the Arab areas of Palestine to maintain law and order . . . (this must) not prevent the execution of any UN decision . . . (and Tawfiq Pasha undertook) not to enter Jewish areas unless the Jews invaded Arab areas.[38]

The annexation of Palestine to Transjordan was nowhere mentioned in that new Anglo-Transjordanian treaty. However, on 22 March Bevin brought the outlines of the new partition scheme for the approval of the British Cabinet.[39] Thereafter, Britain did her best to prepare the Legion for the new task. In February, at a speed unfamiliar to British bureaucracy, guns, Armoured cars, men and equipment were rushed to Transjordan, though with only ten 'contact days' replenishment of ammunition. Towards the Legion's crossing of the River Jordan to Palestine on 15 May, Glubb managed to get an additional special allotment of ammunition to the level of 30 'contact days', including 25 pounders, which were particularly in short supply.[40] This delivery, amounting to over 500 tons, was sent from the British depot of Tel el

Kebir by train to Port Suez and was loaded on two chartered Egyptian ships on 20 and 22 May. The first of the two ships reached Aqaba safely. But the second, the *Ramses*, was stopped by the Egyptian authorities, after it had already weighed anchor. Its cargo, which included most of the Legion's 25-pounder shells and mortar bombs, was confiscated and sent to an Egyptian ammunition dump in El Arish.[41]

Thereafter, a diplomatic tug-of-war developed between Egypt and Transjordan over that portion of ammunition, reaching even the level of Kings, but to no settlement. For the Legion, the painful fact remained that this was the last consignment of ammunition that the British Government, with all due goodwill, felt able to grant. For when it was approved, the Legion had already crossed into Palestine, though it had not yet entered into battle. Later, the British commitment to the embargo and the US Government's sensitivity to the Legion's involvement in the war made it impossible for the British to send another consignment. In fact, following the *Ramses* incident, General Crocker still suggested to compensating the Legion with a substitute allotment, but London objected. On 26 May, it was the British Prime Minister himself who proposed to the American Ambassador a strict Anglo-American supervision of an international embargo, based, of course, on a mutual Anglo-American restraint in arms supply.[42] It was Attlee who insisted that the introduction of the truce resolution at the Security Council 'must not be spoiled by injecting conditions of any sort'.[43] Bevin probably did not know and having been critical about Abdullah's conduct, did not care, that during the first period of its fighting, the Legion squandered its 25-pounder and 3-inch mortar ammunition, shelling Jewish positions and civil quarters in Jerusalem until, according to Glubb, it was left with only 3 contact days of ammunition. Glubb probably was somewhat equivocal. The Legion still had reserves of small arms and 2 and 6 pounder shells at its disposal, but he was correct about the shortage of ammunition for heavier guns and mortars.[44]

THE BRITISH PALESTINE POLICY IN 1948 AND 1949

From the moment Britain decided to transfer Palestine to the UN and up until the end of the war there, in 1949, her Palestine policy underwent four phases. During the *first phase*, from 14 February to 29 November 1947, it was an escapist policy, aimed at passing the issue to the UN 'without recommendations'. For some time, however, Britain still maintained a watchful waiting, to see what course the UN would take. But following UNSCOP's report, the British policy was epitomized by the statement which Arthur Creech-Jones, the Colonial Secretary, made at the UN Assembly. He said that Britain would not help to implement any solution not acceptable to both Arabs and Jews, which amounted to a do-nothing policy. *The second* phase began immediately after the UN Assembly recommended partition, and lasted until 22 March. During that period, Britain was guided by the Cabinet decision of 4 December 1947 aiming at pulling out of Palestine with minimum loss at British lives and resources. Accordingly, Britain refused to allow the UN to take preliminary steps in Palestine towards implementing partition, or to allow Jewish immigration. At the same time, Britain warned the Arab governments not to intervene openly in Palestine before the end of the mandate. But she did not go out of her way to prevent the infiltration of volunteers and military aid sent from the Arab states to help the insurrection of the Palestian Arabs. When it became clear that the UN would fail to implement its partition scheme, new British ideas cropped up and gradually added up to a new policy, which ripened in the Cabinet on 22 March, when it was decided 'not to oppose the setting up of a Jewish State or a move to Palestine from Transjordan'.[45]

The *third phase* began with that decision, and lasted up until early November 1948. Now Britain viewed with satisfaction that the map of Palestine began to depict a *de facto* partition 'sorting itself out', which after the disintegration of the pro-Mufti and the pro-Syrian forces in Palestine, created just the sort of vacuum that Abdullah's authority could fill. Britain was opposed to the armed intervention of the regular Arab armies in Palestine in mid-May, and became critical of Abdullah's joining the fighting. But she hoped to be able to check the military intervention by means of truce and international embargo. When the Anglo-American co-operation was indeed attained, British policymakers believed that, after all, the issue of Palestine would be solved according to their interests. The British policy during the third phase followed three guidelines:

(a) The Palestine war must now come to an end and the sooner the better and a truce, imposed by the Security Council, must retain the military and territorial *status quo*.

(b) A political settlement must follow, in line with the Anglo-American strategic interests, and it must *not* allow a Soviet involvement in its implementation. A close Anglo-American cooperation became

the paramount consideration, even when it temporarily antago-
nized the Arabs.

(c) The method of turning the truce into a permanent settlement
was to make the truce frontiers, *mutatis mutandis*, into partition
boundaries. The parties to the partition settlement should be Israel and the Kingdom of Transjordan, and perhaps Egypt as well.
'We have always thought', Bevin wrote on 26 May,

> that it was King Abdullah's intention to add the central Arab
> area of Palestine and possibly Gaza to Transjordan. It is poss-
> ible that the Egyptians may also wish to appropriate the area
> between the Egyptian frontier and Gaza to their occupation
> of it . . . Transjordan and Egypt would no doubt wish to share
> the Negev . . . The Jews would no doubt claim Western Galilee,
> if they lost the Negev and it seems likely that it is beyond
> the power of the Arabs to turn them out. A solution on these
> lines, particularly if Abdullah had an outlet to the sea at Gaza,
> would have many obvious advantages from our point of view,
> creating a strong barrier against Jewish and Communist (*sic*)
> expansion south and east, and it would provide us with an
> extended area of friendly Arab countries in which we would
> have strategic facilities; whereas a separate Arab state in Pal-
> estine would be so small and weak that it could not maintain
> itself and might well succumb at some stage to Jewish press-
> ure of infiltration.'[46]

In a cable to Kirkbride, 2 days after the commencement of the truce,
Bevin further explained his wish that the truce should be extended
beyond the preliminary 4 weeks agreed and that the present front lines
would in due course turn into boundaries, making the area of the Jewish
state to include only that, effectively under Jewish control.[47]

This third phase, lasted until November 1948, when the IDF drastically changed the frontiers, Anglo-American agreement collapsed and
the UN declined to accept the Bernadotte plan. The fourth phase included Britain's readjustment to a reality, whereby a wider and militarily
stronger Jewish state was there to stay and in which the Arab–Israeli
dispute became permanent.

BRITAIN AND THE EMBARGO AFTER 29 MAY

The involvement of the Legion in the war against the IDF was first viewed in London with alarm. Bevin believed that Abdullah had allowed himself to drift towards joining an 'irresponsible' policy, which undermined Transjordan's interest. Early in July he told the Minister of Defence that, 'It was a pity that the Transjordanian troops had fought in Jerusalem . . . this interfered with the original idea of having most of the Arab areas of Palestine (passed) to Transjordan'. During that phase the British maintained full cooperation with the USA and the strict embargo.[48] Following the successful passing of a Security Council resolution on 29 May and the early steps in the UN Mediator's work, Bevin wrote again:

> The cease fire comes at a time when the Arab forces are . . . bogged down (in Palestine) and before the Jewish forces have had time to increase their numbers and import war material . . . we have preventing the lifting of the American embargo, while it is quite clear that this would have taken place had we adopted any other policy.'[49]

Wasting no time, on 31 May the War Office ordered the General Staff Q Branch, the Ministry of Supply and the Middle East Land and Air Command, that 'All deliveries of arms and war materials including military aid to the Arab armies should immediately be stopped', British officers seconded to the Legion be withdrawn, and the subsidy to Transjordan on account of the Legion, be withheld.[50] In the Security Councils, a list of the items suspended was made and it 'included material already paid for or in a process of shipment'. Detailed instructions and lists of items were cabled by the Ministry of Defence to army commands between 2 and 6 June, with a warning against infringement of these instructions.[51]

These orders were met with dismay among many British military and diplomats and their criticism constantly fed back into the Minister of Defence's disagreement with Bevin.[52] But Bevin remained adamant and he was always backed by the Prime Minister's support. Bevin's ideas were widely shared by his subordinates in the Foreign Office. The Chief of the Eastern Department, Bernard Burrows, explained to an American diplomat, that 'Egypt has more to gain from the American embargo than from the removal of the British one'.[53] Even sober Arab politicians, like former (and future) Iraqi Prime Minister, Nuri al-Said, expressed themselves in the same vein.[54] 'In spite of Arab bitterness against the British and more so towards the United States',

Bevin told the Cabinet in July, 'the governments of the Arab states seemed to recognize that we had acted in their best interests'.[55] When Ambassador Mack in Baghdad pleaded to Bevin for an 'extraordinary gesture' towards Iraq, by which he meant releasing equipment for the grounded Fury aircraft, Bevin replied that he knew that the '. . . orders will be extremely unwelcome to the Iraqis but there is no, *repeat no* possibility of agreeing to infringe the embargo and break the promise made to the USA and in the Security Council'.[56]

One thing, however, which the British could not afford to do was to boast publicly of their orthodox observance of the embargo. The worse the Arab military situation in Palestine turned, the more anxious the British became to muffle praise of success in maintaining the embargo. Zionist and Soviet propaganda, which continuously blamed the British for violating the embargo, was, to some extent helpful to the British image in the Arab world. But when the Zionist accusations began to be taken seriously by the American public, the British felt in a cleft stick. In the autumn, British statesmen and diplomats had quietly 'pledged their word of honour' to their American colleagues, that nothing of the sort had happened. On 13 December the Minister of State in the Foreign Office made a vehement statement in the House of Commons to the effect that his government never infringed the rules of the embargo.[57] Bevin asked Sir Oliver Franks, 'to swear' to Marshall that 'Britain refrained from giving any military aid . . . although she was obliged to do so by her contracts with Egypt, Iraq and Transjordan'.[58] When American politicians remained sceptical, Prime Minister Attlee himself called the US Ambassador to tell him that his government

> scrupulously observed conditions of the truce and has refrained from delivering arms to the Arabs countries in spite of their treaty obligations to do so . . . while Israel has built up a considerable modern fighting force . . . with material from Czechoslovakia'.[59]

THE BRITISH DISENCHANTMENT FROM THE EMBARGO

With the establishment of the first truce, the British idea of a settlement seemed within implementation. Foreign Office experts believed that 'a realistic Arab interest' was to comply with the existence of the 'compact' Jewish state. They continued to believe that keeping the Arab countries devoid of war materials was an essential measure to cool down the Arab wish to go on fighting.[60] The renewal of the war on 9 July, at the Arab League's initiative (against Abdullah's objection), embarrassed the British but did not diminish their hopes. Now pointing out Abdullah again as a 'responsible' Arab leader, Bevin wrote to Kirkbride, on 13 July,

> You should tell King Abdullah that the situation . . . is exactly that which I have been working my hardest to prevent. I will do my utmost to help King Abdullah, but I cannot, *repeat, cannot* do this by the supply of ammunition.[61]

With the establishment of the second truce on 18 July and the repeated warnings now made by the Security Council against a party which would violate the truce, it seemed to London that things were back on the right track. It was not until mid-August that intelligence about the invigoration of the IDF and about Israel's offensive intentions shook the British confidence. Bevin began to fear that the embargo was working non-symmetrically and that its effect on Arab military capability was more devastating than the British experts foresaw. On 26 August he told the Cabinet about a recent exchange of intelligence with the Americans, which brought both governments to the conclusion that 'the only hope . . . lay in the imposition of a settlement by the UN', the sooner the better. Bevin was hinting at an Anglo-American intervention, under the guise of the UN Mediator and the Security Council. He believed that Bernadotte could be brought to propose whatever he was told to jointly by Britain and the USA, namely, the Anglo-American plan of partition. The Mediator plan would then be brought to the Security Council for approval. This was hoped to be either enough deterrence against an Israeli breaking of the truce and, if it was not, the Security Council could use sanctions against Israel, which would enable British or American troops or both, to occupy key positions in southern Palestine and provide a strong footing to dictate the Bernadotte plan.[62]

There were, however, two clouds of danger at the corner of the sky: the approaching US elections and a possible USSR veto at the SC. Thus, the production of the mediator's plan had to be made under heavy secrecy and camouflage. Indeed, Bevin refrained from telling the Cabinet (and Marshall from telling the White House) that he and his American counterpart had conspired to send two emissaries to the Island of Rhodes, to put pressure to bear on Bernadotte, so that the mediator's proposal dovetailed with theirs.[63] That secret mission was carried out on 13–14 September. Meanwhile, the worried British Minister of Defence renewed his pleading to anticipate the IDF offensive by supplying ammunition and spare parts, at least to the Arab Legion. But again, Bevin flatly refused.[64]

Bevin was not unaware of the prospect that his planning might not work or that until it did the Arab Legion might simply be eliminated. So, while continuing to oppose any relaxation in the embargo, he considered favourably a plan, first suggested by Glubb and now strongly advocated by the Minister of Defence, according to which, there was no need actually to renew supplies to the Legion – or if the government wished, to other Arab armies. It would be enough to dump at British bases in the Arab countries well-calculated quantities of ammunition and other expendable equipment, for use by the Arab armies, if and when the truce was grossly violated by Israel. This arrangement was approved in consultation between the Prime Minister and Foreign Minister in mid-November and was conditioned by approval of both. In addition, a shelf plan was made to meet an Israeli refusal to obey the Security Council order, with a British 'surgical strike' against selected Israeli targets. This idea originated from General Crocker. That last plan began to be considered seriously only when it was realized that Israel was going to take full advantage of America's preoccupation with her election to violate the Security Council's orders.[65]

Indeed on 25 October President Truman pledged himself not to force Israel to give up the Negev, an area which the Bernadotte plan excluded but which at that very moment came largely under the IDF control. Now Bevin's heroic resistance to pressure to lift the embargo neared its end. Fortunately, the IDF, as well as the Legion commands, were now doubly careful to evade a clash between the two armies. With the exception of a short front guard–rear guard skirmish at Beit Jibrin on 26 October, no further combat contact was made between the IDF and the Legion until the end of the war. Furthermore, on 30 November a nucleus of an Israeli–Transjordan armistice agreement was signed in Jerusalem between military commanders of both sides. But the IDF continued to deal blows to the Egyptian army and to expand southwards towards the Red and Dead Seas. By then the US delegation to the UN abandoned her support of the Bernadotte plan, and Bevin's scheme was laid to ruin.

DID THE BRITISH INFRINGE THE EMBARGO?

Israeli spokesmen and the Soviet media often accused Britain of violating the embargo by supplying arms to the Arabs. For some time, these accusations were not based on any solid facts. But tactics worked out in New York between Israel's unofficial representative at the UN, Abba Eban and the Chief of the Soviet delegation, Andrey Gromyko, envisaged that depicting the Arab armies as 'British controlled' might be effective anyway, because the British would not dare to deny it.[66] Later, Israeli spokesmen pulled out more specific 'proof'.

One way to check how much the British adhered to the embargo is to check these proofs and also to read British internal reports on their treatment of some of their own misdemeanors.

An Israeli list of British breaches of the truce was published on three occasions: first, on 14 December, at the end of the UN Assembly in Paris, secondly, the next day, by an IDF spokesman in Tel Aviv and, thirdly, on the second week of January, through several newspapers in the USA. Before checking up this list, let us say that each accusation had its roots in some true event, but this does not make any of them more truthful. Of course, one must take into consideration the precarious situation in which Israel found herself in late December and early January 1949, *vis à vis* the UN and the Big Powers. At that point Israel had more vital objectives than telling the whole and nothing but the truth. The list of Israeli accusations about British embargo violations included the following:

1. During the first truce two British supply ships, *Derryheen* and *Bardistan*, allegedly 'unloaded war materials in the port of Basra'.[67] The Israelis did not specify what was unloaded, but British internal exchange did. The two ships left British ports on 16 and 27 April, respectively, long before the imposition of the UN embargo but after the British internal ban on military aid to the Arab states. They called at various ports in Africa and thus reached Basra only on 6 and 14 June. A report from the British Embassy in Baghdad describes their cargo as equipment destined to both the British and the Iraqi army, including a vehicle workshop and optical and electronic equipment.[68] A similar Israeli accusation was made against the British ship *Carinthos* which called at Basra 'in September' and 'unloaded small arms'. Again, no further details were given.[69]

2. It was alleged that 'Between June and October, Britain supplied the Egyptian Army 20 000 6-pounder shells, 5 000 25-pounder shells

and hundreds of other artillery ammunition items'. This has no bearing in the British documents, but may be related either to the *Ramses* affair or to fragments of intelligence leading to the preparation of emergency ammunition loads for the Legion in October,[70] which were in the event not delivered until the end of the war. It may also be that the Israeli intelligence monitored deliveries destined to the British garrison in the Canal Zone.[71]

3. It is alleged that 'Britain supplied spare parts to "Misr" airline which serves Egypt's war effort'. This accusation was based on the long Anglo-American deliberation of this fringe case, which was eventually turned over to the UN Mediator's decision..Dr Bunche's verdict was that these items must be withheld, and so it was.

4. Another allegation was that 'During the second truce . . . the British sold small arms ammunition to the Egyptian army', but no further specification was made. This is probably related to thefts from the British depots at al Geneiffa and Tel el kebir, with which we shall deal below.

5. The Israeli release included 'a suspicion' that during General Glubb's visit to London in August 'it was agreed' to supply war materials to the Arab Legion. Glubb's visit and activities on this occasion are well documented and they clearly show that his request was turned down.

6. The allegation includes what became known that in a secret meeting of the Iraqi Lower House in mid-October, Prime Minister al Pachachi said that Iraq would 'soon' receive American tanks 'at British disposal' to the strength of an armoured brigade. No such or any other AFVs were supplied to Iraq up until the end of the autumn of 1949.[72]

7. British Fury aircraft were supplied to Iraq during the war. It seems that this was an Israeli shot in the dark, with a hope that it would hit 'something' and if not at least embarrass the British Government, when it would have to deny it. The ten aircraft of this sort which the Iraqi Air Force received before the restrictions of March, were never used by the Iraqis, for lack of weapons and other equipment.

8. 'In October or November', an allegation goes, Britain flew 'big quantities of ammunition' from the Suez Canal Zone and from Britain to Amman. This was an inaccurate interpretation of the instruction, actually given to prepare ammunition to be sent to the Legion which never received the green light.

9. Finally, Israel accused Britain of supplying Egypt, during the war, with a 'battalion' of Locust light tanks.

THE LOCUST TANKS AFFAIR

In the first week of December 1948, the IDF was attempting to secure its right flank in Western Negev by pushing the Egyptian forces in the Khan Yunis section further back (operation Assaf). After an IDF contingent captured Bir Ma'ein, an Egyptian counter- attack followed, assisted by tanks of an unfamiliar type. Some of these tanks were hit, then captured and soon identified as the light World War II American tanks Locust, carrying a 37 mm gun. It was well known that during World War II such tanks were specially produced for British airborne units, to be landed by Hamilcar gliders.[73] When these tanks went out of service, in early 1947, they were left, along with thousands of other obsolete AFVs, in an OFLC dumping ground in Egypt. The December operations was the first instance where the Israeli intelligence had noticed the existence of such weapons in the Egyptian OB.[74]

The Egyptian counter-attack, in which the Locust tanks took part, was, by evidence of Israeli intelligence and other officers, 'not very effective' and the performance of the Locusts in particular was, 'surprisingly, not a problem'. Simply, tanks hardly used their guns they moved very slowly.[75] During the skirmishes of 6 and 7 December, more Locusts were hit and nine were captured by Israel.[76]

In London, the Israeli release about the Locust was first viewed as a quibble. On 22 December the British Minister of War, Emmanuel Shinwell, received assurances from internal sources that 'there are no such tanks in Egyptian possession . . . let alone given by Britains.[77] The Foreign Office was less convinced, because the British Consul General in Jerusalem, Sir Hugh Dow, reported that he had seen the captured tanks and because in Washington, Sir Oliver Franks was told that the US Government was unsettled. The riddle was turned over to the BMEO and again the answer was 'categorically' that 'no, *repeat no*, "Locust" tanks could have been obtained from Middle East Army stocks'.[78] The Foreign Office reported this reassurance to Sir Oliver in Washington.

But the Department for Special Affairs in the British Foreign Office, continued its own investigation and soon enough solved out the mystery. It turned out that 26 'neutralized' American L. L. Locusts were bought on 2 July 1948 by the 'Delta Trading Company', an Egyptian civil corporation engaged in scrap metal, with encouragement from the Egyptian Ministry of War. The sale was sanctioned by the local US OFLC officer on the ground these tanks were 'properly neutralized', which indeed they were. It appears that, since British troops practically guarded that particular scrap-yard, approval to take out these tanks was given by a member of General Crocker's staff, namely, Brigadier S. Lamplough, who, along with other officers are on record as suggesting turning such equipment over to the Egyptian Army.[79] The tanks were under repair in Egyptian workshops from July (the British Embassy once mistakenly reported that the Egyptians purchased Shermans tanks formerly in British Service).[80] Apparently, the Egyptian technicians never manged to recondition these tanks properly. From scattered Israeli evidence, it comes about that, when thrown to battle, these tanks either could not use their guns at all, or managed to fire only a few, inaccurate shots. It should, therefore not be a wild conjecture, that after the defeat in October, the Egyptian command had little to lose by throwing these tanks unprepared into battle. But the results indicate that they did not gain much either.

ARAB THEFTS OF BRITISH WAR MATERIALS

While it is clear that the British Government was not involved in any violation of the embargo, it is equally clear that British war materials did reach Arab (and Jewish) forces. The question is, first of all, how this was possible and, secondly, how significant this addition was to the parties' strength.

British military deployed in Arab countries were, generally speaking, prone to support the Arabs and unsympathetic to London's embargo policy. The MELF command continuously warned the Ministries of War and Defence, that the embargo hurt their 'working relations' with the local military establishment and that it worked unsymmetrically in Israel's favour. When the embargo lasted indefinitely, they became prone to be lenient about embargo violations. It was reported in September that General Crocker said that 'it was time to get going with Egypt'[81] and that the British authorities in Egypt are turning a blind eye on thefts of war materials from British stores. In mid-December the Foreign Office was disturbed by the publicity given to the Locust affair and by Israeli accusations published in the American press. Consequently, the Superintending Under-secretary in the Foreign Office, Michael Wright, asked the British Embassy in Cairo to check these matters. He was reported back that, indeed, 'from . . . August there have been highly organised raids on ammunition depots and theft of vehicles . . . organised by Egyptian officer with the rank of Lieutenant

Colonel, whom we now know by name, acting on instruction of the (Egyptian) Ministry of Defence'. British permissiveness was not mentioned, but the report included an alarming assessment of the quantities stolen, based on comparison between the inventories of two periods. The list included, among other things, 30 items of ammunition which the Egyptian army was desperately short of, for instance, half a million 0.303 rounds of ammunition, 27 000 blank artillery cartridges, 5500 3-inch and over 4000 2-inch mortar bombs, 2800 2-pounder gun shells, approximately 1000 3.7-mm gun shells, etc.[82] The report mentioned apologetically the 'difficulty of air-tight guarding' large dumps of equipment and that a protest was sent to the Egyptian Minister of War. In January it was reported that these thefts 'had now ceased'.[83] Surely, the quantities listed, while serving as some form of palliative to the Egyptian supply system, do not represent a meaningful change in the Egyptian ammunition agony.

Thefts on a smaller scale were reported from British depots in Iraq and Transjordan as well. But a large scale daylight ammunition robbery was made on 3 January 1949 by the Iraqi army. A British convoy, carrying over 100 tons of 20-mm shells destined for the British RAF in Habbaniya was held up at gunpoint and forced into an Iraqi military base, where the ammunition was unloaded. The Foreign Office instructed Ambassador Mack to protest and to demand its immediate return. But the negotiation dragged, until many weeks later, in appreciation of the Iraqi Government's decision to withdraw the army from Palestine, Bevin agreed that the said ammunition should be registered as a 'special allotment' on the account of future deliveries.[84] Ironically, the Iraqis had very little use for this ammunition, because they had only few 20-mm guns and none fitted in their Sea Fury planes, which for this and other reasons were grounded.

ISRAELI ILLEGAL AND SEMI-LEGAL ACQUISITION IN BRITISH TERRITORY

The Arabs rarely tried to acquire war materials illegally in Britain, but the Israelis did. These activities included semi-legal as well as totally illegal activities. During the British evacuation of Palestine, there was a series of thefts and robbery of British equipment by the Haganah, the IZL and LHI, sometimes with help of lower British echelons. In this way the IDF acquired two Cromwell and one Sherman tanks, as well as 15 other AFVs, among them four armoured cars carrying 2 pounder guns and three half tracks.[85] Against the background of Israel's failure to build a standard armoured corps, these vehicles formed an important part of the IDF mechanized forces. Legal IDF purchase from the British forces pulling out included three police coast guard boats, which the Israeli Navy received late in June[86] and several Auster aircraft.

The Israelis had little chance to persuade Britain to sell them arms. But they took advantage of the sympathy towards them in sections of the British public, and of the liberal British civil liberties, to develop an underground network of illegal purchase of war materials in British territories. This pertained mainly to used aircraft, which were sold cheaply in the British market. In January 1948, the Yishuv civil aviation company, Aviron – for all practical purposes the Haganah – won a tender on the sale of 24 obsolete J1 Auster planes from the mandatory authorities. The deal was met with criticism in London, so these authorities went back on their decision, but it was too late. On 4 February, the Under-secretary-of-State for Foreign Affairs assured the House of Commons that these aircraft were 'totally unserviceable'. But contrary to this assurance, some of the aircraft were. Five of the Austers were put to use before May, when the infant Israeli Air Force consisted of only a few light aircraft. A few others entered service later, rebuilt with additional spare parts bought illegally in Britain.[87]

Meanwhile an Israeli network for illegally purchasing aircraft in Britain was developed. The project began in February 1948 by Fredie Fredkens, a Haganah member and a former RAF pilot. It was continued by another 'Haganah' pilot, Emmanuel Zur (Zukerberg); both used dummy companies to camouflage their activities. In February, Frendkens bought five old twin-engine Ansons and eight Tiger Moths, under the guise of Australian and Singaporian business enterprises. Since the French Government allowed landing of Haganah aircraft in French territory, during April the Ansons were planned to be flown through France, Italy and Greece. The first Anson was damaged upon landing in Brindizi, Italy, and a British inquiry exposed the true destination of all the rest. None the less, some Ansons arrived in Greece, where they were held on suspicion of serving the Communist underground. By request of the British Embassy in Athens, they were detained and consequently the Tiger Moth deal was also called off.[88] A more successful method was used by Zur in May.[89] He 'chartered' ten civil aircraft from the British 'Mayfair Air Service' and sent them flying to Israel. They included seven Rapides, two Geminis and one M57 Aerovan. Because these aircraft had 'correct' documentation, the British authorities managed to stop only two of them when they arrived in Nicosia. The rest arrived hurriedly in Israel at the worst moment in Israel's air inferiority. They were converted into 'bombers' and did much of the bombing of Arab targets until the first truce. When some of them bombed Amman on 1 June, the Council of the Arab League were sat there discussing the mediator's truce terms. It appears that the bombing helped Bernadotte to goad the heads of the Arab states to accept his terms.[90]

Zur, now under Scotland Yard surveillance, moved to France and continued acting through local agents in Britain. His next move was to buy surplus military aircraft and hire former RAF pilots to fly them directly to Israel. He bought two used PR16 Mosquitos for $18 000 each. The first, flown by an ex-RAF pilot, John Harvey, took off on 7 July from a base in Cambridgeshire, supposedly to Exeter. It soon disappeared from the air control and was believed missing until reported fuelling at Nice. A British air photographer spotted the plane at the Ramat David base in Israel on 10 August. This Mosquito was Israel's only high-altitude photography aircraft during that war. The second Mosquito, took off from Oxfordshire in a similar way, but crashed when trying to fuel in Corsica and the pilot was killed. Zur then bought seven obsolete British Beaufighter bombers, one of which crashed in Britain during a test and four others took off on 1 August from Thame, Oxfordshire 'to shoot a film'. They fuelled in Corsica and were later identified by high-altitude photography in Israel's Aqir base. The remaining Beaufighters were confiscated.[91] The four Beaufighters which reached Israel entered service in September, but their bad condition limited their usefulness.

Egypt was the only Arab state which tried to buy arms abroad. But her purchasers acted less adroitly than the Israelis. After months of negotiations (monitored by Scotlands Yard), Egyptian agents, under the guise of the Brussels-located 'Air Transport', bought nine British Sterling and two Halifax bombers, registering them as destined for Tangiers. Five of the Halifaxes arrived in Egypt in September, but all efforts to make them serviceable failed.[92]

BRITISH DILEMMAS *VIS À VIS* ISRAEL'S OFFENSIVE PLANS

A month after the commencement of the second truce in Palestine, British experts began to suspect that the embargo was not working to

Table 7　Israeli acquisition from British sources

Type of material	Date and number		Number entering service and date	
Aircraft				
J1 Auster	(24)	January	(12)	March–July
Anson	(5)	January		–
Tiger Moth	(6)	March		–
DH89 Rapid	(7)	January	(4)	May–July
A1 Gemini	(2)	April	(2)	May
M57 Aerovan	(1)	April	(1)	May
PR16 Mosquito	(2)	May	(1)	September
Beaufighter	(7)	May	(4)	August
Beachcraft	(1)	?	(1)	June
Boats				
Coastguard boats	(3)	May	(3)	June
AFV				
Medium tanks	(3)	June	?	(gun problems)
Other AFVs	(15)	April	(15)	May
Air spare parts	From	May	Continuously	

maintain the *status quo*. Intelligence reports had reached London about the offensive intentions of the Israeli Government. Bevin, still convinced that full cooperation with the US was more important than the renewal of military supplies to the Arab armies under contract, was persuaded to reconsider the damage to British interests from a possible Israeli offensive if it hit hard the Arab Legion.[93] General Glubb arrived in London and began campaigning for the renewal of supplies, at least of ammunition, to his army. In a memo, sent to the Chiefs of Staff Committee on 11 August, Glubb maintained that the Legion had not had any fresh supplies of ammunition since February and was now left with only 5 'contact days' allotment, and with less still in artillery ammunition. The Chiefs of Staff were agreed that it might be the IDF intention and capability to break the truce and outflank the Legion along with the Iraqi army and possibly destroy them. Of the two threatened Arab armies, the Legion was dearer to them, if anything, as being an integral part of the British Order of the Battle, sharing in the plans for the defence of the Middle East. Glubb's pleadings had many supporters in the Defence Office and in military circles, and even in Bevin's Ministry.[94]

On 12 July and again on 24 July, Alexander, followed by General Hollis, met Bevin to discuss 'the Legion's situation'. In these meetings it was reported that 'the Jews are getting arms and aircraft' and that the 'knowledge that the Legion was so short of ammunition, which was kept secret . . . (but it) will probably have reached the Jews'. Bevin agreed to consider a plan suggested earlier by Glubb and Pirie-Gordon,[95] which involved two emergency measures for such a case. The first measure was to pack up and make ready for quick delivey, stores of ammunition and make them available 'in no time' upon emergency. The second measure was to plan a British 'surgical' strike against the IDF, to deter Israel from destroying the Legion. But no decision was yet made on either of the proposals.[96] Early in August, Alexander again wrote to Bevin that 'if the Legion is now attacked . . . it might mean its total withdrawal from Palestine . . . or a disaster'. Alexander added that:

> The effect of the withdrawal of the Arab Legion from Palestine will almost certainly destroy what military control the Arabs at the present exercise over (parts of) Palestine. The blame will . . . be laid on our shoulders because of our refusal to carry out contracts signed by us'.[97]

This time the appeal prompted a discussion of the proposed two measure at the Chiefs of Staff's Committee's meeting. The Chiefs of Staff were increasingly worried. Lord Montgomery, the outgoing Chief of General Staff, ignored the subtlety of the situation – after all the Legion stayed outside Transjordan – and opined that the British Government must warn Israel that an attack on the Legion would put Britain in a state of war with Israel. His Deputy, General Templer, suggested an open renewal of supplies to Amman, and the Minister of Defence, said he would press the Cabinet to accept flying 15 contact days ammunition to the British base in Mafraq, near Amman, where it would be held by the British Army and be supplied as soon as the Legion was attacked. But in contrast to Montgomery, Alexander maintained that a British strike against the IDF should be sanctioned only if the Israelis crossed to Transjordan proper.[98]

The Foreign Office, however, was reluctant to approve either of these plans, because 'it would be difficult to explain such deliveries, to the US government'.[99] Indeed, Bevin's mind was now preoccupied with the Anglo-American plan dictated to Bernadotte.[100] On 30 August he wrote to Alexander, who on his part informed the COS Committee that:

Unless there is some critical development, it would be better not to run the risk of breaking the embargo ... or appearing to do so ... You may be ready at a short notice to despatch supplies ... by air to Transjordan but not to begin until I instruct you so.[101]

On 9 September a plan was introduced to the Chiefs of Staff Committee for emergency replenishing of the Legion. The plan consisted of two stages: in the first, a small portion of 60 tons of ammunition, calculated to fit the Legion's immediate needs, would be made ready at a British base in the Middle East. The second stage consisted of the delivery of an additional 320 tons of ammunition, made ready in British sea- and airports. When fighting broke out between Israel and Egypt on 15 October an order was given to make the second portion ready for air and sea transportation, with the interim deadline for their despatch fixed for 4 November.[102] But before that date, a truce was again established in Palestine, with the IDF now holding most of the Northern Negev, a wide corridor to Jerusalem and the entire Galilee – an area far beyond the frontiers prescribed by the Bernadotte plan. IDF columns continued to exploit the success in various directions, and one of them was engaged in a clash with a Legion contingent at Beit Jibrin, on the slopes of the Hebron Hills. But apart from that incident, the Legion was not attacked by the IDF.

The Israeli military offensive of October seriously threatened to pull the rug from under the Bernadotte plan, which was now being debated at the UN Assembly. But Bevin still hoped that the Security Council would force Israel to withdraw to the lines which had existed before 15 October. If Israel refused, British planners believed that a British strike might be sanctioned under UN authority, provided the USA did not strongly object. But what if she did? Considering the worst, Bevin wrote to Kirkbride that 'the Legion must not stay in Palestine at all cost'. One thing was 'abundantly clear' to him: 'It would be fatal to do anything which might prejudice ... the prospect of Anglo-United States solidarity on the Palestine question'.[103]

In the second half of October, the USA elections reached their peak with more bad omens for Bevin. On 25 October Truman broke his silence and pledged himself not to force Israel to give up the Negev. When, on 4 November Truman was re-elected, he stood by his word. On 16 November the US delegation at the Security Council switched from the demand for an unconditional Israeli withdrawal, to stressing the need of armistice talks. Following this, the UN Assembly, too, dropped the Bernadotte plan. Now there was perhaps less immediate danger to the integrity of the Legion, but British humiliation had hit a new low.

Typically, Bevin reacted with a new diplomatic offensive in Washington.[104] On 12 November the US Ambassador was called to see Attlee at Chequers, where, in the presence of Cabinet members and the Chiefs of Staff the Prime minister told the Ambassador that the British government was 'greatly perturbed' by the Palestine situation which was 'an immediate danger to the world peace and to Anglo-American cooperation, including Berlin . . . and to the UN'.[105] Attlee said that 'the immediate question' was not only a threat to Transjordan but to Britain's strategic position in the region. Douglas had already been briefed earlier by a memorandum handed to him by the British Minister of Defence, according to which 'as a result of British observance of the Embargo . . . the Arab Legion had been reduced to a position of relative impotence with no more than 2,000 rounds of 25-pounder ammunition'.[106] Attlee also said that he hoped the US Government would understand his Cabinet decision to launch an airlift of ammunition to Amman, beginning on 16 November, and made it clear that this ammunition would be given to the Legion only if Transjordan was attacked. It still did not mean that Britain wanted the embargo abrogated.

Douglas felt the matter was so urgent that he flew to Paris, where Marshall was attending the UN Assembly and the SC meeting. Marshall's opinion was that it would be 'perfectly alright for the British to reinforce their military installations', but advised that the matter be referred to Lovett in Washington and to the White House for approval.[107]

There is no record of Lovett's consultation in the White House, but it is unthinkable that he acted independently. In any event, Lovett replied back to Marshall that 'assuming these contacts were *not* released', he had had no objection. Typically, it was now Bevin's turn to ask for a delay until the Security Council had a chance to make a new resolution on the demand for Israeli withdrawal.

But it was already being said that the resolution was major disappointment for Bevin, because the SC slurred over the need for immediate Israeli withdrawal. None the less, on 17 November Bevin decided to hold the deliveries of ammunition yet further, 'to await the Israeli reply to the UN Acting Mediator . . . [to see] if the Jews refused to comply with the Mediator's order to withdraw in the Negev'.[108] Israel, on her part, procrastinated by sending vague memoranda to low-ranking UN officials (such as J. Reedman and P. Mohn), while preparing yet another offensive in the south. Dr Bunche's visit to Ben Gurion's office on 6 December was made while the IDF launched its preliminary offensive (Operation Assaf) on the Egyptian front, and the meeting with the Acting Mediation only further augmented Israel's conviction that she could get away with a new attempt to eliminate the Egyptian army (Operation Horev).[109]

Towards the end of November Bevin felt it was necessary to send a new warning to Vice-Air Marshal Foster that no war materials were yet allowed to be sent to Transjordan without the Prime Minister's permission.[110] This step might be ascribed to the news that Israeli and Legion officers were now holding talks in Jerusalem.

Now the British military option began to slowly take shape. On 18 November General Crocker sent the sloop *St Bride's Bay* to the port of Aqaba, and on 1 December his air-power support at the Shalouffa base had been reinforced by an additional two squadrons from Britain: one of Tempest fighters and one of Lincoln bombers. A British infantry regiment and two tank squadrons in the Canal Zone were put on alert and a mechanized Legion contingent, commanded by British officers, including an air-support unit, began patrolling the road from the Dead Sea to Aqaba.[111]

THE BRITISH MILITARY OPTION AGAINST ISRAEL

At the end of November it became apparent in London that Israel, encouraged by the atmosphere of the USA election, was not only refusing to withdraw from the areas it had captured after 15 October but that she was preparing further offensives. The Minister of Defence, representing the opinion of the Chiefs of Staff and General Crocker, pointed out to Bevin that the Arab armies had now been largely incapacitated. Lifting the embargo and renewing military assistance to them, notwithstanding the effect in the USA, might, anyway, be too late to change this situation, at least in the short-term. Alexander pointed out Britain's responsibility to see that there was a limit to Israel's expansion in, and perhaps beyond, Palestine. The Minister did not exclude the possibility that such an Israeli expanding 'prepared the ground . . . for a Soviet penetration to the back of the Western defences . . .', 'helped by immigrants arriving to Israel from Eastern Europe'. He was sure that the USA would understand a British drive to restrain Israel. The RAF Commander-in-Chief, Lord Arthur Tedder, was more outspoken. He felt that Israel's actions were an 'intolerable risk to our vital positions . . . in defending the oil fields and the Suez Canal, from which we may need to attack the USSR'.[112]

The first draft for a British plan to strike against Israel was prepared at General Crocker's headquarters on 27 October and was passed
to London, where it was approved by Generals Edelston, Templer and
Sanders, for the new Chief-of-Staff, Field Marshal William Slim. The
plan consisted of two alternatives, 'A' and 'B'. Alternative 'A', given
the code name 'Barter', prepared for a case in which the IDF would
cross the border into Transjordan, whereupon a request from Amman
to apply the defence article in the treaty between the two states be
applied. Alternative 'B' was aimed at assisting the Legion 'if attacked
in violation of the truce', that is, *inside* Palestine. In both cases the
operation was to be opened with a 'surgical' air strike against the Israeli air force, 'with all the power at our disposal . . . in order to destroy it', though 'it may not be sufficient to halt Jewish aggression in
Transjordan'. The air strike was to be followed by a qualified action
of British land forces, including an infantry brigade group plus armour
and artillery, with air support, which would be sent to Transjordan via
Aqaba, by two landing troop ships, escorted by three frigates. A Foreign Office disagreement made the Chiefs of Staff 'hold Plan "B" in
abeyance' and this plan was finally ruled out on 10 December.[113] Probably
the biggest prize British planners hoped to achieve was to be able,
with the help of additional land force from the Canal Zone, 'to capture air fields in the southern part of Palestine'[114] and British control
of the southern Negev.

What did the British Government hope to achieve through either
plan 'A' or plan 'B' if their execution went well? Probably the deterrence of the Israeli Government and the IDF General Staff from further expansion, and maybe the regaining of some British prestige with
the Arabs. Optimists might have still hoped to revive the Bernadotte
plan, although it was not clear who, in the absence of functioning
Arab armies and the failure of the Security Council to issue a firm
resolution, would be responsible for pushing Israel back to the pre-
October front lines on which the plan was based. At the same time,
the failure of this plan might have caused Britain unsustainable damage. Bevin and Attlee were sceptical about its success, partly because
they could not predict how the American government would react to
such a British assault.

What were the chances of a military success of Operation Barter?
The general Order of the Battle of the British combat forces ('Teeth')
under the MELF was quite impressive. It included some 18 infantry
battalions (one third of them colonial forces), 5 armoured regiments
and 12 artillery regiments (of which 7 were field-artillery regiments).
These formations were deployed in several countries around the Eastern

Mediterranean and Africa and some were already heavily involved in vital tasks such as the protection of Northern Greece, where there was a threat of a Communist takeover. In the Suez Canal Zone the British had two infantry brigade groups, one tank brigade and an extended artillery regiment. The main reserve, including the less-than-standard first infantry division, was stationed in Libya. A commando battalion was stationed in Malta and two more infantry brigades were in Eritrea and the Sudan.[115] It seems that in addition to the forces which in mid-November were already seconded to 'Barter', it was possible to amass a divisional expeditionary force for a short-term punitive action against the IDF. However, there was no chance at all of getting reinforcement from the European theatre, where the Berlin crisis was at its peak. There was little help to be expected from the Arab armies in Palestine, unless Britain supplied them well in advance of 'D Day'.

The force available for 'Barter' was superior to the IDF in firepower, command and air support, but not necessarily in morale. But even a full British division was a relatively small force, given the size of the theatre and the Order of the Battle of the IDF. To secure success the preliminary 'surgical' strike must be short and very effective, both militarily and politically. If the initial strike was not very successful – if Soviet forces appeared on the Israeli side or if Israel was able to demonstrate enough resilience for a short time – Britain would have found herself under joint US–Soviet pressure to stop the operation. She could have to cast her veto at the Security Council but then found herself in splendid isolation, which would be disastrous to Western solidarity. Criticism from the British public and in Parliament, perhaps in the Cabinet as well, might have brought the government down. If Bevin and Alexander wanted to secure the support of their party or of the USA, they needed to have some preliminary consultation to expose their plan in advance to wide circles, but then the military operation would lose the surprise effect.

In fact, in a month's time Britain was faced with a somewhat similar test. Following the collapse of the Egyptian forces in the Negev at the end of 1948 (Operation 'Horev'), IDF troops entered Sinai in an attempt to outflank the Egyptian stronghold in Raffah, via El Arish. The IDF forces stayed on Egyptian territory between 29 December and 5 January but no British intervention occurred. This time it was the confused government in Cairo – Prime Minister Noqrashi was assassinated on 28 December, amidst another Egyptian military defeat – which failed to ask Britain to apply the mutual defence treaty provisions, and come to Egypt's aid. Had the Egyptians done so, the Brit-

ish would have probably been more embarrassed than otherwise, because the Chiefs of Staff in London, who wished to intervene in favour
of the Legion, opposed intervention in Egypt on the grounds that such
action could be feasible only on one front, and once an engagement
was started in Egypt, the Legion would remained exposed.[116] However, it was the effective USA pressure on the government of Israel
which prompted the Israeli withdrawal, without bringing this British
dilemma to a head.

Then, on 7 January, Britain seemed ready to face yet another test
when the Israeli Air Force shot down five RAF fighters over Egyptian territory. Although it was very tempting for the British military to
opt for the long-planned air-strike against Israel, Bevin and Alexander
controlled their tempers and as a result Air Minister Arthur Henderson
ordered the stoppage of British flights near the mandatory borders of
Palestine.[117]

AFTERMATH: BRITAIN'S DRIVE TO ABROGATE THE EMBARGO

The embargo began as an emergency measure to save the Anglo–American alliance from '. . . the sorry spectacle of Britain arming one side
in the Palestine conflict, and the US the other, with the Russians the
sole permanent beneficiaries'.[118] It soon developed into a wider policy,
at the end of which there seemed to be a promise of a settlement
which at the time both Britain and the USA adopted, aimed at turning
the truce frontier into political boundaries. In early August both governments still hoped that the embargo served their plans well. The missing
pieces in their appreciation were the pace of disintegration of the Arab
military capability and Israel's success in bypassing the embargo. Later
in August the British government realized that the embargo was working
very much in favour of Israel, and intelligence about Israel's preparation for an offensive increased its discomfort.

Still, their basic confidence in the course taken remained unshaken.
Their belief was that if Anglo-American adherence to the embargo
and to the design of settlement stood fast, the UN would eventually be
able to impose it. In September the British still believed in the successful implementation of the Bernadotte plan in the deterrence of the
Security Council's warnings to keep Israel at bay. But these hopes
collapsed between mid-October and mid-November when Israel attacked

and changed the truce lines, and when the USA changed course at the Security Council and allowed Israel to get away with keeping literally every part of Palestine which the IDF had conquered in defiance of the Security Council warnings. The British had no choice but to accept this *fait accompli*, namely, a reduced version of their original 'partition which sorts itself out'.

Now, at last, supporters of the renewal of arms supply to the Arabs, both as a domestic shot in the arm of the tottering Arab regimes and as means to restore British prestige among the Arabs, had got the upper hand in London. Bevin's himself became convinced that, in order to create a new military balance between Arabs and Israelis, first of all the former must be rearmed. Action was to start where it had stopped early in 1948, that is, with supplying to the Arabs what had long promised. But the process had to start at the UN.[119]

For a while, the main obstacle to changing the Security Council's policy was Dr Bunche, who refused to discuss the renewal of arms supply before the armistice had been signed between Israel and all her neighbours. However, the most ardent objection to lifting the embargo later came from the government of Israel.[120]

The British increased their pressure on both the USA government and on Dr Bunche, until it became acceptable to both that upon conclusion of the last set of armistice talks – that is, between Israel and Syria – the State Department and Dr Bunche would remove their objection to the renewal of the supply of British arms to various Arab governments, 'for internal security needs'. The Security Council's resolution of 29 May 1948, was abolished on 8 August 1949, less than 3 weeks after the Israeli–Syrian armistice had indeed been signed.

5 Assistance from the Soviet Bloc to the Warring Parties in Palestine[1]

THE USSR'S MIDDLE EAST POLICY AFTER THE SECOND WORLD WAR

In the 'Big Three' summit meetings of the Second World War, Churchill and Roosevelt agreed to various territorial and statutory concessions requested by Stalin. In return Stalin recognized the Middle East (he even mentioned Palestine) as within Britain's sphere of influence. But the dynamics of the Cold War which followed undermined these agreements. The shock in Western democracies at the way in which Communist dictatorial regimes were enforced by the USSR in East Europe, Soviet attempts to plant satellite 'republics' in Northern Iran, together with Soviet demands for territorial and statutory concessions from Turkey and involvement in Communist insurgence in Greece, all helped turn the Middle East into the first theatre of the Cold War. When early in 1947 the British exchequer was unable to support the British exertion to contain the Soviets in Iran, Turkey and Greece alone, the United States, which earlier acted firmly to force the Soviet withdrawal from Iran, came to Britain's aid by launching the Truman Doctrine of March 1947. From the Soviet angle, however, these acts looked like a threat to the USSR defences at her soft underbelly. Moscow reacted with an ever-more aggressive strategy, verbally anyway, aimed at undermining the British position in the Middle East from within. One means of attaining such a goal was to support peoples and groups which tried to get rid of the British rule.

One arena in which the Soviets ran these campaigns was the UN. Having been themselves forced by the Security Council, early in 1946, to pull out of Iran, the Soviets took revenge at the same forum and enhanced the evacuation of the British and French troops from Syria and Lebanon shortly afterwards. In May 1947, the USSR delegation tried to persuade the special UN Assembly to vote for the immediate termination of the British mandate in Palestine and on the occasion Gromyko read an astonishing speech in which he recognized the Jewish right for an independent state in Palestine, alongside a Palestinian Arab state. In August, the USSR supported the Egyptian case against Britain at the Security Council and during the Palestine debate at the regular Assembly in the autumn, the Soviets turned champions of the partition of Palestine. In committee, they even resorted to cooperation with the USA, in order to push the partition resolution through. In this part of the world they generally viewed the UN as a useful tool to serve their ends and were careful not to block the work of the Security Council on Middle Eastern matters. They never cast their veto on any issue pertaining to Palestine, up until March 1954, except once, on the entrance of Transjordan into the UN.

THE USSR AND THE PALESTINE QUESTION UNTIL 1948

In 1948, Soviet influence on Middle East politics was meagre. There was a general suspicion and estrangement towards Communism amongst the ordinary people of the Arab world, and local Communist parties were small and, in most countries, illegal. Soviet diplomatic representation was almost a disgrace for a superpower: the USSR had only three legations in Arab capitals, Cairo, Beirut and Baghdad, all served by small staff and low-ranking officials.[2]

In the mandatory Palestine too, the Communist party was legalized only in 1942 and Soviet influence was small, both in the Arab and the Jewish sectors. And although the prestige of the USSR in the Yishuv was in the ascent during the last part of World War II, due to the Red Army's role in defeating Nazism, the large majority of the public, including that which espoused Socialist ideas, rejected the Soviet 'Revolutionary' version. Even most Marxist-minded members of the Yishuv, kept away from the Communist Party. At the beginning of 1948, various Zionist–Marxist factions amalgamated into the United Labour Party, Mapam, which in fact regarded itself 'part of the World of Revolution'. But Mapam continued to lament 'the tragic contradiction', whereby the USSR refused to recognize Zionism as 'the true Jewish national movement self-determination'. The Soviet position following Gromyko's statement of May 1947 was hoped by Mapam to be the beginning of the removal of that 'tragic contradiction', but this is not how the Soviets viewed it. For them the establishment of a Jewish state had been merely an opportunistic, tactical manoeuvre. Mapam was nothing but an embarrassing ally. It is doubtful that they ever contemplated taking advantage of Mapam in order to extend their influence in the Israeli Government, in which Mapam shared, although many in Mapam wished so and many British and American analysts at the time, feared it.[3]

To date we have no access to genuine Soviet position papers dealing with the Middle East and Palestine in 1948; perhaps such papers no longer exist in archives. A small volume of Czech documents is available, but according to Czech military historians, many Czech high-policy elite papers pertaining to Palestine were destroyed in 1953–4.[4] We still had no better choice but to make use, albeit with a pinch of salt, of intelligence reports and appreciations in Western, including Israel's, military archives and complement them by reading between the lines of Soviet official publications.

Through this method, a somewhat different pattern of Soviet Palestine policies than had been held until now, emerges. The Soviet diplomatic support of Israel in 1948 appears hesitant, short-lived and from the Soviet point of view, disappointing. Since it was found barren, it was called off quickly, without any problems. As for the military assistance given to Israel by Czechoslovakia, this, no doubt, was made with Soviet approval. But the question remains whether it was a Soviet plan coordinated from Moscow or merely a Soviet attempt at exploiting relations tailored to fit Czechoslovakia's needs. We are inclined to maintain the second interpretation. The Czech–Israeli arms deal began as a Czech–Yishuv symbiotic affair, motivated by Israel's exigency to survive and by a Czech financial constraint. Czechoslovakia started off by offering arms to the Arabs and for commercial reasons turned to lean more, but never entirely, towards aiding Israel. The Czech–Israeli deal did not end in 1948, but went on long after the USSR ceased to side with Israel. But the main doubt about the existence of a Soviet master plan to support Israel emerges from the records of the Czech military assistance to Israel itself. It depicts a very disorganized and inefficient operation, resulting, to all appearances, from the absence of central direction from Moscow.

THE PATTERN OF SOVIET SUPPORT FOR ISRAEL IN 1948

The Soviet diplomatic support of the establishment of Israel was an attempt to take advantage of the potential Zionist nuisance-value both in the Middle East affairs and in Anglo-American relations. It hoped to thwart Western strategy against the USSR. The Czech military assistance to Israel, however, originated from the Czech craving for foreign currency. A link between the two trends seems to have developed in due course but only up to a point. The Soviet attitude towards the Czech–Israeli arms deal was no more than *laissez faire*.

Until 1947, Soviet policy towards Palestine indicated a mild preference for the Arabs on the Zionist side, but in practice, it was non-committed. It had been pointless for the USSR to side with the Arabs, as it could neither tolerate nor prevent the persecution of Communists in all the Arab countries. Soviet propaganda, which called 'the masses' to throw away the 'capitalist yoke', did not sound attractive to the Arab ear, and the Soviets did not yet teach themselves to speak differently to Arab nationalists. With regard to Zionism, the root of Soviet estrangement was 'self-determination', less pertaining to the problem of Palestine *per se* and more to the Soviet domestic front. The Zionist ideology sharply contradicted both the Soviet dogma on nationalism and their pragmatic handling of the Soviet empire. According to the dogma, the abolition of classes in the USSR and the establishment of a system of autonomous 'republics' and 'regions', had already solved the problem of national aspirations in the USSR. Thus there was no need for any section of the public to seek self-determination elsewhere. But underneath this platitude, there was a well-established fear that if one ethnic group was allowed to choose its historic destination, it would open up a chain-reaction which might bring about the disintegration of the entire Soviet empire.

In the short term, the sitting on the fence with regard to Palestine provided an advantage. The USSR would have a lot to gain once a situation occurred in which it would take sides. At the time when Palestine came before the UN Assembly in April 1947 the Soviets were impressed by the Yishuv anti-British struggle, and the support it gained with the USA public. The partition of Palestine under the UN auspices appeared to them a lever to undermine British control of the Middle East and the new Anglo-American strategy, by confusing Anglo-American relations and by tearing off a central piece in the Western strategic setting. No doubt such reasoning prompted the instruction sent to Gromyko during the Special UN Assembly in May 1947, which made him recite the Zionist credo from the Assembly podium, together with advocating the 'rights' of the Palestinian Arabs. A similar consideration enhanced the Soviet wish to cooperate with the USA at the next UN Assembly, making the passing of the partition resolution possible. Sovietologists rightly point out an interim confusion in Soviet policy between the two Assemblies, and that it was only when there was no escape from taking a definite position, came the 13 October Soviet demarche of joining the drive to push through the partition resolution.[5] None the less hesitation continued through-out 1948.

In March 1948 USA-USSR cooperation at the UN no longer stood. When the USA-convened a Security Council session in February to consider the fate of the partition scheme, the USSR remained the champion of the implementation of formal partition, while the USA looked for ways to bail out. When, at USA request another special Assembly session was convened in April to discuss swaping partition with trusteeship, the USSR contributed to the disarray in which that Assembly ended, on 14 May. The USSR trailed Truman less than two days in recognizing Israel, but was the first to grant Israel a *de jure* recognition. The Soviets were credited with the siting of an Israeli observer at the Security Council in July 1948 and for some filibuster at that Council, when the IDF needed more time to complement some military operation. The USSR supported Israel's requests to join the UN, but never accepted Israel's retention of areas conquered by the IDF in Galilee, which the 29 November resolution had allotted to the Arabs. For a while she was also opposed to the demand that Israel should absorb back Arab refugees. But her vehemence to support Israel subsided as the IDF began to dominate the theatre of the war. For this was a stabilizing factor.

However, the Soviets were often ambiguous. Noticing that behind the truce regime and the embargo there was an Anglo-American plan to impose a settlement which would exclude the USSR from participation, they were not sure whether they wanted the truce to be kept or thwarted. For a while, they toyed with a hope of being invited to share in the supervision of the truce. Their diplomacy, therefore, swung from denouncing the Observers Corps to a request to join it. As late as mid-June Gromyko believed that he would persuade Philip Jessup, acting chief of the US UN delegation, to support the inclusion of a few Soviet observers in the mediator's team. Had the State Department been persuaded to do so (there were those, including Jessup, who believed it should be done)[6] the Soviets might have had to consider a halt on the Czech–Israeli arms deal at an early stage. But the USA decided against allowing Soviet participation in the Observers Corps, which turned them strongly against the truce and Bernadotte. At the same time, they were not interested in a too-strong IDF or in incapacitated Arab armies. Out of these complex considerations, the USSR was doubly careful about giving direct military assistance. At the same time, in 1949, a Soviet offer of arms was made to Egypt.[6]

When in August 1948 the Soviet news agency TASS strongly denied allegations that Soviet military aid was given to Israel this was a true statement of fact and continued to be so for the rest of the war. Not a single military item or a person were sent from the USSR to any side in that war. But, according to intelligence collected in Prague, as early as October 1948, the USSR asked Czechoslovakia to stop military assistance to Israel; afterwards it tolerated with its continuation.[7]

ISRAEL'S ATTEMPT TO OBTAIN DIRECT MILITARY ASSISTANCE FROM THE USSR

Israel made several attempts to obtain direct military aid from the USSR, but failed.

Until August 1948, the only way her representatives could approach the USSR Government was at the UN. Such pleadings, therefore, began in New York immediately after Gromyko's made his statement of 14 May 1947. Ben Gurion, in his capacity as Chairman of the Jewish Agency Executive, who attended the last phase of that Assembly, went to see Gromyko and suggested that a Yishuv delegation be invited to Moscow 'to explain our needs'. Gromyko 'took note' of the request,[8] but no reply came. On 5 February 1948, when the issue of Palestine came before the Security Council, a Czech arms deal with the Haganah had already been signed. Now, Sharett asked to see Gromyko and raised three requests: that Moscow should see that Prague refrained from sending arms to the Arabs, that the government of Yugoslavia be told to be more helpful in the transit of Czech arms to Palestine through Yugoslav territory and that the USSR herself should consider sending arms to the Yishuv. Again, Gromyko 'took a note' of the requests, but to no consequence. On 14 February Ben Gurion noted 'Gromyko said nothing whether they would help'.[9] Early in May, Sharett met Gromyko yet again and after repeating the request for Soviet arms, saw to it, that in Prague, Ehud Avriel would 'check with representative of Yoseff' (Stalin) 'what is going on there'. Again, to no avail.[10]

On the third week in May, when the invasion of the Arab armies was in full swing, Tel Aviv was bombed and Israel lacked air defence, Mapam representatives in the provisional government of Israel demanded that a new approach be made to Moscow for arms. Sharett, now Foreign Minister, cabled his representative in Washington, Eilat, to see Gromyko 'immediately', but balanced this step with a similar request to the State Department. Gromyko was unavailable until 1 June, when he met with Dr Uriel Heiyd, Eilat's adviser who was sent to New York. Heyid told Gromyko that Israel was exposed to attacks against unprotected civilians and 'urgently needed guns, bombers and cargo ships to bring in military supplies'. Heyid suggested 'that two or three of us will go there (Moscow) to negotiate it'. Upon returning to Washington Heyid reported: 'Haro'em [Gromyko] promised to tell his master'.[11] Again, nothing happened.

When a few days later it became known that Bernadotte, who first requested the service of Soviet observers was forced by Britain and the USA to eat his words, Golda Meir, who met in New York with the Haganah wise man, David Hacohen, believed that now the USSR 'must' be more prone to undermine the embargo. Refraining from consulting the Israeli Foreign Office, but consulting Avigur in Geneva, they decided to send Hacohen, who spoke fluent Russian, to see Gromyko on 5 June. At last Gromyko spoke, and his reply was reported to Geneva in code as follows: 'About the Ro'em family [USSR] the reply is totally negative . . . but it does not apply to his relatives [Czechs] with whom we already have contact now. The Ro'em's family must have clean hands.'[12]

On 15 June the Security Council voted down the Soviet request to join the UN observers in Palestine, which again, made Israeli policy makers hopeful that perhaps now the USSR would 'stop hesitating'. Abba Eban, then Israel's observer at the UN who befriended Gromyko, raised the issue with his friend on 20 June, together with a colleague, Gideon Raphael. Again, Gromyko said nothing that could raise Israel's hopes.[13]

Late in August the USSR and Israel exchanged diplomatic missions, and early in September Golda Meir went to Moscow as head of the Israeli delegation. At last a direct channel for Soviet–Israeli contacts was opened and one would have expected that military assistance would be among the urgent subjects the Soviet military would like to discuss with the Israeli Military Attaché, General Yohanan Ratner. In fact, the Israeli delegation found itself isolated from the Soviet Government and Ratner was unable to establish working contacts with the Red Army Command.

However, for a short while it seemed as if the Israeli efforts to obtain Soviet military aid had born fruit. On 5 October Ratner was invited to see the Commander-in-Chief of the Red Army, General Alexey Antonov. The Soviet General asked what were Israel's needs in military equipment, pointing out that Ratner's chances of obtaining what he wanted 'would be better' if he applied *not* for Soviet arms proper, but for 'captured arms (German) which is very good . . . and is located outside the USSR'. But the request had to be addressed to the Soviet Foreign Office. Probably, the idea was to encourage Israel to dare and break the truce, in order to defeat the Bernadotte plan, pending debate at the UN Assembly.

Ratner was unprepared, so he cabled home asking for advice and a purchase list, but the reply was withheld. By the time it arrived, the date was 8 November already. The IDF offensive had by then been crowned with success without the Soviet aid in question and new frontiers were created between the Arab armies and the IDF, threatening to pull the rug from underneath the Bernadotte plan. Nevertheless, the Israeli list was immense. It included far more implements of war than the IDF had altogether and ignored Antonov's advice not to include Soviet weapon proper. Israel requested 70 tanks, of which 45 were medium T34 with a 100-mm guns and 25 others, all of them with an allotment of 1500 gun shells per tank. She further asked for 50, fully armed and equipped, fighter aircraft, with ammunition and spare parts 'for a year', 65 bombers of three types, 150 37-mm anti-tank guns with ammunition, 24 self-propelled 75-mm guns, 110 75-mm field artillerly guns, 24 6 inch howitzers; 250 anti-aircraft guns of various types and 80 towed anti-tank guns, all with 'adequate' stores of ammunition.[14]

What was the rationale behind the Israeli list and how did the Soviets react to it? Obviously, both Moscow and Tel Aviv now had second thoughts about the wisdom of Soviet military aid to Israel. Since the war seemed close to being decided in Israel's favour and the USA had turned less critical of Israel's latest conquests, a supply of Soviet arms to Israel, involving the arrival of many Soviet experts to Israel, was bound to sever USA–Israeli relations, and risk Israel's chances of obtaining American economic aid. Ben Gurion's vacillation in answering Ratner and the nature of the subsequent Israeli request point to an Israeli dilemma. Soviet military assistance was no longer needed for Israel's immediate survival. Yet, if the USSR was ready to give Israel such implements of war as would secure her military superiority for years it might be worth the consequences in America. The Israeli government now published a denial to rumours that it was receiving military assistance from the USSR, but went on to say that Israel was ready to obtain arms from any source. The Israeli list of requests was a way of testing the water which a few believed would bring results; indeed, it did not. Early in 1949, British intelligence reported a Russian offer of arms on easy terms to Egypt, including tanks, guns, etc.[15]

Moscow never repeated such an offer to Israel. The Soviet *Novi Vremia* was up to the mark when it stated that 'Among the foreign volunteers fighting in the Israeli army, there is not a single Soviet citizen.'[16] Members of the Israeli delegation in Moscow were now told that Soviet military assistance to Israel would 'be more than offset by friends of the Arabs who may then decide to open their stores to the Arabs, and allow them to do openly what they are now do secretly'.[17] Early in 1949, Mrs Meir inquired at the Soviet Foreign Ministry what happened to the Israeli request and was told that it could not be approved because the USSR adhered to UN decisions. At about the same time, Ratner mentioned the problem to a high-ranking Soviet officer, who gingerly replied that the USSR 'believed' that Israel was 'building a big army in order to participate in a (Western) pact'.[18] Ratner was never again invited to any meeting of importance with the Red Army Command and had gradually reached the conclusion, to which his successor, General Barne'a succumbed, that keeping an Israeli Military Attaché in Moscow was pointless.[19]

THE NATURE OF THE CZECH MILITARY ASSISTANCE TO ISRAEL

The real military assistance given to Israel from the Communist Bloc came from Czechoslovakia. In this saga, Soviet global strategy and Czech sympathy towards Zionism played only a secondary role. Rather, it was a policy motivated by strong mutual interest which was that the Yishuv desperately needed arms which the Czechs were keen to export and the Czechs desperately needed dollars which the Yishuv could raise in the USA. True, the first contact between the Yishuv and the Czech Government began when there were a number of pro-Zionists in that government. But that same government also offered military assistance to Syria and Egypt and the military assistance to Israel continued long after the pro-Zionists were no longer in government. The fact that in 1948 Israel received 85% of the Czech foreign military aid and the Arabs only the remainder, does not indicate any degree of preference but who was the better customer. A 'reliable source' in the Czech Foreign Office, which used to pass information to the British Military Attaché in Prague, said categorically that the Czech interest in exporting arms 'is just Dollars' and that Moscow understood the

Prague position. The US ambassador in Prague, Lawrence Steinhardt, opined in August 1948, that Prague was likely to continue violating the embargo 'because its government craved for Western currency'.[20]

At the time, not much heed was paid to such reports in Britain and the USA, because their analysts were captivated by a concept, according to which the Czech military assistance to Israel was part of a premeditated plan made in Moscow, with division of labour: Moscow would give Israel diplomatic support and try to sneak agents to Israel through Jewish immigration from Communist countries, until eventually they would take over Israel from within, while Prague would take care of building the Israeli army. Bevin and Marshall believed it and esteemed American diplomats and foreign policy analysts, like Walter Bedel-Smith and George Kennan, related immense sophistication to the Soviet Palestine policy. The Bedel-Smith theory was that 'when checked in Europe the USSR will turn to the Middle East . . . using tactics of penetration, and subversion'. Kennan believed that 'Palestine has opened up an opportunity for exploitation which the USSR will not neglect'.[21]

To date there is no proof of such a premeditated Soviet conspiracy or even that it was Moscow which 'ordered' Prague to supply arms to Israel. Yet, there are plenty of indications to the contrary, the chief one being the course of the Czech-Israeli arms deal itself.

Apparently, at the time it seemed that the'proof' for such a Soviet 'order' to Czechoslovakia was 'found'. It was provided by the Israeli Communist leader, Shmuel Mikunis, who in 1949 attended the funeral of the Bulgarian Communist leader, Georgei Dimitroff, in Sofia, where, according to his own evidence years later, the Deputy Soviet Prime Minister, Marshall Klementi Voroshilov, had whispered in his ear that 'it was Stalin who gave to order to send arms to Israel'.[22]

Now, Mikunis's zeal to glorify Stalin needs little proof. But Stalin's ingenious planning and determination to establish a Jewish state and take control of it badly needs more evidence. Supposing Stalin did make such a plan and did give such an 'order', when did he do so? Was it in May 1947, when Gromyko made his renowned statement but declined to respond to Ben Gurion's wish 'to explain the Yishuv needs' to the government of the USSR? Or in February 1948, when Haganah agents had already signed arms contracts in Prague, but in New York Gromyko remained silent when they asked him to see that Czech arms were not sent to the Arabs or that Yugoslavia, Bulgaria and Poland would be more helpful in the transit of the Czech arms to Israel? Was it when Gromyko vaguely advised Israel 'to continue where they had already been obtaining help', namely, to leave him alone? Was it in

October 1948, when the Soviet Chief of Staff offered Soviet military aid to Israel, only to ignore this offer shortly afterwards? Was it when the best of the goodwill between Prague and Tel Aviv failed to make the Czech Spitfires arrive in time to be of use to the IDF? Or was it merely an order to Prague to fan the flames of the Arab–Jewish conflict by supplying arms to both sides and seeing what happened?

A similar myth which has no proof is that the Czech aid to Israel was planned to suit the Jewish military planning. While it is true that the early delivery of Czech small arms and ammunition to the Jewish forces in Palestine between April and June 1948 sometimes came in the nick of time to save the Jewish forces from a defeat, it is only this context to which Ben Gurion referred in his 1968 interview with Schiff, saying 'without it we could not have held our own'. For the military value of the subsequent more ambitions and expensive parts of the Czech assistance to Israel had little or no effect at all on the outcome of the war. It was largely a waste of human effort and funds which could have been avoided had the USSR played the role many believe she did in orchestrating that aid.

CZECHOSLOVAKIA'S ARMS EXPORT AND HER CUSTOMERS

Czechoslovakia was a traditional arms producer and exporter. But in 1948 the export of arms became her financial deliverance. To survive she intended to sell not only what she produced, but also weapons given to her by Britain during the Second World War, including armed fighting vehicles and 72 Spitfire aircraft, which once formed the 313 RAF Wings.[23] This keenness for export resulted largely from the changes enforced on its economy by its transfer from a free enterprise to an increasingly concentrated system and from production of light consumer goods to heavy industry, geared to serve Soviet plans. Even prior to the coup of February 1948, the USSR had already dictated much of the order of priorities in the Czech economy, through the 'Economic Rehabilitation' and 'Mutual Trade Agreement' of December 1947. These steps involved nationalization of mines and much of the heavy industry. The immediate result was a drop in the Czech national product and a decline in foreign trade with non-Communist countries. Now, raw material of good quality, formerly procured in Sweden, Germany, etc., came at a dictated price from the USSR and Poland or from old Czech mines which were earlier abandoned due to unprofitability.[24] In the spring of 1948, the Minister for Foreign Trade, Dr Antonin Gergor, admitted that the trade deficit had become a permanent phenomenon. The figures for December 1947 showed a 3 million crowns deficit and in May 1948 it was twice as big.[25] In February 1948 the USSR banned Czechoslovakia from joining the Marshall Plan, which might have improved her dwindling foreign currency balances. The Czech Treasury, which emerged from the war with very small reserves of foreign currency and gold in the first place, saw these balances shrink still further to $105 million in 1946, to $95 million in 1947 and $83 million in 1948. These figures indicated *all* foreign currency, including Communist. The last dependable data of the Czech balances in US dollars and gold, of the autumn of 1947, put these reserves at $18.9 million only. Czech industrialists in the shrinking private sector, told Western diplomats that had they been able to get more Western currency, they could have improved the quality of their products.[26] Czechoslovakia was, in fact, nearing the intolerable point of not being able to buy raw materials outside the Communist bloc. The shortage of raw material began even to affect the export of arms.[27]

The Communist coup of February stepped up nationalization. By the end of 1948 it embraced 95% of the economy. Western countries reacted by imposing limitations on trade with Czechoslovakia. Now, not many channels of trade with the West remained open, but weapons remained somewhat more immune to exclusion, because it was a cash-and-carry business, done secretly. Only a few customers outside the Communist bloc were willing or able to buy Czech arms: a few Latin American rulers and some Middle Eastern countries, *c'est tout*.[28] By this elimination, the parties to the Arab–Israeli conflict remained Czechoslovakia's only meaningful customers and among these last only the Haganah, later the IDF, was found ready to buy at any price, at least at the start and were capable of paying immediate cash. Stalin did not have 'to give the order' to Prague to sell arms and ammunition to Israel. It was Czechoslovakia's economic survival instincts which dictated it. Indeed, it was Tel Aviv which, from time to time said 'enough', never Prague.

According to a British report, based on inside information from within the Prague Government, the total Czech dollar income from the export of arms and military services to the Middle East in 1948 was over $28 million. Ehud Avriel, Israel's chief purchaser and soon Israel's Minister in Prague, was below the mark in his estimate, that the Czech dollars earned from selling arms to Israel amounted to one quarter of Czechoslovakia's total dollar income.[29] The percentage was higher.

Czechoslovakia's sales of arms to the Middle East began in a competition between Syria, Egypt and the Haganah for the same quantity of small arms in stock. The Egyptians while remaining generally undecided, offered to barter cotton in return for the arms, whereas the Syrians were unable to pay all in immediate cash. In contrast, Avriel was ready to buy the whole stock and was ready to pay cash immediately. No wonder that a Czech agent, who met Avriel in Paris, paid his flight to Prague and offered him a stock already committed to Syria.[30]

THE COURSE OF CZECH MILITARY ASSISTANCE TO ISRAEL

Israel's arms dealing with Czechoslovakia in 1948,[31] was a highly improvised affair. Some of its projects were not carried out as intended, and some not at all. When it ended, it left a legacy of disagreement between Israel and Czechoslovakia as to what had been agreed to and what was done, and at what cost.

As early as spring 1947, leaders of the Yishuv put out feelers to Communist countries about buying arms. In July 1947, Dr Moshe Sne, formerly Haganah Chief of Staff, now Chief of the European branch of the Jewish Agency, paid a visit behind the Iron Curtain and was impressed by the sympathy towards Zionism in the government of Prague and by the Czech interest in exporting arms. But it also became apparent to him and other leaders of the Yishuv that the potential sources of arms were almost exclusively confined to Czechoslovakia.[32] The most important event in Sne's visit turned out to be his meeting with Vladimir Clementis, Deputy Foreign Minister of Czechoslovakia. Jan Masaryk, the non-Communist and definitely pro-Zionist, was then still Foreign Minister, but he soon lost his position (and his life) with Clementis succeeding him. Sne and Clementis discussed the possibility of a Czech arms sales to the Jewish State when it was established, and the ground was prepared with Masaryk's approval. But the matter was just but academic. The British were still in Palestine, and it was not at all clear what course the Palestine issue would take at the UN. In September, when UNSCOP recommendations became known, the Haganah sent emissaries to Prague, but to little effect.

However, the UN Assembly resolution of 29 November ended the Czech's watchful waiting. When Ben Gurion sent Ehud Avriel to Paris to contact agents of the Czech arms industry who were there looking for clients, two Czech Jews – Robert Adam, a commercial agent, and

Zoltan Toman, Chief of Security in the Czech Communist party – screened Avriel and guided his first steps through the Prague labyrinth. After qualifying to get in touch with people at the top of the government,[33] Avriel was asked to obtain himself the guise of a sovereign government and such accreditation was bought from Ethiopia. He was then introduced to General Ludvik Swoboda, the Minister of National Defence, under whose cloak he started talking directly with the arms-producing firms of 'Skoda', 'Zobrojuvka'. At this point, Masaryk slipped a message to Avriel to the effect that 'the more you buy the less will go to the Arabs', which galvanized Avriel and his superiors in Tel Aviv.[34] The Haganah branch now opened in Prague, received a first priority in the allocation of finance.[35] A cable from Tel Aviv to Avriel said 'speed is more important than low price'.[36]

The first contract between the Czech Government and the Haganah was signed by Avriel on 10 January.[37] It included 200 MG34 machine-guns, 4500 P18 Mouser rifles and 5 million rounds of 7.92 mm ammunition. This particular consignment was 'already packed'. More contracts of small arms followed, as Avriel paid meticulously. Then, just as the United States was about to ban the export of aircraft of all kinds, Avriel began to negotiate with Prague buying Messerschmidts.

During World War II, Messerschmidts were produced at the Czech 'AZNP-Avia' plants in Cakovice and Kunovice, for the Nazi war effort. Later the production line was idle, but in 1947 it was intended to be put back to work, with a capacity for producing 20 aircraft a month.[38] Some delay in the negotiation was caused by the nationalization of the Czech aircraft industry, in February 1948, but General Swoboda was helpful in removing these obstacles. The first contract on the sale of ten S-199 Messerschmitts to the Haganah was signed on 23 April. A month later 15 more were sold, bringing the number of aircraft bought to 25, with more intended to be sold later on.[39]

The Czech offers went further. In May they proposed to sell Israel tanks and artillery and offered an ambitious training programme for Israeli troops and airmen. In fact they had no guns for sale, so they offered their mediation in the purchase of guns and mortars in Finland. By May, Avriel had already signed seven different contracts, worth $13 million, which now also included medium ZB37 machine-guns. Finally, in August Czechoslovakia agreed to sell Israel 50 British IX Spitfires, and a further ten later on. Of these last, only nine were eventually sold, bringing the number of Spitfires sold to 59.[40]

At an early stage of this deal it became clear that there was no easy way to deliver the Czech equipment to its destination. At the early stage the British were still in Palestine, and soon after they left the UN embargo was imposed, supervised by UN observers. Compounding these difficulties was Czechoslovakia's lack of access to seas. The obvious route to move the equipment was thus transit via Communist countries, either those to the south, that is Hungary, Romania, Yugoslavia, Bulgaria and Albania on to the Adriatic or the Black Seas, or to the north, via Poland and the Baltic Sea. The route first chosen was the most practical, not the shortest. It involved transportation by train to Bratislava, then shipment on the Danube River and then movement by rail to the ports of Sibenik or Rjeka, in Yugoslavia. From that point the shipment was the responsibility of the Haganah.[41] Visiting home at the end of January, Avriel estimated that shipment of arms through this suggested route should take one month. He did not take into consideration the various obstacles caused by the Communist authorities, including red tape and often deliberate delaying tactics to increase payment.[42] In practice, the journey took more than 2 months. It also turned out that there was only a limited degree of help Prague could render on this score. A stronger intervention was needed to speed up the process, namely from the USSR, but this was not forthcoming. Israeli agents eventually took this Sisyphean struggle into their hands.

Of course, there was also the possibility of flying the equipment. But here, the difficulties were immense. To begin with, the short civil air routes from Czechoslovakia to Israel crossed British and American military controlled airspace. Probably a firm order from Moscow would have provided the opening of an *ad hoc* new route via the airspace of Communist countries, but even in such a case the airlift would have to cross the British-monitored airspace of Greece or Turkey. When the Stalin–Tito dispute erupted in June 1948, a Soviet intervention to help the arms transit through Yugoslavia became less likely. But it was still possible with regard to Albania and Bulgaria. But such intervention did not come either. Israeli agents themselves had to negotiate every flight and pay outrageously high fees for crossing and landing, if they were allowed to do so. Furthermore, only big aircraft were fitted for this task, both because of volume and of their capacity to go the entire route without refuelling. Such aircraft were obtainable only in the US or the USSR. No Soviet transportation was ever offered and with the severence of the USA embargo measures, it became difficult to charter American carriers such as the 'Skymaster' or 'Constellation', not to mention buying them. Even Israel's newly acquired C46s were actually too small for the task. It took two C46 flights to carry one dismantled Messerschmidt, whereas a Skymaster could do it in one flight. For safety's sake, the C46s still needed one refuelling *enroute*, in Corsica, Sicily or Rhodes, all which had become hazardous sites under the embargo. Landing there, except Corsica, until mid-June, incurred the risk of confiscation of both the planes and the equipment. But the C46s were, anyway, not available before the third week of May.[43]

Facing the unfortunate choice between sending the equipment by sea and waiting many weeks for its arrival or sending it by air under high risk of losing it, the desparate command of the Haganah decided to use both alternatives and incur both risks. The search went on in the US charter market for a company which would be ready to break the law. On 30 March, a chartered Skymaster of the North Carolina-based 'Ocean Trade Airline' arrived in Czechoslovakia and delivered one consignment of small arms to an improvised Haganah landing strip at Beit Daras, in Palestine. But when this plane returned to Czechoslovakia for a second round, the FBI in concert with the US Embassy in Prague, warned the charter company and made the plane return to the USA instead. Just when Avriel optimistically cabled Avigour that from now on there would be 3–4 weekly flights, Avigour (who better informed by his men in the USA) broached the bad news to Tel Aviv: 'No flights until further notice'. The lull in this air transportation lasted until the second week of May. The day was saved by the arrival in Tel Aviv, on 3 April, of the first ship with Czech arms. But, again, the next ship did not arrive until the end of April and the next one only on 25 May.[44]

THE SUPPLY OF CZECH SMALL AND MEDIUM ARMS TO ISRAEL

The Czech supply of small arms began at a small pace but soon increased. Whereas only 5000 Czech rifles, 200 machine-guns and 5 million rounds of 7.92-mm ammunition had been delivered to the Jewish forces by the end of April, an Israeli flotilla of 12 ships was now ready to take any additional consignment which eventually passed through the Yugoslav *via dolorosa*. By the end of May Israel had already absorbed some 20 000 Czech rifles, 2800 machine-guns and over 27 million rounds of Czech ammunition. Two weeks later, an additional 10 000 rifles, 1500 machine-guns and 20 million rounds of ammunition arrived. In September yet another 10 000 rifles and 1200 machine-guns, including 300 ZB37 medium machine-guns, were brought from Czechoslovakia. By October, the IDF had absorbed 46 751 rifles, 6142 machine-guns of two types and over 80 million rounds of ammunition from that source.[45]

In the final account, the Czech small arms and ammunition arrived in time and played a vital role, enabling the IDF both to run its late April and early May operations (the Dalet Plan). From May onwards, the IDF could equip every new IDF recruit with personal weapons. Every infantry section (Kitta) was armed with a machine-gun, and many IDF battalions obtained medium machine-gun support. It also gave the IDF Command the comfort, no longer prevailing in the Arab armies, of having a large small-arms ammunition reserve, in addition to an open line of supply. The level stores of 7.92-mm rounds in the IDF at the opening of the 10 days fighting in July was around 50 million, and it never fell much below this level. The exchange of cables between Ben Gurion and Avigour in June to the effect that 'in small arms we have reached the point of saturation' is indicative of the situation.[46] However, the value of the other, more ambitious and expensive types of the Czech assistance to Israel, particularly the supply of aircraft, was very different.

THE SUPPLY OF CZECH AIRCRAFT

The Czechs undertook to pack the aircraft committed to the Jews to fit whatever transportation method chosen, and to equip them with guns, machine-guns, communication equipment, etc., to reassemble them upon arrival in Israel and to train their air and ground crews. Assuming that these aircraft were brand new, and that the Israeli pilots were usually superior to the Arab ones, in Israeli eyes this more than offset the fact that this German model of aircraft was considered somewhat inferior to the British Spitfires, which the Egyptians had, or which the Czechs themselves intended to sell second-hand ('but not just now', as they told Avriel). It is not clear why Avriel did not insist on buying Czech Spitfires in the first place. His superiors probably failed to assess the situation correctly. According to a *post factum* explanation by General Ahron Remez, the Commander of the Israeli Air Force in 1948, 'this is what the Czechs made available to us at this point, so it was decided to buy [Messerschmitts] as a stop-gap measure. If we refused, we could have been left without air defence.'[47] But when Czechoslovakia later offered the IDF more Messerschmitts as well as second-hand Halifax bombers, the offer was turned down. Now Israel insisted on buying the Czech Spitfires, and got its way.[48]

The Haganah could not afford to wait for the Messerschmitts to arrive by boat. Therefore, it first contemplated flying some of them with refuellings on the way. The maximum standard range of these aircraft was approximately one-quarter of the distance from Czechoslovakia to Israel, but the extension of the aircraft fuel tank (an idea which materialized months later, when the Spitfires were flown to Israel) would have reduced the required stops to two. On 18 May, there was still no solution to the problem of the aircraft delivery so Sharett urged Eilat to plead with the State Department for US intervention with the Greek Government to allow landing in Greece. The UN embargo was not yet imposed, yet the State Department took the request in its stride. Next, Eilat tried to settle the matter directly with the Greek Ambassador in Washington, but to no avail.[49] The other choice was to dismantle the Messerschmitts, fly them on board cargo planes and reassemble them in Israel. In the internal competition over the single available Skymaster which was clandestinely chartered in the USA in May, the priority was given to the Messerschmitts over small arms and ammunition. On 21 May the first dismantled Messerschmitt arrived in Israel together with a group of Czech technicians who, unfortunately, according to an Israeli report, were 'far from first-class'. General Remez remembered that 'the slow pace of assembly stemmed from the low standard of the Czech product, and from defects in the arms gear'.[50] Meanwhile, Schwimmer's nine C46s arrived and in the last week of May joined the airlift, nicknamed Operation Balak. From the end of May, the weekly number of Balak flights went up to seven and the pace of delivery of Messerschmitts up to three a week. Operation Balak was completed by 4 August.[51]

Up to the beginning of the first truce, on 9 June, 11 Messerschmitts were brought to Israel, but only four were made serviceable. General Remez planned to launch a knockout air attack on the Egyptian Air Force, hoping to 'destroy it on the ground'. But the slow pace of reassembling the Messerschmidts in Israel and the threatening situation at the Iraqi and Egyptian front, caused the IDF Command to try and stop the advance of these armies by an early air strike. On 29 and 30 May, the ready Messerschmitts were sent to attack ground targets. A report on their first attack in Isdud shows that: 'Despite the fact that the Egyptian troops and vehicles were densely stationed, no much damage was caused to them. Yet, it appears that the psychological effect on them was great.'[52] In that attack two Messerschmitts were lost. The next day, the remainder two aircraft attacked an Iraqi column near Tul Karem, directly hitting an Iraqi Brigade Command vehicle;[53] but another Israeli Messerschmitt was now lost which left General Remez with one operational Messerschmitt until the beginning of the truce. But on 3 June, that remaining plane, flown by the best native Israeli pilot, shot down two Egyptian Dakotas which tried to bomb Tel Aviv.

These outstanding activities, probably mark the most significant role which the entire fleet of 25 Czech Messerschmitts played in the war. Their main effect, by far, was in demoralizing the Arab commands and governments. The appearance of modern fighter aircraft on the Israeli side was a surprise to the Arabs, and having been served by a very poor military intelligence they had no way of knowing the size of this fleet. In fact, throughout the next 4 weeks of the truce, after 18 Messerschmitts had already arrived in Israel, a report by the Air Force Command to the Chief of Operation warned that 'if the fighting is to be renewed, you may count on no more than 3–4 "knives", which also needs repair'.[54]

The IDF gave the Czech Messerschmitts one more chance in July, during the 10 days fighting, before finally admitting that they had been a great mistake. Thereafter, they were barred from such tasks as dog-fights or straffing ground targets. The few of them that remained servicable were 'confined to escorting tasks'. At last Prague became less adamant in its refusal to sell Israel its Spitfires. On 26 August it agreed to stop selling Messerschmitts to Israel, and instead sell her 50 second-hand Spitfires, at a reduced price. Once again, time was for Israel, and the question of how to deliver the planes quickly became paramount. In Israel, the availability of Spitfires was viewed as an indispensable condition for launching the IDF new offensive.[55]

However, the Czechs no longer dared to renew such an air-lift as they ran for the Messerschmitts, and for the IDF the experience of reassembling dismantled aircraft at home had been a bad one. At the same time, it was similarly clear that shipment by boat would not allow the Spitfires to be available in time for the forthcoming offensive. In distress, the Israelis resorted again to the idea of self-flying at least some of the Spitfires, a mission General Remez termed 'on the margin of the possible'. It involved the extension of the aircraft fuel tank to such capacity that only one refuelling would be needed *en route* to Israel. The refuelling was expected to be arranged at Podgorica (Titograd), in Southern Yugoslavia, after which the planes were expected to reach Israel on their last drop of gas. Twenty-two Spitfires were to be flown in this way (Operation Velvetta) and arrive in Israel before late September.[56]

The improvisation worked well technically, but the operation as a whole was a failure because of a series of delays. Probably, some of the excuses given by the Yugoslav authorities for the delay which now ensued were true: Israel vacillated in the payment of her debt to Yugoslavia, which was claimed to amount to more than $1 million. The Yugoslavs also excused themselves by the proximity of the air runway of Podgorica to the Albanian border, and the presence of Moslem populations in the area of Kosovo. Sometimes they would evade being helpful by resorting to the 'absence' of certain officials. Probably the main reason for the delay, which at times looked like deliberate sabotage, was the recent Yugoslav striding on a narrow and slippery path between the two world blocs. The USA Chargé d'Affairs in Belgrade, Robert Reams, is on record as warning the Yugoslav Foreign Office not to engage in arms trafficking to Palestine.[57]

In mid-September Israel's Minister of Defence was on edge. The deadline for the offensive drew near and not only had the Spitfires failed to arrive, but tanks, bought in Italy as well. Ben Gurion cabled Geneva that he 'stood aghast to hear that Yoram [Yugoslavia] was vacillating on the Yorkim [Spitfires] which were so urgently needed now'. The IDF agent on the spot, Yeshaiahu Dan, suggested trying refuelling in Bulgaria,[58] but at last the Yugoslavs moved. On 28 September, six Spitfires painted the Yugoslav colours but flown by Israeli pilots, left Czechoslovakia. After refuelling at Podgoriza, they set course for Israel, but one of them crashed on the runway and two others, while over the Mediterranean, feared insufficient fuel to complete the journey and landed at Rhodes. Under British pressure, the aircraft were confiscated and the pilots were released, after interrogation. Three other aircraft arrived safely in Israel and were the only Czech Spitfires to take part in the October operations.[59]

Meanwhile, not only the landing of Spitfires in Rhodes received publicity (it was even made public that RAF officers identified these aircraft as once a British gift to the 'Free Czechs'), but as a result of interrogation of the captured pilots, Britain and the USA learned all they needed to know about the Velvetta Operation, which was immediately withheld by the government in Belgrade. However, in December, when the IDF was about to launch more operations on the Southern front, the Bulgarian route was finally negotiated. But to the shock of the Israelis, the Bulgarians demanded $10 000 for the landing of each aircraft, not including fuel. Ben Gurion called this 'a blackmail', but nevertheless was inclined to accept the payment as *eminent domain*, but a concerted opinion in all quarters of the acquisition establishment was that 'If we now pay 10 000 "Stefans" [dollars] per "Yorek" to Beit Baruch [Bulgaria], we risk our future price system in the Slavic countries'.[60]

Eventually the Yugoslavs softened their attitude, and on 8 December the Podgorica runway was reopened. However, due to bad weather, two more Spitfires crashed, before the remaining ten arrived safely in Israel in the third week of December. By then, Operation Assaf was completed and Operation Horev was in full swing. In the nick of time, four of the arriving Spitfires took part in the last belligerent act of the war. On 1 February 1949, an IDF inventory indicates six Messerschmitts and 16 serviceable Spitfires in the Air Force OB, of which 15 originated from Czechoslovakia still a very far cry from the 84 planes bought there.[61] More Spitfires arrived afterwards by boat. Two major consignments arrived in February and March 1949, but the rest suffered further delays. The Danish ship *Lendsund*, which left the port of Gedynia in January 1951, brought the last of them.[62]

OTHER CZECH MILITARY SERVICES TO ISRAEL

In May 1948, Czechoslovakia sometimes looked as if it intended to get involved in all walks of Israel's war machinery, except the navy. In addition to small and medium weapons and aircraft, Prague offered to take care of Israel's armour, artillery and made a rich programme of military training, which included the air force personnel, parachutists, armour commanders, ordnance and logistic officers. It also provided a variety of services such as fitting and repairing Israeli aircraft, hosting a Mahal recruitment centre and running scheduled passenger flights from Tel Aviv to Europe. But this magnanimous attitude did not last long and did not yield very much. The quality of most of the services offered was suspected to be not particularly high or efficient, but its price was usually astronomical. 'Go and tell the people in high places in Prague', Avigour once exploded in a cable to his men, 'that this is supposed to be assistance to a friendly nation and not horse-trading'. It did not help.

In mid-May, Prague offered to Israel 32 light tanks, probably British Mk 6s.[63] As Israel was desperate for tanks, it had showed great interest until she learned that the Czechs wanted $90 000 for each tank. Since brand new tanks of a similar size in France were sold to Israel at $40 000 each (although their number was limited) and since in the USA Colonel Ives was selling such used tanks for less than $8000 each and in Italy 'neutralized' bigger Sherman tanks were on sale for as little as $4000 each, Ben Gurion called the Czech price 'mad' and vetoed the deal. The bargaining continued and the Czechs knocked off 15% of their price. The negotiation was dropped and picked up again in August, only to be dropped again.[64] To be sure, not a single armoured vehicle from Czechoslovakia reached the IDF and the reason was price.

The training of Israeli air and ground personnel in Czechoslovakia began in May. Originally, it was planned that about a hundred flight cadets would be trained, at Olomouc, where they would learn to fly Arada and Cessna aircraft. Those qualified were to join an advance programme of flying CS-199 and S-199 aircraft at Ceske Budejovice, from which they would eventually emerge as qualified combat pilots. The programme also envisaged training 'any number' of ground technicians at the technical school of the Czech Air Force at Liberec, where also Israeli airborne and parachute commanders were to be trained. Finally, an advance course for Israeli airmen was to be held at the Czech Air Academy of Hardec-Kralove.[65] What transpired was quite different. The commanding officer of this Czech programme, Major Jaromir Kotors, bowed to the bare necessities and started 'from the end' by improvising an instant course for the more experienced Israeli pilots, to fly Messerschmitts. Five such pilots were qualified and on 21 May after only 9 days' training, they were rushed back to Israel to operate the first assembled Messerschmitts. During the summer, more Israeli pilots attended similar courses in the hope of grappling with this difficult aircraft.[66] This course was by far the most valuable contribution of the Czech training programme to Israel's war effort.

The elementary course, originally consisting of some 20 Israelis, awarded 'wings' to 13 Israelis in September,[67] but just when they began their advance training, the entire programme was withheld. To all appearances, the reason was the 'shock' suffered in Tel Aviv upon learning the price which the Czechs had charged for the course. But there was also a decline in the enthusiasm of the Czech Ministry of Defence to run this programme, probably due to a combination of American pressure and disenchantment in Moscow. This course was not immediately essential for Israel either, since the Israeli Air Force now had more trained personnel, mostly Mahal, than aircraft to fly. The half-trained Israeli cadets returned home, and when the war was over they had to attend flight-school afresh in Israel.[68]

A Czech–Israeli project which particularly alarmed Western intelligence, for no good reason, was the 'Czech Brigade'. To be sure, it was neither a 'Moscow design', nor a Czech one, but a Zionist idea, prompted by Israeli officials of the Hamerkaz Lsherut Ha'am, a Gahal recruiting centre in Prague, in conjunction with Jewish veterans of the Czech regular army. The idea was to form a legal channel, through which young immigrants, Czechs and others, including families, could emigrate to Israel and serve in the IDF. The term 'brigade' did not mean such an operational unit, but was to serve as a paragon. In May, Avigour cabled Ben Gurion, 'In Ofri (Czechoslovakia) there is a plan to train a "Masaryk Battalion" of . . . Czech Jews and refugees'. Early in June the Israeli mission in Prague approached General Swoboda with this idea and the Czech Minister of Defence agreed to support the project – for *bona fide* dollar payment! The initial price was set at $191 000 not including travel expenses to Israel. Soon, the title 'Masaryk' was dropped and the title 'battalion' was changed for 'brigade'. The number of able-bodied recruits was approximately 800.[69]

Now the Czech army appointed Major Antonin Suchor, formerly a tank battalion commander in the Red Army, bearing a Hero of the USSR decoration, as Commander-in-Chief of the brigade, promoting him to Lieutenant Colonel. Suchor went to Israel twice, 'to get acquainted with the terrain' and met with Ben Gurion and members of the IDF General Staff. His second in command was a Jewish officer (Shechta) from the group which initiated the project. But the rest of the command was a bizarre mixture of Zionist officials and professional soldiers, and the demarcation of authority between them was never clear. 'Ugly arguments' and mutual accusations developed inside this command, and disagreements flourished. Avriel interfered in the appointment of officers and disagreed with members of the IDF Command, namely, Galili and Shaltiel, who arrived from Israel in an attempt to put the house in order. Meanwhile, the first group of recruits gathered, consisting of some 100 volunteers, former Jewish members of 'Free Czechoslovakia' who had fought with the British army during World War II. Next came some 400 young Czech Jews, who were recently recruited. Finally, came the 'Halutzim' – young displaced persons from camps in Germany, who were admitted to Czechoslovakia for this purpose without passports. On 15 August the brigade began its training at four bases: Libava, Milovice, Velka Strena and Straz pod Ralskem. A parachutist unit, formed earlier at Straz under a Palmach officer (Guri) was incorporated in as well.[70]

When the Czech army objected to including families in the project, the number of recruits shrunk and when the terms of service were defined as 1 year, after which servicemen were expected to repatriate, the Israeli officials suddenly noticed 'undesirable elements' in the unit.[71] Avriel started to worry lest, after all, this was some kind of a 'Cominform plot' and cabled his worries back to Israel. Ben Gurion shrugged it off, but on second thoughts decided to arrange that members of the Czech brigade would join the IDF not as a group but as individuals. In December, 600 Czech Jews left for Israel. However, by the time they were ready to join the Israeli army, the war was over.[72]

The affair had some embarrassing consequences. Quite a few members of the brigade demanded a proper salary for their service in the IDF and transportation out of Israel. The issue was quietly settled on individual terms. There was also a residual disagreement over the cost of the brigade and no settlement was reached between Israel and Czechoslovakia. It added to the large volume of unsettled accounts between the two governments, which amounted to millions of dollars.[73]

THE CZECH MILITARY AID TO ISRAEL: TERMS, PRICE AND VALUE

Israel used the Czech aid not because she leaned towards Communism, but because she was fighting for her survival. The price of this Czech aid was outrageously high, and Israel paid it, not because of a particularly high quality, but because it was essential to the survival of Israel. The trouble with sources outside Czechoslovakia was that in most cases the equipment on sale needed reconditioning before it could be put to use. Such equipment had to be bought and shipped illegally and often with no guarantee for the supply of ammunition and spare parts. In Czechoslovakia's case, the equipment offered was either new or in operative condition, with a government sponsorship and with a guarantee of supply of ammunition, spare parts and know-how, and a mutual interest in its speedy supply.

In the arms deal in Prague both parties were genuinely interested that the military aid should be useful. The Czechs were truely keen to go on selling military aid, and the Israelis were keen to do honest business in order to keep the line of supply open. For months, the Israeli representatives in Prague avoided bargaining over the price while receiving the largest share in Israel's resources. Indeed, this section of Israeli arms-purchasing rarely suffered from budget limits. Early in

January 1948, the Haganah mission was still granted barely half a million dollars. But in March their spending had already amounted to 3 million and by mid-April it was 5.8 million. In May Avriel so impressed his Czech negotiators when he pulled out a new cheque for $2 million in a Swiss Bank that he was offered short-term credit of up to $12 million to buy more. In Czech eyes he was a man of unlimited means and in some way he was. It was at this point that Ben Gurion for the first time asked Avriel not to exceed a debit of $5 million.[74]

The shortcomings of the Czech aid to Israel were three-fold: (a) transport difficulties which were never surmounted; (b) the low standard of Czech products and expertise, except small arms; and (c) the price. Israel was asked to pay the 'market price' for the Czech aid which was far from being what economists would call an 'elaborate market', whereby one may choose between several suppliers. In fact at some point these price were monopolistic *par excellence*, literally blackmail. For each equipped Messerschmitt, the quality of which we have already discussed, Israel was made to pay $190 000. This price was one and a half times the price Arazi paid for the carrier ship *Attu* in the USA, 12 times the cost of buying and reconditioning an American B17 bomber and 25 times the likewise cost of each American C46. More absurd, it was seven times the price of each of the Spitfires Czechoslovakia later sold Israel; in this case the price went down drastically after the Czechs got wind that Israel was negotiating to buy used Spitfires elsewhere, for less. Even the price of the Czech small arms was double their price elsewhere. For a rifle Czechoslovakia charged was $46–50, when arms dealers in Italy asked $20–28 for British and American service rifles and an Australian dealer asked £4 Sterling. The Czech price for one 3 inch mortar bomb was $3.57, while in Italy they cost 13 cents.[75] Fortunately, Israel produced such ammunition at home. Only on rare occasions did the Czechs agree to take their own currency for their services to Israel.[76]

But the 'market' was not always in favour of the Czechs. In fact, as soon as Israel looked determined to take no more Messerschmitts, even at a lower price,[77] the Czechs agreed to sell Spitfires to her, which they earlier refused. For these planes they first asked $50 000, then $30 000, and finally sold each for only $23 000. Even in the abortive tank deal Israel's stubborness made the Czechs go down from $90 000 to $75 000, where the negotiation stopped, because the price still seemed outrageously high for tanks of a dubious quality,[78] and against the possibility of M4 Sherman tanks, offered in Italy for as little as $4000 a piece.[79]

One may well point to Israel's long-standing wish for Czech tanks as the reason for her belated decision to buy and recondition Sherman tanks in Italy and, in consequence, her inability to make these tanks available for the war operations at all. The abnormal price of the Czech equipment and the inability of the Czech government to effect the transit of this equipment through other Communist countries can only be explained by the absence of a determined Soviet intervention. This explanation must also stand for the quick Czeck submission to Anglo-American pressure which brought about the cessation, on 11 August, of the use of the Zatec air-field for flying aid to Israel, or the stoppage, in June, of the Czech transport flights to Israel by their BATA airline, which had to go through the Western controlled corridor south of Czechoslovakia.[80] Clearly, when London and Washington put pressure to bear on Prague, a Soviet firm intervention, as well as allocation of alternative air routes would have offset this pressure. If indeed it was Moscow's plan and interest that the Czech arms should help Israel, is this the way the USSR would have acted? Is there any doubt that Soviet intervention in Prague and other Communist capitals would have levelled prices and have made the transit faster and more successful?

But notwithstanding these shortcomings on price or quality, the Czech government truly spared no effort to be helpful to Israel. General Swoboda was personally involved in cutting red-tape and improving the process of delivery inside Czechoslovakia. Under his guidance, a coordinating body was established, headed by Colonels Jan Palla and Leopold Presser of the Czech General Staff, with representatives of the producers, the Ministry of National Defence and the General Staff, who jointly supervised these operations.[81]

How much Israel spent on the Czech aid cannot be calculated exactly. At the end of 1948, Israel was asked to pay a balance of $11 million. However, in Geneva, Sapir only sanctioned payment for purchases and services for which there was proof, and this caused a suspension in payment. According to a reconstructed debt, made by Sapir's auditors at the end of 1948, Israel paid or recognized the validity of Czech claims of approximately $17 million.[82] According to an informant from within the Czech Defence establishment, in 1948 Israel received assistance amounting to $23 million.[83] The temporary suspension of the Czech assistance towards the end of 1948 and its renewal in 1949 further complicated these credit–debit accounts. In the spring of 1949 Sapir assessed that the Israeli debt in Prague was 'just above a million'. However, new purchases were now negotiated and this caused further confusion over the settlement of former debts. The differences were never settled. In 1956 the Secretary-General of the Czech Communist Party, Antonin Novotni, told his Israeli counterpart that Israel owed Czechoslovakia $6 million, but his country no longer insisted on the settlement of that debt.[84]

The value of Czech aid to Israel's military strength in 1948 can be simplified into four main categories: (a) small arms, which was by far the most important part; (b) 84 fighter aircraft, of which only a few were useful to Israel's war effort; (c) various services, including military training and the maintenance of civil air communication with Israel; and, finally (d), aid with no effect at all on the war, such as the 'Brigade', the supply of tanks, guns, etc.

THE SUPPLY OF SMALL ARMS TO ISRAEL

It is hard to exaggerate the significance of the Czech supply of small arms to Israel, particularly the first delivery of some 5000 rifles, 250 machine-guns and 5 million bullets early in April. This relatively small shot in the arm must be viewed in relation to the volume of arms and the number of combat troops on both sides at that moment. The weapons at the disposal of the Jewish forces until then did not suffice even for the defence of the Jewish settlements and the communication lines between them. The shortage of small arms in the Haganah until the end of March was so acute that when preparations were made to pass supplies to the besieged Jewish Jerusalem (Operation Nahshon) the Haganah command had to confiscate rifles and ammunition from Jewish settlements and from military courses.[85] It was this period to which the Chief of Operation, General Yadin, later referred to as 'the most terrible in the war'. The arrival of the Czech small arms made a tremendous difference. It enabled the Haganah to switch to full-scale offensive operations, known as the Dalet Plan, which resulted up in the defeat of the irregular Arab forces in Palestine before the invasion of the regular Arab armies began. The Czech small arms gave the Jewish forces momentary superiority in fire-power and a big boost to their morale. The relatively successful execution of the Dalet Plan, just before the end of the British mandate, gave the embryo Jewish State control over the strategically vital areas of Palestine, of the major lines of communications and sea- and airports. It made it possible for the IDF to hold its own against the joint attack of the regular Arab armies after 15 May. 'After absorbing that part of the Czech arms', Ben Gurion remembered, 'the situation radically changed in our favour'.[86]

It has been mentioned that the USA vigil over the embargo, combined with a sloven Yugoslav cooperation with the Czechs, delayed arrival of further deliveries of Czech small arms to the Jews by boat and by air. However, from mid-May small-arms deliveries began to arrive in big quantities and most of it before the commencement of the UN embargo. During that period the IDF received over 20 000 rifles, 4000 machine-guns and some 47 million rounds of 7.92-mm ammunition. At a time when the embargo was increasingly crippling the Arab armies, particularly in terms of ammunition, the IDF enjoyed the relative comfort of a small-arms ammunition reserve which never went below 50 million rounds. The Czech aid provided the IDF with all its needs in rifles and machine-guns[87] and gave its General Command confidence in the future supply of ammunition. Such an advantage was no longer enjoyed by the Arabs.

THE CONTRIBUTION OF THE CZECH AIRCRAFT TO ISRAEL'S MILITARY SUCCESS

Twenty-three out of 25 Messerschmitts and 56 out of 59 Spitfires sold by Czechoslovakia to Israel eventually entered service in the Israeli Air Force.[88] Their usefulness during the war was another matter. The Messerschmitts were a great disappointment. It was a bad product, unfriendly even for the best pilots, and with dubious performance even when properly maintained. The Spitfire was a far better aircraft and one with which many Mahal pilots were familiar. But these aircraft could only give support to Israel during the armistice talks as they failed to arrive in time for the war itself.

The contribution of the Messerschmitts to Israel's war effort was mainly psychological, particularly their appearance over Arab positions on the eve of the first truce. But this effect was not strong enough to deter the Arabs from deciding to renew the war on 9 July. During the 10 days fighting in July, only five Messerschmitts were available for combat and two of these were lost in what appeared to be mechanical air accidents during engagement with the enemy. This made the Israeli Air Command confine these aircraft 'to escorting missions only'. As from August, Israel's hopes of controlling the air were pinned on the Spitfires, but only three of these aircraft arrived in time to take part in the October operations. Even in December, when 16 Spitfires had already

Table 8 Czech military assistance to Israel in 1948

Type of assistance	Dates of availability
Small arms: Mauser rifles, 470000 MG34 machine-guns, 5300 ZB37 machine-guns, 850 7.92-mm, 80 million	Stages: 1. end of March to early April 2. April 28 until second truce 3. Pre-October offensive 4. During 1949
Fighter aircraft I 23 S-199 Messerschmitt Other weapon, ammunition and equipment.	16 May–July 31 Air bombs, parachutes, radio and other aircraft communication and air navigation equipment: May– September 1948
Fighter aircraft II 56 Spitfires	Stages: 1. 3 towards the October offensive 2. 10 at the end of December 3. The rest throughout 1949 and 1950
Training of air and ground crews: Training flight cadettes advanced pilots on S199 and ground crews	The training of 25 not completed 10–12 pilots trained to fly S199 Most other courses not completed

arrived, only seven were serviceable and not all of were of a Czech origin. Even in the last campaign of the war, that is the Horev Operation, only 13 aircraft of Czech origin were serviceable, half of which were in a limited capacity.[89]

How was it, then, that as from October the Israeli Air Force, nevertheless, controlled the Palestine sky? There were three reasons for this capability. First, during the summer Israel gleaned a variety of combat aircraft from sources other than Czechoslovakia. These included B17s, Dakotas, Beaufighters, Mustangs, Mosquito, and Harvards. In addition, she also managed to turn a few light aircraft into improvised combat planes. Secondly, the Israeli Air Force had more air and ground crews than its aircraft required. Aircraft could thus carry out more sorties than usual. The third factor, and probably the important, was the almost total grounding of the Arab Air Forces as a result of the embargo and technical incompetence.

Table 9   Pace and quantities of Czech small arms and medium arms supplied to Israel

Stage	Date and type of transportation	Mouser rifles	Type of weapon MG34 mach. guns	ZB37 mach. gun	7.92-mm ammunition
Dalet	31.3 flight	200	40	–	160,000
plan	3.4, boat	4500	200	–	5 million
	28.4, boat	10000	1415	–	16 million
Pre-	25.5, boat	5000	1200	–	6 million
truce	30.5, flight	–	–	–	6 million
period	6.6, boat	2500	1230	–	9 million
	June, flight	–	–	224	–
First	Nor recorded	2500	–	–	9 million
truce	27.6 flight	–	–	–	6 million
	July, boat	–	–	117	–
Second	6.8 boat	–	–	–	7.5 million
truce	8.9 boat	10000	594	100	1 million
	19.9 boat	–	100	100	4 million
IDF	10.11 boat	–	–	–	5 million
offen-	Not recorded	12051	521	301	5 million
sives					
					circa:
Total		46751	5300	842	80 million

CZECHOSLOVAKIA AND THE UN EMBARGO

Very few governments in 1948 kept the embargo as strictly as the governments of Britain and the USA. But only one government, that of Czechoslovakia, violated it as a matter of policy. However, even Czechoslovakia did not remain unaffected by the embargo rules, particularly when the USSR was careful not to appear to violating them. There was evident anxiety in the Prague Government not to manoeuvre itself into international isolation. Prague did its best to hide or camouflage its assistance to Israel. Flights of civil aircraft over Northern Bohemia were banned. Israelis receiving training in Czechoslovakia were ordered to wear a Czech uniform and not to use a foreign language in public. A road block and permanent watch was put on the Stalingrad Hotel in Zatec, where the Israeli teams took lodging. Aircraft leaving

Czechoslovakia to Israel were painted the colours of their country of destination, etc.[90]

Nevertheless, details of the Czech aid to Israel quickly diffused to British and American intelligence. The crew of the first chartered Skymaster which flew to Palestine on 31 March were throughly interrogated by the US Military Attaché in Prague. On 23 June, a C46 destined to Zatec made a forced landing at Trevizio, Italy. In its cockpit, the local police found maps and information about the Balak Operation, and this was passed to the British Embassy in Rome. The interrogation of an Israeli crew of a Norsman coming from Zatec and taken prisoner by the Egyptian army in Gaza, brought the British further information. Both the British and the Americans planted their informers inside the Israeli community in Czechoslovakia. A Mahal airman recruited in Geneve, Hans Lehman, reported to the British Military Attaché in Prague from Zatec and then from Israel and a Czech Jew who was trained at Ulomouc was reporting to the American Embassy. On 11 August, Czech airmen, who had asked for political asylum in the US zone of Germany were made to talk to the press on the Czech aid to Israel.[91]

As early as April, the Director of the CIA, Rosco Hillenkoetter, began sending warnings to the White House and to the Secretaries of State and Defence, that Israel had obtained arms and developed an Air Force with the help of Czechoslovakia, now an enemy country. What particularly worried the CIA was that increasing numbers of Americans with military expertise had now crossed to Czechoslovakia. On 8 July, Hillenkoetter wrote an even more alarming memorandum, which made Secretary of Defence Forrestal himself warn the President of the damage caused to the USA defence by the movement of American citizens and aircraft into a Communist territory.[92] Immediately Marshall instructed his ambassador in Prague to make a quiet but firm protest. According to evidence given by Vladimir Clementis in his trial in Prague early in August 1953, the US Ambassador visited Zatec unannounced and although he was not allowed in, he based his protest to the Czech Foreign office on that visit. The British Ambassador, Dixon, followed with his own protest.[93]

Evidently these protests brought about the immediate cessation of the flights from Zatec to Israel. Such flights did not completely end, but were thereafter carried out only piecemeal from Zhelin and Malecki. A Czech army spokesman invited foreign reporters to Zatec to see for themselves that there was no truth in the allegations.[94] 'The rulers of Ofri are becoming more and more sensitive to a UN pressure', Avigour reported upon retiring from his post in Geneva. His successor also reported that 'The Czechs are afraid of the intervention of the Count [Bernadotte] and his superiors'. Ben Gurion, too, remembered that 'after the revelation . . . the Czechs turned much slower'.[95] But on 14 January 1949, new negotiation was opened on the renewal of the Czech assistance to Israel, with Clementis even promising 'to consider the possibility of the Czech army giving up . . . its equipment in its use to Israel'.[96]

THE ABORTIVE ISRAELI ARMS DEAL WITH FINLAND

Late in March 1948 Avriel cabled his superiors: 'No heavy things at all in Ofri',[97] meaning that the Czechs had no guns for sale. However, Prague was more than ready to mediate in the sale of Finnish artillery and ammunition to Israel.

Finland was a *sui generis* Soviet satellite. She took the German side in World War II and in 1945 was conquered by the Red Army, forced to pay compensation and to put on trial her top politicians, including the State President, who led the pro-Nazi policy. Until July 1948, the Helsinki Government was a 'national' coalition of leftist factions and non-partisan politicians, who signed the 1945 Peace Treaty of Petsamo with the USSR. That government did all it could to placate the USSR on matters pertaining to foreign policy in return for retaining Finland's democratic system and institutions. When, in February 1948 Moscow orchestrated the Communist takeover in Prague, many in the West feared that a similar fate was awaiting Finland. Indeed, in February Stalin sent a 'personal message' to Finland's President, Yuho Paaskivi, suggesting a treaty of mutual defence between the two states, which Finland could not afford to refuse. But thanks to the cautious handling of the negotiation by Carl Enckell, Finland's Foreign Minister, the talks held in Moscow in April 1948 ended up with 'a treaty of mutual assistance' and not with an encroachment on Finland's political system. In foreign relations, Finland committed herself to a 'non-alliance' policy, which for all practical purposes meant a Soviet policy. 'Finlandization' became a soubriquet for a relation by which a country near the USSR retains her internal sovereignty but subordinates her foreign policy to Soviet dictate. This may well explain Finland's quick recognition of Israel in June 1948.[98] In July there were general elections in Finland and the 'national government', headed by Munno Pekkala, suffered a defeat. The new government, headed by the Social Democrat, Carl

Fagerholm, consisted of none of the former leftist Ministers, except Enckell, yet it was just as careful not to give the USSR a pretext to remove it.

Finland had a good weapons industry, but no strong motive to sell to Israel. The major principle which shaped the Finnish Government arms export policy was to refrain from opening any such relationship unless Moscow demanded it. Besides, this industry was a private enterprise, though under government supervision, which in 1948 was tightened, after the discovery of arms caches, belonging to a right-wing faction, part of which was illegally exported.[99]

It is against this background that the abortive Finnish–Israeli deal should be viewed. As early as February 1948, Arazi was informed that arms dealers in Helsinki had guns, mortars and mortar ammunition for sale. At that point, Haganah agents were looking desperately for artillery and in their zeal to buy it neglected the rules of safety. They paid $22 000 as a downpayment to a broker who promised to supply them heavy mortars and hand them over at Copenhagen airport. The broker ran away with the money.[100] In May, the Czechs offered their arbitration and a plan was made jointly with the Israelis to buy from Finland 50 120-mm mortars with 50 000 bombs, 24 20-mm Medsen navy guns, with 75 000 shells and 100 flame-throwers.[101] Mistakenly convinced that the attitude of the government in Helsinki was similar to that of Prague, Avriel cabled home: 'the deal is on'. But in Helsinki Enckell vetoed the deal and 'the Yael [code name for Finland] Merchandise was put on ice'.[102] The next idea which cropped up in Prague was that 'Ofri [Prague] will buy Yael merchandise', which would not have to go to Czechoslovakia but sail or fly from a Balitc air- or seaport. Colonel Presser of the Czech General Staff was about to fly to Finland on that score when it became known that 'not only the Foreign Minister, but the Prime Minister of Yael as well opposes the sale, because of [Uncle] Sam's pressure'. Yet, the Finns seemed to be looking for a solution which would enable them to conclude the deal but the blame would be on Prague alone. They asked Prague if Clementis was ready to undertake in writing that the arms were destined for the Czech army. Clementis seemed to have agreed, so again Avriel reported that 'the government of Yael apologized to the Ofri government on the delay'. But on 10 September Avriel again wondered 'why the Yael business is still stuck'. Past October the Finnish deal was still bogged down. In November 1948, Avriel's lieutenant, Felix Doron, flew to Helsinki to see where exactly the deal was stuck and as a result of his visit the deal was abandoned.[103]

MILITARY ASSISTANCE FROM THE SOVIET BLOC TO THE ARAB STATES

Israel was not the only Middle Eastern client for Communist military aid in 1948, nor indeed the first. Syria and Egypt negotiated such aid in Prague before Israel.[104]

However, in 1948 it was very much more difficult for Arab countries to seek military aid from behind the Iron Curtain – or indeed in the open world market at large – than for Israel. For, whereas the Jews had just started to build and equip an army, the Arabs had their armies already established, and they found it hard to accept a change of standards. Egypt, Iraq and Transjordan had explicit conditions written into their treaties with Britain, prohibiting them from seeking military assistance anywhere else. They could, of course, claim that Britain had been the first to violate these treaties by withholding supplies to them. But none of them expected the British interdict to last long, when respected British diplomats and generals encouraged them to think so. Furthermore, none of the Arab governments had at its disposal machinery to handle arms acquisition abroad, particularly not when it turned a clandestine job. There was a world of difference between getting arms on easy terms from Britain, France or the USA and the conditions prevailing in the illegal international arms market. In the first place, one needed a tremendous amount of foreign currency in cash to run such an independent arms acquisition. In 1948 all the Arab governments had severe financial problems. The governments of Iraq and Transjordan were in deep financial crisis, whereas Egypt had to overcome her traditional balance-budget policy with her main reserves of foreign currency being the newly unfrozen Sterling balances in British banks. Finally, all the Arab governments were apprehensive lest arms deals with Communist countries involved Communist penetration into their politics.

Syria was the odd one out. Her army never really had a supporting power and had not been accustomed to uniformity in standards and calibres of weapons. The Syrian Government was also relatively financially better off than her Arab sisters. As early as the fall of 1947, after Syrian officers were looking for military aid in various Western countries, they ended up in Czechoslovakia. In December 1947, when the Arab League decided, to support the Palestinian Arab opposition to the UN partition, Syria had a particular interest in supporting this cause, both against the Zionist and against Abdullah's ambitions. Seeking to combine both ends, she tried to improve the poor state of her army and strengthen the 'Army of Deliverance' by taking advantage of a

Czech offer. Her initial plan was to buy Czech arms and equipment for $11 000. The first contract, for 10 000 rifles, hundreds of machine-guns and explosives, worth $2.5 million, was signed in December.

But when it became apparent that the Syrians were unable or unwilling to pay immediate cash, the appearance of Avriel in Prague, combined with a pro-Zionist sentiment among ministers of the government, prompted what appear to be a slight change of attitude in Prague. It was to give Israel, with a better way of payment, priority in procuring small arms, but not to call off the Syrian deal. The Czechs were determined to keep arms-trade relations with both parties, and they succeeded in this. In February, two consignments of small arms went out almost simultaneously in two directions: the Syrian one went to the port of Rjeka and the Haganah one to Sibenik. The Syrian transport included 10 000 rifles, several hundred machine-guns, 6 million rounds of 7.2-9mm ammunition, thousands of hand grenades and several tons of explosives. In Rjeka, it was loaded onto the *Lino*, a chartered boat which was insured by the Czech company 'Slavia'. According to the British Admiralty report, the ship's capacity was only 270 tons, but its cargo was approximately 400 tons.[105]

On its way, the Syrian consignment incurred bad luck. The overloaded *Lino* left Rjeka on 3 April, in a very rough seas and after a day's struggle sought refuge in the Italian port of Molfetta. The British Navy, which was present in that section of the Italian coast, suspected that the ship was smuggling arms to an Italian subversive group and warned the Italian police, which arrested the *Lino*'s crew and towed the ship to the port of Bari. There *Lino* cast anchor and was guarded by British war ships. Meanwhile, Haganah agents, who earlier failed to impress upon the Czech Government the necessity of withholding arms from Syria obtained knowledge that she was at Bari and sent a Palmach commando team, which stayed in Italy. On 10 April the team managed to blow up and sink the *Lino* inside the port. Meanwhile, the Italian authorities discovered their mistake and sanctioned a rescue operation to draw out the cargo, which was supervised by the Czechs. The reconditioning of the arms took some weeks and when it was completed, the UN embargo was already in effect. But the Italian government decided that since the arms were caught before the embargo was imposed, it could go. It was eventually loaded onto another ship, the *Argiro*, which set sail on 19 August, but was siezed by Israeli commandos in high seas at gunpoint. The arms was then loaded onto a standby Israeli ship and the *Argiro* was sunk.[106]

Syrian negotiations for arms purchases in Czechoslovakia did not end here, but no meaningful military purchases are known to have been been made in Czechoslovakia throughout 1948.

Egyptian inquiries in Prague were made at approximately the same time as the Syrian, embodied in the visit in Prague of Brigadier Hafez, Egypt's Chief of Military Intelligence. Disappointed everywhere else in Europe and the USA, Hafez actually bought a small amount of military equipment, probably to impress the British that he was serious. This consignment, worth a few thousand Egyptian lira, reached Egypt in January.[107] On 3 March, a Soviet delegation, headed by the Soviet Deputy Commissar for Foreign Trade, Michail Menshikov, concluded a trade agreement in Cairo. The British monitored these talks with much interest, but obtained no knowledge of any military subjects discussed. Yet, after a few days Brigadier Hafez left for Prague again, with much publicity. The British Ambassador in Cairo was told that an Egyptian delegation was invited to visit 'Skoda' and 'Zbrojuvka' factories and that the Czechs had offered to help build an arms industry in Egypt. On 12 April, still on his tour, this time of European capitals, Hafez scattered rumours to the effect that if Egypt could not find arms in the West she might well buy them in the East. If the USSR was ready to trade wheat for Egyptian cotton, why wouldn't she trade arms?[108] However, Egypt's arms purchases behind the Iron Curtain did not get off the ground. As for the Czech proposal to build an arms factory in Egypt, the government of Egypt was deterred by the prospect of having to employ hundreds of Czech engineers.[109]

Egypt's negotiation for arms acquisition in Communist countries was renewed only in the spring of 1949, this time with less hesitation or publicity. The first consignment of Czech military equipment was due to go via Gdynia in July 1949. It was now the Israeli Embassy in Prague which tipped off the British Embassy on the matter.[110] But at that point the government of Egypt received strong assurance from Bevin himself that he was working on lifting the UN embargo, and when this was achieved Egypt would be the first to be compensated for the long suspension of British arms supply to her. This prospect killed the Egyptian–Czech deal.[111]

In a report prepared by the British Ambassador in Prague early in 1949, on Czechoslovakia's arms sale to the Middle East in 1948, Israel's purchases were estimated at $23 million, the Syrian at over $2 million and the Egyptian – at a few tens of thousands of dollars.[112]

6 Other Arms Sources to Palestine in the 1948 War

A Western intelligence error, which permeated to the historiography of the Arab–Israeli dispute, ascribed Israel's military capability and success in 1948 mainly to the assistance obtained from Czechoslovakia. It has already been shown that this aid had severe limits: it did not include artillery, armour, or indeed many aircraft that were serviceable while the war was still being fought. To be sure, Israel's military arsenal in 1948 did not come from any dominant single source, but from diverse, world-wide sources, as well as from the production of weapons at home. While much of the assistance bought in Czechoslovakia failed to become useful in the war, many of the weapons which did play a role in deciding the war in Israel's favour came from Western Europe. Most of the weapons from Western Europe arrived at an early stage, before or immediately after the imposition of the UN embargo.

The Israelis had been more familiar and better connected in the twilight world of arms-sales – including governments, police, ports, airports and the underworld – than had the Arabs. This was mainly due to the Israelis' long experience gained through years of running illegal immigration. In some countries in Western Europe the political circumstances were now also particularly favourable to Israeli support.

SOURCES OF ARMS IN WESTERN EUROPE

In 1948 there were three ways by which one could acquire arms: a treaty relations with a patronizing power; buying arms legally on a certificate granted in an arms-producing country; or buying legally or illegally obsolete or neutralized arms and then reconditioning them. Post-war demobilization and the renewal of arms production by a few European countries for export glutted the West European markets with new as well as used arms. The democratic governments were not too keen or capable of controlling this market, either before or even after the declaration of the UN embargo. Skill, experience and diplomacy had much to do with the success or failure of arms acquisition.

In 1948, the European Common Market was still a dream, but in illegal arms trade West Europe was already one market. Arms-dealers sold French-made arms in Switzerland. American equipment held in Belgium was sold in France. Equipment held in one country was transported for shipment to one port or another. Sailings to Middle Eastern destinations were made from Mediterranean ports, intermittently from the French or the Italian Rivieras, or from Southern Italy, Spain or French North Africa. A typical Israeli report, sent to Tel Aviv from Geneva in April reads: 'Freddy bought 31 guns in Denmark, from a Belgic company. Ammunition is in Switzerland... they sail from Marseilles...'[1]

At first sight, the West European arms market looked like a supermarket with everything one needed to equip a big army instantly. An Israeli agent who in August 1948 was looking for tanks in Italy, recalls: 'We entered a huge scrap-yard of armoured vehicles. We counted about 600 "Sherman" tanks alone. We picked up the 40 we chose... and obtained an export licence without a hitch. The tanks prices at the gate was $3175.'[2] Reconditioning and transportation of this equipment was another matter. In July, Arazi reported from Italy that he could 'supply any British ammunition needed' and that 'there is more 75-mm, 6-Pounder and 20-mm shells on sale, than money can buy'. He also 'found half tracks, armoured cars... Spitfire aircraft... you name it'.[3] But to a great extent this market was a mirage, full of useless junk. By the time the said tanks, which Israel was tempted to buy became serviceable, the war was long over.

ISRAELI AND ARAB MILITARY PURCHASES FROM THE WEST EUROPEAN MARKET

The historical significance of Israel's purchases in the West European arms market was that it included implements which Israel failed to obtain in the USA or Czechoslovakia and that it reached its destination at an early stage of the war (and that a good deal of it was absorbed by the IDF at a strategically good time). The main reason for this success was the position of the French Government during the months of April and May. On the Arab side, only Egypt was active in this market, but the outcome of her efforts were poor and belated.

The Israeli search for arms in West Europe began simultaneously with searches in the USA and Czechoslovakia, and for some time this

European supply was considered an auxiliary source only. As elsewhere, the idea was to buy the equipment between January and April, keep it in places where it was bought and transport it to Palestine immediately at the end of the British mandate. In mid-March, as the limits to the American source became apparent and the opportunities in this new area became apparent, Haganah agents, particularly Arazi, prompted the extension of arms-purchasing in the West European market.

By then, sea transportation arrangements had to a large extent been completed. In April, there were 12 cargo ships, bought or chartered, at the Haganah's disposal, with a total volume of 13 000 tons, sufficient to carry the equipment both from the Czech–Yugoslav direction and the Italian–French routes.[4]

The decision by the Haganah command to start the massive arms delivery only after 15 May, for fear of confiscation by the British, was a gamble. It might have come too late. However, the indecisive nature of the first thrust by the invading Arab forces, the absence of any Arab attempt to block the Israeli flotilla, coupled with the delay in the establishment of the UN observers corps, turned the Israeli gamble into a successful one. Meanwhile, the period of waiting was used to check the equipment in question and to try and clear local political and legal aspects, pertaining to its onward shipment.

Arazi, whose methods here were no different than in the USA, had better luck in Europe. He provided himself with letters of authorization to buy arms from three sovereign governments and had some ten fictitious corporations which he supposedly worked on their behalf. 'Dr Jose Arazi representing the government of Nicaragua' was a welcomed customer among scrap dealers.[5] The equipment which he and his colleagues bought between January and April 1948 included 50 65-mm French guns (manufactured in 1906), 12 120-mm French mortars, ten H35 light French tanks bearing 37-mm guns, tens of thousands of gun shells, a great number of US army half tracks (bought in Belgium) and a variety of small and medium French arms. In most cases this equipment was tested, so when it arrived in Israel it could instantly be put to use.[6]

THE VOLATILE POLICY OF THE FRENCH GOVERNMENT

Haganah agents began buying implements of war in Western Europe with little idea of how the equipment would reach Palestine. The government of France solved their problem by opening French territory and the French ports. Without this assistance, which came as a surprise and only lasted from mid-April till mid-June 1948, Arazi's acquisition efforts in Western Europe would have ended the same way as his efforts in America.

The French assistance to Israel was a short phase in a volatile policy, which swung from giving military aid to the Arabs, to neutrality, to helping the Jews, to adherence to the embargo, and then again helping to arm the Arabs.[7] It was a shaky government, headed by the Liberal (MRP) Robert Schuman, one in a series of short-lived governments which, to remain in power, tried their best not to rock the boat. The Palestine issue had the potential of doing so, because of a marked schism inside the Socialist–Republican (MRP) Cabinet. A further destabilizing factor was the National Assembly, where the two strongest opposition parties, the Communists (PCF) and the Gaullists (RPF), were, momentarily, solidly pro-Zionist. In addition, there was strong extra-Cabinet pressure on Cabinet members from their own party elites, to take a pro-Zionist stand. Yet, at the beginning of 1948, the French Government was about to resume a plan, which it dropped in 1946, to help modernize the armies of Syria and Lebanon. This policy stemmed from the strong influence of the pro-Arab Foreign Office, particularly from its Secretary-General J. M. Schauvel, and from the Chief of the Africa-Levant Department, G. Bonneau. These and other French experts had long lamented the way France left the Levant in 1946 and the subsequent distrust and hatred towards her in these countries, which seemed to stand in the way of resuming France's 'traditional' influence in Syria and Lebanon. These experts also held that the mistrust of France was reinforced by the support which the French Government gave in 1947 to illegal Zionist immigration to Palestine. In their opinion, the way to win back the Syrian and the Lebanese goodwill was to give them generous military aid.[8] George Bidault, the Foreign Minister inCEM Schuman's Cabinet, was strongly influenced by this reasoning.

On the Zionist side, the moving influence was Leon Blum, a former Prime Minister in the third and fourth Republics and until recently leader of the Socialist party. Despite being out of Cabinet, and his advanced age, Blum was still an influential figure in his party and nation-wide, particularly among former Resistance members, who were now scattered all across the political spectrum.[9] But the most important factor which momentarily made the political pendulum swing to the Zionist side was the fact that large sections of the French public were pro-Zionist. When it began to appear as if a supply of arms to the

Arabs might antagonize the public and bring down the government yet again,[10] Messers Schuman and Bidault switched to the pro-Zionist side.

Mentally, it was not too difficult for Bidault to switch to the Zionist side, since he was a wartime underground leader, thus a member of a group which after the war remained sympathetic to Jewish causes. Furthermore, Bidault's wife, Susanne, a high Foreign Office official in her own right, was a declared pro-Zionist. So just when preparations were made to send arms to Syria, the head of the Jewish Agency office in Paris, Maurice Fischer, reported that 'the Foreign Minister's attitude towards our cause is no longer unfriendly'. Zionists who talked to Alexander Parodi, the chief French delegate at the UN, reported the latter saying that: 'At the time we opposed partition, but now the establishment of a Jewish state is a French interest'.[11] Soon, France became firm in her demand to implement the UN partition resolution, taking a particularly keen interest in the internationalization of Jerusalem.[12] Still, when in March 1948 the USA reversed her support of partition, the government in Paris was taken aback and Bidault joined the American line. In the face of this development, Blum advised his Zionist friends to urge the Yishuv leaders to proclaim the Jewish state 'immediately'.[13]

For a while, the supporters of military aid to Syria and Lebanon again had the upper hand. For if Palestine underwent a UN trusteeship and the Zionist state was deferred, why not take the opportunity and work for Syria's goodwill? Certainly a green light was given to sending some arms to Syria; for at least one delivery, worth 150 million francs (approximately $800 000) was sent towards the end of March. The relatively small cost of this equipment does not necessarily point to the size of the consignment. France's policy was dictated by political and not commercial considerations and the equipment sent was, anyway, already out of use in the French army. It is not clear what exactly it contained; according to the Haganah intelligence, it had among other things, 105-mm guns, armoured cars, machine-guns and ammunition. According to reports from inside the French Government, more such deliveries were about to come.[14]

But this plan was checked under pressure from the Blum group. When the renewal of arms deliveries to Syria was brought to Blum's knowledge, he persuaded Jules Moch, a Socialist member of the Cabinet, to raise the issue immediately with the Prime Minister. On 31 March, André Blumel, formerly Blum's *chef d'cabinet*, now President of the French Zionist Federation, informed Avigour that 'the next delivery [to Syria] was withheld' and that 'the King of Neter [France]', now in London, 'phoned and asked the pro-Zionist group to meet him upon his return'. Cables of the following day indicated that Schuman had changed his mind. A message from Blumel of 3 April (as a coded Hebrew cable to Tel Aviv tells) was that 'The cabinet in Ir-Perah [Paris], in a stormy session . . . decided to stop arms deliveries to the Yishmaelim [Arabs]'.[15]

However, stopping military aid to Syria was one thing, allowing arms to the Jews was quite another. For at that particular moment, France was a candidate to serve on the Security Council's Palestine Truce Commission, which hardly went along with sending arms to Palestine. But now there was also such a sudden eruption of a pro-Zionist enthusiasm among former Resistance members in public positions, that it transgressed party affiliation and pushed aside other considerations. In mid-April, Fischer reported 'a total change in our favour in the government . . . even among those who earlier supported the Arabs' and Blumel telephoned Avigour (Hebrew coded, again) that 'The King of Neter ordered selling arms to the Jews'. Soon it became apparent that leading members of the French defence establishment, such as the Chief of the General Staff, General George Revere and chiefs of the twin Secret Services, Pierre Boursicot and Roger Wybot, were personally involved in helping the arms accumulated by the Haganah in Europe go through French port facilities.[16]

At that point, France also became a recruiting centre for Mahal and among the French volunteers there were quite a few non-Jewish persons. Several hundreds of French citizens served in the IDF in 1948, many in the so-called 'French Commando' in (Palamach) Brigade 12.

The 'permissive' French policy towards Israel lasted long enough to enable most of the equipment bought in West Europe until then, to go to Israel. The French Government never opposed the embargo, but it quietly postponed its application. Arms-carrying ships sailed from French ports to Israel, with government permission, up until 11 June, the date on which the first truce began.[17]

THE DIMENSION OF FRENCH ASSISTANCE TO THE WARRING PARTIES

The interim summary of military assistance which came to Israel via France and with French assistance up until the end of May, when the embargo was declared, included 30 65-mm guns; 12 120-mm mortars;

25 20-mm guns; 12 75-mm antitank guns and large stocks of ammunition of all sorts, mainly for artillery. During the next 2 weeks, when the embargo had already been in effect, but not as far as France was concerned, the Israeli flotilla brought from France 10 H35 Hotchkiss tanks, more ammunition, small and medium arms. Thereafter, arms bought in French territory continued to be shipped via Italian and other ports. It included 38 75-mm Krup guns, arriving piecemeal between June and August. It was this French assistance which enabled the IDF almost at once to build an artillery corps, and to bring in a sufficient amount of ammunition for it. The French policy also helped to establish the IDF tank corps which, however, did not develop much further than the 10 light French Hotchkiss.[18]

The *Altalena* affair, an IZL's arms ship which embroiled the new state of Israel in a near civil war, also originated from the same French permissiveness. In fact, it was the last Jewish arms ship which sailed from France with government permission. It carried some 5000 British rifles, approximately 300 British machine and submachine-guns, 2–3 million 0.303 small-arms ammunition, a few light British AFVs and a few tons of explosives. Had this transport arrived before the Czech arms, it might have been a significant addition to the still small Jewish arsenal and resulted in a change in the relative power between the IZL and the Haganah. Now, however, this amount was almost negligible (in addition to being incompatible with small arms used by the IDF). Part of the consignment was weapons accumulated separately by IZL, while another part was second-hand British arms once in use by the 'Free France' forces and now donated as a gift.[19]

Notwithstanding the still unresolved Israeli public contention on various moral aspects of this affair, a dispute was later ignited by some historians with the theory that the *Altalena* was a provocation of the French Government to embarrass the government of Israel. To many, this theory does not hold water at all. For while it is true, both by the nature of the preparation of *Altalena*'s sailing and its cargo, that the French government knew she was going to a dissident group, their enthusiasm to help the government of Israel – which was not originally intended, but lurked in the shadow until it abruptly swept the government – was genuine.

For the Israeli Government, the *Altelena* raised another tormenting dilemma. The ship's arrival had received world-wide publicity, because it occurred under the eyes of the UN observers and the press, when the embargo was already in effect. At this point Israel pretended to respect the embargo, but at the same time continued to absorb arms clandestinely. It, therefore tried to reach an agreement with IZL, that before being spotted by UN observers, the ship should be directed at night to one of the sites where the IDF was unloading its own arms. The IZL command, however, objected to 'giving all the arms' to the IDF, claiming they needed it for their forces in Jerusalem. The government was in a cleft stick and decided to report the arrival of the ship to the UN, and when the *Altalena* refused to surrender and set sail at daylight directly to the beach of Tel-Aviv, Ben Gurion decided to turn a bad situation into his advantage, by performing the enforcement of the embargo before the eyes of the UN observers. He ordered opening fire on the ship, using a French 65-mm gun brought earlier, setting the *Altalena* ablaze and destroying its cargo.[20]

But at about the same time that the *Altalena* was prevented from unloading, IDF ships which sailed from French and other ports, continued to unload arms. The IDF General Staff diaries indicate that such unloadings took place on 15, 22, 24 and 27 June, in defiance of the embargo.[21]

But the French Government's attitude soon changed. As from 14 June French observers were on guard with the UN Mediator to see that the embargo was not violated. The French permissiveness towards Israel now changed into observance of the embargo, while the government of Henry Queuille followed suit.[22]

Towards the autumn of 1948 the public sentiment in France steadily changed. Israel no longer looked the underdog, and reports by French observers serving in Palestine which appeared in the French press told of IDF ruthlessness. Some of the French observers in Palestine were wounded and even killed in action, and often Israeli troops were blamed for this. News of bad treatment by IDF soldiers of French religious institutions in Palestine, the failure of the internationalization of Jerusalem, the IDF occupation of Lebanese villages in October and the plight of the Arab refugees, all worked to Israel's detriment. When the French government learned of the ammunition exhaustion in the Syrian and Lebanese armies, the Foreign Office was for lifting the embargo and helping them. In February 1949, a ship, probably French, called at the port of Beirut and unloaded French ammunition for the Syrian army. In March, a Syrian military mission was in Paris, as well as in London. France now joined Britain in putting pressure to bear on Washington and on Dr Bunche to lift the embargo. It was the Syrians who hesitated entering into commitment to buy French equipment, because they hoped that once the embargo was lifted they could, instead, get British or American arms.[23] Suspicion of French motives still dominated political life in Syria. Politicians used the label 'French connections' when they wished to besmear political opponents.[24]

ARMS SUPPLY FROM SWITZERLAND

Switzerland's geographic situation between East and West in Europe, her neutrality, financial dependability and the confidentiality of her bank system, all made her an ideal clearing house for any illegal arms purchase. Switzerland was also a respectable arms producer. Israel bought here brand new 20-mm Hispano-Swiza mini-guns and paid for almost all her purchases in the world with dollars, transferred from the USA to Swiss banks. In March 1948, the headquarters of the Rechesh organization moved from Paris to Geneva. Egypt, too, used secret deposits in Swiss banks to pay for arms purchases abroad and she sought the services of the Swiss arms concern 'Oerlikon', in purchasing arms in other European countries.

The HS 20-mm guns, which Arazi started to buy in Switzerland in January 1948, were the first 'artillery' the IDF had. The first purchase included 50 pieces, of which the first 12 were secretly brought to the port of Tel Aviv on 23 April, under a heavy layer of onions and potatoes. More arrived after 15 May. By the end of May their number in the IDF was 32 and at the end of 1948, following their success, the number of 20-mm guns in the IDF surpassed 100 (the IDF also bought other guns of the same calibre). Israel never suffered any shortage of ammunition for these guns, because the producer sold the guns along with 1000 shells each and provided a written guarantee to supply more upon demand. After the October campaign the IDF still had a reserve of 160 000 such shells, which was soon doubled. Early in 1949, the level of the 20-mm stores in the IDF was 350 000 shells.[25] Diverse use was made of these guns: direct-laying machine-gunning, anti-aircraft and anti-tank defence (though these guns did not have armour-piercing shells), in aircraft and the Navy, etc. Formally, the purchase was made under a Nicaraguan order, but the Swiss knew exactly who the customer was, and allowed Haganah officers to visit the factory and test the guns.[26] The price was $13 000 a piece, including 1000 shells per gun.

Another successful Israeli purchase of artillery, made in Switzerland in May, included 50 used German 75-mm Krup guns, with 100 000 shells. The deal was made here, but the guns had to be collected from several locations in France, Italy and Algeria. These massive field-guns arrived bit by bit between June and September, all in good condition.[27]

In 1948 there was also Iraqi, Egyptian and Syrian searches for arms in Switzerland, but to no practical result – only scandal. Egypt sought the services of the 'Oerlikon' Concern, which its behalf mediated for the sales to Egypt of obsolete 105-mm guns, bad hand grenades and useless artillery ammunition in Spain and in Italy. This deal was one of the main items in the corruption trial held in Egypt in 1950. Militarily speaking, no significant help to the Arab war effort came from any deal made in Switzerland in 1948.[28]

ARMS PURCHASES IN BELGIUM

In Belgium, there was a concentration of American L.L. equipment, now owned by private dealers. Belgium also had an arms industry. But the government, consisting of Socialists and Catholics and headed by Paul Henry Spaak, was a stable one and her foreign policy was unlikely to be swayed by domestic pressure. The Zionists regarded Spaak as a supporter of their cause and, basically, as a Social Democrat he was. But he was more concerned with the strategic strength of the West and with the prestige of the UN, which turned him into a staunch supporter of a Palestine embargo, even before it was declared by the UN.[29] In April, Belgium became a member of the Truce Commission, along with France and the USA and as from 13 June, Belgian officers served as observers in Palestine. Some of these soldiers were killed or injured in action and this cemented the public support of the Prime Minister's arms policy.

As early as March 1948, it became impossible for the Palestine rivals to buy, legally, either used or new equipment in Belgium. In January, Egyptian purchasers still bought several thousand British rifles and 0.303-mm ammunition, worth $1.7 million, to make up for the stoppage of the British supply. But when Brigadier Hafez returned to Brussels in March, with orders of more of the same, the Belgian Foreign Office sought the British advice and on the strength of it turned the request down. Later on, it vetoed an attempt by the Belgian firm 'Armat' to get a licence to export guns produced by the 'Fabrique National' (a private firm) to Egypt. Illegal arms purchase, however, *was* possible. As early as December 1947, Egypt bought in Belgium nine used British Stirling bombers, by a Tangieric order. In the summer of 1948 it managed to import six of them, and three of the six became airworthy. However, their function as bombers was utterly defective.[30]

Israeli agents used Belgium as a market for a variety of spare parts. But another important purchase was some 40 American half tracks, which were sent to Israel by train and boat, via Italy, during the first truce.[31]

ARMS PURCHASES IN ITALY

As the imposition of the UN embargo became more effective, Italy remained the embargo's Achilles' heel. The Apennine Peninsula was not only the biggest dumping ground of L.L. equipment in Europe, but a territory with a long coastline, many harbours and a weak government, which was not particularly interested in checking the illegal expert of military equipment. Italy was not yet a member of the United Nations.

The main concentrations of equipment, known in Italy as 'the RR-RR stores', were at Livorno, Pisa, Caserta, Rome and Milano. As early as September 1946, the USA OFLC in Rome signed an agreement with the Italian Ministry of Trade, to sell all the American equipment in Italy to the government, for $160 million. A *prima facie* condition was the neutralization of every implement of war, before selling it on to citizens. But this principle was not always complied with.[32] Scrap-dealers, in their attempt to upgrade the value of their merchandise, often outwitted the authorities by evading such action. The OFLC established a special authority to supervise compliance with the regulations, namely, the 'Field Compliance Office'. But this body dealt mainly with complaints against discrimination in tenders, not with lax neutralization.[33]

Law enforcement in Italy was loose, particularly at the local level. Trading with military equipment was in most cases in the hands of former army and police officers. Their activities rarely bothered the local police, unless they turned violent or were suspected of serving the Communist underground. In the used equipment market, as Israeli agents recalled, 'one could buy everything on the cheap side, and if one insisted, one could test the equipment, and in some cases even recondition it on the spot'.[34] Israelis, who bought equipment in Italy, were long familiar personalities in this trade and with the fauna and flora in many Italian ports. Arab agents were in most cases newcomers, but some of them were fast learners. Both registered as representing governments or firms of other countries and put fake destinations on their bills of Loading. One Israeli agent reported, that on one occasion, in September, the port bulletin, instead of denoting the cover-up destination, put down Haifa and yet the cargo was allowed to pass without a hitch. Bribe was acceptable as a norm.[35]

The Italian market also sold new implements of war, produced by the Italian arms industry. Its quality was somewhat below the level of the same products elsewhere, but their price was far cheaper. In 1948, the most attractive Italian products were light artillery, aircraft and ships. The embargo hardly bothered the Italian authorities as the government was interested in expanding its country's exports.

The Israelis had an advantage over their Egyptian rivals, with their better knowledge of Italy and their superior technological ability to handle used equipment. Although technically the export of arms from Italy required a licence, it was none too difficult to obtain one.

Nevertheless, much of the equipment bought by the Arabs and the Israelis in Italy in 1948 proved useless, at least for the 1948 war. The trouble with the used equipment was the difficulty of undoing the damage caused by the neutralization, and the trouble with new equipment was that it usually took longer to supply it than the contract obliged and that it proved impossible to learn to use it within a short time. On the whole, there was nothing but deep disappointed with the purchases from Italy.

THE ISRAELI PURCHASE OF ARMS FROM ITALY IN 1948

The Haganah arms procurement in Italy began with the shipment to Palestine of two caches of small arms, ammunition and explosives, which had been hidden in Magenta and Bari since 1945. The consignment, several hundred rifles and a few scores of machine and sub-machine-guns, arrived safely in January 1948.[36] Such an amount of weapons would be almost negligible after May, but in January it served as a significant reinforcement to the Haganah arsenal.

Arms acquisition on a larger scale began in February, when a group of Haganah agents, who had known Italy from their former illegal immigration activities, began searching for naval guns. This group was losely controlled from Rome by Ada Syreni, until Arazi stepped it. These Italian purchases still received only scant attention from Tel Aviv, but with the growing disappointment from the acquisitions in the USA, and the increasing difficulties with Czech aid and Arazi's confinement to Europe, the Haganah purchasing machinery in Italy increased its search (which now included artillery, ammunition, armour, and even aircraft). Following the good use made of 20-mm guns, Israel bought in Italy 30 brand new 20-mm Isetta Fraskini guns with a good deal of ammunition, which arrived in Israel in September. With the help of Israel's military industry at home, Italy became a major source of supply for old artillery ammunition, which was then 'refreshed' at home. A retired Italian colonel-turned-scrap-dealer tested the samples of ammunition. Registration of series of shells was made regularly to prevent the 'contamination' of larger stocks in case some ammunition was found dangerous for use; this was a measure the Egyptians failed to take.[37]

The Israeli search for naval ships yielded few useful results. In 1948 the situation was summed up as follows:

> One towing ship, two Landing Crafts (LCT) and two other ships (which) were moored in Haifa for the duration of the war without use. 6 mini-Landing Crafts, which arrived after the war, and a fuel tanker bought but never arrived . . . only a commando equipment and two coast-guard boats (SS *Haportzim, Galia*) were of real use.[38]

In August 1948, when the IDF Command was preparing for its grand offensive, stress was put on the acquisition of aircraft and tanks. Israel turned down an offer made by the Italian arms concern to buy 'ready to use' *Macchi* and *Fiat* fighter aircraft, mainly because she expected the Czech Spitfires to arrive in time. Meanwhile, Arazi came out with a proposal to buy used Spitfires which he saw in an Italian stock, said to be airworthy 'soon'. However, the bidder for these aircraft was unable to guarantee any deadline for finishing their renovation, so this offer, too, was turned down.

The importation of American-made Shermans from Italy looked more promising. Arazi reported spotting a large stock of such tanks near Milano and he assured Geneva that he could 'send them with all that goes: guns, equipment and ammunition, at the end of the month' (September). If Arazi was as good as his word, Israel would gain an immense advantage on the battlefield, having at her disposal a tank with speed, armour and gunpower far superior to anything the Arab armies had. The trouble was that Israeli experts were not sure that they could fully recondition the sabotaged tanks' guns. But when Arazi's Egyptian counterpart, Abdul Latif (Rudi) Ragayillah, began to take an interest in the same tanks and it became known that Ragayilah was assured by the Italian dealers 'to have the tanks ready for action in a month time', Arazi urged Geneva to outsmart his Arab rival by buying 50 of the best of these tanks, if only to prevent the Egyptians from picking them up. Since the price of the tanks was in the vicinity of $3000 apiece, Arazi independently decided to earmark 41 of the tanks and made an advance payment to the dealer. He acted likewise with regard to 30 000 75-mm gun-shells.[39]

Meanwhile, the IDF General Staff rushed its best Ordnance Officer, Yeruham Kafkafi, to Italy to examine the tanks and opine on the chance to have the Shermans serviceable in a few weeks. But Kafkafi was only ready to vouch for the reconditioning of the tanks themselves, not the guns. Tel Aviv cabled Geneve: (we are) 'Desperate for Leonard's (Italy) Shermans but not without the guns'. A cable of 16 September made it clear what bothered them: 'will the tanks not remain pointless scrap metal?' Two days later a further cable followed: 'if Kafkafi's opinion is positive – send it right away'. Since Kafkafi remained sceptical, the newly appointed Geneva chief, Pinhas Sapir, came to Italy in person and decided on the spot to buy only 30 tanks and he ordered the sending of three ships to load the tanks. On 21 September the first 17 Shermans were sent by train to the port of Civitavecchia, along with 30 tons of onion and canned food, to hide them from a possible UN inspection.[40]

Now another event interfered in the departure of the tanks. On the night of 19 September, Israeli commandoes destroyed four Macchi aircraft, due to be sent to Egypt, at a hanger near Vanguno. On that occasion they also destroyed some innocent Italian planes.[41] The Italian police were alerted and increased their vigil over the Israeli agents. To make things worse, the ship which was due to take the tanks was late arriving at the port of embarkation and the tanks stood exposed at the depot. Arazi tried to save the situation by ordering the train to continue circling in idle routes, but this attracted even more attention. Finally, the police confiscated the tanks.[42] The next consignments of Shermans did arrived in Israel, but this was only towards the end of November and then early in January 1949.[43] By then the IDF decisive offensive was long over. But even if these tanks had arrived in October, it would have been impossible to put them into service because their guns remained defective. With the exception of two tanks, for which replacement guns were found, it took Israel many more months and much technical 'cannibalism', before the Italian Shermans entered the IDF OB. The Egyptian experience with Italian Shermans was similar, only it took even longer to make them serviceable.[44]

Table 10 Israeli arms acquisition in Western Europe, Australia and South
Africa

Source and sort	Amount, number and date of purchase	Entered service
France, Switzerland		
H35 Hotchkiss tanks	(15?) March	(10) June
65 mm guns (including naval guns)	(60) February–March	(5) May
		(49) Until August
75 mm Krup	(50) August	(50) September–December
Artillery ammunition		
20, 57, 65, 75 mm	(180 000)	May–September
20 mm HS guns	(50) January	(12) April
		(15) June–August
	(20) October	(43) October
120 mm mortars	(22) April–July	(12) May
		(10) June–August
Other guns	About 20	(20) September–December
Italy		
20 mm IF	(30) May	(30) October
Mark 4 Sherman tanks	(41) August	(30) Autumn 1949
Artillery ammunition and explosives	'Any amount needed' Problems of quality	From October
Naval equipment		
LCT	(2) April	(2) (Not used)
ML, etc.	(4) April	(2) July–August
Commando boats	(6) June	(6) August
LCM	(6) April	1949
The Netherlands		
C47 Dakota	June (by Van Leer)	
Belgium		
M4 US half tracks	(50) April	(35–40) June
		(10–15) October
Variety equipment		Continuously
Germany (US zone)		
UC64 Noorduyin aircraft	(20) February	(12) May–October
South Africa and Australia		
Light aircraft	(11) March–May	(5) May
Lockheed Hudson	(4)	(4) November 1948–May 1949
Douglas DC5		(1) June

THE EGYPTIAN ARMS PURCHASE IN ITALY

As from mid-May, Egypt's budget was inflated and the Minister of War had at his disposal a huge sum to buy arms in sources other than British. However, lack of knowledge of the market and corrupt motives made the Minister, in conjunction with the King's Court, commission the services of foreign mediators and businessmen to do the job. This combination of inexperience and corruption ruined any attempt to end the shortage created by the embargo. It was already August before the Egyptian purchasing began, but the trouble was not only this delay but the fact that most of the purchases, (of both new equipment or of war surplusses) were made without checking the quality. Meanwhile, high-ranking Egyptian officers such as the Deputy Minister of War, the Commander of the Engineer Corp, the Chief of the Army's Acquisition and scores of other officers, privately pocketed part of the budget.[45]

Many of the Egyptian purchases were made through a corporation called 'Egi-Italia', established for this purpose, which was run by an Italian businessman of Egyptian origin, Abdul Latif Ragailah, helped by Colonel Omar seif al Din and a flight officer, Colonel Jizrin. Egi's agents negotiated small arms, ammunition, artillery, torpedo boats, naval equipment, tanks and, above all, new fighter aircraft. On 13 August Egi signed a contract for the supply of 24 205 Macchi fighters at the cost of 47 millions Italian lire each, with an option of extending it to 48 aircraft. Twelve more Macchis were added to the deal on 13 November and an additional contract in December was for 24 G55 Fiat aircraft, the production of which had not yet started. The cost of the air purchase (perhaps the Macchis alone) was reported as $25 million. In November, a group of Egyptian pilots was sent to Varese to learn how to operate the Italian planes – a terribly late moment to do so. Egi also negotiated the supply by an Italian shipyard of 10 torpedo boats, 3 MAS (anti-submarine) boats for over $100 000 each, and 2 corvettes for over $7 million each. Artillery ammunition worth over a $1 million was ordered in December. To guarantee payment for these large deals Egypt mortgaged her next year's cotton crop for 33 million Swiss francs, and when this was not enough King Farouk volunteered to mortgage one of his bank accounts in Switzerland.[46]

Like the Israelis, the Egyptians were wrong in assessing that they would be able to use their purchases from Italy to improve their position in the war. The Macchis, expected in September, began to arrive piecemeal only in November.[47] When some of them were scrambled for the first time towards the end of December, the result was that three of them were shot down while others were destroyed on the ground.[48] The latter part of Egypt's aircraft deal in Italy materialized months after the signing of the Egyptian – Israeli armistice. Egypt also bought some 50–60 Sherman tanks from the same source as Israel. But the making of some of them serviceable lasted years.[49] The Syrians, roused by the Egyptian purchases, also entered into negotiation in Italy for 24 Macchi fighters and a few Macchi trainers. Their deal, however, materialized only after the autumn of 1949, and during 1950.[50]

MILITARY PURCHASES IN THE US MILITARY ZONE OF GERMANY

In the American military zone of Germany, L. L. equipment was on sale from American ex-servicemen.[51] This favouratism was designed to increase compliance with the law, but it was cunningly exploited by the Sonneborn Institute in New York to the contrary. The Institute made contact with one David Miller, a former US Air Force lieutenant colonel, now a scrap-dealer living in Paris and sent Arazi and Fredkens to him, who negotiated 30 UC64 Nooduyins (Norsman), a cargo aircraft used for landing in rough terrain. Miller arranged for the aircraft to be reconditioned at Schiphol, The Netherlands, supposedly for a company called 'Somoco', said to be engaged in mining in the Congo. A group of Mahal pilots were gathered to fly these planes from The Netherlands to Israel or to Czechoslovakia, as required, via Paris. The planes' fuel tanks were extended to require as few as possible refuelling stopovers. The FBI and the US military authorities in Germany were slow to trace Miller and they were unable to prevent the departure of the aircraft from Schiphol. Early in May, the Norsman aircraft began arriving in France, where for a while they were safe.[52].

Twenty Norsman aircraft were eventually bought by Arazi and Fredkens. However, the Anglo-American cooperation in hot pursuit after them did a lot to complicate their subsequent movement. In addition, the hasty reconditioning of the derelict aircraft made them risky to fly (Israeli pilots nicknamed them 'asses' and 'flying coffins'). Two of them arrived in time for the proclamation of Israel, but one crashed upon landing and the other crushed on 10 May when on a bombing mission in the Jerusalem hills. Three more Norseman aircraft arrived in Israel before the beginning of the embargo and five more managed to leave Schiphol just after the embargo was imposed. But of these last, two crashed in Czechoslovakia and yet another in Italy. The remaining two landed by mistake in Gaza and their crews were taken prisoner by the Egyptians. Following a long judicial struggle in Dutch courts, five more were later released. They arrived in Israel in September. In October, the Israeli Air Force had five serviceable 'Norsemen'.[53]

The Egyptians, too, tried to buy military equipment in the American zone in Germany. In July, a Greek scrap-dealer called Zephirias, acting on behalf of Brigadier Hafez, made an advance payment for old American tanks. The US military authorities were immediately on Zephirias's heels. The dealer was warned that he might lose his licence if he violated the embargo and the deal did not go any further.[54]

EGYPT'S ARMS PURCHASE IN SPAIN

The Franco Government in Spain was the last and only Fascist regime which survived the Second World War. Now, Franco saw a vital interest in obtaining legitimacy from the Western world (particularly from the USA), or at least a *modus vivendi*, without having to give up power or to change the system of his government. Franco desired to join the UN, the North Atlantic Treaty Organization and, if possible, to receive a 'Marshall Plan aid'. The development of the Cold War seemed to provide him with some hope of getting out of isolation and the road towards achieving this looked fairly clear. Franco regarded an improving relationship with the USA as the major aim of Spain's foreign policy and he was ready to go a long way in respecting American foreign interests, even when they somehow negated his own.[55] However, public opinion in the USA at large and more so in Western Europe abhorred his regime. Thus, although Spain was highly interested in developing good relations with the Arab world, it eventually did not appear to Madrid too great a sacrifice to abide by the embargo. This tendency stood in the way of Egypt's acquisition of arms in Spain, which probably was unlikely to help her much anyway.

Spain did not produce weapons, nor did it host L. L. dumps, but it had its own accumulation of scrap arms, trading in which was at the hands of private entreprenuers close to Franco's circle. In February

1948, the US Charge d'Affaires in Madrid, Paul Culbertson, reported Egyptian contacts buying arms in Spain. He wrote that Egypt negotiated buying 'a lot of leftovers of the Spanish civil war', including small arms, small-arms ammunition, hand grenades, 105-mm guns with ammunition, as well as old 25-pounder shells. The surprising part was the large volume of the intended purchase, equipment which was in a bad shape and yet cost some two million Egyptian Pounds, approximately $9 million. The negotiation started when Egypt had already lost her British sources of supply but had not yet decided on sending her army to Palestine. For the time being, no instruction came from Washington.[56]

When Egypt's joined the war in Palestine, her purchases drive in Spain increased. As elsewhere, wherever Egyptian purchases were made, a shoal of middlemen swarmed around. The Swiss 'Oerlikon' firm came in, following its undertaking to equip the Egyptian army with ten batteries of field artillery and ammunition. More dubious characters such as Victor Oswald (who sold equipment to Israel too), Patric Domville, a former RAF officer renowned for 'not taking up any business worth less than a million Dollars' and General Jose Delgado, a member of the Madrid's high society, were involved. These people profitted from the deal and cared little for the Egyptian army. More amazingly, the Egyptian officers involved, too, seemed to care little. As a result, the equipment in question was again bought without being checked.[57] In any event, the deal was far from being completed when in Washington Lovett instructed Culbertson to express to the Spanish Foreign Office concern over Spain's violation of the embargo. As a result, in August the unfinished deal was suspended. The Spanish purchases did more harm than good to the Egyptian army by 'contaminating' larger stocks of ammunition, which then had to be disposed of. The 105 guns in question were also found to be unserviceable. Meanwhile, so many people had dishonestly profited from the deal that it was only a matter of time before it blew up in the Egyptian government's face.[58]

ISRAELI ACQUISITION IN BRITISH COMMONWEALTH COUNTRIES

Israeli acquisition in South Africa and Australia was never part of any plan made in Tel Aviv, but instead was the initiative of local members of the two Jewish communities. South Africa served as a source for Mahal volunteers, particularly pilots and doctors, and was also a source of small aircraft given as a gift. Some of these aircraft arrived at a very early stage in the war and were useful in the improvised bombing of Arab positions. There was, however, a high rate of failures: out of 11 aircraft which took to the road from South Africa during April and May, only five Bonanzas and Fairchilds reached their destination. Israel's acquisition from Australia included one DC5 Douglas plane, which entered service in June and a Lockheed Loadstar plane which entered service in September. An additional four Hudsons arrived – but only after the war.[59]

7 The Value and Effect of the UN Supervision of the Embargo

The task of the UN observers in Palestine was to maintain the cease-fire and keep the military balance intact and the territorial *status quo* unchanged until a political settlement could be attained.[1] The rival parties, on the other hand, tried their best to change the *status quo* and improve their respective positions, in order to decide the war in their favour at the next round of fighting. In a war which was, in fact, an armed truce interrupted by short outbreaks of fighting, the role of the UN observers would be expected to be decisive, but it was not so.

THE UN OBSERVER CORPS UP UNTIL THE END OF THE FIRST TRUCE

The establishment of the UN Observer Corps in Palestine, later called the UN Truce Supervision Operation (UNTSO), was based on the Security Council's resolution of 29 May, which initiated the truce and the embargo. Under that resolution, the UN Mediator in conjunction with the SC Truce Commission was 'to supervise the observance of the truce', helped by a 'sufficient number of military observers' and see 'that no war material or fighting personnel were introduced into Palestine, Egypt, Iraq, Lebanon, Saudi Arabia, Syria and Yemen during the truce'.[2] The resolution did not specify what a 'sufficient number' of observers was, or from which countries they should come, or how they should operate. The UN Mediator, himself inexperienced in this kind of a job, was not able to get the Security Council's advice on these matters, because the Council itself was split over these issues. Bernadotte was not free to make his own decision on the situation: when his decisions were not liked by the USA, the Americans threatened to withdraw their support, and when he changed his mind to follow the American dictate, he was harshly criticized by the USSR. This action left the way open for countries such as Czechoslovakia not to abide by the embargo rules. At least Bernadotte was lucky to have at his disposal an experienced team of UN officials, headed by Dr Ralph Bunche, who knew Palestine well.

Bernadotte's immediate intention was to mobilize observers from both sides of the Iron Curtain, but the USA forced him to accept a formula according to which observers could only come from the three countries which were members of the Truce Commission, namely USA, France and Belgium, with the addition of a few Swedes. UNTSO was clearly designed to be an instrument of the Western powers to implement their plan of a settlement. The small number of observers put at the Mediator's disposal also resulted from the Cold War situation. The manpower establishment chart for the Observers Corps was drawn up by a badly-briefed, low-ranking British soldier, Major Guy Campbell, who had been sent by his uncle, the British Ambassador in Cairo, to give Bernadotte practical advice about Palestine. Campbell knew Palestine well, but had the wrong idea as to what the task of the observers should be. He believed that he was being asked to calculate how to man checkpoints on the Palestine borders and he was not told that they would have to supervise 500 km of twisting front-line in difficult terrain, most of it *inside* Palestine, as well as airfields, ports, coastlines and lines of supplies' in seven countries. Thus, Major Campbell simply multiplied the number of the border-crossings to Palestine by four and added one command post, reaching the figure of 68 observers. Since the UN Secretary-General in New York, Trygve Lie, was desperate to obtain some figures in order to launch the peacekeeping operation, Campbell's temporary assessment was rushed to him, and it was approved by the Security Council.[3] When this assessment turned out to be numerically highly inadequate, the USSR had already objected to the way in which the observers were selected and it was no longer easy to extend the number of observers.

The 68-man establishment was thus divided equally between the USA, France and Belgium, 21 officers from each, with five more officers from the Swedish army. Even this arrangement took too long to implement. When the first truce came into effect not a single UN observer was yet in operational position[4] and when the observers did begin to arrive, they came piecemeal. In its initial strength, the force did not suffice even for the task of supervising the cease-fire, which was the mediator's first priority. Bernadotte's second priority was to supervise food convoys to besieged Jewish Jerusalem and to the Negev and checking Jewish immigration, to which he committed himself in return for the two parties acceptance of the truce. Bernadotte also needed men for headquarters, communication and general services. In the end, not many, if any, were left for the task of checking the seaports, airports and coasts, which came last in the order of priorities. Still, Bernadotte wished to look as if he was carrying out all his duties at once. He would thus often send men to do a superficial checking at one point and then move them to another job.[5]

The mediator's distress became known in New York, and yet for most of the truce period it was impossible to extend the force, at least not by professional soldiers. On 23 June, Trygve Lie, who had been looking for a palliative, mobilized 49 members of the UN Guard Force, and sent them to Palestine. These people had no military expertise or status and were psychologically unprepared for the difficult job which awaited them. Criticism from the USSR and casualties suffered by this group, brought their return to New York early in July.[6] When, at last, Lie managed to extend the establishment strength of the Observers Corps by 27, the truce collapsed and the matter sunk into oblivion. At this point, the USA was quite reluctant to increase her participation in the force, but tried to be helpful in other ways. Rear Admiral Sherman, Commander in Chief of the US Sixth Fleet, stationed in Eastern Mediterranean, sent equipment and experts to build a radio communication system for the mediator. The British, who could not send men at all, lent Bernadotte military vehicles and a squadron of Auster reconnaissance aircraft, which were flown by American pilots.[7] British and American intelligence was extended to Bernadotte on the sailing of illegal arms to Palestine and as from 24 June, three US Navy destroyers were assigned to watch over the coasts of the Mediterranean, with a French Corvette joining in later on.[8] However, the authority given to these ships to act was very limited. They were not allowed to stop a ship at high sea for search, nor to follow a ship into territorial water. On no occasion was a cargo confiscated by a UN naval vessel. Furthermore, no similar naval task was carried out along the coasts of the Red Sea or the Persian Gulf.[9]

During the 4 weeks of the first truce, which ended on 9 July, only one permanent check-point was established at ports (namely, in Tel Aviv) with a very small staff. No checks were seriously made at any other sea- or airport.

THE OBSERVER CORPS DURING THE SECOND TRUCE

Bernadotte's efforts to get more observers won vehement support from the UN Secretary General, but not from the USSR or the USA. The former opposed it because she herself was barred from serving on it, and the latter for fear of being sucked into a growing military involvement in Palestine, which she was determined to avoid. When, at last, the USA was persuaded to add nine more observers, it became apparent that the Arab League would decide not to extend the truce, and the Pentagon was quite relieved to learn that the additional men would not have to go to Palestine. Meanwhile, facing a renewal outbreak of fighting on 8 July, Bernadotte ordered the observers to leave their posts and to go back to their home countries. The force was literally dismantled and the arena was left unattended by observers not only for the duration of the 10 days fighting which ensued, but longer. At the end of July, the supervision apparatus was still not yet operative. For the second truce a new force had to be built afresh and valuable time, experience and prestige were lost.[10]

The main reason for this new delay was a misunderstanding between the UN Secretariate and the government of the USA, which was wholly characteristic of the internal confusion in the US Government about their role in Palestine. When Bernadotte visited the USA after the collapse of the first truce, his appearance before the Security Council was effective and evidently impressed the Americans. It helped to bring about a new, firm resolution which helped restore the truce, this time for an unlimited period. But Trygve Lie and his lieutenants were wrong to conclude that there was a change in the USA policy towards participation in the Observers Corps. Under the advice of Commander Robert Jackson, Lie's Executive Assistant, Bernadotte returned to his headquarters on the island of Rhodes and immediately approached Admiral Sherman, who was also stationed there, with an unusual request. He asked for a 'loan' of US marines, some 1000–1500 men in arms, to maintain the truce in Jerusalem. Bernadotte even pointed out the formation he wanted. The embarrassed Admiral allowed Bernadotte to use his wireless network and Bernadotte sent this request to the Secretary of State Marshall.[11]

This action outraged both the Departments of State and Defence in Washington, first because the very idea was loathsome to them and, secondly, because Bernadotte broke all rules of procedure. It was as if Bernadotte had shot himself in the foot. The immediate decision in Washington was to withhold sending any men to the mediator, pending clarification of the USA commitment to the UN in Palestine. The action confused the other governments which contributed personnel to the Observers Corps.[12] As a result the second truce started, again with the UN Observers not in position. In consequence, there was no way that the Security Council could establish the position of the warring parties in Palestine when the fire stopped on 18 July, if indeed it stopped at all. Both sides continued to try and gain ground, and on several occasions (namely at Kharatiya, Tel Azzaziat, Aslouj, Government House, Latrun, the Southern Carmel enclave) serious fighting continued which created significant changes of the front lines between 18 and 30 July. When eventually UN Observers arrived, their most urgent task was to demarcate the new truce lines. Again, maintaining the embargo remained the least of their priorities.[13]

However, towards the end of July, CIA reports exposed the dimensions of Israel's arms purchases and her preparations to break the truce. This brought an end to the USA evasiveness. Suddenly, both Marshall and Forrestall were of the opinion that the military balance in Palestine, which was considered vital to Western strategy, was at risk and that if the war was to be renewed, the Anglo-American plan for a settlement might be untenable and Anglo-American cooperation thwarted. The panacea now recommended in Washington was 'a true restoration of the truce', which entailed reinforcement of UNTSO. The former principle of 'equality in contribution between Truce Commission members' was abandoned. A senior US marine officer, Brigadier William Riley, was appointed Deputy Chief of Staff to General Aage Lundstrom, Bernadotte's Chief of Staff, and a so far unknown efficiency was demonstrated in the recruitment of more observers. On 25 August, an additional 125 Americans were sent to UNTSO, the strength of which had, in consequence, surpassed 300 men, half of them Americans.[14] After the assassination of Bernadotte by Israeli terrorists on 17 September, the USA practically took charge of the UN mediation. Dr Bunche became acting mediator, Riley was promoted to a Major-General and replaced Lundstrom as Chief of Staff. After the establishment of the third truce in early November, the number of UN observers reached 430. By early 1949 it was 572.[15]

Israel's Foreign Ministry often protested to the mediator on 'the uneven deployment of observers in Israel and the Arab states ... which gave impression that the truce is not supervised on the Arab side'.[16] Of course, from the point of view of the danger to the future of the truce, Israel was now the side to watch rather than the Arab states. However, with the growth of UNTSO, the observers began to be sent to permanent

Table 11   The number of UN personnel and major equipment at the
disposal of the observers corps at selected times[17]

Date	Observers in posts	Reconnaisance aircraft	Patrol ships	Period in the war
11.6.48	None	None	None	Beginning of first truce
20.6.48	55	8	None	First truce
3.7.48	68 (+49)	8	4	First truce
12.7.48	6	None	None	10 day fighting
20.7.48	None	None	3	Beginning of second truce
2.8.48	115	5	3	Second truce
17.9.48	314	14	4	Second truce
12.1.49	430	18	3	End of fighting

positions in the ports and airports in Arab countries as well. In early
September observers were at last permanently deployed in all the major ports in Israel and in most of those of the Arab states and kept a
24 hours vigil.[18] However, this reinforced deployment came, by and
large, too late and still proved insufficient to prevent arms smuggling.

In August, cooperation at the top level on the Palestine issue between London and Washington became more focused. Plans discussed
in Washington during Bunche's visit there in early August turned into
a secret agreement between the State Department and the Foreign Office,
on the practical course of implementing the Anglo-American partition
plan. It was again agreed that this design must be based on the delimi-
tation of the present truce frontiers as the basis for the future political
boundaries between Israel and Transjordan, and on the demonstration
of a determination by the Security Council to maintain the truce and
to punish its violators.[19]

The need for firm Anglo-American action became acute following
an incident in the second week of August, in which IDF troops in
Jerusalem tried to capture Government House. The British and Americans saw this incident as a rehearsal for an imminent Israeli offensive,
which they hoped to deter. Since the incident occurred when both
Bernadotte and Bunche were away, the USA did not wait, but immediately convened the SC, where on 18 August it passed jointly with
the British, a resolution warning the parties in Palestine from trying to
change the *status quo*. In the second week of September, when Bernadotte was back in Rhodes, the two governments, which did not fully
trust him to act as they wished him to, secretly sent two envoys to

dictate to Bernadotte both the outlines of the Anglo-American design and the procedure they wished to follow in attaining it.[20]

THE TRUCE SUPERVISION AT ITS PEAK

After the assassination of Bernadotte on 17 September, the US keenness to get involved in keeping the truce was felt in the field. Many new American officers joined UNTSO, while tired observers were released. But the long neglect of the supervision of the truce until then had already caused irreversible damage to the observers' prestige and authority. As the number of observers increased, their authority continued to plummet, particularly in Israel and Egypt. The governments of these two countries simply barred UN observers from getting to the front when they had something to hide and often the Iraqis, too, acted in the same way. The UN Command became blindfold and could report neither the preparation of the Israeli offensive prior to 15 October, nor, for several days, the situation at the front.

The methods used by the parties to sabotage the observers work was diverse. Basically it was to leave the harrassment and interference with the observers work to lower echelons of officers. But, typically, it took 5 days from the outbreak of the fighting in the Negev in October until General Riley was able to report to the Security Council what was the situation at the front. The process of ordering a cease-fire was delayed until the seventh day of the Israeli offensive. Observers on the Israeli side only got to the Negev front on 24 October and in Galilee, where the IDF offensive ended on 31 October, only on 2 November. By then, the UN Observers found the frontiers so very much changed that there was nothing they could do before a political decision was made by the Security Council.

Riley tried to inspire his men with a more resilient policy. When it seemed obvious in early December that Israel was preparing yet another offensive in the south, he instructed his officers to head to the front without permission from the Israeli Command. In this case, however, he wrongly read the Israeli strategy and unwittingly helped Israel's deception plan, aimed at attracting the Egyptian attention to the Khan Yunis – Raffah section, while the main IDF thrust came further south, at the Halutza-Auja area. However, heroically as the Chief of Staff of UNTSO and some of his men acted, their attention remained focused on the front, not on the prevention of arms smuggling.[21]

THE WARRING PARTIES AND THE UN SUPERVISION

The first truce began when the work of the Israeli arms flotilla and airlift Balak, were in full swing. Israel's leaders and the IDF Command were first greatly perturbed by the fear that their deliveries from France and Czechoslovakia be intercepted. The diaries of the Rechesh chiefs indicate contradictory instructions. In early June the IDF Command urged Geneve to 'send every available equipment quickly to Beit Ilan (Tel Aviv) before the truce started'. Soon, the order was to 'hold all sailing of *kvedim* (artillery, armour)' and then again, 'speed up deliveries'. But on 17 June, when the truce was a week old, the IDF Command cabled Avigour: 'don't hesitate to open new seminars' (meaning keep sending more ships). Subsequent cables were inspired with more and still more confidence and joy: 'We are managing to overcome the UN', said one cable. The small number of observers and the rare prospect of the coming of reinforcements to the few observers, enhanced a rule made by the Acquisition Department in the IDF General Staff, never to hold deliveries of arms or to slow them down because of UN inspection. When the arrival of a certain vessel or a plane carrying arms became known to the UN observers, the practice was to prevent them from approaching the site until the unloading was over. The actual excuse, ploy or trick to keep the observers away was of a secondary importance. This task was carried out with growing 'skill' by the Departments of Acquisition and UN Liaison, of the G. Branch, headed by Lt. Colonel Baruch Komrov.[22]

The Arab governments, which were badly prepared to run independent arms supply, made this part of the UN supervision in their territories easier. During the first truce, there were was no importation of arms to the Arab states at all. The Legion Command, believing that the war was over, expected British supplies to be resumed. When this hope was shattered, it still refrained from looking for sources of supply other than British. The governments of Egypt and Iraq, too, pleaded with London through the British Ambassadors in their capitals. Iraq was financially bankrupt, with an annual deficit of 13–15% in their foreign trade. Her only attempt to obtain supplies from abroad was through Pakistan. This failed because Pakistan hesitated to violate the embargo. Egypt was the only Arab country which was financially and mentally set on buying arms independently in the open market,[23] and it never hesitated to bar UN observers from the ports of Alexandria and Gaza when it felt it was necessary. However, what they were hiding during the first truce was not illegal arms but the despatch of reinforcements by boat to the front which, of course, was also against the truce rules. It was only well into the second truce that Egypt began her independent importation of arms. The Syrians began doing so only in 1949.

THE UN SUPERVISION OF THE ARAB STATES

Shortage of personnel and intelligence about the Israeli import of war material made the UN inspection in Arab ports and airports literally non-existent until August. Thereafter, the UN established permanent supervision posts in most of the Arab sea and airports. Before that, what was done was grotesque. On 11 June, two new observers who arrived in Cairo, a Swedish Colonel and an American Major, were sent to take positions in Tel Aviv. As they arrived there, it became apparent that the fire on the Syrian front had not yet stopped. So the two newcomers' destination was changed to Damascus, from which they were told to check the front at Mishmar Hayarden. When they arrived at the front, it was already quiet. But now the Chief of Staff of the observers, Colonel Thord Bonde, ordered them to stay on the Syrian side and 'make inspection' of Al Maza airport, near Damascus, which was also the command post of the Syrian Air Force. The two rented a car, hoisted a UN flag and paid a 2 hour visit to the place. No further UN checks were made at al Maza for many weeks after that visit. As for the said observers, they were now sent to the Lebanese section.[24] A permanent presence of observers in Syria began to be established at the end of the July, still with only a handful of men who were engaged in watching over the front line. In early August, observers posts had at last been established in Syrian air- and seaports, but the airports of Damir and Al Dimas were not covered. The total number of UN observers in Syria was left at 16 as a maximum. Iraq was treated even more extrinsically. Neither Bernadotte nor Bunche, nor indeed any of their changing Chiefs of Staff, had ever visited Iraq. But on 20 June, a couple of observers, an American and a Frenchman, were sent to Baghdad 'for inspection'. Two days later, the observers advance headquarters, which moved to Haifa, needed them as staff officers. The next inspection of Iraqi installations was made as late as 3 August, when permanent posts were established both in Baghdad and in Basra.[25]

Even after a considerable increase in the number of UN personnel, their deployment in the Arab countries continued to be sparse. According to a plan, worked out in late July by General Lundstrom,

Table 12   The establishment of permament observer posts in sea- and airports – chronological order[26]

Position	Date	Position	Date
Tel Aviv	13 June	Aqaba	2 September
Haifa	22 July	Bagdad	3 September
Beirut	23 July	Cairo	16 October
Damascus	24 July	Alepo	23 October
Aman	25 July	Alexandria*	9 November
Basra*	29 August	Port Said	10 November
Tripoly	1 September	Mafraq	(Occasional)

* A joint sea- and airport inspection post.

the new deployment of observers was to be as follows: Jerusalem 50, Tel Aviv 19, Tiberias 12, Haifa 19, Advanced Command in Haifa 37, Gaza and the Negev area 13, Nablus 17, Hebron 6, Israeli airports 14, and supply convoys to Jerusalem 7. In Palestine there was a total of 214 observers. For the Arab states the allocation was: Iraq 5, Transjordan 19, Lebanon 16, Egypt 9, Syria 16, giving a total of 65 observers in Arab states. Further details of this plan point out to the preference of inspection at the front over ports, and to UNTSO headquarters focusing particularly on Israeli ports. Two Transjordanian airports were allocated 3 observers; Syria and Lebanon with six airports were allocated four observers; Port Said had one observer and Basra with separate sea and airports was allocated three observers. None was sent to Baghdad and none, at that point, to the ports of Alexandria or Gaza. In Israel, the total allocation of observers to ports was now planned to be 36, and the deployment of the UN air reconnaissance unit in Haifa contributed to the relative density of inspection inside Israel.[27]

However, the Arabs rarely gained from the scarcity of the inspection in their ports since they did not import much. An Israeli intelligence review of the Iraqi performance in the war corrects the earlier, erroneous Israeli assumption that, somehow, Iraq continued to obtain British supplies. It concludes that 'The Iraqies never manged to get the arms, the aircraft and the ammunition promised to them by the British for their guns, aircraft and armoured vehicles. This was their main problem.'[28]

Egypt began importing war materials piecemeal in September, but her main acquisitions abroad did not arrive before November and December, which was too late to affect the war. In the case of Egypt, UN observers were unlikely to expose Egypt's main embargo violations.

The 26 Locust tanks were acquired by a civil agent from a LL site on Egypt's soil; the 38–40 Israeli-destined half tracks were confiscated in the Canal Zone; and the Macchi aircraft arrived flying Egyptian colours. Still, Egypt barred UN observers from the Port of Alexandria under the pretext that Israel did the same at Haifa.[29]

UN INSPECTION IN SEA- AND AIRPORTS IN ISRAEL

In the autumn of 1948 the attention of the reinforced Observers Corps had been rightly focused on Israel's military preparation. But how effective was their inspection of Israeli sea- and airports? Evidently, not very. Shortly after the beginning of the first truce, Israel's General Staff already felt that the UN presence was merely a minor nuisance with which one could well live. Israel's heaviest import of arms occurred before the establishment of the UN system or when it was still very thin. That time also served as a testing period for various techniques to deceive the observers. Archive reports sometimes go into details as to how the observers were outsmarted. For example, as early as 12 June, two observers were deployed at the port of Tel Aviv, a main point of Israeli arms unloading. Tel Aviv had shallow water, so ships were anchored away at sea and the cargo was brought to shore on board barges. The two observers rented rooms at the nearby Koete Dan Hotel, on the sea front, from which they could actually inspect the approach to the harbour with the help of a simple telescope. Since there were only two of them, they usually shuttled together between the hotel and the port and when they were informed or noticed that a new ship was about to unload in the distance, they went there by means of a motor launch, went on board and checked if the bill of loading corresponded to what they could see in the ship's cargo halls. Obviously they were helpless when to do this they had to dig into layers of food stuff, which the Israelis deliberately sent in bulk. The observers, however, did not attend the actual unloading of the barges, especially when it took place at night.[30]

Two days after the establishment of the observers post in Tel Aviv, the arms ship *Borea* arrived, with ten French H35 tanks, 75 mm guns and gun ammunition on board. The Israeli deception procedure went as follows: the *Borea* was held out of sight of the shore until darkness. It then changed places with a similar ship which had already been checked by the observers and which now sailed out of sight.

Unfortunately, it was feared that the *Borea*'s cranes were not strong enough to lift the tanks, so the captain of a third ship, whose vessel brought tracks to Israel, was intimidated to allow his crane to be used to unload the *Borea* and to keep quiet about it. The tanks, ammunition and guns were brought ashore when the observers went to bed. The next day, the operation log book at the UN Advance Command in Haifa, kept by one Lieutenent Lichley, reported various port problems, including the arrival of immigrants, tracks, etc., but there is no mention of the *Borea*.[31]

The concealment of arms deliveries to Israel by air was at this point a smaller problem. Israel controlled over a dozen good runways and the observers' command was in the dark as to where the airlift actually unloaded. The Balak Operation, carrying mainly Czech Messerschmitts was at its peak towards the end of June. When Lt Colonel Martin, commander of the UN reconnaissance squadron approached Major Harold Simon, chief of Israel's air operations and asked for a list of airports and air installations 'to coordinate our mutual work', Simon replied that if the UN Command wanted to carry out an inspection, they must forward a written application not to the Air Force Command but to Colonel Komrov of the Liaison Office, Operation Branch. He added icily, that, 'UN pilots would be risking their lives if they flew in the vicinity of Israeli air installation without permission'. That 'written application' procedure was designed to enable the IDF to keep the movement of UN observers under control and to avoid a spot inspection. The Aqir airport, where the Messerschmitts were assembled, was kept totally out of bounds for inspection. During the second week of the first truce, the chief of the IDF Acquisition Department, Pinhas Vase, cabled Avigour: 'you may fully continue with "Balak" except Haifa (airport. Which was held by the British until 30 June)... we are uninterrupted by the observers'.[32] During the first truce the airlift and the sea flotilla brought over 3 thousand tons of arms and ammunition to Israel, of which there is no specific mention in any report of the UN Observers. Deliveries of equipment went at a pace of six to seven ships a month and four to five flights a week.[33]

When the truce collapsed on 9 July, the observers vanished from the scene for 4 weeks until 4 August, but ships and planes carrying arms continued to reach Israel. When, at last, the observers returned to their positions, their new Chief of Staff, General Lundstrom of Sweden, tried a harder hand with the Israeli authorities. The case of the UN Chief air observer, Lt Colonel Eric Gardin, illustrates what happened.

With Lundstrom's encouragement, Gardin began to make spot-checks, landing with his Auster at Israeli Air Force installations without any written permission. After landing at the Aqir base on 7 August, during which Gardin was physically prevented from walking straight into a hanger where Messerschmitts were assembled, the Chief of Israel's Air Command, General Ahron Remez, ordered Israeli air base commanders that in any such future event they should arrest the intruder. This, indeed, was the orders which Colonel Dov Ben Zvi, commander of the Ramat David base and the chief of the Air Force Security, Captain Andre Stanek, carried out when Colonel Gardin next landed unpermitted, this time at Ramat David.[34]

Colonel Gardin actually gave a warning to the Israeli security when he telephoned Colonel Komrov, on the morning of 12 August, announcing his intention to check the alleged arrival in Ramat David of an aircraft smuggled from Britain. The IDF was ready. When Gradin, followed by another UN pilot landed their two Austers at Ramat David, without written permission, security officer Stanek arrested them. When one of Gradin's companions produced a printed page signed by Bernadotte, including their rights to carry out inspection, Stanek replied: 'this isn't the Bible'. The three observers were held in detention until Colonel Komrov arrived. Then, a most obnoxious argument developed, in which Komrov told Gardin that 'if he could not stick to the rules he would not be able to fly in Israel's skies'. Gardin repudiated this ruling, so Komrov and Ben Zvi decided to allow the other observers to take off, but kept Gardin detained until land transportation arrived to take him to Haifa. That same day Israel's Foreign Minister, Sharett, filed a strong protest about the incident to Bernadotte.[35] But as it happened, on that same day Bernadotte left for a three week vacation in Sweden and the gloomy General Lundstrom ordered his men back to abide by the Israeli procedure. For all practical purposes, Israel's air bases remained out of bounds for the UN observers.[36]

A similar mixture of harassment and deception was used to prevent inspection at seaports. Measures to incapacitate the inspection included the prevention of observers from setting up permanent positions inside the port precinct (they had to get fresh permission and a liaison escort each time they wanted to make an inspection), and the covering of the imported equipment with a bulk of other goods, such as coal, building materials or food stuff, which required clearing before the observer could ascertain the nature of the entire cargo.[37] Duplicity in the bills of loading was also used: one form was filled and signed upon sailing while the other was only signed but kept clear, until new details were added upon arrival to the port of embarkation. Radio contact was kept between ship and land, to enable the Departments of Acquisition and UN Liaison to decide, at a late stage, where and when to approach the harbour.[38]

Finally, there were the cynical tricks. A Rechesh agent who came from Italy to Israel with the first consignment of Sherman tanks on board the *Arsia*, reported watching with amazement how UN Observers, who probably knew what was on board, were prevented from entering the port of Haifa. First, the approach to the port was blocked by a train which manoeuvred backwards and forwards on end, with the barrier rod down. Then, an Israeli policemen violently attacked and arrested a UN Observer for carrying a camera. An excited argument flared and when the man was released, the observers were asked where was their escorting naval liaison officer, who was deliberately not made available.[39] Since the observers eventually stayed out, the next day General Riley sent a complaint to IDF acting Chief of Staff to the effect that 'Our observers have been denied access to a vessel because they came unaccompanied by liaison Naval officer ... but they did so, because the Naval liaison officer was said to be 'unavailable'.[40] At about the same time the British Ambassador at the UN reported:

> Dr. Bunche said that the Jews had agreed to inspection of their airfields only on condition that a similar inspection was permitted in all the Arab states. Bunche had obtained the agreement of all the Arab state (for such inspection) except Egypt. So the inspection in Israel was also prevented.[41]

Israeli liaison officers saw their main mission as wearing down and frustrating the UN Observers efficiency, taking advantage of their social seclusion, unfamiliarity with the climate, etc.[42] Indeed, the morale among the UN Observers sunk and their action turned cautious and undaring. Characteristic is a piece of advice given in December 1948, by a veteran French observer nicknamed 'Clement', to a compatriot freshman:

> First and foremost: take care of your own personal safety. Do not show zeal to do your duty; do only what you have to do. When you act, remember that your real commitment is to France. Never do anything not in line with our country's interest.

The observer who passed this piece of aphorism to an Israeli officer added bitterly: 'Only French observers are sent on field duties. The Americans all sit in offices.'[43]

The observers' only weapons in this war of attrition was filing complaints or endorsing ones made by a Jew or an Arab. It was then passed on to the Truce Supervision Board (TSB), which consisted of senior observers, whose task was to help the mediator to sort the complaint out and decide whether or not to send it on to the Security Council. The TSB dealt with hundreds of complaints every month. They included breaking the cease-fire, civilian casualties, interference with the observers work and, lastly, complaints about arms smuggling.[44] These last usually came in form of 'suspicion', with little solid detail.

The mediator himself had a strong interest in neither appearing to side with one party against the other, nor rocking the mediation boat altogether by showing how unstable the truce was. Consideration of his own political (and physical) survival often made him 'balance' a denunciation of one party with a similar denunciation against the other. The ever-growing number of complaints, after which usually nothing happened, decreased the value of making a true complaint in the first place. The parties and the observers knew it.

THE FAILURE OF THE UN SUPERVISION

The embargo of 1948 was relatively successful in preventing war materials from reaching the warring parties in Palestine. However, if any did manage to slip away, the UN observers in the field were usually unable to stop it. In an appreciation sent to the British Minister of Defence 9 months after the establishment of the Observers Corps, General Crocker wrote: 'experience shows that the presence of UN observers was no safeguard at all against the build-up of Israeli military power and [against] the operation of Israeli forces'.[45] Indeed, Israel was the only party whose army gained considerable military strength from bypassing the embargo and thereby greatly influencing the outcome of the war.

There were five reasons for the failure of the UN supervision.

First, the prevention of arms smuggling was never a high priority of UNTSO Command; prevention of violation of the cease-fire was always their first priority. This preference was outstanding in the allocation of men and means when the number of observers was small, but remained steady when the number of observers grew. When their number had already surpassed 200, General Riley demanded 300 more.[46]

Secondly, the prevention of arms smuggling was technically almost an impossible task. In order to seal off all routes of arms running into Palestine and the Arab states, one had to deploy observers 24 hours a day in approximately 25–30 airfields and active runways[47] and at some 12 active harbours and twice as many other jetties (like the Israeli one at Kefar Vitkin). The multiplication of such a task by teams of four to six to enable them to take shifts, plus the need for regional headquarters to control such a ramified network, required several hundred observers, which were never available.

Thirdly, authority was not given to the UN Observers to stop a suspected ship at high sea, let alone to confiscate its cargo. Similarly, observers on land had no authorization to hold equipment, or any idea what to do if the local authorities tried to prevent their inspection by force. The Security Council of 1948 was impotent to delegate a stronger authority to its representatives in the arena.

Fourthly, UNTSO work had a very bad start, as well as a lot of interruption to their work. Observers were not present during the periods of fighting, nor at the beginning of any of the three truces. In fact, they were absent when they were most needed. Their early work was derisive and, later on, it was difficult to regain respect from the parties. The superpowers bore much of the blame for this; the USA because of her initial hesitation to get deeply involved in the observers work, and the USSR for vituperating the very existence of the Observers Corps and casting doubt on their legitimacy.

Finally, UN politicians, from the Trygve Lie and his lieutenants in New York, down to Bernadotte and Bunche in the Middle East, while carrying out their missions, were also struggling for their own political and institutional survival. Admittance of their failure to maintain the truce, no matter the reasons given, was tantamount to admitting the failure of their project. They were afraid that if they expressed themselves openly on the weakness of their organization, it could bring about its total collapse. Between the hammer and the anvil, they usually felt obliged to choose the lesser evil. Bernadotte's practice *vis à vis*, Soviet rancour, to either sweep failures under the carpet or else 'balance' accusation of truce violations equally between the parties, so as not to rock the mediation boat too much, was passed on, after his death, to Dr Bunche. The fact that Israel benefitted from the truce more than the Arabs, which was known to both, was by and large absent from their reports, enhanced by the reality in which, except in the *Altalena* case, neither the Israelis nor the Arabs were ever or could ever be caught in *flagrante delicto*.

Bernadotte and Bunche put their trust, wrongly as it turned out in the ultimate action of the Security Council to punish gross violators of the truce. Rather than brandishing Generals Lundstrom's and Riley's reports to the effect that (the parties) 'are doing everything to under-mine the UN authority ... ignore, obstruct and circumvent (UN) mis-sion except when it can serve their own interests ...' (and that) 'the UN observers had lost whatever authority and moral force they may have had at one time',[48] Bunche continued to express himself to the effect that 'the political settlement is very near' and that it would not be wise to stop this process by criticizing either side or both.[49]

The UN supervision, therefore, was not a serious obstacle to the import of war materials by a party which had the sources and the financial and technical means to buy, deliver and assimilate them. In all these aspects Israel turned out to be superior.

8 Conclusion

Arab and Israeli efforts to augment their military power in 1948 were hampered by three sets and stages of embargo: first, the American embargo of December 1947, then the British embargo (imposed by degrees from February 1948) and, finally, a universal embargo, imposed by the Security Council on 29 May 1948, into which the former two embargo policies amalgamated, and which together held until the autumn of 1949.

Post-World War II experience shows that, given favourable circumstances, the big powers – in cooperation with the UN – are capable of imposing an efficient embargo. It also shows that with any degree of international cooperation and determination, the subject of the embargo will always try to bypass it and import the forbidden materials. There will always be governments and non-governmental elements in the international arena interested in supplying these materials and there will be chinks in the embargo barriers through which such materials will pass. In the case of a 'coercive' embargo, it is reasonable to assume that a relatively small violation of the embargo will not prevent the attainment of the ends for which it was imposed. However, in the case of a 'neutralizing' embargo, aimed at maintaining the *status quo* in the level of fighting capability of warring parties and which is imposed symmetrically, relatively small violations may be enough to jeopardize the entire effort by creating or expanding a power gap between these parties.

This is what transpired in Palestine in 1948. The embargo was aimed at diminishing the military capability of both rival parties, who had earlier reached a point defined as 'exhaustion at a near draw'. Its imposition was quite efficient and it was further elaborated during its course. But, although it damaged both sides' efforts to retain or to augment their military capability, its effect was grossly unsymmetrical. The different character of the rival parties and their different ways of adapting to the embargo situation, enhanced a process by which the dominant trend in the Arab armies was disintegration of their military power and on the Israeli side military invigoration went on. When the power gap had moved markedly in Israel's favour, UN warnings were insufficient to prevent Israel from capitalizing on her advantage on the battlefield. As a neutralizing instrument of conflict resolution, this embargo was a failure.

THE UNITED STATES AND THE WAR IN PALESTINE

In the USA, as a result of a built-in conflict between the professional Foreign and Defence policy-makers on the one hand (who were hostile to the Zionist aspirations) and the American elected politicians on the other hand (who, particularly in a wayward election year, tended to bow to the strong Zionist pressure), the United States Palestine policy in 1948 followed a tortuous line. However, on the issue of the embargo both politicians and 'professionals' supported it throughout. Zionist pressure to get the President to lift the embargo proved to be in vain. By the end of April 1948, the Zionist hope of turning the USA into a major source of either legal or illegal armament for Israel foundered on the rocks of a well-managed embargo policy, both within and without the USA. Almost the only equipment which had reached the IDF in time for the war was that which sailed or flew out before severance of the US embargo restrictions in mid-April. Most of the Israeli purchases which did not leave the American territory before that date were either confiscated or stayed put.

It was different with regard to issues pertaining to the general settlement of the Palestine problem. On this, the tug-of-war between the politicians and professionals continued, ending up in Israel's favour. The two most celebrated occasions in which this result manifested itself, were Truman's recognition of Israel on the night of her proclamation, and his commitment on 24 October not to force Israel to give up areas which the IDF conquered in defiance of the Security Council orders.

But these acts came only after the US policy had swung wildly from support of the 29 November resolution to trusteeship, then to attempts to find a caretaker for Palestine and prevent the proclamation of the Jewish State. Only then came the Presidential recognition, about which neither the Secretary of State nor the US UN delegation were warned. When a full-scale war erupted in Palestine, and the IDF managed to withstand the immediate assault of the armies of the Arab League, the baffled State Department began to concur with a British plan, according to which Palestine be partitioned between a compact Jewish state and Transjordan, along the existing front lines. Thereafter, with President Truman's concurrence, the USA succumbed to yet another British idea, according to which the conflict should be resolved through a controlled process of truce, embargo and pressure on the parties to accept the said design. The paramount principle guiding both powers was not to allow a situation to develop in which Britain and the USA would support opposing sides in the Palestine conflict.

From a domestic point of view, this was a none too easy line to adopt in an election year. But pretty soon it became discernible that the embargo worked in favour of the Israelis, and this made the Truman administration's task easier. While the American Zionists continued to accuse the embargo policy of being an evil conspiracy aimed at forsaking Israel, with a strong innuendo about the past conduct of the US Government during the Holocaust, the better-informed Zionists knew that from Israel's point of view it was better to leave the American embargo intact. Indeed, towards the end of 1948 it was Israel which begged Washington not to lift the embargo. After the armistice was signed between Israel and her neighbours in 1949 and the embargo was of-ficially lifted, with no further progress reached towards a political resolution of the conflict, Truman asked his National Security Council to prepare a fresh appreciation of trends in the military balance between the Arabs and the Jews. The NSC, having still been under the impression of the poor performance of the Arab armies in the war, of the failure of the embargo and of the failure of the Security Council to punish the truce violator, tended to exaggerate Israel's military strength and expansionist impulses and at the same time to view the Arab states as retarded governments, which cannot even take care of their own internal security and which urgently needed military assistance. The NSC report concluded

> Israel's military establishment although small, is . . . a modern and effective fighting machine. (It) proved itself adequate to resist the poorly equipped, ill trained and badly led armies of the Arab League states . . . occupy considerable territory beyond that awarded under the partition plan, and it can be expected that the future effectiveness of the Israeli Army will increase. So long as there is the present discrepancy . . . there remains the danger of Israel's resorting again to military action.[1]

Further NSC appreciations in 1950 were written in the same vein and were clearly supportive of Britain's wish to resume military aid to the Arab governments, with the USA sharing in the overall supervision of the process. It was this attitude which turned the USA in May 1950, the moving spirit behind a Tripartite Statement signed by the USA, Britain and France, on armament and boundaries policy in the Middle East and on Western control of the balance of power in that region.

BRITAIN AND THE 1948 PALESTINE WAR

At the beginning of 1948 the British were pulling out of Palestine in an ugly mood, determined to have nothing to do with the UN partition scheme. They set the deadline of mid-May for the end of their mandate. However, the combination of the collapse of the UN scheme, the civil war in Palestine, King Abdullah's ambitions to annex Palestine to his kingdom and the USA perplexity, began to give the British Government a ray of hope, that, after all, some salutary results might emerge from the imbroglio. When the USA announced her abandonment of partition on 19 March, the British Cabinet quietly decided on the contrary to accept partition as a solution; not one imposed by an external force, but one which seemed to have been 'sorting itself out' between a 'compact' Jewish State and what looked to be a vacuum, which might well be filled by Transjordan.

Meanwhile, for reasons not directly connected with Palestine, early in 1948 Britain's relations with the governments of Egypt and Iraq turned sour. Following this development, British military assistance to these governments slowed down and soon was brought to a halt. What began as a response to the abuse of the British honour and reconsideration of a policy, soon turned into a deliberate policy of preventing British arms and British-trained troops to be introduced into the Palestine conflict. In March 1948 it amounted to a *de facto* embargo which only excluded Transjordan.

As a result, the armies of Egypt and Iraq entered the war in a disorganized manner, and in a desperate state of supply. More suprisingly, this was also the case of the Transjordanian Legion. For although the entrance of the Legion to Palestine at the end of the mandate dovetailed with the British ideas, after warning Abdullah that he must refrain from entering areas allotted to the Jews by the 29 November resolution, the British Government gave Abdullah's plans its blessing and began carrying out an intensive plan to enlarge and equip the Legion. But Abdullah's subsequent decision to join the other Arab armies and to send the Legion to fight the Jews, forced the British to suspend supplies to his army as well; soon afterwards came the embargo. The robbery by Egypt of the ammunition ship *Ramses*, destined for the Legion, made the ammunition situation in that army just as bad as that of the other Arab armies. Bevin wanted to compensate the Legion for this loss, but feared lest President Truman would use that act as a pretext to lift the American embargo. Instead and despite opposition from within his government and from British diplomats and the military,

Bevin became the moving spirit in the government behind a strict adherence to the embargo throughout the Palestine war.

For some time, the British believed that the combination of truce, embargo and the presence of the UN Mediator in Palestine under the SC's auspices would serve their goal well. When they began to suspect that this was not so, their greatest fear was that another Israeli offensive might destroy the Legion and, consequently, Israel might expand over the whole of Palestine or even beyond it. Still, the government in London did not dare resume military supplies to the Arabs. Instead, she took two anticipating emergency measures, to prevent such a calamity. One measure was to prepare consignments of ammunition for the Legion in British bases, ready to be supplied at a short notice; another measure was a plan for a short, 'surgical' air and, perhaps, land strike against the IDF, aimed at cooling down Israel's proneness to launch any more offensives. A possible bonus of this alternative, if it worked well, was British reoccupation of southern parts of Palestine. But three reasons rendered the execution of either of the two plans quite remote and they were never on the point of execution: first the fear of a bad impact on Anglo-American relations; secondly, a doubt about the nature of response to it at home; and, thirdly, the fact that as from mid July Israels' refrained from attacking the Arab Legion.

However, the fact remains that Britain was the holder of the military balance in the Palestine war. Had it decided to resume supplies to the Arabs in time, the Arab fighting capability could have been improved and the outcome of the war might have been different. Britain watched the disintegration of the Arab armies with growing dismay, but it was her strategic alliance with the USA against the USSR which remained the paramount consideration. It was only in 1949 that Bevin began to seek US agreement to abrogate the embargo. France had allowed the passage of arms to Syria, without British or American consent.[2]

THE USSR, CZECHOSLOVAKIA AND THE PALESTINE WAR

From the moment Britain decided to throw Palestine into the lap of the UN, the USSR tried to complicate the Palestine situation in order to get it out of Western control. But the Soviet means of achieving this were scant. At the UN, they supported the establishment of the Jewish State and in another arena they allowed Czechoslovakia to send arms to both warring parties. But the Soviet support of Israel was short-lived, hesitant and indecisive. It was no more than an experimental manoeuvre to which the USSR never committed herself. Ideologically she remained strongly anti-Zionist and it soon looked as if her moves achieved little to advance her global interests. But, meanwhile, what the USSR involvement contributed to the future of Palestine and the Middle East is history.

Three factors brought about the Soviet failure. First, Britain and the USA put their strategic alliance above their particular interests in the Middle East. Their adherence to the embargo was symptomatic of this attitude. Secondly, the war in Palestine did not develop into a quagmire, as the USSR might have hoped, but ended up conclusively in Israel's favour, which restabilized the region again under Western hegemony. Finally, the USSR herself did not take any decisive action to intervene in the war and herself persistently adhered to the resolution of 29 November 1947, which had now lost its feasibility. At the Security Council the USSR never used her veto on any Palestine issue, even when she was prevented from joining the Observers Corps. The fact remains that not a single Soviet soldier or an implement of war reached Palestine in any form in 1948 and 1949. Not a single Soviet vessel or aircraft had landed or set anchor in Palestine.

In view of the nature of the military aid given by Czechoslovakia to Israel and to the Arabs and of the USSR herself refraining from giving any direct aid (although at sometime she offered aid to both) it is doubtful whether there had ever been a Soviet master-plan to help Israel particularly or to intervene directly in the Palestine conflict, as British and American experts believed at the time. Communist Czechoslovakia offered arms to both sides and ended up assisting mostly Israel. But this was so largely because Israel proved by far a better customer. While there is no doubt that the Czech arms sales were sometimes sanctioned by Moscow, the Soviet attitude towards the Czech–Israeli arms deal was merely a pragmatic *laissez faire*. The USSR never went out of her way to remove the complicated obstacles from the transportation of the Czech equipment to Israel or to the Arabs or to see that this equipment was sold at a resonable price, etc. As result of this neglect, a good deal of the Czech aid failed to reach its destination or came too late or was useless for the war effort. The real Czech aid to Israel was the export of small arms and ammunition in the early phase of the war. The value of its subsequent, more ambitious and expensive part, including 84 fighter aircraft, to the outcome of the war was small.

OTHER SOURCES OF ARMS SUPPLY TO PALESTINE IN 1948

While the equipment and know-how in the important Arab armies came exclusively from British sources, the IDF equipment and doctrines originated from diverse sources, not mainly from Czechoslovakia, as many believed at the time. Israel's relative success to bypass the embargo also was not achieved in one specific area, but resulted from the proliferation of her acquisition efforts over five continents.

Israel's arms purchases in Western Europe, particularly in Switzerland, Belgium, Italy and France, coupled with a short-lived pro-Zionist policy of the French Government in the spring of 1948, account for much of the IDF ability to contain the first assault of the regular Arab armies in May and for Israel's early offensive capability. Over 90% of the IDF effective artillery came from these sources, as did artillery ammunition and much of the IDF improvised 'armour'.[3] Of the rest of the IDF artillery, 32 out of the total of 40 pieces imported from Latin America, proved useless and not a single piece of armour, artillery or artillery ammunition came from the Soviet bloc.[4] Even the Israeli snatch import of aircraft from Britain served as an important stop-gap for the Israeli Air Force when the arrival of aircraft from Czechoslovakia lingered. In contrast, the Arab import of arms from Western Europe either failed or proved useless or was late.

In 1948, France never took the embargo too seriously. Until April 1948, she occasionally supplied arms to Syria, and between April and June 1948 she was a despatch house for military aid to Israel. Then in 1949 she renewed sending military equipment to Syria, before the SC decided to lift the embargo altogether.[5] But there was a world of difference between the utility of the French assistance to either side. Italy was the main arena in which Egypt and Israel directed their main armament efforts during the latter part of the embargo. But the exertions of both parties here contributed next to nothing to the strength of their respective armies at the war's outcome, with the exception of old artillery ammunition, which both bought, but only Israel managed to use. In Belgium, Israel purchased American half tracks, which were useful in her improvised mechanized striking forces.

THE UNITED NATION SUPERVISION OF THE EMBARGO

The UN Observer Corps utterly failed to prevent arms smuggling to Palestine and to the Arab states. The lingering in the establishment of this force, resulting partly from the Soviet wish to participate in its activity and partly from the USA fear that extending the American contribution to the UN force might lead to a deeper American military involvement in Palestine, led to the immediate loss of authority of UNTSO, which later could not be restored. UN Observers were absent from the arena when they were most needed, namely, at the commencement of the three truces. They were literally absent when Israel imported most of her arms and when the Arabs underwent a major reinforcement of their forces. Even when the UN force quadrupled and was better equipped, it was never large enough even to carry out its most important task, namely keeping the cease-fire. Preventing arms smuggling had always been a low priority to the UN mediators and their Chiefs of Staff – maybe because they felt that it was technically futile and politically hazardous for them to attempt it.

ARAB AND ISRAELI ATTEMPTS TO INVIGORATE UNDER THE EMBARGO

The difference in methods between the efforts of the Arabs and the Israeli armies to strengthen themselves during the truce, tells much of the war's story. The Arabs sent more and more reinforcements to the front, without managing to improve their supplies, while the Israelis improved their arsenal *and* increased their OB. Between mid-May and the commencement of the second truce on 18 July, the Arab armies nearly tripled the number of their troops in and around Palestine, but hardly managed to bring any fresh supplies or to introduce any new weapons that could make a difference. Thus, the same stocks of ammunition which served the relatively small Arab troops which invaded Palestine in mid-May, minus ammunition spent and wear and tear, were to serve far bigger Arab OBs, which obviously made the shortage per unit more severe. In contrast, Israel imported and produced more and more implements of war and ammunition, so that the larger the IDF grew the bigger the army's stores of expendable supplies became.

None of the Arab armies entered the war with anything nearing the standard level of ammunition stores required for a long warfare. Worse still, at the outset the Arabs squandered much of their artillery ammunition as though they were assured of future supply, which they probably believed they were. They were convinced, as were some of the British, that the war would be short, either because the Jewish resistance would be crushed or that the UN would stop the war. It was only at the commencement of the second truce that it became apparent to their commands that the war would probably drag on longer and that in the meantime there would be no renewal of the British supply to them. Now, their ammunition stores stood at near exhaustion, particularly in artillery and mortar ammunition. Even where some such stocks still existed, the commands lost their confidence in their capability, logistically to plan any large-scale operations. 'If you ran out of ammunition', Napoleon is once said to have told a General, 'save the rest of your excuses'.

What earlier seemed a great disadvantage to the Palestine Jews, namely, that they did not have a spoonfeeding nursing power, as Britain was to three Arab armies, turned out to be an advantage under the embargo. For from as early as the summer of 1945, the Yishuv was busy developing a world-wide organization for the clandestine purchase of war materials, supported by Jewish communities abroad and a home military industry. In 1948 this organization was quite ready for the task. Its activity was not without painful failures, but what it managed to provide was sufficient to arm and equip an army strong enough to beat an embargo-stricken foe. August came, and British and American experts learned that the Arab armies could no longer open an offensive, whereas Israel not only could, but would. These experts were shocked to realize the degree to which the embargo worked in Israel's favour. In October, astounded by the collapse of the Egyptian army in the Negev, the British Minister of Defence wrote:

> The Chiefs of Staff point out that the circumstances are exceptional and that it was never foreseen, still less intended, that the embargo, which has lasted for months instead of weeks, would have such serious effect on the Arab forces.[6]

THE IRAQI ARMY IN PALESTINE BETWEEN TRUCE AND WAR

Had Iraq's relations with Britain in early 1948 developed as the British and the Iraqi governments of the time wished, the Iraqi army would have entered the war better equipped and with larger stores of expendable supplies. But the Iraqis entered the war with empty stores, bad gaps in the standard equipment in their existing units and a nil chance of tapping alternative supply sources.

Iraq joined the war with a relatively small force and then reinforced it with every single combat unit it could spare, without compromising internal security. In spite of a volatile public in her cities and the danger of Kurdish insurgence, eventually barely a brigade or small contingent of second-rate armour and artillery was left at home. The Iraqi OB in Palestine grew from two brigade groups at the end of May to an equivalent of two army divisions by the second truce, consisting of five brigade groups and including local Arab forces, organized in several separate battalions, which often proved superior to Iraqi standard units. Their total strength reached 18 000 men. However, the larger the OB, the more acute became the shortage of ammunition and the proper maintenance of equipment.

The opening performance of the Iraqis, at the battles of Gesher and Kaukab al Hawa, was a disgrace considering that the best units took part in them and that the Iraqi artillery did not yet economize on ammunition. Thereafter, at the battles of Jennin, Lajun and in the Gilboa Hills, the Iraqi army did better, probably because it was engaged in defensive activity, for which the British had trained it. When the strength of the expeditionary force increased at the end of the first truce, the Iraqi advance positions in the central part of Palestine were only a few kilometres from the Mediterranean. They could have at least tried to slice Israel into two, right down the middle and perhaps would have succeeded. However, the IDF offensives in July, against their left flank at Ras al ein and against an Arab enclave in southern Carmel which was under their command, resulted in the loss of these positions and in a fear of encirclement. Thus, their command chose a defensive disposition by reducing their strength at the front and deploying considerable force (including the main armour) to take care of an Israeli thrust along the Jordan Valley. Up until mid-August their command still toyed with the idea of launching a concerted offensive with the Legion. But the state of their armour, air force and ammunition, and King Abdullah's reluctance to go on fighting, put paid to this plan.

Meanwhile, a deepening financial crisis, made acute by loss of oil revenue, prevented the government of Iraq from trying to alleviate the situation through self-supply. In September, when an Italian company called 'Icarro' offered to sell Iraq armour, ammunition and aircraft on the cheap, the deal was called off 'in view of the financial situation'. In consequence, both Defence Minister, Sadeq al Bassam and Finance Minister, Ali Moumtaz resigned.[7] The new, pro-British Defence Minister, Shakir al Wadi, believed that pleading with the British Ambassador might change the British policy, but in vain. 'We were unable to

Table 13   Major sorts of ammunition in the Iraqi Army, July 1948[8]

Type	In Iraq	In Palestine
0.303 (small arms)	15 million	2 million
3-inch mortar bombs	3 600	1 800
2-inch mortar bombs	5 900	5 000
25-mm gun shells	13 000	4 000

make use of the arms, aircraft and armour at our disposal', al Wadi explained later, 'because we could not get ammunition'.[9] Israel's evident strengthening helped diminish the Iraqi Command's enthusiasm to carry on with the war. Had the government in Baghdad not been terrified of the street mob and its reaction, Kirkbride wrote to Bevin in October, it might have already pulled out of Palestine.[10]

In the second truce, the Iraqi artillery and armour almost totally ran out of 37-mm and 2-pounder 25-mm pounder shells. Even small-arms ammunition was rationed. A British estimate in mid-July, of the entire stock of ammunition in the Iraqi army of the main sorts is shown in Table 13.

Just for comparison, at approximately the same time the IDF stores of similar sorts were 7.92-mm 57 million, 65 and 75-mm shells 90 000 and 20-mm shells 180 000. As for mortars, Israel produced these at home.

Since there was no further significant replenishment of the Iraqi army thereafter, this level of ammunition stores, minus what had been since spent, is what the Iraqis had throughout the rest of the truces and the war. A memo of early Obtober in the British War Office explained that: 'The Iraqis are no longer seeking means to continue the war against the Jews, as all their supplies are exhausted. They only seek small quantities (of supplies) to enable (their army) to exist'.[11]

On 22 October, when the Egyptian front in the Negev collapsed, the Regent of Iraq, Abd al Illah, inspected Iraqi troops on the front line where it was feared that the next Israeli attack might come. After talking to officers he opined gloomily to a British diplomat: 'Nothing can be done anymore . . . in the absence of arms and equipment . . . the army would not hold more than one day . . .'.[12] A piece of Israeli intelligence of the time similarly explains 'Iraqi inaction' due to their 'very bad shortage of ammunition'[13] and Israeli intelligence research, written shortly after the war, correctly dismissed the notion that fresh ammunition had somehow reached the Iraqi army during the war from

British sources. It concluded that 'The Iraqis never managed to get the arms, aircraft and the ammunition promised to them by the British for their guns, aircraft and armoured vehicles. It was their main problem'.[14]

Thus, if for no other reason than this, it is quite clear why, when other Arab armies were under attack, the Iraqi army remained relatively inactive. In October, Iraq's assistance to Egypt was confined to two local raids at Megido and Ein Shemer, after which the relative tranquillity was resumed. In November, an Iraqi battalion was put on alert for a possible concerted Arab operation to relieve the encircled Egyptian brigade at Faluja. But this battalion soon returned to its original layout, because an IDF attack in the Jordan Valley was believed to be imminent. In December, when the IDF again attacked at the Southern front and the Egyptian Command explicitly asked for Iraqi action, Prime Minister al Pachachi made a statement in Baghdad to the effect that his army 'was ready to help Egypt', but the Iraqi commanders in the front said he could not act unless he received a fresh supply of ammunition. When this did not happen, he paid his due in a day's raid at the Tira section, which did little to help the Egyptian situation. The Iraqi Air Force was now totally grounded, but three of its unused Furies were lent to Egypt in December, because Egypt believed she could install guns in them. All three aircraft were lost in accidents or immediately upon making contact with Israeli planes.[15]

The Iraqi Government was looking for an opportune moment to call its army back home. The progress in the Israeli–Transjordanian talks provided it. On 6 January, a new government was established in Baghdad, headed by Nuri al Sa'id. It announced that its main task was 'to save the situation in Palestine'. The Minister of Defence told the prime Minister that the government 'must do something' about the supply situation or 'solve the problem by other means'. In March, Nuri sent certain opposition leaders to prison and then brought his Cabinet to make the difficult decision of bringing the army back home.[16]

THE EGYPTIAN ARMY DURING THE WAR[17]

From the beginning of the second truce up until mid-October, the Egyptian forces in Palestine were deployed in more or less the same defence positions. During the 10 days war which proceeded, the Egyptians managed to consolidate their grip over a strip of a few kilometres width which cut off the IDF forces in the Negev from the rest of the area held by the IDF. However, the strategic value of this achieve-ment had been more than offset by the establishment of the Egyptian defences devoid of strategic depth. The IDF forces, including Brigade 12 and quite a few fortified Jewish settlements which were soon rein-forced by Brigade 11, were deployed right at the back of the Egyptian line, in addition to their lines of communication being threatened by Jewish settlement all the way to the old mandate border. The Israeli forces in the Negev were thus supposedly encircled, but by the same token they threatened to encircle the main corps of the Egyptian expe-ditionary force.

The Egyptian forces in Palestine operated in two, almost totally in-dependent groups, which until the end of May were on the offensive and thereafter they switched to a defensive disposition. The main group in the West formed a narrow wedge pointing to the Jewish rural and urban area south of Tel Aviv, which widens south-easterly near Kib-butz Negba, which they tried in vain to capture and widens further, north-easterly towards the Hebron Hills. At this point, the Egyptian forces thinned out and never really fully encircled the Jews in the Northern Negev. When the Israeli Southern Command began to pre-pare for the offensive, it did not find it too difficult, to move large, fresh forces through the Egyptian lines to the Negev. The second Egyptian group was positioned at the northern part of the Hebron Hills, point-ing at Jerusalem south of Kibbutz Ramat Rahel, which they also failed to take. The Egyptian defences of this group loosely overlapped with the left flank of the Legion to the east and to the west, with local Arab units filling the gaps between the Egyptians and the Legion, down at Latrun. But in their midst the IDF held a corridor, in which, from early July, it managed to construct a road ('Burma') through which supplies went to the 100 000 Jews and the IDF forces in Jerusalem, unchecked by Arab forces or, later on, by UN Observers.

In October, the Egyptian Order of the Battle in Palestine was as follows: the Western group in the coastal plain consisting of two rein-forced infantry brigades (the second and fourth) with seven regular battalions (nos 3, 4, 5, 6, 7, 8, 19) and two Support battalions of medium machine-guns and mortars. In addition, there were many non-standard units, including reservist battalions (Ihtiat)[18] and foreign troops: Saudi Arabians, Sudanese, Yemenites and Libyans. The non-standard battalions, which were of a lower quality and were intended to serve as the guard of military installations in the rear. But the fatigue of the regular troops enhanced the allocation of more and more untrained troops to first-line tasks. The infantry was supported by an improvised armoured brigade, consisting of a mixture of all kinds of AFVs, including the remains of a Mark 6 tank battalion, which in September counted only 16 serviceable tanks, 33 Humber armoured cars (half of them of type 3, with no gun) plus a few half tracks, armoured cars without a turret and armoured Bren carriers. The Egyptian artillery included a battalion of 24 25-pounder guns, in a relatively good shape and four separate batteries of 18-pounders, 4.5- and 6-inch howitzers, which due to wear of bore were no longer in use. The AA artillery consisted of four batteries of 3.7-inch and 40-mms guns and the anti-tank guns, which were mainly 6-pounders were allocated permanently to infantry units.

The Eastern Egyptian group, sometimes called 'the light forces', consisted of the original Muslim Brotherhood units, as well as remnants of the Palestinian 'Jihad al Makdas' and other local volunteer forces from the Hebron area. In October its total strength was approximately 2000 men. This group was not organized in standard battalions, except the Reservists Battalion No. 1, but in independent companies, commanded by section commanders. They had very few heavy weapons: six old 6 inch howitzers, which in other sections were already put out of use, four anti-tank 6 pounder guns and a limited number of medium mortars. These forces had no armour at all.

Like Iraq, Egypt invaded Palestine with a relatively small force and thereafter did her best to reinforce it. Fresh officers were sent from the central training base of Abassiya; reservists were called and hastily grouped into battalions and the selective conscription was extended. In June, seven Saudi companies arrived, equipped with small arms and eight armoured cars. After these came other foreign contingents, which, with the exception of three Sudanese companies, had a poor standard of training. In September the Egyptian expeditionary force numbered 15 000 strong;[19] twice its size in May. But it would be wrong to consider that it was militarily twice as powerful. The additional troops not only lowered the standard of soldiery, but they did not bring additional ammunition. Obviously, this further increased the severity of shortage.

During the first truce, at the request of the British Foreign Office, the British Ambassador in Cairo made an inquiry about the state of ammunition in the Egyptian army. He reported that in order to bring the Eyptian infantry stores to a standard level, an additional 50 million 0.303 rounds of ammunition and approximately half a million 3- and 2-inch mortar bombs were needed.[20] The ambassador did not report the state of artillery ammunition, because in the short-run the Egyptians could depend on the amount confiscated from the *Ramses*. Indeed, IDF reports of May and June indicate massive use of gun-fire by the

Egyptians. But in the second week of July, when General al Muwawi was ordered to go on the offensive, he grumpily cabled Cairo, that while carrying out the order, 'his ammunition would not suffice to maintain himself or ensure withdrawal if he does so'. Doubting his superiors understanding of his desperate situation, al Muwawi demanded an immediate inspection to verify his complaint.[21] Egypt, which had earlier squandered good gun ammunition, now often used inferior shells. As from mid-July, IDF intelligence reported the Egyptians 'economizing' on artillery fire, the cessation of counter-battery fire and a growing number of Egyptian duds, some of which were found to be 30 years old.[22]

The Egyptian Air Force, the strongest among the Arab air forces, rapidly declined as well. In October, while on paper it still consisted of nine squadrons with 82 aircraft, among them 36 fighters (32 Spitfires and four Macchis) and 16 bombers, suffered a debilitating shortage of spare parts and maintenance know-how.[23] During the October operations, this air force carried out less that 50 sorties, against 240 sorties by the Israeli Air Force,[24] which had even less serviceable combat aircraft.

EGYPT'S ARMS PURCHASING OPERATIONS IN 1948

Egypt was the only warring Arab country which took unorthodox emergency budgetary measures to provide her army with financial means to buy war materials. But these means and efforts were, by and large, wasted away, by lack of experience, bad organization and corrupt conduct of the project's chiefs.

Particularly affected by corruption were the purchase in Italy and Spain of guns and ammunition, which proved useless. The facts about these deals were exposed in trials, held in Cairo in 1949 and 1950, of high ranking government officials and officers who in 1948 managed the arms acquisition. Among those put on trial were Deputy Minister of War, Tawfiq Ahmed, Commander of the Engineer Corps, General Saad al Mesiri, Chairman of the Army Procurement Committee, General Ibrahim al Mesiri, Commander of the Navy Admiral Ahmed Nader and two dozen other generals and officers of lower ranks. They were charged with stealing over a million pounds from the public purse, in addition to getting fat commission from foreign middlemen, who more often than not sold these officers useless war materials.

According to Egypt's Public Prosecutor, up to 42% of the ammunition bought by Colonel Jaffar Osman, Chief Inspector of Explosives in the Egyptian army, who during that summer spent much time in Italy and in Spain, 'risked its users more than the enemy'. Since there was not even registration of ammunition series, much wider stocks became 'contaminated' and it necessitated disqualifying the entire bulk as unserviceable. The obsolete ammunition was subsequently quietly sent to dumps; the worst part to Wadi Nuf 'where no one dared come near', and the rest to a ground near the Cairo citadel, where they were blown up, or to the northern Delta area, where they were defused.[25]

Arms bought by General Ahmed from the Swiss company 'Oerlikon', which mediated for the purchase of 16 105-mm Bofors guns in Spain, at the price of £15 000 each and of several thousand old British rifles and many tons of 0.303 ammunition, from the same source, was found already obsolete before its shipment to Egypt. Yet, the money paid could not be recovered. Sixty used Sherman tanks, bought in Northern Italy by the 'Egi-Italia' company, proved useless for any foreseeable future and many of them never entered service.[26]

However, the charges made in these trials must be treated cautiously. To begin with, they completely bypassed War Minister Haidar and some his associates and, even more so, the King's Court. These last were earlier deeply involved in judging offers for arms supply. Probably justice stopped short of intercepting the major culprits.[27] Moreover, the shame and agony of Egypt's defeat made the public all too eager to punish someone who supposedly had stabbed the nation in the back. Someone had to be come the scapegoat. But corruption in foreign trade was the norm in the Faroukian Egypt. The root of trouble was, probably, the exemption of the War Ministry from the duty to report how the special war budget was spent.

The Egyptian acquisition was seemingly more efficient in the purchasing of aircraft and navy vessels from a reputed Italian arms-producing concern. But the money spent in this quarter did not help Egypt in her immediate war effort, either. In October the Egyptian Air Force received the first eight (or ten) Macchi fighters, which were first (and lastly) put to use in December. But on the two occasions in which these planes scrambled out, the low standard of the training of the pilots and the inferior performance of the aircraft themselves showed. All the Macchis in Egypt's service in 1948 were destroyed, either in the air or in accidents on the ground. The 26 Locust tanks bought in June as scrap-metal through a civil company were reconditioned during the summer, but their guns remained neutralized. They were put into battle at Khan Yunis in December and one-third of them were soon destroyed by the IDF infantry. Ironically, the most useful Egyptian armour acquisition was the confiscation in November of nearly 40 American half tracks, destined for Israel. Since in December the entire Egyptian armoured corps consisted of six Mark IV tanks, nine to ten Locusts and two dozen modern armoured cars (with some additional inferior AFVs), the addition American half tracks were a shot in the arm.[28] The Egyptian army was saved from final destruction only by the armistice talks.

THE ARAB LEGION UNDER THE EMBARGO[29]

According to the original British plan, at least the army of Transjordan had to be better equipped and supplied when it entered Palestine. This plan however, was based on the assumption that the Legion would not join the war against the Jews. When this hope foundered and it coincided with the Anglo-American agreement to push the embargo at the Security Council, the British Government had no choice but to include the Legion in the same category of restrictions. The unfortunate loss of the *Ramses* ship, consisting of the last delivery of British artillery ammunition to the Legion, robbed this army of its reserve. In August General Glubb wrote that 'the British Command still agreed to replace the (*Ramses*) ammunition, but the UN embargo was imposed before it could be done'.[30] Glubb and the British command had hoped that with the first truce the war in Palestine would be over, so supplies to the Legion could be resumed. This hope was further augmented by talks about the resumption of the British subsidy to the Legion, which was earlier suspended. Glubb became alarmed only in early August, when he suddenly realized that the war might soon be renewed, and that the Legion might be a main Israeli target and perhaps be liquidated.[31]

The Legion received its last allotment of 25 Pounder and small-arms ammunition in February 1948. The *Ramses* portion was to suffice for an additional 30 contact days. In its absence, Glubb reported that his army had already 'fought for forty days on ten days (allotment of) 25 Pounder ammunition' and that 'the present stocks of ammunition for all arms (perhaps he should have excluded 0.303) are at about 5 contact days'.[32] Indeed, already during the 10 days battle of July, the Legion fire-power, not counting small arms, had shrunk. Twenty-five pounder guns were hardly put to use, mortar ammunition was used miserly and, by improvization, 2 and 6 pounder guns were used as field artillery.[33] At the same time the IDF increased its artillery fire-power by absorbing a great number of guns and mortars, which in contrast to the Arabs, had an abundance of ammunition.

Following the loss of Lydda and Ramle in July, with the Legion casualties surpassing 400, King Abdullah painfully realized that the Arab League would not hesitate to turn The Legion into cannon-fodder. He also realized that if the Legion power was further diminished in battle, his political position in the Arab world would decline – and perhaps vanish altogether. Furthermore, Abdullah shuddered at the thought that his army might face a choice between having to withdraw from Palestine with nothing in hand or be liquidated.

Abdullah was not alone in such fears. When Israel's preparations for the offensive became evident and no British expert to which Abdullah could refer was sure where the IDF would next strike, not only Glubb, but General Crocker and the British Chiefs of Staff were near panic. It was of little comfort to them that the Israeli thrust, in October, came on the southern and northern fronts, particularly when, following the Israeli conquest of Beer Sheva, the IDF shifted part of its effort to the Hebron Hills section, and a clash between an IDF front guard and a Legion near guard contingent took place on 26 October at Beit Jibrin. At a meeting of the British Chiefs of Staff of 29 October, the spirit was that the Legion 'must be saved'.[34] However, Israel had its own red lines; no serious fighting took place anymore between the Legion and the IDF. At the same time, no British supplies were sent to the Legion either.

THE ARAB ARMIES AT THE NORTHERN FRONT OF PALESTINE[35]

The Syrian and the Lebanese armies went to war even worse prepared and equipped than the other Arab armies. All Syria's pre-war exertions to consolidate the state of the army had failed: the USA embargo ended the Syrian hopes for a comprehensive American army-building programme. Britain continuously refused Syrian requests for small arms and when Damascus reluctantly resorted back to French assistance and the *Quay d'Orssay* reacted positively, this French supply programme was suspended in April 1948. Finally, most of Syria's small arms and ammunition bought in Czechoslovakia, went down or was lost in the *Lino-Argiro* affair.

Yet, in the Arab League Syria's voice was loud for military intervention in Palestine, first by irregulars and then by regular forces. 'The Syrians,' reported the British Minister in Damascus, 'were the first and the last ... convinced that the defeat of the Jews was within reach'. But they were also concerned lest, without such intervention, Transjordan alone might get control of Palestine. Early in 1948, Syria's contribution to the training and the command of the 'Army of Deliverance' was material, but it was less so in the Arab offensive after mid-May. Still, Syria kept a cognitive dissociation between the state of the Arab armies and her own, on the one hand and her fervent desire to fight Israel, on the other. She was the most reluctant to accept the truce and only round about the second truce did 'the Syrian Government and the President of the Republic became greatly concerned at the lack of arms and ammunition in their army'.[36] There was no serious replenishment of the Syrian and Lebanese armies througout 1948 and early 1949. In the Qawukji forces, which in matters of supply depended mosly on the Syrians, the ammunition situation was always the worst.

In the autumn of 1948, the strength of the Syrian army was approximately 15 000 men, but this was nominal. Many sections of the army were totally stagnant and efforts to resuscitate them were not crowned with any particular success, much of it due to lack of proper equipment. In mid-July, the Syrian army was proud of its local success in capturing segments of Palestine along the Upper Jordan Valley. It dug in and refrained from becoming involved in any more offensive activity. When the Egyptian army was defeated in October and the IDF turned against Syria's ally, Qawukji, the single act of coming to Qawukji's aid was the despatch on 29 October of two infantry companies to defend the village of Jish. However, by the time this force arrived, Qawukji's defences had already collapsed and the Syrian unit was overwhelmed by an IDF mobile force and destroyed.

After Israel captured the whole of Galilee and occupied a segment of Lebanon as well, Syria was left isolated. The British Military Attaché in Damascus, Lt Colonel O'Harmar, reported that he was approached by the Syrian Minister of Defence with a ridiculously small request for 'any amount' of ammunition, 'say, half a million rounds of 0.303 ammunition ... otherwise Syria will have to turn to the USSR'. In January, a special Syrian envoy, Edmund Homsi, was in London and Paris, asking again for 'any amount of ammunition'.[37] In London, Homsi was told that the British themselves 'were acutely short of ammunition' and he was referred to the French.[38] Ending up pleading with the hated French government, Homsi found a favourable attitude. In December a new government was formed in Damascus, the last to do so in a democratic process. It was headed by Khaled al Azzam, formerly Syria's Minister in Paris, who was respected there. Almost immediately, talks began on the completion of the aid which had been withheld the previous April[39] and one French consignment, containing AFV's and ammunition, was quietly unloaded at the port of Beirut in February by a non-French vessels. However, a new disagreement over the outstanding financial issues between Paris and Damascus arose and again interfered in the process.[40]

On 30 March a *coup d'état* was carried out in Damascus, by the army Chief of Staff Colonel Husni Za'im. The French government quickly extended recognition to Za'im, and in response to congratulations to the Colonel by Vincent Oeriol, the President of France, Za'im promptly asked for resumption of French arms delivery. But he also renewed the Syrian requests for aid in London.[41] Here, Bevin was 'strongly against it', because 'he thought it had been agreed that we should leave Syria to the French'. Indeed, the French Government was now keen to resume their foresaken plan of 1946 of rebuilding the Syrian army, pending the lifting of the UN embargo and the settlement of some outstanding problems between the two states. A French envoy to Damascus, De Mergerie, promised Za'im an urgent consideration of his request. But Syria, which at that moment was embroiled in tough negotiation over the terms of the armistice with Israel, felt threatened by Israeli military manoeuvres and needed material supplies immediately. When Za'im got the French to offer him a written plan of rearmament, he rushed and brandished it before the British eyes, hoping that they would offer him a still better deal.[42]

As for the Lebanese army, in the fall of 1948 it ceased to be a force to reckon with, as did Qawukji's 'Army of Deliverance'. When Qawukji was attacked by the IDF at the end of October, his defences promptly collapsed, but he managed to evade encirclement by sneaking most of his army into Lebanon, where it finally disintegrated.

ISRAELI IMPORT OF ARMS DURING THE SUMMER AND AUTUMN OF 1948

At the outset, Israel's leaders viewed the embargo as a conspiracy aimed at helping the Arabs eradicate the Jewish State. Their main complaint was against the USA State Department, but their real fear was that while they would be denied military aid, Britain would continue to supply the Arab armies. This, of course, was not the case. However, the Anglo-American agreement of May, in which the embargo was to play a key role, had been secretly made and camouflaged to the best of the two governments' ability. This was done because the British Government did not wish to be stigmatized as 'betraying the Arabs' and the USA Government of 'abandoning the Jews'. This attempt at concealment, coupled with Zionist anti-British prejudices, made it difficult for the Israelis to immediately grasp one of the most important causes of the Arab military weakness in the war. It was not that IDF intelligence failed to monitor that there was a severe shortage of supplies and bad maintenance in the Arab armies – their files were filled with fragmented information to this effect. But Israeli analysts continued to take for granted that somehow the Arabs did replenish, during the war, from British sources.

During the rest of 1948 and early 1949, Israel continued to import war materials from the same sources as earlier. But they came with growing difficulties. The IDF could never depend on any specific source to provide a specific weapon to match a strategic or a political deadline. The offensive planned for September was put off several times, when weapons defined as 'indispensable' did not arrive. When the government of Israel realized that further vacillation would allow the Bernadotte plan to be adopted by the UN Assembly and be implemented by the Security Council, it decided to launch the offensive without the weapons it planned to have.

Thus, of the 25 Messerschmitts bought in March, only eight (or less) were serviceable for the offensive in October and these ones were in a bad shape. Of the 50 Spitfires bought in August, only three were available for the October operations and only half of the additional 12 Spitfires, which arrived late in December, were serviceable in the December operations. One American Mustang and a few American Harvards completed the reinforcement of the air force. Of the 12 tanks at the disposal of the IDF in October, seven were knocked out at Iraq al Manshiya within an hour of their first engagement with the enemy. The surviving Hotchkiss tanks were stripped of their guns, which were installed in more useful AFVs. Not a single tank was added to the IDF OB until the end of the war. Thirty-two of Israel's 75-mm field guns, bought in Mexico, proved unserviceable. Bad acquisition also affected the Israeli Navy. All in all, the implements of war which played a major role in the IDF, at the most crucial junctures of the war, were almost totally those imported before the first truce, or produced at home.

THE ROOTS OF ISRAEL'S MILITARY SUCCESS IN 1948[43]

In 1948 the IDF was a badly equipped, under-trained body of recruits, grouped around a small nucleus of more, but not much more, experienced soldiers. It lacked conventional armour or significant air and naval forces. Most of its artillery was pre-World War I guns or 20-mm guns, used for purposes other than those originally specified. Its local arms industry, which was of great help in some aspects, was a failure in others. (The locally produced 160-mm mortar, called Fritz, was inaccurate and dangerous to its users.) The IDF anti-tank weapon was usually limited to the infantry short-range PIAT. A few 6-pounder or 57-mm AT guns had been inaccurate because of wear of bore. Against earlier hopes, the IDF failed to attain numerical superiority over the Arab forces in any single weapon, although it came close to it in artillery pieces. The morale of the IDF troops was usually high, partly because they could afford to be on the offensive, but the standard of the Israeli soldiers and commanders was, on average, not superior to the Arabs. The highest command course any IDF officer had attended was that of platoon commanders. Commanders in the field were promoted not through acquiring additional professional knowledge in courses, but for showing leadership or courage. But the better the officer, the less was the chance that he would be spared for anything other than combat tasks. Common knowledge of the use of new equipment was hastily diffused to troops by individuals moving from unit to unit in the front. As a result, the assailing practice of the best IDF units was smattering. In the main battles of the 1948 war, when Israeli frontal attacks on fortified positions suffered unnecessary defeats because of ignorance of elementary standing operation procedures (SOP – Nohal Krav) and absence of planning of the fighting to the objective, and on the objective. An Israeli military historian concluded recently that

> given the standard of training, organization, discipline, means of control . . . and intelligence capability in the IDF in 1948, this army was incapable of capturing a . . . locality, held by British-trained and British-commanded, army.[44]

Ben Gurion himself often lamented that: 'our boys are good Zionists but not soldiers' or that 'we did not win because our army worked wonders, but because the Arab army is rotten'.[45] But considering the high standard of most of the Legion officers and the military learning of many Iraqi and Egyptian army officers, the definition 'rotten' for the conduct of the Arab command in the war is indicative of a lack of understanding of the factors which incapacitated the Arab armies.

What then really decided the war in Israel's favour? What circumstances, weapons, strategy, tactics or other factors enabled Israel in the autumn of 1948 to defeat some of the Arab armies and force the rest to give up or sign an armistice with her? What advantage did Israel have in the fall of 1948 which it did not have earlier?

The 1948 war was decided by ground forces. The air forces and navies played little role in any particular campaign and had little effect on the war's general course. True, in October 1948 the Israeli Air Force gained control over the sky of the war theatre. But what did this control mean? This Israeli advantage did not result from any large-scale Israeli success in the air, but from the dismal state of the Arab air forces at that stage and the small number of serviceable aircraft at their disposal. There is much to be said about the resourcefulness of the IDF Air Force operators in carrying out air assaults by improvised combat aircraft. However, the damage these assaults inflicted on enemy communication, layouts and logistics was minimal. If it had an important effect, it was in the psychological realm. The very appearance of Israeli planes in the theatre took the Arab commands and governments, which were badly served with intelligence about the size of the Israeli Air Force, aback. It enhanced their decision to switch to the defensive, perhaps too early. The value of the air support to the IDF ground forces and its strategic bombing of enemy targets in the rear were almost negligible. By far the biggest contribution of the Israeli Air Force to the war's outcome was air transportation, namely, the delivery of arms from Czechoslovakia and the reinforcement of IDF troops in the Negev. Still, the crucial delivery of the Czec small arms was made by foreign, chartered planes (American and Czech) and by boat and most of the men and equipment moved to the Negev towards the Yoav Operation, went on foot or by vehicular means. As for the task of the C46s carriers, these aircraft delivered mainly Messerschmitts, whose role was very limited. What were of importance were the auxiliary air services such as communication and reconnaissance.

Israel's control of the air in the last phase of the war stemmed from two factors: the general down-grading of the Arab Air Forces and the great number of good airmen and technical teams in the IDF service. However, in the final account these advantages did not amount to much, due to the limitations of both the number and type of Israeli aircraft.

The few Israeli–Egyptian engagements at sea were carried out on the Israeli side mainly by air or naval commando forces. Fortunately for Israel, there was no Arab attempt or capability to block the supply route to her.

Table 14   The strength of the Israeli Air Force, mid-October 1948[46]

Squadron name/no.	Squadron	Number and type of aircraft	Aircraft available for operation	Number of air crews
LTA	Transport	6 C-46 (Commando)	12 (the rest on flights abroad)	74
35		6 Norseman		15
101	Fighters	5 Spitfires 15 Messerchmitts 4 Mustangs	5 8 serviceable Not yet serviceable	20
103	Transport bombers aircraft	5 C-47 (Dakota) 3 Beaufighters 1 Mosquito 2 Hudson	Only 2 serviceable Non-serviceable Not serviceable 2	31
69	Heavy bombers	3 B-17	3	41
Galilee		5 light aircraft	5	15
1		20 light aircraft	20	
Negev		4 light aircraft	7	7

Indispensable factors in Israel's strength were the large IDF infantry force and the relatively large field artillery. In October, the number of IDF troops, excluding women, was 88 000,[47] as opposed to the 67 000 troops on the Arab side of the front and at its immediate rear.[48] Since the Israeli figures include at least 28 000 troops in non-combatant tasks, which on the Arab side were not included in the forces counted, the number of combat troops on both sides may be considered, numerically equal. In circumstances whereby the Arab forces lacked unity of command, suffered from shortage of ammunition and essential supplies and fought in 'external disposition', this ratio amounted to a marked Israeli advantage. The IDF General Staff could shift forces from one section to another and create local superiority wherever it chose to strike. Sometimes, as in the case of the Yoav Operation, the IDF command did not originally see it necessary even to create local numerical superiority,[49] because it depended on its other advantages. The IDF ability to break through the Arab defences without the use of tanks or air force is largely ascribed to its superior fire-power and penetration capability, resulting from the development of mechanized units, which replaced 'classical' armoured forces.

In the autumn of 1948, artillery was the one domain in which the IDF came close to a numerical equality with all the Arab armies put together. But since the Arab artillery suffered a debiltating shortage of ammunition and the IDF artillery enjoyed good supply, the Israelis were in fact superior in artillery fire. Whereas in the Arab armies stores amounted at best up to 100–200 shells per a gun, the IDF, with 147 serviceable field artillery pieces (including 120-mm mortars, but excluding 20-mm guns) had an average of over 1200 shells per barrel, with the 20-mm guns having 2500 shells per barrel. The IDF command was thus far more confident in planning its future operations. At that time the level of IDF stores of small-arms ammunition stood at approximately 80 million rounds.[50]

In 1948 Israel lacked tanks and other standard AFVs, but necessity combined with creative innovation and some successful acquisition provided an adequate offensive alternative in the form of mechanized foray units, with which, eventually, every IDF Brigade was reinforced. Following the early success of improvised mechanized 'columns' behind enemy lines, notably in May at Malakiya and in July at Lydda and Karatiya, the General Staff increased the use of such contingents, varying from a platoon up to a battalion. These forces were nothing but standard and they consisted of a variety of vehicles: home-made armoured cars, with or without turrets and with or without guns; captured enemy AFVs; half tracks (often fitted with with 2 or 6 pounder or 57-mm guns); and, last but not least, machine-gun-mounted Jeeps. While these units were poorly shielded, their trafficability in rough terrain, their speed and fire-power, combined with the shortage of ammunition in the Arab armies, compensated for their weak or absence of armour and turned them into effective means of disrupting enemy defences.

Thus, essentially, three factors gave the IDF superiority, and made possible the victory it attained against the Arab armies in the autumn of 1948:

1. The neglect by the Arab armies of some of the basic principles of war, particularly the unity of command, the maintenance of the objectives and the concentration of the effort.
2. The gradual build-up of an overwhelming Israeli advantage over the Arab armies in terms of expendable supplies, particularly am-

Table 15 The build-up of improvised Foray units in the IDF[51]

Formation	Type or name of unit	Date of establishment
Brigade 1	Foray battalion	July
Brigade 2	Scouting company	August
Brigade 3	Scouting company	November
Brigade 4	Special Foray unit	November
Brigade 5	Mechanized company	June
Brigade 6	Special Foray unit	September
Brigade 7	Armoured battalion	May
Brigade 8	Tank battalion	June
	Foray battalion	June
Brigade 9	Scouting company	December
Brigade 10	Scouting platoon	November
Brigade 11	Mechanized company	(May) September
Brigade 12	Foray battalion	June

munition, resulting from the embargo situation, and from the difference between the parties' ability to cope with it.

3. Israel's genuine war-like capability: namely, her better adherence to the principles of war; her fighting in 'internal lines'; and her success in building-up and maintaining a large, highly motivated and sufficiently equipped infantry and artillery force.

It was these three factors which helped to provide the Israeli forces with the necessary superiority to break through the Arab defences in the Negev and Galilee. The starting-point of all Israel's other military and political achievements can be traced back to these conquests.

Table 16 The growing military strength of Israel: implements of war in the use of the IDF, April 1948–July 1949*

Item/amount	1 April 1948	20 May 1948	15 October 1948	1 January 1949	July 1949
Rifles	16 000	35 800	62 600	Same	Same
Light machine-gun	1200	6 567	6 351	6 455	6 547
Medium machine-gun	150	219	1 290	1 646	1 728
120 mortars	–	12	32	35	68
20-mm guns (ground forces)		25	70	79	96
Field artillery	–	5	147	149	173
Tanks**	–	3	(11) 8	(45) 8	53
Half tracks	3	15	46	96	?
Fighter aircraft**	–	–	11	(24) 19	58
Bombers (originally)	–	–	15	17	25
Ammunition stores, selected items					
Rifles (millions)	1.5	6	60	80	57
20 mm	–	60 000	178 000	603 000	1 200 000
65 mm and 75 mm guns	–	48 400	83 000	124 000	175 000
75 mm	–	–	42 000	60 600	105 000
120 mm mortar	–	?	9 000	9 000	11 000

*Not including sub-machine-guns, light and medium mortars and navy vessels.
**Under reconditioning or rebuilding are in parentheses.
***Data are mostly from File 163, 28/60, IDFA. Vase quotes somewhat different figures.
Selected items. The thickly defined area indicates the war decision.
Figures are sometimes rounded.

Notes

Notes to the Introduction

1. For the pace of the rearmament of the IDF see Chapter 8, Table 16.
2. Annex 9 to W. Khalidy, *From Haven to Conquest* (Beirut, 1971).
3. For a pro-Israeli presentation see Table 2 in the latest revised edition of N. Lorch, *Korot Milhemet Ha'atzmaut* (Tel Aviv, 1989), English version: *The Edge of the Sword* (New York, 1961). See also J. Wallach, M. Lissak and N. Lorch, *Atlas Karta Letoldot Medinat Yisrael, Shanim Rishonot* (Jerusalem, 1978) pp. 13, 36, 53–5.
4. The author is aware of the somewhat controversial use of the 'inner lines' argument, in view of the twisting frontline prior to the October 1948 campaigns. None the less, this definition stands by the criteria of communication, location of the command and the ease of moving reinforcements from one section to another.
5. Memo by the British Chief of Air Staff, 14.6.48, DEFE5/11, COS(48)125; 'The Royal Iraqi Air Force', Note by VCAS, 7.10.48, and Vice Air Secretary Foster to FO, 22.12.48 FO371/68419; also Bevin to Attlee, 4.2.49, FO800/457.
6. FO371/69188. J6828 and *passim*.
7. Yanai to Da'at, File 92, 260/51, IDF archives, henceforth, IDFA.
8. A. Kaplsnsky (Israeli Air Force History Branch), *The First Fliers* (Tel Aviv, 1993); discourse in the IDF Air Force History Section, April 1993; FO371/75396, E313, and E1065. See Table 14, p. 000.
9. FO371/69188, E6828; A. Shatkai, *Heil Avir*, No. 45, pp. 63–4, No. 46, p. 15; Lorch, op. cit., p. 506.
10. These are just a few of over 30 cases of international embargo imposed or attempted in growing numbers after World War II. See G. von Glahn, *Law Among Nations* (London, 1981), pp. 568–70.
11. Memo of 2 January 1948, RG 84, US National Archives, Suitland MD Annex, henceforth, WNRC. Interview with Beeley, London, 25.1.78.
12. CAB 128/12, 24(48)6.
13. For the periodization acceptable in Israeli historiography see M. Pail, 'Hakochot Halohamim', in Y. Ben Aryeh (ed.), *Milhemet Ha'atzma'ut*, Vol. 10 of *Hahistoria Shel Eretz Yisrael* (Jerusalem, 1983); also in Lorch, ibid.

Notes to Chapter 1: The Security Council's Arms Embargo of May 1948

1. DEFE4/13–15, *passim*; DEFE5/7.
2. *Foreign Relations of the United States*, 1948, Vol. V/2, p. 1031.

3. *FRUS*, 1949, Vol. VI, p. 661. Anglo-American Palestine relations will be discussed extensively in Chapters 3 and 4.
4. Bunche papers, DAG13/3.1.0, Boxes 1–7, UN Archives, henceforth, UNA (New York).
5. *FRUS*, 1948, vol. V/2, p. 1008.
6. I deal at length with these affairs in my book, A. Ilan, *Bernadotte in Palestine 1948, A Study in Modern Humanitarian Knight Errantry* (London, 1989).
7. CAB128/12, 24(48)6.
8. For day-by-day reports on this process the best source is *FRUS*, 1948, vol. V/2, pp. 1032–77.
9. Despatch from R. H. Hadow, 10.5.48, FO371/68554, E6420, and see FO371/68555 *passim*.
10. Exchange with the UK Delegation, 25.5.48, FO371/68553, E6331.
11. *FRUS*, 1948, vol. V/2, p. 1041.
12. Bevin to representatives in Arab Capitals; his memorandum 'Mediation in Palestine', 26.5.48, FO371/68558, E7166; also E7208.
13. *FRUS*, 1948, Vol. V/2, p. 1072, fn. 3.
14. *NYT*, 3.6.48.
15. The accusation that 'Western Imperialism was responsible for the Arab invasion of Palestine', however, continued unabated in the Soviet media: see *Pravda*, 29.5.48. See also the US Moscow Embassy to the Secretary of State, 29.5.48, RG59, 501.BB Palestine/5-2948, USNA.
16. Reports by Kirkbride, by Mack and by Campbell of late May and early June, FO371/68555 and 68556, particularly E6880, E6885 and E6908.
17. *UNSCOR*, third Year, No. 74.
18. *UNSCOR*, 1948, Res. 50, p. 20.
19. Ilan, op. cit., pp. 73–97.
20. DEFE2/225–6; FO371/75359, E5004; *UNSCOR*, nos 73 and 38, and resolution, p. 8; *FRUS*, 1949, vol. VI, p. 1435; *FRUS*, 1950, vol. V, pp. 122–35, 184, 883.

Notes to Chapter 2: The Warring Parties in Palestine

1. Exchange, Bevin–Campbell, early February 1948, FO141/1265; FO to Air Ministry, 20.5.48, DEFE7/833; Bevin to Kirkbride, 24.5.48, FO371/68555, E6790.
2. WO261/549; DEFE7/833, *passim*.
3. FO371/69202, J4582, J7602. See also FO371/68413, E7561/G.
4. Yehuda to Hillel, 15.6.48 and Fredie to Rami, 27.6.48, telegram record book of Avigur's headquarters, henceforth, TRBA. The record of telegrams of Avigur's successor, Pinhas Sapir, will be marked TRBS, units 1–8, 24/54, IDFA..
5. For background to the militarization of the Middle East see J. C. Hurewitz, *Middle East Politics: The Military Dimension* (New York, 1974).
6. Minutes, 5.4.46, CAB131/1, DO(46)10.
7. Memo by General Renton, August 1947, FO371/61593, E7401/G.
8. Ibid.; *Iraqi Parliamentary Inquiry on the War in Palestine* (I have used

the Hebrew version of 1954, henceforth, IPI), pp. 104–5.

9. 'Brief for the Secretary of Defence on the Iraqi Army', 8.8.47, DEFE7/ 833; FO371/68475, E1858; W. R. Louis, *The British Empire in the Middle East 1945–1951* (Oxford, 1986), pp. 324–8.

10. See Chapter 4..

11. FO371/68476, E1858; exchange FO–Mack, ibid., E3132 and E3140.

12. Mack to FO, FO371/68476, E4313, E4366; 'The Inspector-General's half-Yearly Report for the Period Ending 31st March 1948', FO371/ 68477, henceforth, Renton. See also DEFE7/834 and WO261/18.

13. 'Sandown' was a British shelf plan for 'the defence of the Middle East and control of our Mediterranean communications in the event of hostilities breaking with Russia'. (COS(48)144(0) DEFE5/12 and DEFE 5/9, COS(48)209.) It assumed a Soviet onslaught aimed at Britain's vital area of the Suez Canal Zone, possibly via Iraq and Transjordan. (DEFE 5/13.) 'We must hold the Russian advance at least as far from Egypt as Southern Syria . . . or Iraq'. (DEFE6/7 JP(48)108, 109.) See also the C.I.G.S in C of S meeting, of 9.9.48, DEFE4/16.

14. FO371/68476, E3132, E3140.

15. FO371/68476, E4336; see also retrospective report on the 'Iraqi Army in Palestine' in FO371/82450. Note also IPI, pp. 119–22.

16. FO371/68413, E8059; 'Hagorem Hairaqi Bemilhemet Ha'atzmaut', 922/ 45, IDFA..

17. Intelligence File 10, 4332/50, IDFA. For the Iraqi command list of spring of 1948, see Renton, ibid.

18. Semi-annual reports of inspectors of artillery, armour, ordnance and staff, March 1948, FO371/68477; Ha'artileria shel Tzivo'ot Arav Bemilhement Hashihrur Hyisre'elit', 64, 137/53, IDFA.

19. 'Half Yearly Report on the Royal Iraqi Air Force, March 1948' henceforth, Fisher, FO371/68477, Appendix 'B' and minutes.

20. IPI, pp. 151–2; Mack to FO, fn. 12, above.

21. The Consul in Mosul to Mack, 3.8.49, FO816/94; 'Hagorem Ha'iraqi . . .' IDFA, ibid.

22. IPI, pp. 26, 85–8; FO371/82450; 'Lehimat Ha'arvim Bemilhemet Ha'atzmaut', proceedings of the Galili Institute, 10.4.89; A. Sela, 'She'elat Eretz Yisrael Bama'arechet Habeinarvit Mehakamat Haliga ad Plishat Tziv'ot Arav Le'eretz Yisrael', PhD dissertation, the Hebrew University (Jerusalem, 1986), pp. 547–62.

23. 'The Iraqi Army in Palestine, . . .' memo by Brigadier Orlebar, the British Military Attaché in Baghdad, February 1950, FO371/82450; FO371/68591, E368, E7371; 'Hagoerm Ha'iraqi', IDFA, ibid.

24. 'The Iraqi Army in Palestine . . .', ibid.

25. 'Hagorem Ha'iraqi', IDFA, ibid.

26. Kirkbride to FO, 18.5 and 1.6, FO371/68591, E7368, E7371.

27. Hurewitz, pp. 58, 63ff.

28. See FO371/68476, E6436.

29. 'Half-Yearly Report No. 31 on the Egyptian Army by the Chief of the British Military Mission . . .', 31 December 1947, FO141/1265, henceforth, Arbuthnot. Also Embassy to FO, of January 1948, FO371/69200, J46 and J337.

30. Arbuthnot, ibid., FO371/69202, J5487, J7491.

31. A. M. Sabit, *A King Betrayed* (London, 1989), pp. 162–75.
32. Campbell to FO, cables of January 1948, FO141/1265.
33. Talk to Yusuf Bey at Abdin Palace, 17.12.47, FO141/1265.
34. FO371/69201, J2521/G.
35. Campbell to FO, 17.1.48, FO141/1265; WO261/18.
36. 'Demands Which Can be Met from WO Stocks' and 'Items on Production', DEFE7/181.
37. Sabit, op. cit., p. 166.
38. 922/45, IDFA. And see Campbell to FO, FO371/69202, J4098.
39. A. Sela, 'She'elat Eretz Yisrael . . .', pp. 462–3, 582–5; idem., *Arviye Eretz Yisrael Umedinot Arav Lifnei Milhemet Ha'atzmaut*, The Y. Galili Publications, vol. 76, pp. 48, 60.
40. FO371/69190, J606; FO141/1246/1; FO371/69201, J3809; FO371/69200, J337; FO371/69188, J2040/G & WO216/18.
41. FO141/1246; Campbell to FO 11–16 May FO371/68372, *passim*; FO371/68373, E6405; FO371/69190, J2890 and J2890. *Al Tali'a*, March 1975. M. Naguib, *Egypt's Destiny* (London, 1956), pp. 15–20.
42. Stevenson to Bevin, 10.2.51, FO371/90178, JE1196/2; C. Issawi, *Egypt at Mid-century: An Economic Survey* (London, 1954), pp. 166, 169 and 172; P. J. Vatikiotis, *Egypt from Muhammad Ali to Mubarak* (London, 1991), p. 368. On Egypt's ill-fated arms purchase see Chapter 8.
43. 'Mitzraim vehatzva . . .', IDFA and note Lorch, op cit., pp. 567 and 587–8.
44. Arbuthnot, ibid.; FO371/69202, J7491; 'Ha'artileria shel Tzivo'ot Arav . . .', IDFA, ibid.
45. FO69202, J4582; WO261/549. 'Ha'artileria Shel Tziv'ot . . .', ibid.
46. FO371/69188, J3612; cf. also exchange FO–Supply, 2.4.48, op. cit., J2368 and FO800/457.
47. FO371/69188, J6828.
48. Arbuthnot, ibid.
49. Order 7 of the Minister of War, 24.4.48, File 8, 2168/50, IDFA. BMEO to FO, 22.1.49 (*sic*), FO371/75099, E1080, and E1099.
50. Violent street demonstrations in January bewildered Nokrashi's government, which readily accepted the 'Ehwan' demand to be sent to fight in Palestine. After a brief training at Hextaff and Mersa Matruch, the main force landed at El Arish on 8 March. The Egyptian General Command appointed the force's commander and its other officers. FO141/1260; S. T. Mayer, 'The Military Force of Islam, The Society of the Muslim Brethren and the Palestine Question', in E. Keddouri and S. Haim (ed.), *Zionism and Arabism in Palestine and Israel* (London, 1981); Sabit, op cit., p. 174.
51. Order No. 7, ibid.; FO371/69223. Seven Egyptian Spitfires were lost within a week of the fighting: five of them in the mistaken attack of 22 May on the Ramat David base while still in British hands, due to bad Egyptian intelligence. Two others were lost in flight accidents, one above Israel.
52. Arbuthnot, ibid.
53. FO371/69177, J7385, J7518.
54. Brigadier Rose to P. Gooch, 20.5.48, DEFE7/180.
55. DEFE7/833, COS1732; for Bevin–Alexander correspondence on embargo

issues, see CAB21/1922. On Alexander–Bevin terms see A. Bullock, *Ernest Bevin, Foreign Secretary* (Oxford, 1985), p. 77.

56. Arbuthnot, ibid.

57. 8/k2 and 2168/50, IDFA; M. Naguib, op cit., p. 20.

58. Kirkbride to FO, 23.5.48, FO371/68373 and E6800. FO371/73562, *passim*; also FO371/69289, J8290 and J7385. FO371/68822, E325. Appendix 'C' to RE48–48 CIA of 5.8.48, courtesy Freedom of Information (CIA) 1984.

59. Intelligence 1, Files 10, 2384/50, 361, 922/75 and 8/k2, 2168/50, IDFA. See also FO141/1246/1 and Chapter 8.

60. Bevin to Kirkbride, 9.2.48, FO800/477. See A. Shlaim, *Collusion Across the Jordan* (Oxford, 1988), pp. 132–40. On Britain's policy see Chapter 4.

61. CAB128/12, 24(48)6.

62. For sources, P. V. Vatikiotis, *Politics and the Military in Jordan, A Study of the Arab Legion 1921–1957* (London 1967), pp. 58–74; J. Lunt, *Glubb Pasha: A Biography* (London, 1984, pp. 74–5; A. S. Kirkbride, *From the Wings* (London, 1976), pp. 34–6; Suleiman Musa, *Ayyam al Tunsa, Al Urdun fi Kharb* (Amman, 1982); S. A. el Edroos, *The Hashemite Arab Army, 1908–1979* (Amman, 1980), pp. 250 and 749. For a list of British serving in the Legion in 1948 and 1949 see FO816/477.

63. 'Reorganization of the Arab Legion', 19.1.48, WO261/18; DEFE5/10, COS(48)16(0); 'Ever Hayarden Ve' Halegion Betasach', File 658, 922/45; and 'Halegion Ha'aravi', File 103, 1046/70, IDFA; WO32/13351.

64. Quoted by W. R. Louis, p. 345; and see, 'Reorganization of the Arab Legion', ibid. and 'The Part Played by the Arab Legion in the Arab–Jewish Hostilities 1948–49', FO816/170.

65. Interview with Major-General Lunt (Wadham College, Oxford), 18.4.92.

66. Vatikiotis, pp. 70–1.

67. CAB21/1922, COS(49)423, Annex II, Appendix 'B'; FO816/147. In his book *A Soldier with the Arabs* (London, 1957), Glubb quotes smaller figures, counting only the trained echelons which crossed the Jordan on 15 May. Abdullah al Tal in *Karitha Filastin* (Cairo, 1959) mentions 9000 men. The differences stem from al Tal's inclusion of 2500 untrained men in Brigade 3 and over 1000 irregulars.

68. Even junior commanders in the Legion could in combat be given command over AFVs and use gun-fire. Interview with Colonel T. N. Bromage at the time SinC, Second Battalion, London, 24.4.92.

69. Edroos, pp. 245–51; according to IDF intelligence of July 1949, in the summer of 1948 the Legion had 16 25 pounders plus four 3.7 howitzers and by the end of the war, 24 25 pounders. 'Ha'artileria shel . . . ', IDFA, ibid. These figures are accurate with the exception of howitzers, which the Legion did not have at all.

70. 'Reorganization . . .', ibid.; DEFE 5/10; FO816/152; WO216/18. Lt-Colonel C. N. F Coaker to the author, 12.6.92; Major-General Lunt to the author, 8.5.92; interviews with Lunt and Bromage and a telephone interview with Lt-Colonel Coaker, all during April 1992.

71. Glubb skipped most of the military schooling line leading to the rank of General; his permanent rank in the British Army was Captain. Lash, who served as Glubb's Deputy since 1939, had a police background and is

not on the British Army List. Kirkbride, pp. 34–6; even Glubb, p. 85.
72. Brigade commander Desmond Goldie fought with the Scots Fusiliers, John Ashton, with the Welsh Guards and James Newman (who after reorganization took command of Brigade 4 from the Arab Colonel Ahmed Sidki al Jundi) served with the Northamptons. Chief of Operations Charles Coaker had combat experience, but Administration Chief Broadhearst, sprang from the mandatory officialdom. Ordnance Officer Faire, Signallers Chief Robinson, Supply Chief Cliff, Artillery Chief Hirst and REC Horn, were all professionals. Only one Arab officer, Habs al Majali, had held the position of battalion commander; all the battalions deputy commanders were British. FO816/152; Annex II to COS(49)423; CAB21/1923.
73. The Middle East Garrison, DEFE6/7, JP(107 and 108); also WO32/13351.
74. Brigadier K. A. Timbers of the Royal Artillery Historical Trust to the author, 24.6.91.
75. Interviews: Bromage, Coaker.
76. FO141/1246 and FO371/68822, E10325. Colonel Coaker to the author, 12.6.92, Colonel Bromage to the author, 8.5.92. See also in Sir Alan Cunningham's papers, St Antony's College, Oxford, cables, 7.2.48, and 17.3.48.
77. 'The Part Played . . . ', FO141/1246, ibid. Coaker, Bromage, ibid.
78. A. Sela, 'Transjordan, Israel and the 1948 War: Myth, Historiography and Reality', *Middle Eastern Studies*, vol. 28, No. 4 (1992), pp. 627 and 652 ff; Musa, pp. 126–8; Y. Levy, *Tish'a Kabin* (Tel Aviv, 1986), pp. 179, 246–56.
79. 'The Part Played . . . ', FO141/1246. Edroos, pp. 252–7; Levy, ibid.
80. Bunche to Cordier, 15.6.48, DAG1/2.1.4, Box 5, UN Archives, New York, henceforth, UNA.
81. A. H. Hourani, *Syria and Lebanon* (Oxford, 1968), pp. 199–229; Hurewitz, pp. 59–60.
82. 'Hagorem Hasuri Vehalevanoni Bemilhemet Ha'atzmaut', 922/45, IDFA; Amin al Nafuri, 'al Jeish al Souri fi Filastin aam 1948', *Al Fakhr al Askari*, Damascus, July 1979; for the CIA Report see n. 57 above. See also WO261/54 and CAB21/1923, COS(49)423.
83. Ibid. See also A. Shatkai, 'Soleley Ha'atzmaut Ba'avir', *Heil Avir*, 1955, Vols 44–5.
84. Bevin's hand scribble added 'You should call the American's attention to this'. FO371/68798, E528, E4524, E4539/G and E6478.
85. See Chapter 5, p. 179; CIA report, ibid. Also P. Seal, *The Struggle for Syria* (London, 1965), pp. 33–4.
86. 'Hagorem Hasuri . . . ' IDFA, ibid; CIA report, Appendix 'C', ibid.
87. 'Hagorem Hasuri', ibid.; Nafouri, ibid.; WO261/549; Lorch, pp. 258–64.
88. H. Levenberg, 'The Military Preparation of the Arab Community in Palestine 1945–1948', Ph. D. thesis, LSA, 1989.
89. Taha al Hashemi's Diary, IDFA; 'Tene' and Intelligence 1 File k2, 2168/50, IDFA; 'Shai' reports of February 1948, S/25/3999, CZA.
90. In April at the peak the pro-Mufti 'Jihad al Makdas' forces attempt to control the Jerusalem–Tel Aviv highway, Qawukji proposed to the Haganah terms of a *modus vivendi*.

91. Report by General Lundstrom, September 1948, DAG1/2.1.4, UNA.
92. Report of August 1948, File 10, 2384/50; 'Tzva Ha'hatzala', intelligence appreciation, Stav/a, 289/50, IDFA.
93. Rachish reports, 1948, the, Galili Papers, Section 25M, Series 6. The Kibbutz Meuchad Archives (KMA). See also Lorch, p. 703.
94. Debate among Israeli historians of this issue is alive, yet to date affected by political nostalgia. For the best study of this issue see M. Pail and A. Ronen, *Kera Betasah* (Tel Aviv, 1992).
95. Y. Greenberg, 'Financing the War of Independence', *Studies in Zionism*, vol. 1, no. 9, 1988; Pail and Ronen, pp. 9–22.
96. BGD, 15.5.48.
97. P. Govrin, *Tzav Kri'ah Tashah* (Tel Aviv 1976), pp. 25 and 82–90; BGD, 16 and 25 April, 7, 15, 16, 22 and 26 May; 6 June, etc.
98. E. Sivan, *Dor Tashah, Mitos, Dyoken Vezikaron* (Tel Aviv, 1991), pp. 36–7.
99. D. Niv, *Ma'archot Hairgun Hatzvai Hale'umi*, Vol. 6, pp. 213–18.
100. A compilation of data from J. Matras, 'Israel: Absorption of Immigration, Social Mobility and Social Change', PhD dissertation, University of Chicago, 1962, p. 38.
101. M. Sicron, 'Immigration to Israel . . . ', Statistical *Supplement*, vol. II, Jerusalem, 1957, Table A3; B. Gil and M. Sicron, *Rishum Hatoshavim* (Jerusalem, 1957), Chapter 1 and with some variance, A. Gertz, *Statistical Handbook of Jewish Palestine* (Jerusalem, 1947), p. 47; Sivan, p. 258.
102. P. Gouvrin, *Tzav Kri'a Tasha* (Tel Aviv, 1976), pp. 25, 82–90.
103. Sivan, p. 29.
104. BGD, 5.1.49.
105. Greenberg, Table 5, Appendices A and B and *passim*. BGD, 30.12.47, 12.1.48, 2 and 6 March, 4 and 5 April; Itay to Or, 29.5.48, TRBA and 29.9.48; G. Meir, *Hayai* (Tel Aviv, 1975), pp. 171–2.
106. Yadin's lecture in a Yad Galili symposium, 20.1.82, *Yad Galili Publications*, vol. 76.
107. An ample volume of epic, biographical and monographical literature on Israel's arms acquisition (Rechesh), written by Israelis and Zionist enthusiasts, unfolds valuable information, but is better be taken with a pinch of salt, particularly in regard to the use of those arms. See particulalrly, P. Vase, *Hamesima Rechesh* (Tel Aviv, 1966); M. Mardur, *Shlihut Aluma* (Tel Aviv, 1965); L. Slater, *The Pledge* (New York, 1978); B. Kagan, *Hem Himri'u Ba'alata* (Tel Aviv, 1957). For our documentary sources, see n. 110, below.
108. Or to Amitai and Hilel, 6.6.48, TRBA.
109. 'Cheil Hatothanim Bemilhemet Ha'atzmaut', 1046/70, Files 124–6; Mitzraim ve'hatzava hamitzri' ibid., IDFA. See also FO371/69177, J8257.
110. The atmosphere and daily work of Israel's arms acquisition is vividly found in three working diaries of the time: Prime Minister and Minister of Defence's David Ben Gurion (BGD) and Chiefs of the acquisition organization in Geneve, Shaul Avigour (TRBA) and Pinhas Sapit (TRBS), IDFA. Useful is also the Yehuda Arazi file, 'Eduyot', HA; Rechesh correspondence, Files 189, 633/56 and 407 and 922/175, IDFA.

111. BGD, February, *passim* and 15.3.48 and 20.3.48.
112. Avigour, *Im Dor Hahagana*, (Tel Aviv) vol. 2, pp. 158–9, 162–7 BGD, 1.12.48.
113. Avigour, *Im Dor Hahagana*, ibid.; Shkolnik to Shaul, 18.6.48, File 189, 633/56, IDFA; TRBA, *passim.*
114. M.Na'or, 'Pinhas Sapir Bitkufat Hashanim, 1930–1949', Ph.D dissertation, Tel Aviv University, 1983, pp. 461–76.
115. For more details of Rechesh operations see Chapters 3–9.
116. DBG 7.7.48; Y.Evron, *Ha'ta'asiah Habitchonit Beyisrael* (Tel Aviv, 1980), pp. 68, 76, 79, 80, 82–3, 121, 124–6; *Davar*, 19.1.73; 'Heil Hatothanim . . .', ibid., IDFA.
117. In BGD, 6.6.48, the number recorded is 40 825, but the Minister of Defence mistakenly omitted the Artillery Corps.
118. *Ibid.* 'Detailes of the brigades' strength were: Brigade No. 1 – 3500; No. 2 – 2200; No. 3 – 3000; No. 4 – 2000; No. 5 – 3200; No. 6 – 3100; *Palmach* Brigades (Nos 10, 11, 12) – 5000. Figures for Brigades in building, Nos 7, 8 and 9, figures are not fully given by the source.
119. From Czechoslovakia, 25 700 rifles: 'Arms bought until 31 May but not yet Delivered', memo by Brenner, 31.5.48, 4982/11, HA.
120. Rachish reports for June 1948, Galili Papers, 25M, Series 6, Box 26, KMA. 'Sikumey Tzevet Shirion', File 420, 922/175, IDFA; tele-interview: Colonel (Res.) A. Porath, July 1992; BGD 26.5.48; Y. Gelber, *Gar'in Letzava Ivri Sadir* (Jerusalem, 1986), pp. 117–36, 198 and 260–6.
121. E. Ambar, A. Eyal and A. Cohen, *Shorshei Heil Aa'avir* (SHA), Vol. 2 (Tel Aviv, 1988), pp. 354–8; NYT 5.2.48. The author's exchange of views with the History Branch, the Air Force, November 1992 and April 1994.
122. *SHA*, pp. 188, 211, 326 and 358; General Remez to the author, 15.2.92; E. Weizmann, *Lecha Shamayim Lecha Aretz* (Tel Aviv, 1975), pp. 54–7 and 66–7; Shataki, ibid.; author's exchange of views . . . ibid.
123. E. Tal, *Mivtza'ei Heil Hayam Bemilhemet Ha'atzmaut* (Tel Aviv, 1964). See particularly Annex 8.
124. BGD, 18.10.47.
125. BGD, 2.3.48, 7.3.42. And see Chapter 9.
126. E. Kaflansky, *The First Fliers, Aircrew Personnel in the War of Independence* (Tel Aviv, 1993).
127. FO317/68558, E7166 and E7208.

Notes to Chapter 3: The United States, The War in Palestine and the Embargo, 1947–9

1. J. W. Spanier, *American Foreign Policy since World War II* (New York, 1972) p. 285; R. J. Donovan, *Conflict and Crisis* (New York, 1977), pp. 31–2.
2. Department of State, Office of the Foreign Liquidation Commissioner, henceforth, OFLC, Operating Directive No. 4-C, 27 August 1946, RG59, OFLC Records, Box 10, US National Archives, Washington, DC, hence-

forth, USNA; *US Government Manual, 1947* (Washington, DC, 1947).

3. The OFLC activities are documented in the following series: OFLC, RG59 711.00 Armament Control and RG353, both in USNA. See also WO185/233 and various *USIS Bulletins* of 1946.

4. OFLC Records, Box 1 and FO371/68380, E1538, E2054.

5. RG353, PAC, Country File, Box 1; RG59, 711.00111 Arms Control, 8-1049 (*sic*).

6. *FRUS*, 1947, Vol. V, pp. 525–9, 1300; *FRUS*, 1948, Vol. IV, p. 8; minutes by Acheson and McGhee, RG59, FW68.24/4-2947, USNA.

7. Their records, in Lot 388, USNA were, at the time of writing, only miserly cleared through the Freedom of Information Office.

8. For MD records, see RG353 Armament Control 711.00111, particularly Lot 66D428, USNA and Lot 68A5098 at the Washington National Record Center, WNRC, Suitland, MD, Boxes 403–53.

9. RG59 711.00111 Armament Control/8-1049; RG353, OFLC Records Country File, Box 1.

10. 'Suspension of Arms and Ammunition to Palestine and Neighbouring Countries', Memo by Loy Henderson, 10.11.47, *FRUS*, 1947, vol. V, p. 1249. Cf. also, Vatikiotis, *Egypt*, p. 364.

11. Memorandum, of July 1947, RG59 867.248/8-847, USNA; D. Little, 'Cold War and Covert Action; The United States and Syria, 1945–1958', *The Middle East Journal*, vol. 44, 1990.

12. Memo by Henderson following Bevin's visit to the State Department, 9.9.47, *FRUS*, 1947, vol. V, p. 523.

13. *FRUS*, 1947, vol. VII, p. 782.

14. March–May correspondence, RG84, Lot Missions 890D.20/4-2947, WNRC.

15. Appendix 'A' to memo of 2.12.47, RG59, 711/00111/12-247 and RG59 867.248/8-847, USNA. See also *FRUS*, 1947, vol. V, p. 523.

16. *FRUS*, 1947, vol. V, pp. 523 and 806; a memo for the Anglo-American discussion of the Defence of the Middle East, September 1947, RG59, Lot55-D36, USNA; Swett to Wisner, RG353, PAC, Country File, Box 1.

17. 'Suspension of Arms . . .' (Henderson's memo) ibid; debate at the Executive of the American Branch of the Jewish Agency in New York, 5.10.47 (38th meeting); note Shertok's argument. Silver Archives (SA), Temple, Cleveland, Ohio.

18. 'Suspension of Arms . . .', ibid.

19. US UN Delegation, Summary of Meetings and Telegrams 1947, RG84, Box 57; recorded oral interview with Henderson, the Harry S. Truman Library (HSTL), Independence Mo; E. Eilat, *Ha'mavak Al Hamedinah* (Tel Aviv, 1982), vol. 2 pp. 15–18.

20. Memo by Saltzman, 20.10.47, RG84, Box 32, 867.01/20-1147, USNA.

21. Eilat, op. cit., vol. 3, pp. 520–4; interview with Clark Clifford, Washington, DC, March 1978; C. M. Clifford, *Counsel to the President* (New York, 1991), pp. 5–6, 9–10, 14 and 23–4.

22. *Department of State Bulletin*, 14.12.47; *FRUS*, 1947, vol. V, p. 1300. Swett to Wisner, 26.11.47, RG353, PCA Country Files, Box 1; *FRUS*, 1947, vol. V, p. 1249; see also Armour's talk to Congressman A. Somers, RG59, 867N.113/3-148.

23. 'Munition Division: Task Force on the Organization of Arms Policy 1948', RG353, PCA, Box 1, *passim*. Memo in of the MD, 10.5.48, RG84, Lot 800, Box 87, WNRC. RG353, FLC Box 5; USNA, Israeli State Archives, *Documents on the Foreign Policy of Israel*, DFPI (Hebrew), December 1947–May 1948, p. 385; TRBA 26.5.48.

24. PJP to NE, 10 March 1948, Rusk File, James G. McDonald Papers, University of Columbia, New York. See also RG353, Box 5, USNA.

25. *FRUS*, 1947, vol. V, pp. 1302–5, 1317; Shertok to F. D. Roosevelt junior, 24.12.47, *DFPI* (December–May), pp. 102–4.

26. RG84, Box 87, 867N.01/12-1247, USNA.

27. *FRUS*, 1947, vol. V p. 524; FO141/1265; WO202/958; Swett-Wisner, ibid.

28. Eilat, vol. 3, p. 530.

29. Report on AZEC Activities in 1948 by Abe Tuvim, 12.12.48, SA; *NYT*, 16.2.48; FO371/68410, E1105; FO68502, *passim*.

30. Leo R. Sack to H. Shapiro, end of 1947, 'Sack' drawer, SA; see also *The Near East Report*, 6.4.92.

31. On this subject see: S. Lubel, *The Future of American Politics* (New York, 1951) and his 'Who Really Elected Truman', *Saturday Evening Post*, 22.1.49; Z. Ganin, *Truman, American Jewry and Israel* (New York, 1979); R. J. Donovan, *Conflict and Crisis* (New York, 1977) and *Tumultuous Years* (New York, 1982); and the recent M. J. Cohen, *Truman and Israel* (Berkeley, 1990).

32. 'The Politics of 1948', 19.11.47, Clark M. Clifford Papers, Box 12, HSTL; C. M. Clifford, 'Serving the President: the Truman Years', *The New Yorker*, 25.3.91. Eilat, vol. 1, pp. 206–8; Judith Epstein at the Jewish Agency Executive, 28.9.48, HZ/93/03/85/3, ISA.

33. Weizmann to Truman, 9.12.47, *DFPI* (December 1947–May 1948), pp. 40–1; various reports by Lord Inverchapel, the British Ambassador in Washington, FO371/68410; *NYT*, 21.1.48.

34. FO371/68502, *passim*; *NYT*, 13.2.48.

35. See, for instance, the Sol Blum Papers, NY Public Library, Misc. and the Herbert Lehman Papers, Columbia University.

36. Inverchapel to Bevin, FO371/68410, E1105; *FRUS*, 1948, pp. 581–4.

37. *NY Herald Tribune*, 10.2.48; *NYT*, 4, 5, 10, 11, 13 and 21 February; *Washington Post*, 12 and 15 February and Tuvim, ibid.

38. *FRUS*, 1948, vol. V/2, pp. 629–30, 637–40 and 666–75ff.; Minutes, Jewish Agency Executive, New York, 8.2.48 and 8.3.48, HZ/93.03/67/10, ISA.

39. Memo by Ruffer, 20.3.48, Epstein to the Executive Members and Shertok to Shiloah, 29.3.48, *DFPI* (December 1947–May 1948) pp. 483, 528–31 and 536; *Ha'aretz*, 23.3.48.

40. *FRUS*, 1948, vol. V/2, pp. 972–6, 993; Silver–Fahy, correspondence of March–April, 'Fahy' and 'Agency' drawers, SA.

41. Exchange of telegrams between Israel's Foreign Office and delegations in New York and Washington, *DFPI*, vol. 1 (May–September), pp. 5, 16, 59, 77 and 86; *NYT* 26.5.47.

42. *DFPI*, loc. cit. pp. 302, 309, 311 and 487.

43. *NYT*, 11.9.48; Comay to Shapiro, 3.8.48, HZ/93/03/85/20, ISA; Memo by Lovett, 23.10.48, *FRUS*, 1948, vol. V/2, pp. 1507–8.

44. Ilan, *Bernadotte ...*, pp. 177–91.
45. *FRUS*, 1948, vol. V/2, p. 1509; Eilat to Sharett, 3.8.48, *DFPI*, vol. 1, p. 411.
46. *DFPI*, op. cit. p. 525.
47. The documentary sources we have used on this affair include correspondence between the Haganah and IDF Mission in New York, Files 189, 633/56; 51, 2521/50 and 64, 245/50; Periodical Ordnance Tables, File 163, 28/60, IDFA; various files in the 'Eduyot' series and in the Arazi archives, HA. For the US Administration's point of view, we used the PCA Papers in 'Neutrality Matters', RG353; FBI correspondence with MD, in RG56, and MD papers in RG59, 711.00111 Armament Control. Some illumination was obtained from the 12 volumes of *The United States vs. Adolph Schwimmer et al.*, of the District Court, Southern California. Israel's arms acquisition in the USA was described in various monographs and biographies, which, however, must be taken with a pinch of salt. The most useful among them are L. Slater, *The Pledge* (New York, 1976); W. S. Green, *Taking Sides* (London, 1984); T. Kolek, *For Jerusalem*, (New York, 1978); Y. Eshkol, *Ish Hashura* (Tel Aviv, 1990); and D. Almog, *Harechesh Beartzot Habrit, 1948–1949* (Tel Aviv, 1987).
48. Report and debate at the Jewish Agency Executive (USA), 28.9.48; Y. Slutzky, *Sefer Toldot Hahaganah*, vol. 3 (Tel Aviv, 1972), pp. 1234–6. For record of the establishing meeting (typed on the UJA headed paper) see 'Montor' drawer, SA.
49. Oral report by Polak at the Executive of the Jewish Agency, New York, 28.9.48, HZ/93.03/85/3, ISA; Slater, *passim*; T. Kollek to the author, 9.9.91; Y. Eshkol, p. 199.
50. Kollek, pp. 32, 40–2, 47–8, 89 and Chapter 6; FBI reports to MD, January 1949, RG59, 711.00111/Armament control, USNA.
51. Slater, pp. 104–7; BGD, 31.8.48; Polak Report, ibid.; FBI correspondence with MD, including reports on Schwimmer, Weisman and Miller, RG59, 711.00111, Armament Control and on Agronsky and Fliderblum in R59, FW867N.243, USNA.
52. See File 189, 633/56, IDFA; Slater, Chapter XVII, RG59, 711.00111 Armament Control, 8–1049, 7–2649, 10–1449 and *passim*; Kollek, p. 74 and Chapter 6 and his letter to the author, ibid.; *Davar*, 22.9.78.
53. Slater, pp. 62–5, 160–2, 192–3 and 211–18; Y. Eshkol, p. 199; *Ha'aretz*, 7.3.48; File 189, 633/56, IDFA.
54. Meeting, Jewish Agency Executive, 28.9.48, HZ/93.03/85/3, ISA.
55. BGD, 4.2.48; Davar, 12.1.73.
56. Report by the Assistant Chief of the Explosive Department, FBI, RG59, 867N.241–948, USNA; *NYT*, 8 and 15 January; Slater, pp. 155–64 and 170–4; Davar, 22.9.78.
57. BGD, 21 January, 3, 8, 10, 12, 19 and 29 February; cables from Mati and Teddy, 28.3.48, 'Alon has signed ...', 23.4.48, 'Phone calls from Alon', 25.3.48, 8.4.48; Or to Amitai and Ben Kedem, 10 and 20 May, cables from Teddy and Mati, 21, 23 and 31 May, all in TRBA.
58. FBI reports to MD and MD internal exchange, 26.3.48, 9.4.48 and 10.5.48, RG59, CS/A 867.N113, USNA; FO371/68412 and E3991; Zeev to Pino,

4.8.48, TRBA; Kollek, pp. 72–3; Eshkol, p. 213.

59. Houch to CRB, to IA and to ARA, RG59, 867N.113/5–1048, USNA.
60. File 21, 907/51, IDFA; BGD 16, 28 January, 10 March 1948; Lt Colonel G. Sarig 'A history of the Israeli Signals Corp', *Kesher Ve'electronika*, vols 8 and 10; G. Sarig's private papers.
61. Mati to Ben Yehuda, 11.6.48; Teddy to Amitai and Shkolnik, 19.7.48 and Or to Teddy, 8.2.48, File 189, ibid. 'Inventory of Tanks and Guns in Brigade 8, 15.11.48', File 163, 28/60, IDFA.
62. FBI-MD reports, February–December 1948, RG59, 883.801, USNA; Campbell to FO, 3.12.48, FO371/69202, J7491; FO371/68412, E3745, E3991; Dicky to OR 28.3.48, TRBA; BGD, 29.2.48 and 19.8.48; Mati to Kozlovski, 10.9.48, File 189, ibid., *IDFA*; Galili Papers, 25M, Box 4, KMA; 'Inventory of Armour', 1.2.49, File 4, 714/68, IDFA.
63. SHA, pp. 199 and 260–3.
64. TRBA (a summary list of proposed deals); SHA, pp. 211 and 333–4; BGD 26.1.48, 12.2.48, 12.4.48 and 9.5.48; 'Teddy's proposal' 21.5.48: *Ma'ariv*, 26.12.86.
65. RG59, OFLC, Boxes 5, 10; Joe Eisen to Or, 9.4.48, TRBA; Slater, pp. 141–7 and 221–36.
66. Mati to Ben Yehuda, 11.6.48, ibid.; RG59, 867N.113/4–948, USNA; Teddy to Amitai and Shkolnik, 19.7.48, File 189, ibid.; Summary of Balak flights, TRBA; *SHA*, pp. 199–211, 316 and 342.
67. Report by Alon, 25.4.48, Berg for Teddy, 10.6.48, TRBA and Mati to Ben Yehuda, 11.6.48, File 189, IDFA, ibid.
68. Salztman to Lovett, 28 and 30 June, RG59, 711.00111, Armament Control/6–2848; Appendix 1 to memorandum by Majors Jiri Dufek and Vladimir Slosar of the History Department, the Czech Air Force, March 1992, henceforth, Dufek-Slosar; report of interrogation of Charles Philip at the District Court of Southern California, Schwimmer, vol. 1, pp. 227–338, and prosecution summary, vol. 10, ibid.
69. Saltzman to Lovett, 30.6.48, RG59, 7111, Armament Control/6–2848; Russel to Elliot, ibid.; Cummins to L. B., 4.10.48, RG353, PAC Country File, Box 4; Mati to Viniya and Ben Yehuda, 13 and 14 June.
70. RG353, PAC Papers, 9.8.48 and 4.10.48. Kollek to Ben Gurion 9.7.48. Teddy to Amitai and Shkolnik, 19.7.48 and summary of conversation between Gad and Teddy, 5.1.49 (*sic*) File 189, ibid.; see also in BGD, 21.6.48.
71. Touri to Arazi and other letters, Arazi Papers, Files 26, 27 HA, FO371/68636 and E9974; Dani to Or, 24.4.48, TRBA; Gad to Hadod, 23.11.48, File 189, ibid.; RG319, COS Office, G2, USNA.
72. The 'rate' charged by 'the President', namely, Latin American rulers, began with 3.5%, then 2% and, finally, 3%. It is not clear, however, how exactly this levy was allocated. In 1948 the President of Nicaragua was Victor M. Romain-Reis, a nebulous figure, while the man with which the Institute negotiated was the Minister of Defence and former President, Anastasio Somoza. The letters of introduction were signed by Foreign Minister Louis M. de Bayle. Probably three Ministers shared that income.
73. Sir Oliver Franks to FO, 14.9.48, F371/68638, E13313; FO371/68636,

E9974; FO686387, E11673; Report in RG59, Lot 890.D20, USNA.
74. Telephone conversation, Gad–Teddy, 5.1.49 and a message through Or to Teddy, 8.2.49; Hadod to Gad, 23.11.48, TRBS.
75. See Mati to Ben Yehuda, 11.6.48, Teddy to Ben Yehuda, 22.6.48 and Teddy to Amitai and Shkolnik, 19.7.48, File 189, IDFA, ibid. From Pino, 11.8.48, TRBA.
76. Humbleton to FO, ibid.
77. Mati to Ben Yehuda, a compilation of three letters of 11, 14 and 22 June, 1948, File 189, IDFA, ibid.
78. 'Kniyot Be Dromi', 6.7.48, Mati to Or, 7.7.48, Gad to Teddy and Mati, 5.10.48 and Daniel to Mati, 19.10.48, all in File 189, IDFA, ibid.; 'Heil Hatothanim...', IDFA, ibid.
79. Gad to Mati, 22.11.48, File 189, ibid.
80. Teddy to Ben Gurion, 9.7.48; Mati to Viniya, 13.6.48; Hadod to Gad, January 1949.
81. Kollek and Mati to Ben Gurion, 9 and 19 July and Mati to Koslowsky and Pino, 19.9.48; Or to Amitai, 22.11.48 (*sic*) all in File 189, ibid. O. Abarbanel, 'Harvardim Tzolleim Al Falouga', *Heil Avir*, 1954, vol. 43.
82. Exchange, Campbell–FO, November, FO371/68639, *passim*. Tedder to the Chiefs of Staff, 21.12.48, DEFE5/9, COS(48)216.
83. E. Tal, pp. 224–9; 'Inventory of the Navy', November 1948 and 1.2.49, File 163, 28/60, IDFA.
84. Gad–Laish exchange, 23.8.48, 11.9.48 and 27.9.48, TRBS; BGD, 15.12.48.
85. For air crews, see Kaplansky, pp. 18–25; for others, (Shahan, *Kanfey Havitzahon* (Tel Aviv, 1966), p. 294
86. Salaries sometimes reached $600 a month (Green, p. 54).
87. DEFE5/9, COS(48)216 of 21.12.48; Report on Bunche's meetings in the State Department, 26.8.48, RG353, PAC Country File, USNA; Exchange Campbell–FO, FO371/68639, *passim*. See also Ilan, *Bernadotte...*, Chapter 8.
88. Memo by Hamilton, RG59, Lot 800, WNRC; *FRUS*, 1948, vol. V/2, p. 1177.
89. DEFE7/180.
90. W. S. Green, op. cit., p. 61.
91. RG59, 867N.113/4–948, USNA; Yeshaiahu to Or, 1.4.48, and Oskar to Or, 2.4.48, TRBA; Hillenkoetter to Truman, 12.4.48, OF File (CIA), HSTL.
92. RG59, 501.BB Palestine/7–148 and 8–11/48; oral evidence by Uri Brier, Eduyot, HA; Dufek-Sluser, *ibid.* And see below, Chapter 4.
93. Culbertson–Lovett exchange, RG535, PAC Boxes 116 and 161; FO371/68636, FO371/68638, FO371/68639 and FO371/71261.
94. See below, Chapter 5.
95. Reports from Prague, 29.10.48 and 3.11.48, with comments by EUR, IS and GTI in the State Department, RG59, 867.113/10–2248 and 11–348, USNA; *FRUS*, 1948, vol. V/2, pp. 1292 and 1361.
96. *FRUS*, 1948, vol. V/2, pp. 1279–80.
97. See below, Chapter 8.
98. Minutes by Niles, Clifford, Lowenthal, Bowels and Lovett, throughout early 1948, Clark M. Clifford Papers, Boxes 12 and 13, HSTL; see also

The New Yorker, 25.3.91; the author's interview with Clifford, ibid.
99. BCD, 11.12.47; Kollek, p. 76; Mati to Ben Yehuda, 11.67.48, File 189, ibid., IDFA.
100. See below, Chapter 6.

Notes to Chapter 4: Britain's Middle Eastern Policies

1. E. Monroe, 'Mr Bevin's "Arab" Policy', *St Antony's Papers*, II (London, 1961), p. 46 and pp. 12, 20, 24 and *passim*.
2. 'Review of Soviet Policy', memo by Bevin, 5.1.48, CAB129/23, CP(48)7. See also 'Communism', memo by Defence Secretary A. V. Alexander, 31.3.48, DEFE5/10, COS(48)74(0).
3. DEFE4/3–9, *passim*.
4. Bullock, pp. 34–5.
5. *Hansard*, Commons, vol. 445, pt 2, col. 420.
6. Memo in the Eastern Department, 9.2.48, FO371/68798, E1331.
7. In 1936 the title of the British High Commissioner of Egypt was substituted by 'His Majesty's Ambassador' and Egypt was allowed to have diplomatic relations with other countries. But in February 1942 the British Ambassador, helped by tanks, deposed a disloyal government and appointed another.
8. Chiefs of Staff Meetings, March 1947 till February 1948, DEFE4/3–9, DEFE6/5–7, DEFE7/102. Louis, pp. 105–25 and 226–64.
9. Louis, ibid.; FO371/68373, E6405.
10. Ibid., and see also Vatikiotis, *Egypt*, pp. 364–5.
11. Inverchapel to Marshall, 20.2.48, FO115/4350; Vatikiotis, ibid.
12. 'Warlike Stores in the Pipeline to Arab Countries', memo in the Defence Office, CO537/3938 (*sic*); minutes by Group Captain Plant, ibid.; minutes in the Foreign Office of 9.2.48, FO371/68798, E1331. Under British pressure, the purchase by Egypt of nine used Sterling bombers from the Transport Society in Belgium was also suspended, although eventually carried out. See below, Chapter 8.
13. Minutes by McNeil, 27.1.48, CO537/3938.
14. McDermot to Googh, 6.4.48, FO371/69200, J2013.
15. Minutes by J. S. Beth, FO371/68798, E528.
16. FO371/69201, J3247, J3807; FO371/69202, J4098, FO371/75099, E446
17. Louis, p. 328.
18. Renton, ibid.; Exchange with Mack of September 1947, DEFE 7/833.
19. Louis, p. 329.
20. DEFE7/833.
21. *The Times*, 16.1.48; and see M. Khaddouri, *Independent Iraq, 1932–1958* (Oxford, 1960), pp. 262–6, and Louis, pp. 333–4.
22. Renton, ibid.
23. Bevin to Mack, 16.2.48, FO371/68446, E3182; interview with Beeley.
24. 'Collapse of the Treaty of Portsmouth', in Renton, ibid.
25. Harold Wilson, 'Prime Minister on Prime Ministers', a BBC2 series, 6.2.78.

26. Minutes by Beeley, 11.3.48, FO371/68412, E3557, and interview with Beeley, ibid. See also CO537/3938, *passim*.
27. Bevin to Alexander, 13.3.48, FO371/69188, J2040/G.
28. DEFE7/833 and 834; DEFE5/11, COS(48)125; correspondence with Mack, June 1948, FO371/68143, E9016; IPI, pp. 64–5, 108, 120, 150 and 178.
29. FO371/68142, E4326; FO371/69188, J2368.
30. FO371/68412, E3491, E6515, and CO537/3938.
31. For instance, Bevin to Campbell, 29.4.48, FO371/69201, J2845 and 12.5.48, J2868, and to Mack
32. Minute by M. T. Walker, 23.5.49, FO371/75101, E6515/G.
33. RG353, PAC, Country File, Box 1, USNA; WO261/18; Louis, p. 325.
34. Louis, p. 345.
35. 'Requirements Suspended by the Embargo' FO371/68413, E9016; 'Capital Equipment for Iraq', FO371/68420, E14974; CAB21/1922, COS(49)423, Annex 'B'; DEFE7/833 and 834; WO256/549; and Renton, ibid.
36. Glubb to Lt Colonel Palmer, 27.3.48, WO216/677.
37. See A. Sela, 'Transjordan, Israel and the 1948 War: Myth, Historiography and Reality', *Middle Eastern Studies*, vol. 28, no. 4 (1992) pp. 625–80.
38. FO800/477; exchange FO–Amman, January–February, FO371/68836 and FO371/62226; Glubb's exchange with his Political Liaison in the War Office, London, Colonel R. W. Palmer, WO216/677; see A. Shlaim, *Collusion across the Jordan*, (Oxford, 1988), pp. 122–40.
39. CAB128/12, 24(48)6.
40. See Chapter 2.
41. FO371/68822, E11049/G; FO371/68373, E6800; interview with Colonel Bromage who was in charge of the Legion depot in Aqaba.
42. FRUS, 1948, vol. V/2, p. 5. Interview, Bromage, ibid.
43. Bevin to Kirkbride, 25.5.48, FO371/68556, E6885. Also FO371/68558, E7165, and a retrospectively by Beeley, 8.7.48, FO371/68572, E9387.
44. Pirie-Gordon to FO, 25.7.48, FO371/68822, E10325; Kirkbride to FO, 12.7.48, FO800/477; interview with Bromage, ibid.
45. CAB128/12, 24(48)6.
46. 'Mediation in Palestine', by Bevin, 26.5.48, FO371/68558, E7208.
47. FO371/68374, E7887/G and E7960/G.
48. FO800/457.
49. Bevin to various legations, 30.5.48, FO371/68558, E7166.
50. The subsidy was renewed on 22 July, CAB128/13, 53(48). Most of the officers returned to their positions within a few days 'at their own risk'. Interview with Bromage, ibid.
51. WO cables, FO371/69202, J4582, J6946/G; FO371/68798, E4468 and E15702; General Crocker to the Egyptian Minister of War, 9.6.48 and WO to MELF of 2.6.48 and 7.7.48, DEFE7/180.
52. Their exchange is in CAB21/1922 and in DEFE7/833.
53. FO371/68373, E6613; see also FO371/69201, E2845.
54. FO371/68413, E7629. Also FO371/68373, E6637.
55. See also minutes by Beeley, 8.7.48, FO371/68572, E9388.
56. Bevin's exchange with Mack, 26 May–20 June, DEFE7/833.
57. *Hansard*, Commons, vol. 459, col. 838; *Guardian*, 14.12.48; 'Britain – Arms', cables in Jewish Agency Drawer, SA; FO371/68411, E3399.

58. CAB21/1922.
59. *FRUS*, 1948, vol. V/2, p. 1585.
60. Minutes, FO371/68566, E8409.
61. Bevin to Kirkbride, 13.7.48, FO371/68572, E9447.
62. CAB128/13, 57(48)4; Bevin's memoranda, CAB129/29, CP(48)207 and CP(48)225.
63. Ilan, *Bernadotte*, Chapter 8.
64. CAB21/1922, *passim*.
65. Ibid.; see also Bevin–Alexander exchange, 11 June–26 November, FO371/68822 and 68419, *passim*.
66. The author's interview with Eban, March 1982. For the Soviet media of June, see Y. Ro'i, *Soviet Decision-Making in Practice, the USSR and Israel, 1947–1954* (New Brunswick, 1980), p. 233.
67. 'Britain Violates UN Ban on Arms Shipment to Participants in the Palestine War', an Israeli release, Paris, 14.12.48, Jewish Agency Drawer, SA; Sir Hugh Dow to FO, 17.12.48, DEFE7/181; *Ha'aretz* 16.12.48; *NYT* and *NY Herald Tribune*, 7 and 10 January, 1949.
68. DEFE7/833.
69. 'Britain Violates UN . . .', ibid.
70. For a possible trace, see Shin Mem 1 October–November, 1948, IDFA.
71. 'Size and Shape of the Armed Forces', DEFE5/10–14.
72. WO185/233; FO141/1314.
73. DEFE7/180.
74. Cf. Front Dalet/Intelligence, 'Hakohot Hapoalim Bemerhav Hadarom Vehanegev', 31.10.48, File k/2, 2168/50 and 'Kohot Hatzava Hamitzri Hapoalim Baaretz', 10.12.48 (*sic*), File 361, 922/75, IDFA. For British pondering over the event see WO32/13351 and a note by Wheeler, 21.1.49, *DEFE7/180*.
75. Telephone interview with Colonel (Res.) Galil Elyashiv, April 1993. According to the evidence given in 1949 by the commander of an Israeli Jeep Platoon, whose unit hit five Locusts helped by one 6 Pounder gun, with no casualties to itself, the Egyptian tanks did fire three shells. Affidavit by Ran Bargiora, File 354, 922/75, IDFA.
76. File 10, 2384/50; Shin Mem 1, File 420, 922/175. See also list of captured tanks in BMB 683, File 211, 652/56, IDFA.
77. DEFE7/181.
78. FO–BMEO exchange, and WO–CinC MELF exchange, December 1948, FO371/75099, E1080.
79. Minute by Thirkell, 18.1.49, FO371/75099; FO371/68380, E9635; exchange, Gresswell–Jones-Weeller, January 1949, DEFE7/180; WO261/18; WO185/233.
80. FO141/1314; cable, 22.12.48, FO371/68421. It was in a similar procedure, through which General Renton proposed to supply Iraq with Sherman tanks in 1947, WO261/18.
81. FO371/69177, J8206.
82. FO371/69177, J7385, J7518, J8257; FO800/477.
83. 'Quantities of War materials Stolen from British Service Depots, Between 14 May and 6 November', FO371/69177, J7385, J7518.

84. DEFE7/834.
85. Summary of Rachish operations, July 1948, Galili Papers, 25/6, Box 6G, KMA; oral evidence by Y. Zenyuk, Eduyot, HA.
86. Tal, Appendix 8.
87. FO317/69200, J1404; *SHA*, pp. 183–9; Or to Yeshayahu, 14.6.48, TRBA.
88. CIA Reports to MD, RG59, 711.00111, Armament Control, Country File (microfilm) USNA; BGD, 12, 24, 25 and 30 January, 1, 12 and 27 February, 12 and 14 April, *SHA*, pp. 197–8, 252–3.
89. Fredkens moved to illegal smuggling of aircraft from Germany.
90. *SHA*, pp. 324–5; evidence of Mr Towel, 'Mayfair's' owner, FO371/68369, E15597. Ilan, *Bernadotte*, pp. 87–8.
91. Scotland Yard Inquiry, FO371/68638, E12671, E12330; report by Group Captain Plant, 2.11.48, FO371/68638, E14202/G; RG59, 711.00111, Armament Control, Country File, USNA. Captain Harvey served with the IDF as a Mahal pilot.
92. Exchange Ministries of Supply–Air–Foreign Affairs, FO371/68638, E14202/G; Bartlet to Heyns, FO371/68420, E15204, and CIA, ibid.
93. CAB129/32, CP(49)10; Bevin–Alexander exchange, FO371/68413, E8059, E8756, and FO371/68415-19, *passim*.
94. FO800/477; FO371/68822, E11049/G. But Colonel Bromage, in an interview of 1992, 'believed' that the cry about shortage of ammunition was 'hot air' and that shortage was only in 25-pounder and mortar ammunition. Interview, ibid, and Bromage to the author, ibid.
95. FO800/477
96. FO800/457.
97. CAB21/1922.
98. Minutes in CAB21//1922; see also FO371/68822, E11049/G and E11403.
99. Alexander to CinC MELF, 30.8.48, CAB21/1922; FO800/457.
100. CAB129/29, CP(48)207; summary of the two Ministers contacts, FO371/68414, E10121 and CAB21/1922.
101. Alexander to CinC MELF, 30.8.48, CAB21/1922. DEFE7/833 and minutes by Walker, FO371/68822, E11318/G.
102. Bevin to Kirkbride, 28.10.48, FO371/68418, E14097; exchange in the Ministry of Defence, 27 October – 4 November, and Bevin memoranda 'Assistance to the Arabs' COS(48)149, DEFE5/8, and 'Assistance to Transjordan', 9.11.48, CAB21/1922.
103. Ibid.
104. CAB128/13, 71(48).
105. *FRUS*, 1948, vol. V/2, pp. 1585–9.
106. *FRUS*, 1948, vol. V/2, p. 1571.
107. Marshall's report from Paris, 15.11.48, *FRUS*, 1948, vol. V/2, pp. 1585–9. Bevin–Attlee exchange, mid-November, FO371/68822, E14814. See also a retrospective account in CAB129/32, CP(49)10.
108. COS 1887/9/11/8, CAB21/1922.
109. *DFPI*, vol. 2, pp. 198–201, 265 and 270; RG59, 501.BB Palestine/11-1748, USNA.
110. DEFE7/833.
111. Annex to minutes of COS meeting of 17.11.48, and 'Assistance to

Transjordan', CAB21/1922; Crocker to Field-Marshall Slim, 19.11.48; FO exchange with Amman, November, FO371/68420; interview with Colonel Bromage, ibid.

112. Bevin, Alexander and Tedder in a talk to Ambassador Douglas, 20.12.48, FO371/68152, E16134, E15091.

113. Exchange GHQ/MELF–Ministry of Defence, 27.10.48 and 7, 9 and 19 November; Annex II to note by the Chiefs of Staff, 16.11.48, all in CAB21/1922; General Redman to Michael Wright, 26.11.48, FO371/68822, E15341/G and CAB128/13, CM(48)61.

114. Memo by General Templer, 16.11.48, a cable to General Crocker, 18.11.48 and 30.11.48, CAB21/1922.

115. Sources: 'Distribution of teeth Arms Units in MELF on August 1948', Appendix A to 20/Gen. WO38/13351; 'Order of the Battle, Middle east Land Forces', 21.10.48, WO212/670; See also: FO371/69176, J67970.

116. FO371/68419, *passim.*; General Redman to Michael Wright, *ibid.*

117. FO371/74399, E289; FO371/75400, E804.

118. *FRUS*, 1949, vol. VI, p. 660.

119. Bevin's memorandum, of 2.2.49, CAB21/1922, DO(49); FO371/75100, E5239/G. The evolvement of the change in the FO attitude towards the embargo is documented in FO371/75099-105; see particularly FO371/75103, E7993/G.

120. *DFPI*, vol. 4, pp. 118 and 262–63; *FRUS*, 1949, vol. VI, pp. 953, 958–9, 1091, 1115 and RG59, 501.BB Palestine/7-649, USNA. *The Times*, 9.6.49.

Notes to Chapter 5: Assistance from the Soviet Bloc

1. For earlier research on the USSR and other Communist countries' involvement in the first Palestine war see Y. Ro'i, *Soviet Decision Making in Practice: The USSR and Israel, 1947–1954* (New Brunswick, NJ, 1980). This is a pioneering, credible and meticulously researched work; U. Bialer, *Between East and West: Israel's Foreign Policy Orientation, 1948–1956* (Cambridge, 1990) and his 'Czech–Israeli Arms Deal Revisited', *Journal of Strategic Studies*, vol. 8, no. 3, 1985. An earlier work, now somewhat outdated, is A. Krammer, *The Forgotten Friendship* (Urbana, 1974). Details about Soviet involvement in the Czech–Israeli arms deal were first broached in the much quoted article by Z. Schiff, 'Stalin Natan et Hahora'ah', *Ha'aretz*, 3.5.68, but this also helped to plant a certain misconception. Our own documentary sources, were mainly: (1) TRBA, TRBS, BGD and IDF Inventory Tables 1948-9, all in IDFA; (2) oral evidence of Rechesh agents in the Eduyot section, HA and the memoirs and biographies of some of them; (3) a summary of the Czech military assistance to Israel, by Majors Jiri Dufek and Vladimir Slosar of the Czech Army History Department (quoted, Dufek-Slosar); (4) British intelligence reports in the series FO371, 'N', 'E' and ADM223; and (5) US Documents pertaining to FBI-MD activities, Department of State, series: RG59, RG84, RG353, USNA.

2. CIA resume, June 1948, RG84, 800, WNRC; FO371/75527, E1457. In

Cairo, the largest Soviet legation consisted of four diplomats. In Damascus the Soviet Minister in Beirut took charge.

3. See Bevin's memo, 'Review of Soviet Policy' CAB129/23 of January 1948 and Alexander's memo 'Communism', 3.3.48, COS178, (48)74, DEFE5/100. See also memoranda by Walter Bedel-Smith, *FRUS*, 1948, vol. IV, pp. 909 and 946.
4. Dufek-Sloasar, ibid.
5. G. Golan, *Soviet Policies in the Middle East from World War Two to Gorbachev* (Cambridge, 1990), pp. 35–6.
6. Record of a telephone conference between Jessup, Rusk and Lovette, 10–13 June, RG84, Box 87, USNA. Report from Moscow, 14.7.50 (*sic*), FO371/91921, E10212; FO371/81955, E1192/28G.
7. Monthly Intelligence, January 1949, FO371/77257, N1276/G. For Israeli arms acquisition activities in Czechoslovakia after 1948 see Zitron to Sapir, 19.10.50, and *passim* in HZ/1552/52, ISA.
8. Jewish Agency Executive, minute, 22.5.47, CZA.
9. Sharett to Ben Gurion, 12.2.48, report by Lifschitz (probably of), 15.2.48, *DFPI* (December 1947–May 1948), pp. 338–9 and 347–8; BGD, 14.2.48 and TRBA, 6.4.48.
10. Itai to Or, 5 and 22 May, TRBA. The Kimche brothers write (*A Clash of Destinies* (New York, 1960), pp. 75–6 that the Czech arms deal resulted from a meeting between Sharett and Gromyko in January. The Israeli document, however, indicates just the contrary, that from December through to January no meeting with Gromyko took place; *DFPI*, (December–May), p. 300.
11. *DFPI*, vol. 1, p. 59; Teddy to Or, 1.6.48, TRBA.
12. Mati to Ben Yehuda, letters: 11 and 14 June, File 189, 633/56, IDFA; Teddy to Or, ibid.
13. Exchange, Ben Kedem–Or, 20 and 22 June, TRBA.
14. Ratner's exchange with Ben Gurion, 6.10.48 and 8.11.48, HZ/A/2/2325, ISA; *DFPI*, vol. 2, pp. 29–30; Y. Ratner, *Hayai Va'ani* (Jerusalem, 1978), pp. 394–400.
15. *DFPI*, vol. 2, fn. p. 163; MacEwan to Gresswell, FO371/73549, J3020; FO371/91921, E10212; and E1192/28G; see also FO371/68500, E616.
16. Ro'i, op. cit., p. 154. However, a few IDF officers, who formerly served in the Red Army, reached some prominence in the IDF; the most outstanding were a tank battalion commander (Biatos), an artillery battalion commander (Gorodetzky) and six air crew members.
17. M. Namir, *Shlihut Bemoskva* (Tel Aviv, 1971).
18. Ratner to Shin Mem, 9, 27.6.49, HZ/238/29, ISA; Namir, op. cit., pp. 73–6.
19. 'To Moshe from Yohanan', 16.11.48; Ratner to Shin Mem, 9, ibid; Barne, 'An Exchange with the Foreign Office, 1950', *passim*. See also Namir to Sharett, 25.1.50, HZ/2383/29, ISA.
20. Dixon to FO, 12.8.48 and 7.1.49, FO371/68637, E10781/G and FO371/75396, E312; Steinhardt to the Secretary of State (undated, probably July) OF204, HSTL.
21. *FRUS*, 1948, vol. IV, pp. 909–10 and 946 and vol. V/2, pp. 547–54.
22. Schiff, ibid.

23. Minutes in the Ministry of Air, FO371/68638, E13372 and E14202/G.
24. Monthly Intelligence, 5.12.48, ADM223/228; B. Busek and N. Spulber (ed.), *Czechoslovakia* (London, 1957), pp. 227–36; R. Selucky, *Czechoslovakia: The Plan that Failed* (London, 1970), pp. 27–33.
25. 'Al hamitrachesh bechehoslovakia', HZ/2509/6 and HZ2509/6, ISA; Monthly Intelligence, 5.7.48, ADM223/228.
26. FO371/71264, N6885; monthly intelligence, 5.7.48, ADM223/227.
27. Shortage of aluminium hampered production of aircraft, FO371/77257, N290/G; and of tin, the production of bullets, BGD, 4.1.48.
28. Monthly intelligence, FO371/77257, N290/G; Dixon to FO, 12.8.48, FO371/68637, E10781/G.
29. Bialer, 'Czech Arms Deal...'; report by Dixon, 7.1.49, FO371/75396, E312.
30. 'Letter from Egypt', 18.11.47, Box 6A, File 2, KMA; BGD, 19, 23, December 1947, and 25.1.48; cables and intelligence in File S25/1700, CZA; E. Avriel, *Pithu She'arim* (Tel Aviv, 1976), pp. 258–60.
31. For a summary of Israel's arms purchase after 1948 see Asher to Gad and Amnon, 19.10.50, HZ/52/1559 and HZ/2492/20, ISA; the first-hand sources at our disposal were the work diaries of the 'Rechesh' headquarters at Geneva, and the Czech account by Dufek-Slosar. See also 'Sales of Arms to Syria by Czechoslovakia', 25.1.48, FO371/68798, E528 and *passim*. Minutes by Beith and McAlpin, 14, and 29 January, FO371/69200, J3064, *passim* and FO371/69201.
32. BGD, 14.1.48, 17.5.48, and 21.5.48; see also Itai to Or, 22.5.48, TRBA; Ro'i, pp. 151–2.
33. Avriel, '*Pithu*..., pp. 259–61; BGD, 14, 19 and 22 December 1947; two telephone interviews with Ze'ev Hadari, 27.6.92 and 22.11.92. Toman soon lost face with the Soviets on account of his contacts with Jewish organizations abroad. He was jailed, but managed to escape to the West. *The Jewish Journal* (NY) October 1992.
34. BGD, 25.1.48; Itai to Or, 28.3.48 and Hadari to Or, 30.3.48, TRBA.
35. BGD, entrees, 14 December–29 January, 22 February and 20 March; Or to Amitai, 21.5.48, TRBA; the author's talks with Hadari, ibid.; M. Mardur, *Shlihut Aluma* (Tel Aviv, 1965), pp. 187–9.
36. TRBA, 4.1.48; BGD, 25.1.48; see also a report from the US Consul in Bratislava, RG59, OS/A, 867N.113/10–1848, USNA
37. Mardur, p. 181.
38. FO371/77257, N290/G.
39. TRBA, 23.3.48; *SHA*, p. 334; Dufek-Slosar, ibid.
40. TRBA, cables, 23.3.48 and 21.5.48; DBGD, 23.5.48; and 10.6.48; *SHA*, p. 334; Dufek-Slosar, ibid.; *Letectvi a kosmonautika*, 1991, vols 4 and 5.
41. BGD, 22.2.48; TRBA, 26.3.48; cf. B. Kagan, *Hem Himri'u Ba'alata* (Tel Aviv, 1960), pp. 47–8.
42. BGD, 19, 21 and 25 January, 21 February; TRBA, 18.1.48.
43. Yehuda-Ofri to Hilel and Argov to Or, exchange around mid-June, TRBA, *SHA*, pp. 338–7.
44. Oskar and Itai to Arnon, 1.4.48; Arnon to Yeshayahu, 1.4.48; Balak Records, TRBA, IDFA; 'Rikuz mishlohey himush mihul', Galili Papers, Box 4, File 6; Brenner, 'Neshek Shenirkash...', ibid.; P. Vase, pp. 279 and 282–3.

45. 'Rikuz Mishlohey . . .' ibid.; Vase, ibid. See Table 9 below.
46. TRBA, 8.6.48; BGD, 26.5.48, 26.6.48.
47. Remez's letter and a telephone conversation to the author, 15.2.92, 21.2.92.
48. Itai to Or, 8.4.48; Or to Dicky, 21.5.48; Hilel to Or, 29.5.48, and 12.6.48, TRBA; *SHA*, p. 334.
49. RG353, PAC, Country File, Box 1 and RG59, 711.00111 Arms Control, 6–248 USNA; *DFPI*, vol. 1, p. 21. For the issue of the Czechs' own landing rights in Greece, see *FRUS*, 1949, vol. V, pp. 190–1.
50. Remez to the author, ibid. The Czech assemblers never fully managed to coordinate the propeller with the guns and machine-guns, so the pilot was constantly in a danger of 'gunning himself down'.
51. 'Reshimat Balak', Notebook 2, 24/54, IDFA; Itai to Or (2 cables), 22.5.48; Matkal to Or, 1.6.48, TRBA.
52. Quoted in Shatkai, ibid.
53. 'The Iraqi Army in Palestine', FO371/82450; 'Hagorem Hairaqi . . .' IDFA, ibid.; reports by Campbell, 4.6.48, FO816/120 and by Kirkbride, 31.5.48, FO371/683712, E7283.
54. Oren to Yadin, Baer and Mundek, 29.6.48, File 895/52/71, IDFA.
55. Itai to Or, 8.4.48, Laish to Or, 6, 17 and 26 August, TRBA. Remez to the author, ibid. Shatkai, *Heil Avir*, vol. 46, pp. 14–15; Dufek-Slosar, ibid.; File 163, 28/60, IDFA. The author is grateful to the Israeli Air Force History Section for their advice on this point, though the conclusions are his alone.
56. Cables exchange, Gad-Alon, end of August; Laish- Yeshaiahu and Gad-and Norman, 26, 28 and 29 August, 6, 8 and 13 September, TRBS; Shatkai, pp. 61–3; Remez to the author, ibid.
57. Shaike to Gad and Ben Yehuda to Gad, 28.9.49; a note by Boikin, RG353, Country File, Box 1; RG59, 800.00B, Summaries/8–2348 USNA.
58. Laish to Gad, 13.9.48; exchange Shaike–Ben Yehuda and Gad–Laish, 28–9 September.
59. Hoyland (Rhodes) to FO, 30.9.48, FO371/68638, E13372; FO371/68591, E13258; RG59, 711.00111, Armament Control, 10–248, USNA.
60. Exchange Or–Yeshaiahu, and Felix–Gad, end of November, TRBS.
61. 'Taktziv lehashlamat taken', 28.11.48 and 'Matzevet Heil Ha'avir le', 1.2.49, Files 4, 714/68; 161 and 163, 28/60, IDFA.
62. Doron to Amir, 11.1.51, HZ/530/10; exchange, Asher–Amnon, November–December 1949, File 3, 400/62, IDFA; Galili Papers/25b, Box 6g, File 2, KMA; *FRUS*, 1949, vol. V, pp. 190–1.
63. Or to Amitai and Ben Kedem to Kaspi, 21.5.48; Itai to Pino, 5.7.48; Hagai to Or, 12.7.48, TRBA.
64. Dufek-Slosar, ibid.; exchange cables, Or–Yeshaiahu, 4 and 9 May, TRBA; BGD, 2.6.48.
65. Or to Hilel, to Amitai and to Ben Kedem, 27.5.48 and 4, 5, 6, 12 and 16 June and Pino to Felix and to Laish, 19.8.48.
66. Exchange Or-Yeshaiahu, 4, 5, 9 and 29 May and 10 June. Exchange summaries between Israel's embassy in Prague and the IDF History Department, Autumn 1991 (courtesy of Col. B. Michelson).
67. Assaf to Or, 29.5.48; Yeshaia Gazit to the author, May 1992.
68. Hilel to Or, 4.6.48; A. Shatkai, ibid.; *SHA*, p. 383; E. Stiegman, *Me'atzmaut Lekadesh* (Tel Aviv, 1990), p. 323.

69. Berg from Avni, 30.5.48, TRBA; interview with Dan Segre, 16.5.93.
70. Department of History, embassy, ibid.
71. Reports by Gary Fried of June and of Michael Huter of December 1948, HZ/2501/3, ISA; Uri Brier, Eduyot, HA. Interview with Segre, ibid.
72. Huter, ibid.
73. Correspondence in HZ/2501; HZ/2383/29; HZ/2329/3, ISA.
74. For the process of financing the Czech deal, see BGD, 25.1.48, 24.3.48 and 26.5.48 and 10.6.48; Or to Amitai, Ben Kedem and Kaspi, 21 and 22 May; Itai to Or, 29.5.48; Hilel–Or exchange, 11, 19, 21, 24 and 30 May, TRBA; Gad–Laish and Chay–Pino, 11, 16, 17, 28 and 29 August and 6, 8 and 13 September, TRBS. Letters, Mati-Gad, File 186, 633/56, IDFA.
75. BGD, 13.1.48 and 24.3.48; Chay to Pino, 11.8.48; Hay to Laish, 16 and 20 August, TRBS.
76. When they did, it was to finance the Israeli delegation, for the balances of Zionist organizations in Czech banks had been confiscated earlier. Gera to Eliashiv, 14.11.51, HZ/530/10, ISA.
77. Remez to the author, ibid.
78. BGD, 1.8.48.
79. Felix to Or, 12.6.48; Eliahu to Pino, 20.7.58, TRBA; Alon to Gad, 25.8.48; Gad (and others) to Laish, October 18, 20, 28, TRBS. For details of Israel's arms deal in Italy see below, Chapter 7.
80. Cables, July 1, 17, 30, TRBA, and 28.9.58, 6.10.48, 16.10.48, 26.11.48, 16.12.48 and 21.12.48, TRBS.
81. Dufek-Slosar, ibid.
82. Gad to Laish, 21.11.48; correspondence between Sapir and Ministry of Defence, March–May 1949, File 189, 633/56, IDFA.
83. Dixon to FO, 7.1.49, FO371/75396, N312.
84. Schiff, ibid.; Prague to FO, 14.6.51, HZ/530/10, IDFA.
85. A. Peled, 'Mahleket Himush Bahagana, 1941–48', in G. Rivlin (ed.), *Ale Zait Vaherev* (Tel Aviv, 1990).
86. Ben Gurion to Shertok, 16.4.48, *DFPI* (December 1947–May 1948), p. 647; and see Schiff, ibid.
87. For details see Tables and 8 and 9 below.
88. Two Messerschmidts and two Spitfires crashed on their way. Two others Spitfires made a forced landing at Rhodes, of which one was returned by Greece after 2 years. Balak Diary, TRBA; FO371/82826, E1223; Zitron to Amir, HZ/530/10, ISA.
89. Of the serviceable Spitfires in December two were locally assembled from parts available not from Czechoslovakia. The author is grateful for members of the History Section, Israel's Air Force, for checking this point with him.
90. Exchange of cables, Aron–Or and Or–Yeshaiahu, first and second weeks, June, TRBA; report by Dixon, FO371/71264, N9915; see also FO371/68637, E10781 and FO317/68638, E12195/G and E13691.
91. Penfield to the Secretary of State, 2.9.48, RG59, 711.00111 Armament Control; report from Rome, RG59HH 501. Palestine/7-1048; Kakic to the Secretary of State, 6.8.48, RG59, all in USNA. Green, pp. 300–1; cf. Ro'i, p. 158.

92. Green, pp. 294–95; *FRUS*, 1948, vol. V/2, p. 1200; the full document by the courtesy of CIA Freedom of Information coordinator, 9.7.85.
93. File 263, 137/51, IDFA.
94. Or to Yeshaiahu, 2.9.498; Dufek-Slosar, ibid.; Uri Brier, Eduyot, ibid. Ro'i, p. 159.
95. Gat to Laish, 16.9.48, TRBS; Brier, ibid.; Schiff, ibid.
96. Avriel to Sharett, *DFPI*, vol. II, pp. 406–7.
97. TRBA, 26.3.48.
98. Dr K. J. Jutila to the Secretary of State, RG59, Country File, Box 191, USNA; M. Jakobson, *Finish Neutrality* (London, 1968), pp. 33–44; E. Erling, *Nordic Security* (Adelphi Papers) (London, 1983), p. 7.
99. TRBA, 30.7.48; TRBS 16 and 18 August. FO371/71421B; Utila, ibid.
100. A note from Fredy, 26.3.48, TRBA.
101. Berg to Arnon, 15.5.48; also 23 and 27 May, TRBA.
102. BGD, 10, 15 and 26 June; Itai to Pino and others, 2, 5 and 20 July, TRBA.
103. Felix to Or, Hagay to Pino, and Gad to Laish, 16, 18, 19 and 31 August, 10, 15 and 29 September; Felix to Arnon, 23 and 29 November, TRBS; RG59, A/JB711/00111, Armament Control; File 147ID in RG319, ID.
104. Galili Papers, Section 25-m, KMA; British reports in DEFE7, FO141 and FO371/69190; A. Sela, dissertation, quoted above. See also Krammer, pp. 63–4.
105. BGD, 19, 22 and 26 December, 1947; DEFE7/211; 'Sales of Arms to Syria by Czechoslovakia', 25.1.48, FO371/68798, E528; FO371/77257, N290/G; ADM223/227; Mardur, pp. 218–56.
106. Cables, 22–28 August, TRBS; ADM223/227; M. Mardur, ibid.
107. *DFPI* (December 1947–May 1948), p. 347; annex to Cummins's memorandum of 2.12.47, RG59, 711.00111, Armament Control/12-247, USNA.
108. Minutes by Campbell, Jones, Randall and others, FO371/69190, J794, J1341, J1706; FO371/69201, J3064.
109. FO371/69201, J2521/G; Dixon to FO, FO371/75396, E312.
110. Dixon to FO, 8.7.49, FO371/73561, J5640.
111. British Embassy in Washington Files, March–April 1949, FO115/4444; *FRUS*, 1949, vol. VI, pp. 953, 958, 1249, 1279.
112. FO371/75396, E312.

Notes to Chapter 6: Other Arms Sources to Palestine

1. BGD, 5.4.48.
2. Oral history transcript by Dickenstein, Eduyot, HA; Alon to Gad, 25.8.48, TRBS.
3. Alon to Gad, ibid.; exchange Or–Laish and Or–Admon, 21 and 30 July, TRBA. Reports in 516b, 400/62, IDFA; Shimon to Gad, 25.8.48, TRBS.
4. Vase, *passim*; minutes, 5.6.48, Or to Amitai and Ben Kedem, 9.6.48 and Yehuda to Hilel, 15.6.48; *Santa Chiara* to Itai, *Resurrection* to Alon; Avigur's cable, 29.3.48, all in TRBA.

5. Dickenstein, ibid.; Files 28–35, Arazi's archives, HA. Galili Papers, Section 25-m, Series 6, Box 6g, KMA. For fictitious authorizations, Arazi paid 2–3.5% of the gross value of his purchases to bank accounts in New York City.

6. Still Arazi and his men sent the 65-mm guns without sights.

7. This description is based on a series of reports by the Paris Director of the Jewish Agency, Maurice Fischer, *DFPI* (December 1947–May 1948), and *DFPI*, vol. 1, and by reports on the French situation in TRBA. On French politics see P. Avril, *Politics in France* (London, 1969).

8. *DFPI* (December 1947–May 1948), pp. 202–3, 284, 386 and 484–5. See also FO371/68799–68802, particularly FO371/68802, E125532.

9. Ibid.; see D. Lazar, 'Tzarfat ve Ysrael, Reshitam shel Yehasim', *Medina Mimshal Veyehasim Beinleumyim*, vol. 1, no. 2 (1971).

10. The fragility of the government when faced with a controversial domestic problem is exemplified by the July–September 1948 crisis, whereby a dispute over the military budget, which spilled over to the public, brought down the Schuman cabinet. A new Cabinet headed by André Marie lasted only a few days and was replaced by one headed yet again by Schuman, which lasted only a week, and was replaced by yet another, headed by Henry Queuille. That last cabinet held its own for about a year, but it survived various votes at the National Assembly by a margin of three to six votes only. See Avril, pp. 29–46.

11. For the steady development of this attitude see *DFPI* (December 1947–May 1948), pp. 138–9, 202, 183, 311, 320–2, 443 and 559.

12. Fischer to Goldmann and to Shertok, *DFPI*, op. cit., pp. 249–50, 283–4 and 322; cable from Paris, 12.2.48, TRBA.

13. *DFPI*, op. cit., p. 320.

14. Oscar and others to Avigour, 26 and 30 March and 4 April, TRBA; BGD 26.3.48; Note Lazar, fn. p. 85; RG59, 890D.20, missions, USNA.

15. Cables by Oscar, ibid. 'Report on the activities of the Neter Group'; 'Report on Alon purchases' and 'cables from Zvi' and others, 31.2.48, 26.3.48 and 4.4.48, TRBA.

16. 'Silver from France', 15.4.48, TRBA; Fischer to Shertok, 28.4.48, *DFPI*, op. cit., p. 694; Vase, p. 187; BGD, 5.4.48 and 15.5.48; see also S. Nakdimon, *Altalena* (Jerusalem, 1978), pp. 30–32.

17. BGD, various entries for that period; 'Reports from Sydney', 15 April, and then 25 April–16 May, and Or–Hilel exchange of cables 21 May until 15 June, TRBA. See also Vase, pp. 282–83.

18. Daniel from Sydney (Marseilles), 29.11.48 and 4.12.48, TRBS.

19. See, U. Brenner, *Altalena* (Tel Aviv, 1978) and Vase, p. 220.

20. Vase, ibid. Except 1815 rifles, 118 sub-machine-guns, 206 Bren machine guns and 2 million rounds of ammunition, captured by the IDF during the ship's early attempt to unload its cargo.

21. Galili Papers, Section 25m, Series 6, Box 6b, KMA.

22. Fischer to Shertok, 14.7.48, *DFPI*, vol. 1, esp. p. 332; review of acquisition in France, Galili Papers, Section 25m, series 6, Box 6a, KMA; Vase, pp. 187, 198–9.

23. Minute in the NE, RG59, 890D.20, missions, USNA; Broadmead to FO, 10.12.48, FO371/68798, E15701; FO371/75100, E3745; *NYT*, 20.3.49;

Broadmead's talk to Abdullah Atfe, FO371/75560, E5472; *FRUS*, 1950 (*sic*) vol. V, pp. 36, 160.

24. Broadmead, ibid.; Harvey's to FO, FO371/75560, E2901, E6545; *FRUS*, 1950, op. cit., pp. 678 and 1203. See also A. Rabinovich, *The Road Not Taken* (Jerusalem, 1991), Chapter 3.

25. Files 4, 714/68 and 163, 28/60, IDFA; 18.10.48, 25m/6, Box 6g, KMA.

26. BGD, 8.2.48; 'Heil Hatothanim . . .', ibid.; 'About Alon's Purchases', 25.3.48 and 'Alon vehavkvutza haneterit – Hazmanot', 26.3.48, TRBA.

27. BGD, 20, 26, 27 and 31 May; 11, 15 and 30 June.

28. FO371/90178, *passim.*; report in the Galili Papers, 8.4.48, Section 25m, Box 6a, KMA. And see below, Chapter 8.

29. Reports by Locker, 21.4.48, *DFPI* (November–May), p. 682; *DFPI*, vol. 1, p. 99; FO371/69201, J4078/G.

30. FO371/68420, E15204; FO68421; FO371/68638, E14202/G; FO371/68412, E3444, FO371/69201, J2521/G; FO371/73559, J4640; BGD, 4.1.48; Shin. Mem, 1, 27.1.49, IDFA; Tuck to the Secretary of State, 883.24/3-2348, USNA.

31. A telephone report from a British informer on 'Isgo' (must be 'Inco'), FO371/68638, E12742; Section 25m/6, Box 6a, KMA; File 23, 4254/50, IDFA. The author is indebted to Ami Bresner, Israel's Armour historian, on his useful comments.

32. For documentation see RG59, Records of the OFLC, Box 1a.

33. OFLC Records, op. cit., Boxes 6 and 10, USNA. Note particularly 'Instruction for Neutralization', 27.8.46 and ff.

34. Ibid.; Dickenstein, ibid.; FO371/90178, *passim*; Ahron to Or, 10.6.48, TRBA; Yossi to Gershon, File 15, 2541/50, IDFA.

35. 'Skira al tnaei harechisha beitalia', Galili Papers, Section 25n, Box 6a, KMA' Appreciation by Russell (Rome) sent to the British Embassy in Paris, 13.3.50, FO371/90178, JE1196.

36. 'Hovala vehavtachat Rechesh', memorandum by Z. Rotem, File 407, 922/175; Dickenstein, ibid.

37. Or to Hilel 29 and 31 May, TRBA; Dickenstein, ibid. Galili, ibid. FO141/1331; FO371/90178, JE1196/2. 'Hrechisha hamitzrit beitalia', 26.1.49, and other intelligence reports of April, Galili Papers, 25m, Box 6a, KMA; cf. also Naguib, p. 17.

38. E. Tal, op. cit., pp. 219–24; File 51, 2521/50, IDFA.

39. Gad–Laish exchange, 29 August, 1, 5, 11, 16 and 21 September, TRBS; report of 25.8.48, Galili Papers, Section 25, Box 6g, KMA.

40. Ibid. Borshi to Aviv, 24.8.48, Alon to Gad, 25.8.48, TRBS; Dickenstein, ibid.; Galili; FO371/68421, E15734 and FO81966, *passim*.

41. Gad to Laish, 20.9.48, and cables from Ben Yehuda–Gad, end of September, TRBS. See also Eduyot by David Frumer, HA.

42. Dickenstein, ibid. An Italian court later ordered the return of the tanks to their owner and a payment of compensations to him. See also A. Avneri, *Sapir* (Tel Aviv, 1976), pp. 43–4.

43. Exchange Gad-Laish, 28.8.48, 6, 9, 16, 20 September, 6, 7, 13, 15, 28 October; Yehuda to Gad, 16.11.48, all in TRBS. Report on the unloading of *Arsia*, January 1949, File 2, Section 25m, Box 6g, KMA; Seasonal OB of IDF Armour for 1948–9, Files 4, 714/68 IDFA.

44. FO371/81955, E1192/39; 'Oren', Files 92, 102, 260/51 IDFA; FO371/ 81966, *passim*.
45. Stevenson to Bevin 10.2.51 (*sic*), FO371/90178, JE1196/2; 'Harechisha hamitzrit . . .', Galili Papers, ibid.; DEFE7/181; FO371/73559, J4650; FO371/69188, J4090; Campbell to FO, 3.2.49, FO141/1367; 'H. C.' to Michael Wright, 8.4.49, FO141/1331. See also Chapter 8.
46. Ibid. See also 'Egyptian Acquisition in Italy', by P. Jones, FO371/73559, J4650 and FO371/90178 JE1196/2, passim.
47. Cables, 20, 21, 24 September, and Sireni to Gad, 29.9.48 and 2.10.48, TRBS; Alon to Ben Yehuda, 27.11.48, Arazi Archives, HA.
48. Shin Mem 1, 2.10.48, 28.12.48 and 13.1.49; 'Harechisha hamitzrit . . .', Galili Papers, ibid. Intelligence summaries, Hazit Dalet, File 361, 922/ 75; FO371/73559, J4650.
49. Cairo to FO, 22.12.48, FO371/68421, E15734, and 10.2.51 (*sic*) FO371/ 90178, JE1196/2 and FO371/81966.
50. FO371/81955, E1192/39.
51. 'Task Force on Organization of the Arms Policy', Report, April 1949, RG353, PAC, Subject File, Box 1, USNA.
52. Miller's Affidavit under oath, 28.2.49 and a memo by Saltzman, 17.2.4, RG59, 711.00111 Armament Control/2–2849; FBI-MD exchange, June– December 1948, RG59, 711.00111 Armament Control, *passim*. 'David Miller' must not be confused with 'Albert Miller', which was one of Arazi's code names in the USA.
53. *SHA*, pp. 322, and 326–27; Or and Chai to Dickey and Yeshayahu, 14.6.48, TRBA; BGD, 1.8.48; 'Rshimat Metosim Shenitke'u', TRBA, Annex 2; Kaplansky, pp. 58 and 63.
54. Report of 8 June 1948, RG59, 883.24/6–848, USNA.
55. P. Preston, *Franco: A Biography* (London, 1993) pp. 568–82.
56. Culbertson to the Secretary of State, 23.2.48. See also March, RG59, A/ FK883.24/2–2348, USNA. Also *FRUS*, 1948, vol. III, pp. 1028–34.
57. FO371/90178, JE1196; Naguib, ibid.
58. Exchange with the Madrid, August, RG353, PAC, Box 161 and RG59, EJH883/8–348, USNA; Sabit, pp. 170–1; and see Chapter 8 below.
59. *SHA*, pp. 326–9; cables from Dany to Chai, December 1948, TRBS; a paper by Lt Colonel Z. Lachish, IAF, Tel Aviv University, September 1991.

Notes to Chapter 7: The Value and Effect of the UN Supervision of the Embargo

1. See the discussion in my *Bernadotte in Palestine*, mentioned above. See also D. W. Wainhouse *et al.*, *International Peacekeeping at the Cross-roads* (Baltimore, 1973).
2. *UNSACOR*, 1948, Resolutions, p. 20.
3. Papers of Sir Guy Campbell, Padbury, Bucks, and the author's exchange with Sir Guy, 1980; diary of Barbro Jerring, 1–2 June 1948.
4. Bunche to Cordier, 12.6.48, DAG1/2.1.4, Box 5, UNA.

5. Ilan, op. cit., pp. 95–120.
6. DAG1/2.1.4, Box 4, *passim*, UNA.
7. On the work done by these aircraft see DAG1/2.1.4, Box 5, particularly the report of 2.9.48, UNA.
8. Cordier to Bunche, 19 and 24 June, DAG1/2.1.4, Box 5; Marshall to Trygve Lie, 24.6.48, DAG1/2.1.4, Box 8. On the naval patrols see Box 7, *passim*, all in UNA.
9. Marshall to Lie, ibid.; 'Instructions to UN Observers', DAG13/3.3.1, Box 2, UNA.
10. Pelt to Sobolev, 17.7.48 and other cables of the Secretariat of July, DAG1/2.1.4, Box 7, UNA.
11. Exchange Jackson–Bernadotte, 22–23 July, DAG1/2.1.4, UNA; *FRUS*, 1948, vol. V/2, p. 1231; Ilan, pp. 150–62 and 174–5.
12. 'Assistance to Bernadotte', an interdepartmental inquiry of 4.8.48 ordered by Marshall, RG59, FW 501.BB Palestine/8–448, USNA.
13. Cordier's exchange with Seward, Bernadotte and Bunche, 4.8.48, DAG1/2.1.4, Box 5, UNA; Mohn to Eitan, 29.8.48, File 44, 2618/50, IDFA; also File 26, 2168/50, IDFA and Ilan, pp. 150–6.
14. Correspondence Lie–Lovett, end of July, Box 8; Bunche (from New York) to Bernadotte, 11.8.48, Box 9, DAG1/2.1.4, UNA.
15. Personnel reports signed by Malania and by Riley, 1 and 12 January 1948, DAG1/2.1.4, Boxes 8, 9 and 13, UNA.
16. Sharett's talk to Bernadotte, 22.7.48 and Eytan to Lundstrom, 26.8.48, *DFPI*, vol. 1, pp. 414 and 552–3; 65a and 57, 2168/50, IDFA.
17. Guy Campbell Papers, ibid.; File 65a, 2168/50, IDFA; DAG1/2.1.4, UNA; 81 Congress, Senate Committee on Foreign Affairs, *Hearing to Ammend the UN Participation Act* (Washington, DC, 1950); R. Higgins, *Peace-keeping Operations, 1946–1967* (Oxford, 1969), pp. 66–71.
18. Reports signed by Ortiz, DAG1/2.1.4, Box 5, UNA.
19. *FRUS*, 1948, vol. V/2, pp. 1266–71, 1319–20, 1342–5 and 1991–4.
20. Ilan, pp. 178–83.
21. DAG1/2.1.4, Box 7; File 43, 2168/50, IDFA.
22. Cables, Or to Ben Yehuda, 9, 13, 17 and 24 June, TRBA; Agam–Baruch files are mainly in 2168/50, IDFA.
23. DEFE7/834; *IPI* (Hebrew translation), pp. 106 and 177–80; 'Basra, Considerations generales sur la mission d'observateur dela ONU', October 1948, DAG13/3.3.1, Box 3, UNA; Bevin to Alexander, 5.11.48, DEFE7/833. Colonel Bromage to the author, 8.5.92; Major R. G. Young to the author, 3.6.92; exchange between Bevin–Mack, DEFE7/384; Bevin to Campbell on his talk with the Egyptian Ambassador, FO800/457 and FO371/73549, J409.
24. Operation diary (Haifa) of Captain (US Navy) Daniel Eddy, 12–15 June, DAG13/3.3.1, Box 3, UNA; ibid., cables in Box 1.
25. Colonel Bonde to Major Wimberley and other papers, DAG13/3.3.1, Boxes 2 and 29, UNA; FO371/68567, E8727.
26. Sources: files in Series DAG1/2.1.4, Boxes 6, 7 and 9, UNA.
27. Ortiz to the UN, New York, early August, DAG1/2.1.11, Box 5.
28. 'Hagorem hairaqi . . .', *IDFA*, ibid.
29. DEFE/181; FO371/73559, J4650; FO371/69188, J4090. Reports in File

25, 21681/50, IDFA; Report by Dr Azcarate, DAG1/2.1.4, Box 7, UNA.

30. DAG1/2/.4 Box 26; notes in Captain Eddy's Diary, 14.6.48, and in Paul Mohn's papers, June 1948, Box 431/K, Uppsala University; interviews with John Reedman, Tunbridge Wells, 31.10.80.

31. Captain Eddy's Diary, 14 and 15 June; Vase, pp. 238–46; BGD, 15.6.48, Victor Mills, New York, 6.11.84.

32. Exchange, Simon–Komrov, 20, 21 and 23 June, File 57, 2168/50, IDFA; Ahron to Or, and Yeshaiahu to Ben Yehuda, 17, 24 and 27 June, TRBA.

33. 'Oniyot ufeulot', summary by Vase, Galili Papers, Series 6, Box 6g; DAG13/3.3.1, Box 3, UNA; 'Sikumey Balak', TRBA; Vase, pp. 190–1.

34. Stanek File; 65a, 2168/50, IDFA; DAG13/3.3.1, Boxes 3 and 7, UNA.

35. Reports by Stan, 7, 8, 10, 11 and 12 August, Stanek File, and Sharet to Bernadotte, 11.8.48, all in 65a, 2168/50, IDFA.

36. Stan to Baruch, ibid.; Sharett to Bernadotte, 12.12.48; 21, 2168/50, IDFA; 'Airfields, Coasts and Forts', January 1949, DAG1/2.1.4, Box 9, UNA

37. 'Instructions to send things' and letters from Borshi to Hilel, June–August 1948, Galili Papers, Series 6, Box 6g, KMA; Ben Yehuda to Gad, 30.9.48 and 7.10.48 and Alon to Gad, 6.10.48, TRBS.

38. Or to Yeshayahu, Hilel to Or, and Yeshayahu to Or, 3, 6 and 12 June, TRBA; Dickenstein, ibid.; Borshi to Zvi, 24.8.48, Galili, ibid., etc.

39. Dickenstein, ibid.

40. Lundstrom to Yadin, 12.11.48, 25, 2168/50, IDFA.

41. FO371/68591, E13258; see also Riley to Komrov and Yadin, 12.11.48, 21681/50, IDFA.

42. Examples are reported in the files of the chief Israeli liaison officer of the Southern Command, Major Michael Hanegbi, GSD, 2168/50, IDFA, ibid. See also the P. A. Mohn papers, Box 431/K, Uppsala University.

43. Baruch to Eytan, 25.12.48, 81, 2168/50, IDFA.

44. See 'Informal Lecture by Dr Bunche' (given to members of the UN Secretariate), 16.6.49, DAG1/2.1.4, Box 9; Ilan, pp. 114–20.

45. CinC MELF to the Minister of Defence, 1.4.49, CAB21/1923.

46. 'Informal lecture by Bunche', ibid.

47. In Israel's alone, there were 13 active or serviceable runways for cargo planes; 65a, 2168/50, IDFA.

48. Lundstrom at a meeting with Bunche, 18.9.48 (following the assassination of Bernadotte), Bunche's notes, DAG1/2.1.4, Box 9; Riley to Bunche, 10.12.48, DAG1/2.1.4, Box 7; Lovett to Marshall, 2.11.48, *FRUS*, 1948, vol. V/2 p. 1541.

49. Fisher to the UN Secretariate, 6.11.48, DAG1/2. Box 2, UNA.

Notes to Chapter 8: Conclusion

1. Report to the President by the NSC, 17.10.49, NSC47/2, USNA.

2. Bevin to Franks, 7.3.49, CAB21/1922; *FRUS*, 1949, vol. V, pp. 952–9.

3. See Table 16.

4. BGD, 30.6.48 and 19.9.48; 'Heil Hatothanim . . .' IDFA, ibid.

5. British reports from Damascus, March–July 1949, FO371/75547.
6. Alexander to Bevin, 22.10.48, FO371/68419, E14450.
7. General Saleh al Jubury to the Minister of Defence, 25.9.4 and 16.11.48, IPI, pp. 65, 108, 113–15 and 126–32; FO371/68413, E8059; a memorandum by Brigadier Orlebar, FO371/82450.
8. Mack to FO, July FO371/68414, E9358.
9. IPI, pp. 107 and 180; Khadduri, p. 273; Orlebar, ibid.
10. FO371/68376, E11518.
11. 7.10.48, FO371/68419.
12. FO371/68689, E13669. See also a memorandum by Mack, FO3712/68413, E8059.
13. Shin Mem 1, 20.1.49, IDFA.
14. 'Hagorem hairaqi . . .' *IDFA*, ibid.
15. IPI, pp. 167–72; FO371/82450; intelligence summary of 16.2.49, 8/k2, 2168/50, IDFA; 'Hagorem Hairaqi . . .', IDFA, ibid. Israel, indeed, had a concrete plan to attack the Iraqi army, but political considerations suspended it. See Stav Files, 2289/50, IDFA.
16. Al Wadi to the Prime Minister, 29.1.49, IPI, pp. 137–8; FO371/82450; FO371/68412, E3444; FO371/68478, E16332; Khadduri, pp. 273–4.
17. See FO371/90178, JE1196; FO371/68418 E14137, FO371/81966 *passim*; IDF intelligence reports, Southern Command, Files 361, 922/75 and 8k/2, 2168/50, IDFA.
18. A standard infantry battalion was 850 men strong, including support. A reservist battalion included 650 men and no support.
19. FO371/68418, E14137; Brigadier Baird to WO, WO202/958; FO371/68488.
20. FO371/692021, J4098; FO371/69201, J3247. Campbell recommended that this ammunition be supplied as a special gesture.
21. Campbell to FO, 16.7.48, FO371/68574, E9645.
22. 'Ha'artileria shel tziveot arav . . .', IDFA, ibid.; Shin Mem 1, October 1948, IDFA.
23. FO371/69188, J6828, and see the Introductory chapter above.
24. A. Shatkai, *Heil Avir*, no. 45, pp. 63–4 and no. 46, p. 15.
25. FO371/90178, JE1196/2. Also FO141/1331.
26. FO371/68421, J15734; FO81966; FO371/90178, ibid.
27. Stevenson to Bevin, FO371/90178, JE1196, and JE1202/1, *passim*; *Egyptian Gazette*, 16.1.51; *Neue Zuricher Zeitung*, 17.1.51.
28. FO371/68421, E15734; FO371/69188, J6828; 'Horev' 365, 922/75, IDFA.
29. Sources: a summary of August 1950, FO816/170; Bevin's Legion Files FO816/132 and FO800/477; Glubb's report, 12.8.48, FO371/68822, E11049; interviews and correspondence with Lunt, Coacker, Young and Bromage.
30. 'The Ammunition Situation Today', 12.8.48, E11049/G.
31. FO816/121; FO68414, E10431.
32. 'The Ammunition Situation Today', ibid; see also minutes by Beeley, 5.7.48, FO371/68822, E929, and Lunt, pp. 148–51.
33. DEFE6/6, JP(48)76. Interview with Colonel Bromage, ibid.
34. See Chapter 4. For the Chiefs of Staff consideration of the situation see DEFE4/16 and DEFE4/17, COS(48)153.
35. See 'Hagorem Hasuri . . .', ibid.; intelligence appendix to Operation Oren,

Files 75, 260/51 and 102, 922/57, IDFA; a British report of 31.1.49, FO371/75527-E1457 and FO371/75527-8 *passim*; see also a British appreciation of the Syrian army, FO371/82821.

36. Reports by Broadmead, FO371/68798, E11457 and E11664/G.
37. Minutes by Makins of May 1949, on reports by Sir Oliver Harvey, FO371/75560, E6483.
38. Exchange: Broadmead–FO, 10.12.48, FO371/68798 and 19.1.49, FO371/75556, E1691; Harvey to FO, 3.3.49, FO371/75556, E2901.
39. FO371/75528 and *passim*.
40. FO371/75527, E1457; FO371/75556; FO371/75560; FO371/68801 and E4493.
41. FO371/68799, E1518; FO371/75528, E3887. 'Supply of Arms to Syria', FO371/75560, E5472/G.
42. O'Harmar to MI 2(c), 23.5.49; 'Commandement Superieur del l' Armee et des Forces Armees Syriennes, Demande du Materiel de Guerre', all in FO371/75560, E7326 and *passim*.
43. Sources: Periodical IDF Q Branch Weapons and Ordnance Tables, November 1948–July 1949, Files 163, 28/60, 19, 652/56, 12, 128/60 26, 425 4/49, 23, 1184/50, 39, 893/8 4, No. 19, 652/56, 4, 714/68, IDFA; Boxes 4 and 6a, Galili Papers, KMA; BGD *passim*. Y. Gelber, *Gar'in Letzava Ivri Sadir* (Jerusalem, 1986), M. Pa'il, ibid.; résumés of the Proceedings of the Israeli Society for Military History, published by the Galili Institute, for the years 1986–1990.
44. See S. Shamir, *Behol Mehir – Liyrushalaim* (Tel Aviv, 1994); and comment on in Y. Gelber, *Ha'aretz* (Sefarim), 18.5.94.
45. BGD, 18.10.48 and 27.11.48.
46. Figures are from a draft to Shatkai's publication (1954) and are somewhat different in other IDF publications. Courtesy of the History Branch, IDF Air Force.
47. BGD, 9.10.48.
48. Iraq 18 000, Egypt 15 000, Syria 15 000, the Arab Legion 13 000, Lebanon 2000 and Qawukji 4000 (Arab Palestinian troops).
49. To be brief, this confidence was shaken during Yoav when Brigade 9 was rushed from the Norhern Command to the Southern front.
50. Between 50 and 60 million 7.92-mm rounds, with an open supply line to Czechoslovakia, and 14 million 0.3-inch and 10 million 9-mm rounds of ammunition, which were locally produced.
51. Files 19, 652/56; 39, 893/84, IDFA; File 6, Box 4, Galili Papers, KMA; 'Sikumey Tzevet Shiryon', 2.9.53, 365, 922/75, IDFA.

Bibliography

ARCHIVES

Israel
Israel's Defence Forces' Archives (IDFA).
  Various files.
  'The Diary of David Ben Gurion' (BGD), for the years 1947 till 1950.
  Telegrams Record Books, Avigour (TRBA).
  Telegrams Record Book, Sapir (TRBS).
The Central Zionist Archives, Jerusalem (CZA).
Israel's State Archives, Jerusalem (ISA).
The Kibbutz Hameuhad Archives, Efal (KMA), Y. Galili Papers.
The Haganah Archives, Tel Aviv (HA), mainly the Series *Eduyot* (oral history recorded).
Lt. Col. G. Sarig Papers, Katzrin.

Britain
CAB, Series 21, 128, 129, 131.
CO, Series 537.
DEFE, Series 2–19.
FO371, Series E, J, JE, N
FO115, FO141, FO800, FO816.
WO, Series 32, 38, 185, 213, 216, 261.
Sir Alan Cunningham Papers, St Antony's College, Oxford.
The papers of Sir Guy Campbell, Padbury, Bucks.

USA
US National Archives, Washington, DC (USNA).
  OFLC Records, Country Files.
  Records in the series: Armament Control 711.001111, RG59, RG84, RG353, Lot D428, Lot 55-D36 and Lot 68A5098.
  The National Security Council Papers.
  National Archives, West Record Center, Suitland, MD (WNRC), Series: RG87, Lot Missions 890D.20.
The Harry S. Truman Library, Independence, MO (HSTL), including the C. M. Clifford Papers, the Oral History Library, and the Series OH, and OF.
CIA Papers: RE48–48, Langley, VA (Freedom of Information release).
The Abba Hilel Silver papers, Cleveland, OH (SA).
The James G. MacDonald Papers, Columbia University, New York.
The Sol Blum Papers, New York Public Library (Annex).
The Herbert Lehman Papers, Columbia University.

UN Archives, New York (UNA)
DAG13/3.1.0,
DAG13/3.3.1 Missions and Commission.
DAG1/2.1.4, Office of the Secretary General.
DAG1/2 Papers of the UN Secretariate.

Sweden
The Paul Mohn Papers, Uppsala University (Box 231/K).
The Diary of Barbo Vessel, Stockholm.

UNPUBLISHED SOURCES

Summary Papers of the Czeck arms deal with Israel (Dufek-Slosar), IDF,
Department of History.

PUBLISHED SOURCES

The Army List (Great Britain), 1948, 1949, 1950.
Department of State Bulletins, 1947, 1948.
Documents on the Foreign Policy of Israel (DFPI), vols 1, 2, 3, 4 and the
December 1947–May 1948 volume.
US Senate, 81 Congress, *Hearing to Amend the UN Participation Act* (Wash-
ington, DC, 1950).
Kaplansky, E., *The First Flyers: Aircrew Personnel in the War of Indepen-
dence* (Tel Aviv, 1993).
Foreign Relations of the United States, 1947, vols V and VII; 1948, vols V/2,
IV; 1949, vols V, VI.
Gil, B. and Sicron, M., *Rishum Hatoshavim* (Jerusalem, 1957).
Hansard, Commons and Lords, various volumes.
Iraqi Parliamentary Inquiry on the War in Palestine (IPI) (Hebrew version,
1954).
UN General Assembly, Official Record (UNGAOR), 1948.
UN Security Council, Official Record (UNSCOR), 1948.
UN Security Council, 1948, Resolutions
Lehimat Ha'arvim Bemilhemet Ha'atzmaut, proceedings of a meeting in the
Galili Institute.
Statistical Handbook of Jewish Palestine (Jerusalem, 1947).
The United States Government Manual, 1947 (Washington, DC, 1947).
The United States vs Adolph Schwimmer et al. (Lost Angeles 1952).
Yad Galili Publications, proceedings of various meetings pertaining to the
history of the 1948 war.

BOOKS

Almog, D., *Harechesh Beartzot Habrit, 1948–1949* (Tel Aviv, 1987).
Ambar E. *et al.*, *Shorshei Heil Ha'avir* (*SHA*), vol. 2 (Tel Aviv, 1988).

Avigour, S., *Im Dor Hahaganah*, vol. 2 (Tel Aviv, 1978).
Avriel, E., *Pithu She'arim* (Tel Aviv, 1976).
Avril, P., *Politics in France* (London, 1969).
Ben Ami, S., *Sfarad Bein Dictatura Ledemocratia* (Tel Aviv, 1977).
Ben Aryeh, Y. (ed.), *Milhemet Ha'atzmaut*, vol. 10 of *Hahistoria Shel Eretz Yisrael* (Jerusalem, 1983).
Bialer, U., *Between East and West: Israel's Foreign Policy Orientation, 1948–1956* (Cambridge, 1990).
Brenner, U., *Altalena* (Tel Aviv, 1978).
Bullock, A., *Ernest Bevin, Foreign Secretary* (Oxford, 1985).
Busek, B. and Spulber, N. (eds), *Czechoslovakia* (London, 1957).
Cohen, M. J., *Truman and Israel* (Berkeley, Calif., 1990).
Donovan, R. J., *Conflict and Crisis* (New York, 1977).
Donovan, R. J., *Tumultous Years* (New York, 1982).
Eilat, E., *Hama'avak Al Hamdinah*, vols 2 and 3 (Tel Aviv, 1982).
Erling, E., *Nordic Security*, Adelphi Papers (London, 1983).
el Edroos, S. E., *The Hashemite Arab Army, 1908–1979* (Arman, 1980).
Eshkol, Y., *Ish Hashura* (Tel Aviv, 1990).
Evron, Y., *Hata'asia Habitchonit Beyisrael* (Tel Aviv, 1980).
Ganin, Z., *Truman, American Jewry and Israel* (New York, 1979).
Gelber, Y., *Gar'in Letzava Ivri Sadir* (Jerusalem, 1986).
von Glahn, G., *Law among Nations* (London, 1981).
Glubb, J. B., *The Soldier with the Arabs* (London, 1957).
Golan, G., *Soviet Policies in the Middle East from World War Two to Gorbachev* (Cambridge, 1990).
Gouvrin, G., *Tzav Kri'ah Tashah* (Tel Aviv, 1976).
Green, W. S., *Taking Sides* (London, 1984).
Higgins, R., *Peacekeeping Operations 1946–1967* (Oxford, 1969).
Hourani, A., *Syria and Lebanon* (Oxford, 1968).
Hurewitz, J. C., *Middle East Politics: The Military Dimension* (New York, 1974).
Ilan, A., *Bernadotte in Palestine, 1948* (London, 1989).
Issawi, C., *Egypt at Mid-Century: An Economic Survey* (London, 1954).
Jakobson, M., *Finish Neutrality* (London, 1968).
Kaddouri, M., *Independent Iraq, 1932–1958* (Oxford, 1960).
Kagan, B., *Hem Himri'u Ba'alata* (Tel Aviv, 1957).
Kaplansky, A., *The First Fliers* (Tel Aviv, 1993).
Khalidi, W, *From Haven to Conquest* (Beirut, 1971).
Kimche, J. and D., *A Clash of Destinies* (New York, 1960).
Kirkbride, A. S., *From the Wings* (London, 1976).
Kollek, T., *For Jerusalem* (New York, 1978).
Krammer, A., *The Forgotten Friendship* (Urbana, Ill., 1974).
Levy, Y., *Tish'a Kabin* (Tel. Aviv, 1986).
Lorch, N., *Korot Milhemet Ha'atzmaut* (Tel Aviv, 1989; rev. edn).
Louis, W. R., *The British Empire in the Middle East, 1945–1951* (Oxford, 1986).
Lubel, S., *The Future of American Politics* (New York, 1951).
Lunt, J., *Club Pasha: A Biography* (London, 1984).
Mardur, M., *Shlihut Aluma* (Tel Aviv, 1965).
Meir, G., *Hayai* (Tel Aviv, 1975).
Musa, S., *Ayyam al Tunsa, Al Urdun fi Kharb* (Amman, 1982).

Naguib, M., *Egypt's Destiny* (London, 1955).
Nakdimon, S., *Altalena* (Jerusalem, 1978).
Namir, M., *Shlihut Bemoskva* (Tel Aviv, 1971).
Niv, D., *Ma'archot Hairgun Hatzvai Hale'umi.*
Pail, M. and Ronen, A., *Kera Betashah* (Tel Aviv, 1992).
Rabinovich, I., *The Road Not Taken* (Jerusalem, 1991).
Ratner, Y., *Hayai Va'ani* (Jerusalem, 1978).
Ro'i, Y., *Soviet Decision-Making in Practice: The USSR and Israel, 1947–1954* (New Brunswick, N.J., 1980).
Sabit, AM., *A King Betrayed* (London, 1989).
Seal, P., *The Struggle for Syria* (London, 1965).
Sela, A., *Arviye Eretz Yisarel Umedinot Arav Lifnei Milhemet Ha'atzmaut* (Efal, 1989).
Selucky, R., *Czechoslovakia: The Plan than Failed* (London, 1970).
Shahan, A., *Kanfey Hanitzahon* (Tel Aviv, 1966).
Shamir, S., *Behol Mehir – Liyrusalaim* (Tel Aviv, 1994).
Shlaim, A., *Collusion across the Jordan* (Oxford, 1988).
Sivan, E., *Dor Tashah, Mitos, Dyoken Vezikaron* (Tel Aviv, 1991).
Slater, L., *The Pledge* (New York, 1978).
Slutzky, Y., *Sefer toldot Hahaganah*, vol. 3 (Tel Aviv, 1972).
Spanier, J. W., *American Foreign policy since World War II* (New York, 1972).
Stigman, A., *Me'atzmaut Lekadesh* (Tel Aviv, 1990).
Tal, E., *Mivtza'ei Heil Hayam Bemilhemet Ha'atzmaut* (Tel Aviv, 1964).
Vase, P., *Hamesima Rechesh* (Tel Aviv, 1966).
Vatikiotis, P. J., *Egypt from Muhammad Ali to Mubarak* (London, 1991).
Vatikiotis, P. J., *Politics and the Military in Jordan* (London, 1967).
Wainhouse D. *et al.*, *International Peacekeeping at the Crossroads* (Baltimore, Md, 1973).
Wallach, Y., Lissak, M. and Lorch, N., *Atlas Karta Letoldot Medinat, Yisrael, Shanim Rishonot* (Jerusalem, 1978).
Weizmann, E., *Lecha Shamayim Lecha Aretz* (Tel Aviv, 1975).

ARTICLES

Abarbanel, O., 'Harvardim Tzolellim Al Falouja', *Heil Avir*, (1954) p. 44.
Bialer, U., 'Czech–Israeli Arms Deal Revisited', *Journal of Strategic Studies*, vol. 8 (1985).
Clifford, C. M., 'Serving the President, the Truman Years', *The New Yorker*, 25 March 1991.
Greenberg, Y., 'Financing the War of Independence', *Studies in Zionism*, vol. 9, no. 1 (1988).
Lazar, D., 'Tzarfat ve Yisrael, Reishitam shel Yehasim', *Medina, Mimshal Veyhasim Beinleumyim*, vol. 1, no. 2 (1971).
Little, D., 'Cold War and Covert Action; The United States and Syria', *The Middle East Journal*, vol. 44 (1990).
Lubel, S., 'Who Really Elected Truman?', *Saturday Evening Post*, 22 January 1949.
Mayer, S. T., 'The Military Force of Islam, the Society of the Muslim Brethern

and the Palestine Question', in Keddouri, E. and Haim, S. (ed.), *Zionism and Arabism in Palestine and Israel* (London, 1981).

Monroe, E., 'Mr. Bevin's "Arab" Policy', *St Antony's Papers*, vol. II (London, 1961).

al Nafuri, A., 'Al Jeish al Souri fi Filastin Aam 1948', *Al Fakhr al Askari*, Damsacus (July 1979).

Pail, M., 'Hakohot Halohamim', in Y. Ben Aryeh, op. cit.

Peled, A., 'Mahleket Hiumush Bahaganah', in G. Rivlin (ed.), *Ale Zait Vaherev* (Tel Aviv, 1990).

Sela, A., 'Transjordan, Israel and the 1948 War: Myth, Historiography and Reality', *Middle Eastern Studies*, vol. 28, no. 4 (1992).

Shatkai, A., 'Soleley Ha'atzmaut Ba'avir', *Heil Avir* (1955) vols 44–5.

DISSERTATIONS

Lachish, Z., 'Harechesh Ha'aviri Meaustralia Bemilhemet Ha'atzmaut' (Tel Aviv University, 1990).

Levenberg, H., 'The Military Preparation of the Arab Community in Palestine, 1945–1948' (London School of Economics, 1989).

Matras, J., 'Israel: Absorption of Immigration, Social Mobility and Social Change' (University of Chicago, 1962).

Na'or, M., 'Pinhas Sapir Bitkufat Hashanim, 1930–1949' (Tel Aviv University, 1983).

Sela, A., 'She'elat Eretz Yisrael Bama'arechet Habeinarvit Mehakamat Haliga ad Plishat Tzivot Arav Le'eretz Yisrael' (Hebrew University, Jerusalem, 1986).

NEWSPAPERS AND MAGAZINES

Al Tali'a
Davar
Egyptian Gazette
Ha'aretz
Heil Avir
Jewish Journal (New York)
Kesher Ve'electronika
Letectvi a Kosmonautica (Prague)
Manchester Guardian
Ma'ariv
Near East Report (New York)
Neue Zuricher Zeitung
New York Herald Tribune
The New Yorker
New York Times (NYT)
Pravda
London Times
Washington Post

INTERVIEWS AND CORRESPONDENCE

Sir Harold Beeley, London (January 1978).
Clark M. Clifford, Washington, D.C. (January 1978).
Sir Guy Campbell, Padbury (July 1980).
John Reedman, Tunbridge Wells (October 1980).
Abb Eban, Jerusalem (March 1982).
Victor Mills, New York (November 1984).
Brigadier K. A. Timbers, London (June 1991).
H. Goury, Tel Aviv (December, 1991).
Z. Hadari (January, 1992).
General A. Remez (January – February 1992).
Colonel T. N. Bromage, London (April 1992).
Colonel S. Gazit, Zahala (May 1992).
Major General J. Lunt, Oxford (April and May 1992).
Lt Colonel C. N. F. Coaker, London (June 1992).
Col. A. Porat, Tel Aviv (July 1992).
Major Galil Elyashiv (April 1993).
Lt Colonel Z. Lachish and Major A. Cohen, Division of History, Israeli Air
    Force (November 1992 and April 1994).
Dan Segre, Jerusalem (May 1993).

Index

Abd al Illa, Regent of Iraq, 33, 117, 121, 228

Abdullah Ibn Hussain, King of Transjordan, 9, 30, 33–4, 43–6, 50, 53, 56, 121, 123–4, 127, 178, 221, 227, 235

Abu al Huda, Tawfiq, 44, 121

Adam, Robert, 157

Ahmed, Tawfiq, General, 232–3

Aircraft, acquisition and contribution to military decision: 4–6, 31–2, 69; Anson, 31, 35, 134–5; Arada, 166; Auster, 69, 134; A20, 99; B17, 99–101, 169, 173; BT13, 99; Beaufighter, 135, 173; Bonanza and Fairchild, 69, 200; C46 Commando, 69, 96, 99, 159–60, 162, 169, 173; Constellation, 69, 99, 101; Dakota, 69, 74, 99, 163; Dove, 31–2; Fury, 32, 118–20, 130, 133, 229; Gladiator, 31; Harvard, 52, 77, 99, 103, 238; Lincoln, 140; Macchi, 193, 196–7, 211, 233; Messerschmitt, 64, 70, 99, 138–9, 161–5, 172–3, 238; Mosquito, 135, 173; Mustang, 99, 102, 169, 173, 238; Nooduyin (Norsman), 69, 165, 197–8; Rapide, 69, 134–5; Skymaster, 99, 159–60; Spitfire, 40–1, 115, 118, 158–65, 163, 169, 172–3; Sterling, 135; Tiger Moth, 30, 31, 52, 134–5; Tempest, 140

Airports and airbases: in the Middle East, 209, 212–13; in Communist countries, 166, 175: Podgorica, 163–4; Zatez, 174–5; in Western Europe, 175

Alexander, Victor, 20, 42, 112, 115, 117–18, 125, 128, 137, 140, 142–3, 226

Antonov, Alexei, General, 151–2

Arab armies, 19–20, 26, 34–5; 37, 39–5; Command and Organization, 12–14, 64; Order of Battle, 33–5, 39–47, 225–37; supply and production of arms, 27, 29, 31, 37, 41–2, 45–9, 178–9; disposition: Egypt, 5, 13, 35–42, 74, 229–32; Iraq, 5, 28–35, 226–9; Lebanon, 51–4, 56, 236–7

Arab League, 18, 30, 33, 50, 53, 55–7, 127, 135, 204, 235–6

Arab Legion: 13, 20, 43, 49–51; Qawukji, 13, 25, 37, 51, 55–7, 236–7; Saudi Arabian and Sudanese, 230–1; Syria, 5, 51–4, 56–7, 76–7, 236–7; losses, 54, 235

Arazi, Yehuda, 65–6, 76, 91–101, 169, 177, 182–4, 192–3, 197

Arbuthnot, Robert, General 36–9, 41, 114

Armoured fighting vehicles (AFV), acquisition and OB, 31, 38, 40, 54, 58, 74, 98, 119, 130, 134, 169, 251

Tanks: Cromwell, 69, 133; Hotchkiss, 183, 187, 238; Locust, 39, 129–32, 233; Mark VI, 39, 165, 169, 231; Mark V, 74, 98, 101; Renault, 52; Sherman, 74, 119, 133, 166, 169–70, 182, 193–5, 197, 214, 233

other AFVs: 69, 98–9; Daimler, 31; Dingo, 119; Humber 3 and 4, 31, 231; Marmon Harington, 47, 52, 119

Artillery, acquisition and OB, 31, 38; 20-mm, 31–2, 58, 96, 177, 183, 187; 37-mm, 52, 131; 65-mm, 34, 54, 64, 183–6; 75-mm, 52, 54, 56, 68, 102–3, 113, 186,